Deviance
Conformity
and
Control

SHARYN L. ROACH ANLEU

LONGMAN

An imprint of
Addison Wesley Longman

for Patricia and Una

Addison Wesley Longman Australia Pty Ltd
95 Coventry Street
South Melbourne 3205 Australia

Offices in Sydney, Brisbane and Perth, and associated
companies throughout the world.
Copyright © Addison Wesley Longman Australia Pty Ltd 1995
First published 1991
Second edition 1995
Reprinted 1996 (twice), 1997, 1998

Edited by Louisa Ring Rolfe
Set in Palatino 10.5/12.5

Produced by Addison Wesley Longman Australia Pty Ltd
Printed in Malaysia through Addison Wesley Longman China Limited, VVP

National Library of Australia
Cataloguing-in-Publication data

Anleu, Sharyn L. Roach.
  Deviance, conformity and control.

2nd edn.
Bibliography.
Includes index.
ISBN 0 582 80056 0.

1. Deviant behavior. 2. Conformity. 3. Social control.
I. Title. (Series: Australian sociology (Melbourne Vic.)).

302.542

Contents

Preface to the first edition

There is a pervasive view that the study of deviance involves the investigation of people who are defined as 'bizarre', 'weird', 'non-conformist', 'a drop out' or somehow 'alien' and 'different' from the rest of society. For many students this might herald an exotic and exciting course far removed from the perceived tedium of sociological theory or research methods. For others, it conveys a somewhat morbid or voyeuristic fascination with individuals and groups defined by mainstream society (but not by themselves) as deviant and consequently subject to prejudice, discrimination and oppression. This concentration, it is argued, effectively reinforces their deviant status and justifies their condemnation and victimisation.

Both these views are simplistic and inaccurate. As with many sociological concepts, considerable disagreement exists on what constitutes deviance, and this is further complicated by the parallel use of the term in everyday life. This does not mean that the notion of deviance is useless. Rather, deviance is a polymorphous concept comprising a range of diverse activities and persons with little or no common strand of similarity other than negative evaluation within particular time frames (Sagarin 1985, p. 169; Sagarin & Kelly 1987, p. 18).

Another source of confusion seems to be the assumption that discussions of deviance focus principally on *deviants*. However, the processes whereby individuals or groups come to be defined as deviant, or not, is problematic for the sociologist and a topic of inquiry rather than being taken for granted. I suggest that the most useful focus is deviant behaviour and activity, not deviant persons. This book starts from the premise that deviance is a pervasive aspect of social life. There is no person who has not engaged in deviant behaviour or been identified as such. The sociology of deviance is not the study of others and their 'strange' practices; it is the investigation of all of social life and its members.

The impetus for writing this book came from a suggestion that I contribute to a new series on Australian sociology. I welcomed this unique opportunity to provide more literature published in Australia about Australia and accessible to students. However, the book represents the culmination of almost a decade of work in the area. My interest in the topic 'took off' during the years I worked with Albert K. Cohen, my dissertation adviser at the University of Connecticut. His influence, and I hope his high standards of logic and clarity, is evident in these pages. As part of a general series in sociology the immediate audience will be undergraduate students. However, a wider readership, including students of social administration and criminology, policy makers, and practitioners in the fields of community welfare, corrections, health and corporate affairs, may also find the substantive and theoretical analyses of contemporary issues of particular interest.

A number of people have provided invaluable assistance in the preparation of this book. I am grateful to Margaret Cameron and Lorraine Green for assisting with the research, and to Sue Manser for typing the tables and assistance with the bibliography. I thank Andrew Hopkins and Adam Sutton for reading sections of the book and providing some excellent comments. The continual encouragement and thorough editorial assistance of Malcolm Waters is greatly appreciated. It has been a pleasure to work with Ron Harper, an extremely well organised and professional publisher. Finally, the crew of family and friends, especially Edmer, have been marvellous in expressing interest and helping me to maintain the momentum to complete this book.

Sharyn L. Roach Anleu

Preface to the second edition

This edition of *Deviance, Conformity and Control* extends and updates the discussion and material contained in its predecessor. The overall aim is to incorporate new theoretical developments and directions into the discussion and to address some of the salient contemporary issues and public debates, including the moral panic and changing approaches to youth crime, the enormous corporate collapses in the wake of the 1980s, and the controversial laws surrounding homosexuality, abortion, tobacco use, and marijuana consumption. Specifically, the second edition offers new sections on the theory of reintegrative shaming, the fear of crime, victimisation, the juvenile justice system and youth offending, organised crime and the special agencies established to control corporate and organised crime. It expands the discussions on control theory, feminist theories, abortion, homosexuality, pornography, drug use, community policing, the mass media, mental illness and corporate crime. The chapter dealing with religion, morality and sinners has been refocused to emphasise the shifting boundaries between criminalisation and decriminalisation and there are now two chapters specifically dealing with criminal deviance: chapter 4 examines the nature and extent of the so-called crime problem and provides updated and new tables, while chapter 5 investigates crime control and details the criminal justice system.

Significant changes have occurred regarding the availability of officially collected data since the first edition in 1991. First, comprehensive results from the 1989–90 National Health Survey have enabled the revision of tables in the illness, medicine and deviance chapter. Second, new sources of crime data are now obtainable: the Australian Institution of Criminology has updated the crime statistics that constitute the 1989 *Sourcebook of Australian Criminal & Social Statistics*; the 1993 Crime and Safety survey provides new information on victims of crime; and perhaps most significantly, the first set of uniform national crime statistics were released in May 1994. This latest innovation will make discussion of criminal deviance in Australia more reliable as state idiosyncrasies in data collection will be minimised.

As with any publication, this book is not just the product of the author. I would like to thank Margaret Cameron for her assistance in updating the bibliography; Clayton Reeves for library research; Marie Baker for so painstakingly typing the tables and the new references; Rick Sarre for comments on the first edition which were valuable in formulating the second and Jill Rashleigh for assistance with preparing the final version. I appreciate the opportunity to prepare a second edition of *Deviance, Conformity and Control* and acknowledge the continuing encouragement and support of Malcolm Waters and Ron Harper. Finally, my thanks to Edmer for helping me to reach the deadline, and to Oliver for keeping his.

Sharyn L. Roach Anleu

Figures and tables

Introduction: what is deviance?

Deviance is an elusive concept. It encompasses a wide variety of behaviour including drug addiction, property theft, witchcraft, corruption, tax fraud, prostitution, abortion, drug-trafficking, pollution, rape, shoptheft, rudeness, lateness, illness, drunkenness, being too fat or too thin, women employed as truck drivers or lawyers, men employed as nurses or ballet dancers. The list is infinite. This introductory discussion examines some of the complexity in the concept of deviance.

One aspect of the complexity is the considerable disagreement about what constitutes deviance. Even though deviance pervades social life, little consensus exists on the types of behaviour or activities the term includes, or on the causes of behaviour deemed deviant. Many people might agree on the status of an activity or practice as deviant, but disagree on what constitutes the activity or practice. For example, most people would accept that rape, drug addiction, domestic violence and pollution are deviant but disagree on the behaviour to be included. This is because deviant behaviour occurs in the same social situations as conformity and, indeed, deviance may be an extension of activities which are not deemed deviant. For example, neither consuming alcohol (within certain limits) nor driving a motor vehicle (for which the driver has a licence) is deviant, but they are in combination.

Another dimension of the complexity is that conceptions of deviance change over time and differ across societies. As Erikson writes: 'Every human community has its own special set of boundaries, its own unique identity, and so we may presume that every community also has its own characteristic styles of deviant behaviour' (1966, p. 19). Behaviour defined and sanctioned as deviant in one society or social situation may be 'normal' in another. Cross-cultural norms about food consumption illustrate the relativity of deviance. Eating pork is taboo for practicing Moslems and Jews but not for Christians; eating Chinese dishes with chopsticks is normal but to eat French or Greek cuisine in this way would be deviant. Other societies' customs and norms in specifying arranged marriages, physically painful initiation ceremonies, or the separation of women during menstruation, for example, may appear barbaric and highly deviant to us, whereas these practices might form integral components of the particular society's organisation.

Varying conceptions of deviance raise difficult questions in such multicultural societies as Australia. The notion of multiculturalism emphasises recognizing the values of other cultures. According to the Commonwealth government: 'We need to adapt and reform the institutional processes of Australian society in order to accommodate and respond to the cultural diversity of today's community' (Office of Multicultural Affairs 1989, p. 16). Questions emerge about the extent of such accommodation: Does it go as far as the legal system? Will it mean that different laws or rules get applied to different groups of people? Australian courts have held that members of different ethnic groups, specifically Southern Europeans, are more likely to be provoked than others and possess less self-control because of cultural emphases on expressiveness. This suggests that different rules will be applied to different groups (Yeo 1987, p. 81). If a person on a murder charge can demonstrate that provocation and the loss of self-control caused her or him to kill the victim then the conviction will be reduced from murder to manslaughter, which carries lesser penalties. A further example involves the controversy over the book *The Satanic Verses* by Salman Rushdie. Moslem groups claim that English blasphemy laws, though applicable to the whole community, are unjust and discriminatory because they reflect specifically Christian beliefs and values.

Deviance and illegality are not synonymous. Moreover, not all illegal activities are criminally deviant. Even though an act may be legal some groups may consider it deviant and intolerable. Neither homosexuality, abortion, nor being Asian are illegal (in most states) but some people define these attributes as deviant. Alternatively, some groups may define certain illegal activities as appropriate and normal. In the USA, during Prohibition, wine consumption remained an essential component of many people's daily lives despite its illegality. Another example is petty pilfering from the office, which is widespread but tolerated, although such actions violate laws prohibiting theft. Moreover, the same behaviour may be defined differently in different situations. Acceptable, indeed expected, behaviour at a football game would be unacceptable at a dinner party or in a class room. Nevertheless, there are limits on the types of behaviour that are acceptable at sports matches as discussions of football hooliganism and violence in sport illustrate.

These examples suggest that it is not the *act* but the *definition* others place on it, or the *norms* they apply, that makes action deviant. Definitions of deviance ebb and flow and some segments of society have more power and influence to alter, maintain or apply specific conceptions of deviance.

Currently, there are movements to decriminalise such activities as homosexuality, prostitution, personal marijuana consumption and public drunkenness. Simultaneously, some efforts are oriented to defining various practices as deviant, ultimately to be sanctionable by the criminal law. A good example is cigarette smoking. From the 1950s through to the 1970s smoking cigarettes was entirely acceptable, even expected, behaviour. The deviantisation of smoking is exemplified by the growing number of restaurants and other public places, including all Commonwealth government buildings and aeroplanes, with 'no smoking' areas, often with penalties attached for violation. Further examples of increasing deviantisation include dangerous workplaces, employer negligence, employment discrimination, rape, domestic violence, even drinking coffee.

Rather than being an objective entity and independent of society, conceptions of deviance are linked to social organisation. A widely accepted definition of deviance is: 'behaviour that violates the normative rules, understandings, or expectations of social systems' (Cohen 1968, p. 148). The normative rules specify appropriate and inappropriate or conforming and deviant behaviour and may or may not be codified into law. In determining whether certain activities are deviant, reference must be made to the rules that are applied; the activities or behaviour in themselves are not deviant. From this conception, rule infraction creates social instability and dislocation which requires remedy or management. Students of deviance often adopt this normative conception of deviant behaviour, yet it raises a number of questions:

1 *Whose norms?* The normative conception of deviance assumes a high degree of consensus regarding the norms or rules operating in a situation. However, in a complex society many conflicting and competing norms exist in the form of laws, regulations, standards, organisational rules, and generally as social expectations. Dissensus may be more frequent than consensus in determining the relevant rules to be applied. Moreover, a certain amount of deviance is usually tolerated, for example being five minutes late for work, class or a meeting will be treated differently than being one hour late. The margins of tolerance are diffuse and often ambiguous and unclear until they are transgressed.

2 *How do some norms become official or legal?* Where disagreement and conflict prevail the development of laws and official rules which have universal application (at least formally) cannot result from consensus. Economically and politically powerful individuals and groups will be more successful in codifying their norms into laws than will others lacking such power.

3 *Why are some norms more important than others?* The violation of some norms provokes more serious sanctions than others. One explanation for this is that some norms are more central or important to the whole society. Again, the problems of consensus arise: are norms equally important to the whole society or only to segments of it, and, if so, to which segments?

4 *Does visibility make a difference?* Everybody breaks norms but not everyone is caught or accused of norm violation. If deviance is not detected then

presumably it does not threaten social stability or restrict interaction. For example, a group of middle-class people gambling or smoking marijuana in their own home is not likely to be arrested by the police, unlike a group of Aboriginal people in a city park or even on a reserve. Such factors as gender, ethnicity, appearance and social class all affect visibility. Black or working-class people are more likely to come into contact with the criminal justice system than are white middle-class people, even though there might be the same incidence of norm-breaking behaviour within the groups. More importantly, the person who witnesses norm-breaking activities must be motivated and have the authority to do something about the perceived deviance. If students are asked how they would respond to someone cutting an article from a journal with a razor blade, most will agree that the behaviour is deviant but only a minority will indicate that they would confront the perpetrator or report the incident to someone with authority to sanction the deviance. Motivation to obtain compliance will depend on whether the rule violator is a friend or acquaintance, whether the journal is of particular interest to the observer, and whether she or he is in a hurry.

5 *Deviance without breaking norms?* The notion of deviance as norm-breaking implies an intention on the part of the actor alleged to have broken the norm. This conception does not cover accidents, or incidents where the person was set up or framed, and evidence was planted. In law, crime usually requires both a physical act, the *actus reus*, and a subjective intention, or *mens rea*. Even if an action violates the criminal law the courts may not convict an alleged offender if there is no evidence of the requisite intention. Additionally, some people may be defined as deviant because of physical or other characteristics even though they have not consciously broken any rule. Members of ethnic and other minorities, including people with mental or physical disabilities, may be deemed deviant, not because of their activities but because of their ascribed statuses. Goffman (1963, p. 13) uses the term *stigma* to signify relationships in which attributes become deeply discrediting, thereby relegating the possessor to a deviant status. It is not the attributes, *per se*, that are discrediting and separate the stigmatised from the normal, but the nature of the social relations which link attributes to particular stereotypes.

These issues underscore the multiplicity of questions arising in the study of deviance and, not surprisingly, a variety of theories constitute the sociology of deviance. Many theories and much research focus on one particular type, namely criminal deviance. This might be because the criminal law clearly defines this type of deviance, or because people who have come into contact with the criminal justice system are relatively easy to identify and locate for research purposes. Nevertheless, it would be foolhardy to suggest that criminal deviance is synonymous with the activities and individuals with whom the criminal justice system deals. The discussion here encompasses a wider range of deviance than criminal deviance.

A number of important concepts are related to an understanding of deviance, namely *social control*, *conformity*, and *social problems*. Social control is important because it is usually considered to be all those mechanisms aimed at achieving conformity, the antithesis of deviance. The term social problems refers to many of the same issues as deviance. However, discussions of social problems usually entail explicit value commitments and a concern to change public policy.

Generally, the term *social control* applies to all the sanctions, responses or reactions oriented to the eradication or containment of deviant behaviour (Black 1976, p. 2; Parsons 1951b, p. 298; Ross 1896, p. 519). If deviance disturbs social equilibrium, then social control attempts to restore it. Deviance and social control can be conceptualised as two sides of the same coin, for example Parsons says: 'the theory of social control is the obverse of the theory of the genesis of deviant behaviour tendencies' (1951b, p. 297). However, while the term social control is important in sociological theory it has never been central, because it is secondary and contingent upon deviance (Gibbs 1982, p. 10).

Mechanisms aimed at achieving social control and conformity are known as *sanctions*, which can be rewards for conformity to social expectations, or punishments for norm violations. Radcliffe-Browne, an anthropologist, distinguishes between broad structural influences or expressions of official group sentiment, that is, formal social control, from interpersonal influence or evaluations of conduct related to group membership, or *informal* social control (1952, pp. 205–6). Formal social control includes the legal system, specifically the police, regulatory agencies, courts and tribunals, which administers such sanctions as fines, probation and imprisonment. The point is that only the specialised legal system has the authority to mete out formal social control. Medicine, including psychiatry, welfare and education also manifest social control functions but they are less overt than the criminal justice system and usually are legitimated by goals other than control, such as serving the client or eradicating illness. Informal social control is embedded in everyday social interaction and involves sanctions ranging from ridicule, praise, gossip, smiles and glances to ostracism. These sanctions can be administered by any member of the social group.

The amount of formal, or governmental, social control varies inversely with informal social control (Black 1976, p. 107). Where other types of social control operate recourse to the law is unlikely, indeed legal remedies often do not exist. Anthropological research suggests that informal sanctions are adequate in controlling deviance where strong primary relationships prevail and the extended family retains authority, in communal settings with collective participation and ownership and little privacy, and where cultural values emphasise harmony not competition or conflict (Kawashima 1982, pp. 70–4; Nader & Metzger 1963, pp. 589–91; Schwartz 1954, pp. 484–8). Indeed, the distinction between formal and informal social control is analytical and many situations involve both types of control. For example, while prisons are formal sources of punishment and control, informal groups emerge with distinct norms and values and mechanisms for achieving conformity (Carlen 1983, pp. 89–116; Cressey 1958; Giallombardo 1966, chapter 8; Sykes 1956, 1958).

This conception of social control emphasises the integrative function of sanctions which respond to norm violations. Framing the concept of social control in this way precludes the possibility of envisaging rule enforcers as contributing to deviance. Ironically, agents of social control can actually encourage rule-breaking through escalation, non-enforcement and covert facilitation (Marx 1981, p. 222). The existence of certain rules and enforcement mechanisms may not result in social control but lead to rebellion, or even revolution. Deviance can escalate when police intervention, for example, creates new opportunities for crime including resisting arrest, indecent language, assaulting a police officer, or even manslaughter during high speed car chases. Non-enforcement tacitly legitimates the continuance of norm-breaking activities, while covert facilitation occurs where agents of social control create opportunities to increase the probability of law breaking, for example by initiating 'set-ups' or 'entrapment' (Young 1971, p. 44). Moreover, the designation of people as deviant alters the way others interact with them and may change their position in the social structure by making it more difficult to obtain employment. This increases the probability of further law-breaking and encourages the development of a deviant self-identity.

The mass media contribute to this process of deviance amplification, escalation or dramatisation. News reports present stereotyped images of activities and individuals whom the public perceives as threatening deep-seated societal values and interests, which might lead ultimately to 'moral panics' or the establishment of 'folk devils' (Cohen 1980, pp. 16–17). This process may stimulate the development of full-blown social problems, a concept used differently by proponents of the functionalist and symbolic interactionist perspectives.

The concept of social problems has emerged alongside that of deviance and, in many instances, it is difficult to distinguish the two concepts. Nisbet, for example, in a widely read text, *Contemporary Social Problems*, states: 'A social problem is a way of behaviour that is regarded by a substantial part of a social order as being in violation of one or more generally accepted or approved norms' (1971, p. 1). This definition is indistinguishable from the normative conception of deviance. Most commentators of social problems recognize that value judgements inform definitions of what constitutes a social problem, and that some groups have more power and authority to affect the relative importance assigned social problems (Merton 1971, p. 803). However, in a highly critical discussion of social problems textbooks

C. Wright Mills (1943, p. 171) argues that concepts such as social disorganisation and social problems indicate more about sociologists' own background experiences and values eulogising rural community life than about the conditions in inner city areas where so-called social problems flourish.

By contrast, Blumer, a symbolic interactionist, suggests: 'Social problems are fundamentally products of a process of collective definition instead of existing independently as a set of objective social arrangements with an intrinsic make-up' (1971, p. 298). The process of collective definition consists of stages making it useful to talk about the emergence, the career and the fate of social problems. In other words, a social problem is not a set of objective conditions waiting to be defined as such, but it is an achievement, a result of organised and concerted social action, or claims-making (Kitsuse & Spector 1973, p. 415; Schneider 1985). Claims-making activities can lead to the emergence of social movements whose aim is to re-organise the existing normative structure and mechanisms of social control. This theoretical approach enables an understanding of why some activities or individuals are defined as social problems while others are not, and shifts attention onto the key groups which successfully redefine activities and practices as deviant.

Summary and organisation of chapters

This chapter examines the concept of deviance and explores some of the difficulties in defining the term. A frequently used definition is deviance as norm violation, which assumes a consensus exists regarding norms and values in society. Many theories view deviance as disturbance, as upsetting the smooth flow of everyday activities.

This book follows the broad conception of deviance as behaviour which violates social rules. However, this does not imply a consensus on norms or notions of deviance. The process of defining certain activities or individuals as deviant requires analysis of the distribution of power and the activities and values of various interest groups, not just consideration of the person or groups subject to the application of norms. A distinction between activities which break rules and the emergence of a deviant self-identity is also crucial and points to the importance of social control in contributing to deviance in some circumstances while minimising it in others. Subsequent chapters deal with these issues in greater detail.

Chapter 1 outlines various conceptions of deviance and crime which attempt to locate the causes within individuals' biological make-up or personality type. Chapter 2 surveys four main sociological theories of deviance, namely normative theories, the labelling perspective, political economy theories and feminist approaches. Chapter 3 examines the processes of criminalisation and decriminalisation. It investigates conceptions of morality, moral entrepreneurs, and so-called crimes against morality including abortion, homosexuality, prostitution and pornography.

The nature and distribution of crime in society is the concern of chapter 4 and chapter 5 discusses crime control and examines the criminal justice system. The following chapter addresses the notion of illness as deviance and investigates the role of the medical profession in maintaining social control. Chapter 7 looks at women and criminal deviance, both as the main victims of rape, domestic violence and sexual harassment, and as perpetrators of various deviant and criminal activities. Corporate crime provides the focus of chapter 8 which also discusses organised crime, while chapter 9 analyses poverty and social disadvantage. The concluding chapter pulls together the diverse examples and theories presented in the preceding discussions.

Key terms

Deviance	Sanctions
Deviants	Formal social control
Deviantisation	Informal social control
Actus reus	Crime
Mens rea	Illegality
Conformity	Social problems
Norms	Stigma

Main points

1 A common definition of deviance is behaviour or activities which violates social norms or laws.

2 The kinds of activities deemed deviant depend on the social norms applied, which, in turn, are relative to societies, social contexts and situations. No behaviour is deviant *per se*.

3 Not all norm-breaking is visible, obvious or sanctioned. Some people are able to 'get away with it'.

4 The development of deviant self-identities requires negative sanctioning or social control. Social control can include a glance, a verbal reprimand, exclusion from certain jobs or opportunities, and criminal sanctions such as a fine or imprisonment.

5 Ironically, social control can actually increase the incidence of norm-breaking through escalation, nonenforcement and covert facilitation.

6 The emergence of social problems involves certain groups or social movements identifying and defining activities as deviant and problematic. This process often involves attempts to mobilise public sentiment and agreement and efforts to alter government policy and legislation.

Further reading

Black, Donald 1976, *The Behavior of Law*, Academic Press, New York.

Cohen, Albert 1966, *Deviance and Control*, Prentice Hall, Englewood Cliffs.

Conrad, Peter & Joseph W. Schneider 1980, *Deviance and Medicalization: From Badness to Sickness*, C.V. Mosby, St Louis, Missouri.

Erikson, Kai T. 1966, *Wayward Puritans: A Study in the Sociology of Deviance*, Macmillan, New York.

Goffman, Erving 1963, *Stigma: Notes on the Management of Spoiled Identity*, Penguin, Harmondsworth.

Kitsuse, John I. & Malcolm Spector 1973, 'Toward a Sociology of Social Problems: Social Conditions, Value-Judgements, and Social Problems', *Social Problems*, vol. 20, pp. 407–19.

Pitts, Jesse R. 1968, 'Social Control: the Concept', in *International Encyclopedia of the Social Sciences*, ed. David Sills, Macmillan, New York.

Sagarin, Edward & Robert J. Kelly 1987, 'Deviance: A Polymorphous Concept', *Deviant Behavior*, vol. 8, pp. 13–25.

CHAPTER

1

Individualistic theories

Many early theories of deviance and crime attempt to explain why some people violate rules by distinguishing the deviant's characteristics from those of the non-deviant. Individualistic theories seek to locate the 'causes' of deviance within the individual; they pay little attention to the motivational and situational processes resulting in deviance or to the social, economic and ecological factors creating opportunities for deviant behaviour. These theories accept current, dominant definitions of deviant behaviour and do not inquire into the processes whereby some behaviour and practices or individuals come to be defined as deviant while others are not. Individualistic theories seek to explain deviance by identifying the deviant's characteristic physical or psychological traits and peculiarities rather than assessing the social situations under which norm and law violations are most likely to occur, or the circumstances where activities are likely to be deemed unacceptable.

Explanations of crime and deviance which focus on the individual, like biological and psychological approaches, are sometimes called 'kinds of people' theories. Such theories are developed largely by medical personnel or psychiatrists and psychologists adopting a medical framework that emphasises scientific diagnosis, assessment, individual treatment and medical control. While the medical model is not currently the dominant paradigm in understanding crime and deviance, it periodically reappears, particularly with respect to serious crimes like murder, and is applied frequently to explanations of alcoholism, drug dependence and homosexuality.

In our society we are used to holding individuals accountable and responsible for their actions or failures. Indeed, our legal system is based on this principle. Given this focus, it is not a big step to ask what it is about an individual that predisposes her or him to do certain things which some people define as unacceptable. This chapter examines a sample of 'kinds of people' theories, namely religious approaches which focus on evil in the individual, biological theories which seek to identify critical inherited traits and psychological approaches locating explanations within individual personality. As a preface to the following chapter, the discussion maps out how a sociological approach to deviance differs from 'kinds of people' theories.

Religious approaches

The most fundamental distinction in pre-industrial societies is between the sacred and the profane. Societies from ancient Greece to the Middle Ages considered deviance to be a manifestation of evil or, in the Judeo–Christian tradition, of original sin. Durkheim maintains that the dominant form of law (namely repressive) in these societies was essentially religious in origin, which defined and prohibited various forms of sacrilege, failure to observe religious rituals and ceremonies (Lukes & Scull 1983, pp. 64–5). Many religious theories focus on the role of evil or the devil in causing rule-breaking behaviour, often defined as madness or lunacy.

The ancient Hebrews perceived madness as divine retribution for failing to obey God's commandments and violating his ordinances. Interestingly, both madness and prophecy were abnormal to the Hebrews; both involved unusual behaviour attributable to divine intervention. However, the interpretation of the behaviour was radically different. A diagnosis of madness or prophecy depended on who exhibited the behaviour rather than on the nature of the behaviour itself.

In contrast, the Greeks had two explanations for madness. The most popular view was the cosmological–supernatural explanation that madness was a possession caused by the gods or the spirit underworld. Justice was considered to emanate from Zeus, and the sentiment as a vengeance from the god. Secondly, the Greeks elaborated the first natural–medical explanation in recorded history which defined madness as a disease with natural causes. Physicians recommended a variety of treatments ranging from diet to hot and cold baths and even a form of electric shock using electric eels (Conrad & Schneider 1980, p. 40).

The emergence of witchcraft, or at least a particular conception of it, in Renaissance Europe provides a focus for discussions of religion and deviance. Witchcraft was considered to result from an individual entering a pact or covenant with the Devil, indicating the wilful renunciation of the Faith, and thereby obtaining power to manipulate supernatural forces for anti-social and un-Christian ends, including the killing of unborn children.

In both Europe and England the dominant concern was to identify individuals engaged in the practice of witchcraft and then to punish them. The European approach centred on confession, often obtained by torture, whereas the English looked for external signs, such as particular marks or peculiar characteristics attributed to witches. The techniques of identification included pricking, which was based on the notion that witches invariably possessed a Devil's mark characterised by insensitivity to pain, and swimming, to see whether or not the person sank or floated, the latter evincing evil (Currie 1968, pp. 17–20). These techniques for identifying the characteristics of witches parallel medical or psychiatric diagnoses aimed at identifying the individual characteristics or traits which are assumed to explain deviant activities or lifestyles. For many people, the causes of deviance are still rooted in ideas of good and bad people, and the notion that evil emanates from connections with the supernatural, thereby justifying punishment as a form of divine retribution. However, with the emergence of scientific rationality, religious ideas on the causes of deviance gave way to biological explanations.

Biological theory

In the 1870s, Cesare Lombroso, an Italian physician, developed the theory of the biological inferiority of criminal deviants as compared to non-criminals. He was responsible for establishing the 'positive school of criminology' which applies the inductive scientific method to the study of crime and criminals. The spread of Darwinism and application of the concept of evolution in the social sciences, combined with the rise of the medical profession, members of which set about documenting the history of criminology as a branch of medicine, contributed to the popularity of Lombroso's ideas (Lindesmith & Levin 1937, pp. 667–9). Lombroso's interest and activity in criminology falls into four phases:

1 as a physician in the Italian Army his observations of the background and behaviour of the tattooed soldiers;
2 the application of physical measurements in his research on mental illness and conclusion that the patient and not the disease should be the focus of attention. Although he was concerned with psychical processes he considered them too elusive for direct observation, thus he sought a typology based on organic factors;
3 the extension of his research approach to the study of criminals, in order to identify their traits and differentiate them from other deviants;
4 the direct comparison of criminals with normal individuals and the insane (Wolfgang 1972, p. 237).

According to Lombroso, peculiar physical traits, or stigmata, separate dangerous offenders from the law-abiding. Based on studies of inmates of Italian prisons and a post-mortem of a famous bandit named Villela, he describes the 'born' criminal as exhibiting characteristics similar to animals and humans lower on the evolutionary scale. Lombroso argues that criminality is a manifestation of atavism, that is, a biological throwback, characterised by the re-emergence of primitive traits, such as a narrow forehead, protruding cheekbones and jawbones, eye defects and abnormalities, large ears and lips. Lombroso writes:

> I found in the skull of a brigand a very long series of atavistic anomalies, above all an enormous middle occipital fossa and a hypertrophy of the vermis analogous to those that are found in inferior vertebrates. At the sight of these strange anomalies the problem of the nature and of the origin of the criminal seemed to me resolved; the characteristics of primitive men and of inferior animals must be reproduced in our times (1968, p. xiv).

For Lombroso, criminality is inevitable, a biological imperative, over which the individual has no control. The criminal is not a variation from a norm, but practically a separate human species possessing characteristic physical and mental attributes. Later, Lombroso adds the theory of degeneration which includes a pathological condition in the criminal. The degenerate is the result of diseased ancestral elements which indicate the failure to evolve; pathological individuals manifest the basic physical and mental attributes of so-called primitive people. He also emphasises the similarities between the criminal, the insane and the epileptic.

In addition to physical attributes, Lombroso observes in the born criminal such characteristics as:

1 sensory and functional peculiarities, including greater insensibility to pain, more acute sight, greater agility and marked strength in the left arm;
2 absence of moral sense, involving the lack of repentance and remorse, the presence of cynicism, treachery, vanity, impulsiveness, vindictiveness, cruelty, idleness and a penchant for gambling;
3 a special criminal slang, the tendency to express ideas pictorially and extensive tattooing (Wolfgang 1972, p. 251).

In response to widespread criticism of his atavistic theory, Lombroso recognises the importance of environmental factors which precipitate crime commission. He subsequently incorporates some social and motivational factors into a typology of criminals, but they remain secondary to his theory of atavism. Lombroso (1968, pp. 365–76; Wolfgang 1972, pp. 251–4) identifies four major criminal types and several sub-types:

1 *born criminals* constitute one-third of all criminals and exhibit atavistic traits;
2 *criminal insane* are impulsive, obscene and cruel, frequently suffer from epilepsy or are born criminals suffering melancholia. Hysterical persons, alcoholics, pyromaniacs, dipsomaniacs and kleptomaniacs are examples;
3 *epileptic criminals* combine the attributes of born criminals and the criminal insane. Lombroso found that many of the anomalies he

discovered in the criminal could not be explained by atavism and he identified epilepsy as the other pathological condition causing the slow development of certain organs, especially the nerve centres. All born criminals are epileptics, but not all epileptics are born criminals;

4 *occasional criminals* do not possess atavism or epilepsy but fall into crime for very insignificant reasons. Lombroso identifies specific types of occasional criminals:

a *pseudo-criminals* involuntarily commit acts which violate the criminal law even though they do not threaten or morally outrage the community. Examples include crimes undertaken in self-defence or protection of honour and the family;

b *criminaloids* differ from born criminals in degree, not kind, as they have some connection with atavism and epilepsy but often engage in crime because of greater opportunities for fraud, lack of self-control and other unfavourable exogamous factors. Most criminaloids become habitual criminals as a result of long periods of imprisonment and association with other prisoners, and can only be distinguished from born criminals because they lack the physical marks of criminality;

c *habitual criminals* do not possess the physical or innate attributes of criminality, but poor education combined with insufficient parental training leads them to digress continually lower into the primitive tendency toward evil. He provides the example of the Mafia, which recruits members through association. Lombroso comes closest to demonstrating a sociological perspective in this aspect of his work;

d *crimes of violence* are not caused by organic factors but stem from emotion. Lombroso includes political criminals who, he suggests, have powerful intellects, exaggerated sensibilities, great altruism and intense patriotic, religious or scientific ideals. He suggests that the high incidence of suicide among criminals of passion indicates a pathological state of mind.

Lombroso refutes the accuracy of crime statistics showing women to be less criminal than men. He argues that as women operate in different spheres from men their crimes differ. Although he asserts that female born criminals are fewer in number than males, he contends that the former are much more ferocious (Wolfgang 1972, p. 255). Women's crimes include abortion, bigamy, infanticide, prostitution, and mistreatment of children. Lombroso does not consider that most of these acts involve men in some capacity, nor does he reflect on why only one person, the woman, is defined as deviant. He writes:

> The crimes mentioned above to which women are particularly addicted are just those which are most easily concealed and most rarely lead to trial. To this may be added the well known fact of the greater obstinacy and intensity of criminality when it appears in a woman (1968, p. 187).

Other important members of the Italian school of criminology were Ferri (1856–1929) and Garofalo (1852–1934), both of whom were lawyers, thus their research emphases differed from those of Lombroso. The positive school, according to Ferri, has two missions: the scientific study of crime as an individual phenomenon, and the study of crime as a social fact distributed throughout societies in order to develop and reform criminal laws, punishments, and prisons (Sellin 1972, pp. 378–9). Ferri felt that Lombroso dealt with a narrow aspect of criminality and he sought to incorporate individual, physical and social factors into a typology of crime, he in fact coined the term 'the born-criminal', but was much more explicit in incorporating social factors. Ferri argued that scientific principles within the court, especially training judges in the social and psychological sciences, would enable better disposition of offenders compared with jury trials. He maintained that punishments be determined on the basis of the degree of danger the offender posed to society and the extent his or her motives were blameworthy, rather than the objective nature of the act (Sellin 1972, pp. 380–1). Similarly, Garofalo was concerned with the practical reform of the criminal justice system, especially regarding criminal sanctions. He criticised previous writers for failing to distinguish between the criminal and the crime and proposed the concept of natural crime which consists of actions which offend the basic moral sentiments of pity regarding harms to the individual and probity regarding the protection of property rights (Allen 1972, pp. 320–1). In line with positivism, Garofalo developed a typology of crime comprising:

1 *the murderer* who lacks altruistic sentiments;
2 *the violent criminal* commits crimes of passion against individuals, often under the influence of alcohol;
3 *the thief* lacks respect for property rights and certain environments and associations contribute to crimes against property;
4 *the sexual offender* has a low level of moral energy, deficient moral perception and also may be a violent criminal (Allen 1972, p. 329).

Lombroso's positivism dominated European criminology for thirty-five years. However, two basic methodological and theoretical lacunae flaw his conception. Firstly, as he enumerates prison inmates' characteristics without a control group he has no foundation for the claim that the atavistic traits cluster in convicted offenders. Early this century, Charles Goring, a physician in the English prison system, compared large samples of prisoners with university students and professors, soldiers and hospital patients with regard to the physical attributes Lombroso identifies as indicators of atavism. Goring concludes that a distinct criminal type does not exist and suggests that the differences he observed could be attributed to social class and occupational choice. He found a predominance of crimes of violence, stealing and burglary in the lower class, sexual offences among the poor and destitute and fraud in the middle and upper classes (Cohen 1966, p. 50; Driver 1972, pp. 433–7). While it is often argued that Goring is responsible for refuting Lombroso's positivism, he did not so much disagree with

Lombroso's theory and orientation as with his misuse of scientific technique. Moreover, some of the empirical criticisms he made of the concept of the born criminal had been articulated by French anthropologists and sociologists in the 1880s and 1890s (Beirne 1988, p. 334). Secondly, Lombroso assumes that the categories of prisoner and criminal cover the same people. He cannot account for violators of the criminal law who are able to avoid arrest, trial, conviction or imprisonment. Conversely, he does not consider that some prisoners may have been wrongly convicted and indeed did not commit the alleged acts.

Another type of biological theory is Sheldon's (1949) constitutional typologies of the body. Sheldon, a psychologist and physician, was interested in the overall pattern of body shape rather than specific characteristics. He sought to document a relationship between the human physique and personality and ability. Sheldon delineates three body types:

1 *endomorph*—round, soft, fat bodies with short limbs and small bones;
2 *mesomorph*—muscular, large trunk, heavy chest, large wrists and hands, heavy bones;
3 *ectomorph*—light, delicate body, small face, droopy shoulders, delicate bones.

Sheldon attempts to link temperamental patterns with each body type in a study of 200 boys at a rehabilitation centre for juveniles. He finds juvenile delinquents to be predominantly mesomorphic, with some endomorphy and slight ectomorphy. According to Sheldon, the mesomorph is highly active, energetic, often loud and aggressive, and acts impulsively and adventurously, but lacks conscience, sensitivity and reflectiveness. This combination makes for a predatory person who acts out of self-interest with little regard for others. Few controls operate on the mesomorph to prevent delinquent or criminal actions. In contrast, endomorphs are easy-going, self-indulgent and relaxed, while ectomorphs are introverted, nervous and sensitive.

Again, other interpretations of this data are plausible. The research only deals with boys who have been identified and formally processed as juvenile delinquents, therefore the research findings might have more to do with social class, neighbourhood, ethnicity, or family relations than body shape. Sheldon's work has been strongly criticised both for its methodology and for its imprecise conception of delinquency as 'disappointingness' (Cohen 1966, p. 52). Even so, his work led to a series of prediction studies designed to identify potential delinquents at an early age.

Sheldon Glueck and Eleanor Glueck (1956, 1974) persistently compared delinquent and non-delinquent boys. Their research supports the suggestion that mesomorphs apparently have a greater predilection to deviance than other body types due to their relative aggression, physical strength, energy, insensitivity and tendency to express their frustrations coupled with few feelings of inadequacy or emotional instability. The Gluecks were interested in identifying the development of criminal careers and in assessing the effectiveness of correctional responses in reducing criminal behaviour. Their methodological approach entailed longitudinal and follow-up prediction studies, including control groups where available, the study of serious persistent offenders and the incorporation of various sources of information from parents and teachers as well as from official records. They found a relationship between age and crime and concluded that the most important factor distinguishing delinquents from non-delinquents was the family and its disciplinary practices. Laub and Sampson suggest that the Glueck's unpopularity within sociology stems, in part, from a strong anti-psychiatry ideology on the part of Sutherland who dominated sociological discussions of crime during the 1940s and 1950s, at least in the USA. Even though the Gluecks had inter-disciplinary backgrounds in the social sciences, and were not medically trained, they were perceived as interested only in the biological causes of behaviour, despite the fact that they did not argue for biological determinism but aimed to identify empirically the interplay between social, or more accurately social psychological, and biological factors. Their approach, however, was atheoretical and they ignored such central sociological variables as stratification, peer group, and community characteristics (Laub & Sampson 1991, pp. 1421–7).

Biological theories re-emerge periodically with new claims of evidence of a link between an extra Y (male) chromosome and violent behaviour. This theory became prominent after 1965 with research in Scotland involving 197 mentally sub-normal male prisoners. Although all the men were described as 'dangerously violent', only seven carried an additional Y chromosome, which was considered high as the general population was thought to contain only 1.3 per 1000 live births (Jacobs, Brunton & Melville 1965, p. 1352). According to the researchers, the Y chromosome possesses greater potential for aggressiveness whereas the X chromosome increases gentleness. Other characteristics, including tallness, low intelligence, and a high rate of epilepsy, have also been associated with an additional Y chromosome (Moran 1978, pp. 343–4).

Attempts have been made, usually unsuccessful, to argue the possession of an extra Y chromosome as a defence in murder trials, the defence being that the genetic anomaly caused the violent behaviour and diminished the individual's responsibility. Even so, some research indicates that convicted offenders with an extra Y are more likely to have been convicted of property offences than of crimes against the person (Fox 1971, p. 64). Moreover, as the bulk of research involves examining groups of men held in institutions dealing with behavioural disorders, it is hardly surprising to discover that the majority of extra Y males detected have had a history of antisocial behaviour (Fox 1971, p. 69).

A recent biological, more precisely hormonal, theory of crime relates to Pre-Menstrual Tension (PMT) or Pre-Menstrual Syndrome (PMS). Despite the lack of agreement on the etiology or symptoms, most medical experts maintain that insufficient amounts of the hormone progesterone cause psychological problems such as depression, increased irritability, reduced concentration, restlessness, impaired judgement and volatility, resulting in a loss of self-control. In a number of controversial murder cases medical evidence suggested that the women on trial were extreme sufferers of PMT which was causally linked to their behaviour (Allen 1984, p. 20; Chait 1986, pp. 267–72; Horney 1978, pp. 33–5). A successful argument of diminished responsibility or loss of self–control reduces the crime from murder to manslaughter, which carries lesser penalties. In Britain, in the early 1980s, trial courts found two women guilty of manslaughter, not murder, on the grounds that severe PMS prevented them from controlling their actions. The trials stimulated the first widespread public discussion on the effect of premenstrual symptoms on women's behaviour (Rittenhouse 1991, pp. 413, 415). One consequence of this defence is the increased role of the medical profession in the criminal justice system. Another is reinforcing a conception of women as inherently irresponsible and controlled by their hormones and emotions, thereby placing them in the sick role rather than having criminal intent.

Despite a continual interest in biological causes of deviant behaviour no conclusive evidence exists. Indeed, no consistent personality or behavioural qualities have been successfully predicted from the XYY condition (Owen 1972, p. 209). Much of the research on chromosomes is methodologically inadequate because of biased samples containing only offenders convicted of violent crimes. More importantly, it is impossible to focus on biology and exclude opportunities, learned motivations, and various definitions of behaviour. The most that can be said, perhaps, is that biological factors account for deviant behaviour to the same extent that they explain conformity (Cohen 1966, p. 54). Given these problems, it is surprising that genetic theories hold so much appeal, and sociologists are criticised frequently for expressing animosity toward genetic explanations of behaviour (Rowe & Osgood 1984, p. 526).

Psychological theory

Psychological approaches to deviance focus on defining then identifying and classifying behavioural abnormalities and personality disorders. The dominant conception of abnormality seems to be any behaviour or feelings which are statistically infrequent, that is, they occur at the extremes of a normal curve. The activities and emotions of most members of a population cluster within a certain range; anything beyond that range the psychologist deems a deviation or abnormality (Duke & Nowicki 1986, pp. 7–13). The standard classification adopted in the USA, and widely used in Britain and Australia, is the Diagnostic and Statistical Manual (DSM), first published in 1952 by the American Psychiatric Association. The third edition of the DSM in 1979 details sixteen major diagnostic classes and a total of 187 specific diagnostic categories encompassing every kind of deviance that would be discussed in a sociology course. DSM IV is due for publication in 1994. The diagnostic categories specify such disorders as alcohol, cocaine, cannabis, tobacco abuse or dependence, and disorders relating to anxiety, eating, schizophrenia, depression, sexuality and personality.

Sigmund Freud's work constitutes a major influence on psychological explanations of criminality. Freudian theory maintains that an examination of the unconscious, or inner feelings, explains behaviour. When incompatible personality elements exist mental conflict occurs in the subconscious. The Freudian mode of treatment, known as psychoanalysis, involves confronting the subconscious and becoming aware of repressed feelings. Freud divides the personality into three components:

1 *id*—the most asocial portion of the personality which is the source of all the innate, basic biological drives, including eating drinking, comfort and sexual pleasure. The id is oriented to short-term gratification and pleasure-seeking;
2 *ego*—the conscious personality, reflecting attitudes and ideas developed through interaction with the social and material environment. The ego tries to satisfy the id, that is, to maximise pleasure, but pragmatically, in accordance with the constraints of the real world;
3 *superego*—arises out of relations between the id and the ego and manifests group mores and norms shaping the individual's social experience. The superego provides an individual with a moral awareness and capacity to evaluate actions as good or bad, according to social ideals.

A delicate balance obtains between the id, the ego and the superego. For Freud, mental conflict and illness derive from social morality's repression of individuals' basic desires, energies, urges and instincts (the id). Despite repression, people constantly seek to express these human drives and so release repressed energies. Through socialisation individuals learn to control the innate deviant tendencies with which all humans are endowed. In explaining deviance, Freud's focus is on childhood experiences and family, particularly parent–child, relationships. The improperly socialised child does not learn the inner controls, and either acts out inner impulses and engages in delinquent or criminal activity or projects them inward and becomes neurotic. Freud considers that homosexual adults and prostitutes have not progressed through all the stages of sexual development and therefore do not attain sexual maturity. If the superego fails to develop at all, the result is a 'psychopathic personality' (sometimes called sociopath), or a completely amoral person characterised by selfishness, callousness, impulsiveness, irresponsibility and relatively little guilt or anxiety (McCord 1983, pp. 1315–16).

The notion of psychopath or criminal psychopath is often used to explain such especially heinous crimes as mass murders or massacres, like the incidents in Hoddle and Queen Streets in Melbourne and the slaying of a group of women engineering students in Montreal in 1989. During the coronial inquest legal counsel described Frank Vitkovic, the man who shot dead eight people in a Telecom building in Queen Street in 1987, as 'a "psychotic gunman" running amok in an office building' (Ricketson 1988, p. 6). One reason why mass-murder cases are sensational is that they are so infrequent; most deviance is commonplace and single killings are not headline news unless they are peculiarly odd. The notion of a psychopathic personality is appealing because it is difficult to believe that any sane or normal person could commit such violent and destructive acts. Nevertheless, the conceptualisation of psychotic is problematic and widely criticised in sociological writing (Lindesmith 1938, pp. 593–9; 1940, pp. 914–16; Sutherland 1950, pp. 142–3). Moreover, such distinctive personality traits as emotional instability, or temperament, are not associated consistently with the propensity to break the criminal law (Schuessler & Cressey 1950, p. 483).

The first major problem is psychiatrists' imprecise use of the term 'psychopath' to cover a wide range of behaviour. This conveys an absence of consensus and diagnostic reliability suggesting that value judgements, not scientific principles, inform the conceptualisation of the psychopath (Hakeem 1958, p. 666). A more serious issue is the conceptual indistinguishability between the assumed mental condition and crime commission. The view that persons are psychopaths merely because they persistently engage in deviance or commit particularly violent or self-destructive crimes like murder, drug addiction or suicide, denotes circular reasoning. Many attempts to link psychopathy with crime define the symptoms of psychopathy in relation to the criminal behaviour; the mental condition is seen as causing the crime at the same time as the crime is held to indicate psychopathy. In this line of reasoning, all people who commit particularly serious crimes are psychopaths, by definition; it is difficult to imagine a person with a psychopathic personality conforming to social norms. According to one critic of psychiatry: 'Psychopathy is nothing but a synonym for crime and delinquency' (Hakeem 1958, p. 675).

The popularity of these individualistic explanations for certain types of deviance indicates the increasing importance of psychiatry in the fields of criminology, law and corrections. Judges, for example, may request psychiatric reports for individuals accused of murder, delinquency, drug-use, shoplifting, illegal gambling and offences involving alcohol, including drink-driving. The court order may specify that the convicted offender must participate in a drug and alcohol rehabilitation program, undergo counselling and therapy, or be committed to a mental hospital. This indicates that certain types of crime are beyond the criminal law which emphasises punishment and the assignment of moral guilt to individuals, and are within the domain of medicine which stresses treatment and rehabilitation of individuals who are deemed sick, defective or maladjusted.

Psychological conceptions of deviance as an outcome of insufficient socialisation or the inability to control innate drives and aggression present many problems, although they may be useful in explaining some forms of deviance and treating specific individuals. Among the problems are:

1 an assumption that deviance is impulsive and irrational, which cannot explain norm infractions that are rationally planned and orchestrated;
2 the problem of tautology. If insufficient or inadequate socialisation explains deviance then how can we know or measure the extent of socialisation? If the degree of deviance becomes an indicator the explanation is circular and tautological. This is also an issue in sociological theories which stress the socialisation process. If evidence of a personality disorder is commission of a violent crime or addiction to drugs or alcohol then the deviance cannot be separated analytically from the mental condition. Can people dependent on drugs or alcohol be psychologically 'normal' (however defined); can people exhibiting personality disorders conform to rules and norms? Psychological explanations seem to answer both questions in the negative because they frequently explain deviance as evidence of some underlying problem which becomes the rationale for the behaviour's emergence. Overcoming this problem of logic and conceptualisation requires evidence of the psychological problem independent of the deviance;
3 a more general problem with 'kinds of people' theories (of which the biological and psychoanalytic theories are prototypes) is their difficulty in explaining why deviant individuals violate *some* norms but most of the time conform. The focus on individuals—their physical characteristics or personalities—displaces attention from the pervasiveness and distribution of deviance throughout society. If some societies or regions have more crime and deviance than others, psychologists should expect that the distributions of people with personality disorders reflect the quantity and quality of deviance. However, a more reliable explanation would be that different societies have different norms and laws which affect the type of deviance that exists. Cohen's (1974) notion of the 'elasticity of evil' clearly makes the point that as conceptions of deviance are always changing the amounts and types of deviance also change;
4 over-emphasis on childhood experiences. Psychological theories usually assume that adult behaviour and personality are almost wholly determined by childhood experiences, most of them in the family. For example, McCord says that most psychopaths experience rejection by at least one parent in early childhood, which results in mistrust, insensitivity and hostility (1983, pp. 1316–17). However, socialisation is a life-long process and action varies according to situations and social expectations.

In sum, 'kinds of people' theories seek to account for differences in individuals' behaviour by identifying differences among persons and their situations. A major concern is the identification of factors and processes contributing to deviant or conforming motivations and inclinations. This means that any attempts to reduce the incidence of deviance are directed at the individual in the form of drugs, surgery (including sterilisation), therapy and counselling. In contrast, sociological explanations focus on the ways in which the society or social group defines deviance and impinges upon individuals' motivations and tendencies to rule violation or conformity. Some sociological theories seek to explain the distribution of deviant behaviour which exists independently of individual motivations or desires. Rates of deviance and crime are characteristics of societies, or social structures, not individuals. Durkheim's analysis of suicide is an example.

Durkheim and the sociological analysis of deviance

Durkheim's study of suicide was part of his enterprise to delineate an exclusively sociological subject matter amenable to scientific analysis. He demonstrates that suicide rates made up of intensely individual acts are social not just individual phenomena. Durkheim tries to:

> determine the productive causes of suicide directly, without concerning ourselves with the forms they can assume in particular individuals. Disregarding the individual as such, his [sic] motives and his [sic] ideas, we shall seek directly the states of the various social environments (religious confessions, family, political society, occupational groups etc.) in terms of which of the variations of suicide occur (1970, p. 151).

In other words, the suicide rate is a phenomenon *sui generis*, that is, the aggregate of suicides occurring over a time period in a society form a separate and distinct fact, rather than a series of unconnected events requiring specific analysis. The suicide rate with its own nature and unity becomes a subject of sociological research.

Durkheim refutes arguments ascribing suicide to extra-social factors ranging from mental alienation, race, heredity, climate, temperature or imitation. He suggests that psychopathic states do not bear regular and indisputable relations to suicide, and demonstrates statistically that the numbers of neuropaths and alcoholics do not affect suicide rates. Durkheim's central proposition is: 'Suicide varies inversely with the degree of integration of the social groups of which the individual forms a part' (1970, p. 209). He distinguishes between three types of suicide:

1 *egoistic suicide* results from an individual's lack of integration into a collectivity. Here a person's duties, rights and obligations to the group are weak, resulting in dependence on individual resources. To the extent that individuals are loosely integrated, excessive individualism results, increasing the probability of suicide. Durkheim finds that Roman Catholics are less likely to commit suicide than Protestants, women less likely than men, and married people less likely than unmarried. Weak

links to a collectivity and a dependence on individualism explain the various rates of suicide across social groups, according to Durkheim;

2 *altruistic suicide*, in contrast to egoistic suicide, emanates from an overintegration in the group. The collective norms and duties override the individual's sense of survival. Durkheim observed that soldiers are more inclined to suicide than civilians because they are prepared to take their own lives to further military strategies and goals. Examples include the Second World War Japanese kamikaze aircraft pilots, whose military attacks resulted in their deaths;

3 *anomic suicide* results when customary social norms lose their regulatory force, resulting in deregulation. Dramatic or unexpected change tends to sever the ties and commitments which bind people to the social order, and from a social psychological point of view they reduce a sense of belonging. An example is suicide resulting from sudden wealth or sudden poverty where the newly enriched or impoverished are unable to cope with the unfamiliar circumstances.

The distributions of egoism, altruism and anomie within a society all positively affect the social group's rate of suicide and are the sources of all individual inclinations. According to Durkheim, suicide rates vary across societies not because different societies have more or less of certain types of individuals but because societies are differentially integrated. Collective force or social control restrains suicide (as long as it is not too embracing so as to increase altruistic suicides) but it increasingly weakens with the development and structural differentiation of society. Durkheim writes: 'When society is strongly integrated it holds individuals under its control, considers them at its service and thus forbids them to dispose wilfully of themselves. Accordingly, it opposes their evading their duties to it through death' (1970, p. 209). Rapidly increasing suicide rates indicate the breakdown of the conscience collective and the emergence of basic social structural problems.

In sum, Durkheim attempts to explain suicide rates in terms of the characteristics of the social structure, specifically the degree of integration. Individual motivations or reasons for committing suicide do not concern him. Suicide, which in commonsense terms is an individual, perhaps the most individualistic and asocial act, is a social product. Whereas biological and psychological theories seek to discover why a particular individual is deviant while others conform, Durkheim's interest is why some societies or social settings have more deviance than others.

Moreover, deviance is universal: all societies define some behaviours as deviant, as offensive to legal or moral norms. The very notion that a society has social norms or rules ensures the existence of deviance. This is not to say that certain forms of behaviour or activities are regarded as deviant in all societies or historical periods. Even though some types of behaviour may change or definitions of what constitutes deviance alter, there will always be some activities and practices which some members of a society agree are inappropriate and require eradication or control. Without deviance conformity would be impossible and vice versa. The benchmark of what constitutes deviance is a comparison with what constitutes conformity. Our conceptions of deviance are premised on notions of conformity, which in turn depend on views about deviance. Recognising this Durkheim writes:

> Imagine a society of saints, a perfect cloister of exemplary individuals. Crimes, [or deviance] properly so called, will there be unknown; but faults which appear venial to the layman [sic] will create there the same scandal that the ordinary offence does in ordinary consciousness. If, then, this society has the power to judge and punish, it will define these acts as criminal [or deviant] and will treat them as such (1938, pp. 68–9).

In this passage Durkheim encapsulates many of the attributes of a sociological perspective on deviance: deviance is universal yet variable; deviance is a social phenomenon; social groups make rules and enforce their definitions on members through judgement and social sanctions; deviance is situational; and definitions of deviance and its control involve power. In other words, a society of saints is impossible because a process of social redefinition continuously operates to ensure that all the positions on the scale from wickedness to virtue will always be filled and that some people will always be holier than others. The scale of social definitions of deviance expands and contracts, denoting an 'elasticity of evil' (Cohen 1974, p. 5). This elasticity reflects the fact that individuals' identities contain moral aspects which place value on 'doing the right thing' which involves defining and responding to others who are not doing likewise. Some people develop such high stakes in their moral identities that they take the initiative in locating deviance and legislating new prohibitions, thus helping to maintain the supply of the deviance which reinforces their own identities. Becker (1963, p. 147) calls these people 'moral entrepreneurs' (discussed further in chapter 3). The expansion of deviance accommodates those whose identities would be enhanced by creating new scales of virtue, by changing the saliency of existing scales, or by enlarging the moral significance of differences along these scales (Cohen 1974, p. 17).

Every human community has its own special set of boundaries, its own unique identity, thus every community also has its own characteristic styles of deviant behaviour. Any community which feels jeopardised by a particular form of behaviour will impose more severe sanctions against it and devote more time and energy to the task of rooting it out (Erikson 1966, p. 19). Drug trafficking is viewed as a particularly heinous crime and many governments, including those in Australia and the USA, have turned their attention to fighting the 'war' against drugs and the crime syndicates. Newspaper headlines read 'Drug barons declare war', 'Drug lords seek safer havens', 'Colombia's drug lords declare war'. A drug-free society has become a moral catchcry. The so-called war on drugs is not directed at medical practitioners who over-prescribe anti-depressants or at the multinational pharmaceutical companies 'pushing' drugs via the legitimate avenue of advertisement.

Experimenting with drugs is seen as something bad and unhealthy, in stark contrast with the ideology in the 1960s that drug use was a source of liberation and discovery. Newspaper stories recount the police victories in uncovering the largest marijuana plantation or the biggest heroin cargo. In late 1989, the Panamanian Army Chief Manuel Noriega was cast in the role of demon, providing work for the military forces of the USA in furthering and protecting democracy and a drug-free society (Stothard & Bone 1989, p. 7). A United States Senate report describes him as 'a tough and devious adversary who has mastered the art of covert operations' (Boswell 1989, p. 1). News accounts depict him as a truly evil person and report that US troops dubbed one of his houses the 'witch house' because of the bizarre black magic paraphernalia and signs of animal entrails and 'vats of blood' found (*The Weekend Australian* 23–24 December 1989, p. 7). Alternative explanations are rarely offered: there is no discussion of the fanciful nature of such stories or any suggestion that the evidence may have been planted or imagined. Ironically, Noriega had been an ally of the USA and co-operated with the Central Intelligence Agency (CIA). Certainly, his transformation into a highly deviant identity cannot be explained by individualistic theories, such as his possession of distinct biological traits or a personality disorder. The emergence of Noriega as a scapegoat and the re-definition of his activities as deviant reflect issues of political power, United States foreign policy and the rising international concern about drug trafficking.

Summary

This chapter discusses theories which focus on individual characteristics in order to explain why some persons break rules while others conform. Biological theories compare physical attributes of deviants and non-deviants and attempt to associate distinct physical traits with deviant tendencies. Psychological theories examine tensions located in the subconscious mind which allegedly stem from inadequate socialisation. This results in an inability to control innate human drives which lead to deviant behaviour. 'Kinds of people' theories do not inquire into the socially constructed nature of deviance and treat social factors, like opportunities and group associations, as peripheral to individual peculiarities. Durkheim's theory of suicide does not seek explanations in individual motivations but in social organisation. Unintegrated groups where individuals possess weak ties to the collectivity, and are not enmeshed in a complex of duties, manifest high suicide rates. The suicide rate is a characteristic of the social group, or the society, not an individual phenomenon. As well as having social causes, deviance is a result of social definitions which often arise from the activities of individuals and groups aiming to locate evil and enhance perceptions of their own moral virtue. The following chapter looks more carefully at various sociological conceptions of deviance.

Key terms

Biological theory
Positivism
Atavism
Psychological theory
Durkheim
Egoistic, altruistic and
anomic suicide

Italian school
Born criminal
Stigmata
Psychopath
Elasticity of evil

Main points

1 'Kinds of people' theories focus on the individual and ask what is distinctive about a particular person which leads her or him to engage in deviant activities.
2 The concern of biological and psychological theories is to modify an individual's behaviour through treatment or rehabilitation in order to stem deviance.
3 Much of the research in this tradition is problematic because of the researchers' failure to incorporate comparison groups and their analyses remain restricted to enumerating the characteristics of people who have been identified as deviant.
4 Because proponents of individualistic theories focus on individual behaviour they are unable to account for changing social definitions of deviance.
5 Cohen suggests that deviance is 'elastic', that is, even if some forms of deviant behaviour are non-existent in a society new forms will emerge so there will always and necessarily be deviance and conformity.
6 Durkheim examines the social structure in order to explain the ostensibly most individual act—suicide. He argues that suicide rates and types reflect the level of social integration.

Further reading

Cohen, Albert K. 1974, *The Elasticity of Evil: Changes in the Social Definition of Deviance*, Basil Blackwell, Oxford.

Durkheim, Emile 1970, *Suicide: A Study in Sociology*, trans John A. Spaulding & George Simpson, Routledge & Kegan Paul, London.

Fox, Richard G. 1971, 'The XYY Offender: A Modern Myth?', *Journal of Criminal Law, Criminology and Police Science*, vol. 62, pp. 59–73.

Hakeem, Michael 1958, 'A Critique of the Psychiatric Approach to Crime and Correction', *Law and Contemporary Problems*, vol. 23, pp. 650–82.

Laub, John H. & Robert J. Sampson 1991, 'The Sutherland–Glueck Debate: On the Sociology of Criminological Knowledge', *American Journal of Sociology*, vol. 96, pp. 1402–40.

Lindesmith, Alfred & Yale Levin 1937, 'The Lombrosian Myth in Criminology', *American Journal of Sociology*, vol. 42, pp. 653–71.

Mannheim, Hermann ed. 1972, *Pioneers in Criminology*, 2nd edn, Patterson Smith, Montclair, New Jersey. Especially chapters on Lombroso, Ferri, Garofalo, Goring and Durkheim.

CHAPTER

2

Sociological theories

Within sociological theory little consensus exists on the causes of deviant behaviour or on the social processes involved in categorising certain activities as deviant. Nevertheless, there are four basic perspectives. First, normative theories ask what motivates individuals or groups to violate generally agreed upon social norms. Researchers usually investigate such factors as family background, socioeconomic status, opportunity structures, peer groups and learning processes. Second, the labelling perspective separates rule-breaking from the process of defining acts or actors as deviant and examines the consequences of negative labels for self-identity and subsequent career. Third, political economy theories posit that norms, in particular the criminal law, do not reflect social consensus but perpetuate the interests of dominant groups, thereby operating against those of subordinated groups. Fourth, feminist theories criticise all theories of deviance for their inattention to women. Proponents argue that existing theories cannot be general because, for the most part, the research supporting them deals only with samples of men and boys. Some feminists argue that more research is needed to assess the applicability of theories to female deviance, whereas others maintain that the existing theoretical perspectives cannot be salvaged because of inherent bias. This chapter surveys each of these four general theoretical strands in the sociology of deviance.

Normative theories

Normative theories conceptualise deviance as all behaviour that breaks the norms that are shared by most members of the social system. These norms which reflect some level of consensus can take the form of laws, organisational rules, regulations and standards, or unspoken expectations and obligations. Within this group of theories two themes are evident. Some normative theories focus on opportunity structures to explain deviance, while others pay most attention to social interaction. The former tend to be concerned with the implications of deviance for the social structure and social integration while the latter emphasise learning processes and inter-personal associations. Normative theories share at least four central features:

1 they all treat deviance and norm violation as synonymous, even though their explanations for the origins of deviance differ;
2 these theories conceptualise social control as the non-problematic response to rule infractions, that is, deviance occurs and social control follows the disturbance;
3 normative theories often classify or identify different types of deviance;
4 they attempt to identify the factors—psychological, economic, social, environmental—leading to deviant actions, that is, they seek to explain why individuals or groups are motivated to break norms.

This section outlines the central theorists within the normative tradition by commencing with Durkheim.

The French sociologist, Emile Durkheim, is the first sociologist to offer a conception of deviance within this normative tradition. Although Durkheim is not interested in the general field of deviance, he examines whether crime is pathological or normal; whether criminal behaviour has positive or negative consequences for the social system. Theorists of deviance usually accept Durkheim's discussion of crime as constituting a functionalist theory of deviance (Abrahamson 1978, p. 76). According to Durkheim 'normal social conditions' are those which are distributed generally throughout and across societies, whereas other conditions are 'morbid' or pathological. While Durkheim observes that crime (or deviance) is universal because no social system—even a society of saints—avoids criminal behaviour, he argues that the specific forms of deviance vary. Crime, then, is normal as it occurs in all societies (1938, p. 66). This does not imply that any amount of crime is normal, nor that the individual who violates the criminal law is biologically or psychologically normal. What is normal is the existence of criminality, so long as the rate does not go beyond a certain level. However, Durkheim does not clarify how to determine whether the level of crime is pathological or normal. Moreover, he suggests that criminal motivations or tendencies are not social products but have biological and psychological causes 'given the incorrigible wickedness of men [sic]' (1938, p. 67). The implication is that in any society there exists a normal distribution of individuals motivated to break the criminal law.

Because crime exists in all societies it contributes to social cohesion by offending collective sentiments. This is the core of Durkheim's functionalist perspective on deviance. For Durkheim, crime (and by extension other forms of deviance), rather than creating social disorder unites people in shared indignation and outrage when valued rules of conduct are broken: 'Crime brings together upright consciences and concentrates them' (1933, p. 102). The common expression of anger increases social solidarity and reinforces morality. It makes people more conscious of shared interests and values, thus reaffirming agreement on standards or social norms.

Durkheim also takes interest in what gets done about crime, in particular the law. For Durkheim, different types of law, as signified by the sanctions attached, indicate the prevailing social solidarity (Lukes & Scull 1983, p. 37). He identifies two major types of sanctions:

1 *repressive sanctions* aim to punish an offender. The penal code or criminal law specifies repressive sanctions which reflect the heart and centre of the collective consciousness, that is, the shared sentiments of the community. For example, general agreement that murder and rape are serious crimes is reflected in the fact that imprisonment is the usual penalty. In criminal cases the dispute is not directly between the alleged perpetrator and the victim but between the society, represented by the public prosecutor (in Australia a police officer or a lawyer employed by the Department of Public Prosecutions) and the accused person.

2 *restitutive sanctions* do not necessarily cause any suffering on the part of the perpetrator. They aim to re-establish relationships disturbed from their normal form. Civil law, commercial law, administrative and constitutional law are all examples of restitutive laws whose aim is enforcement of obligations not punishment. The sanctions ordinarily take the form of damages, that is, a monetary payment or an order to perform the specific contractual requirements. For the most part, the collective consciousness is not offended. Most people would not be outraged when business contracts are broken, but the party affected may suffer financial loss or other damage and seek a remedy through litigation. Rules with restitutive sanctions are not established directly between the individual and society, but between individuals or groups, especially corporations. It is up to individual or corporate persons who have been harmed or disadvantaged, not the public prosecutor, to initiate legal proceedings and seek restitution.

According to Durkheim, in societies with little division of labour law is wholly penal in character; the whole society participates in the administration of repressive justice. As society becomes more complex restitutive law increases and punishment performed by special officials becomes less severe. Deprivation of liberty, varying in time according to the seriousness of the crime, increasingly becomes the normal means of social control. The penal law of primitive societies almost exclusively specifies and controls offences against the whole society, its mores, traditions and religion.

As evolution advances, crimes against the collectivity decline while outrages against the person—murder, theft, fraud, violence—take up increasing space. There is less moral scandal and less violent repression (1973, pp. 285–300).

There is little evidence to support Durkheim's evolutionary view of law and sanctions. Diamond (1971, p. 62), for example, argues that in the early stages of social development repressive law covers only a few serious offences, such as incest. He suggests that early law generally takes the form of a regulated or semi-regulated system of private vengeance or feuding, whereas the rise of repressive law parallels the emergence of economic class divisions and state forms. In a cross-cultural survey of fifty-one societies, Schwartz and Miller find that restitutive sanctions—damages and mediation—exist in many societies that lack even rudimentary special-isation (1964, pp. 163–7).

Despite little empirical support for some of Durkheim's ideas, discussions of the positive functions of deviance for the maintenance of the social group flourish. Kai Erikson's (1966) examination of three crime waves (as indicated by official records) in seventeenth-century colonial Massachusetts is a good example. In *Wayward Puritans*, Erikson argues that the Puritan community of Salem, Massachusetts, began to censure forms of behaviour which previously had been present and tolerated by the group, as a way of re-asserting its identity and moral boundaries. As the sense of mission and zeal began to diminish due to the growth and differentiation of this religious community, a spate of witchcraft trials occurred which had the effect of reinforcing the community's religious identity. The identity crisis led to frantic displays of Puritan zeal and public witchcraft trials whose object was to clarify the moral meaning of membership in the colony. The trials were less of a response to an increase in witchcraft than to the need for the minions of the Devil to provide work for God's agents.

Erikson suggests that any community feeling jeopardised by a particular form of behaviour will impose more severe sanctions against it and devote more time and energy to its elimination (1966, p. 20). The deviant is a person whose activities have moved outside the margins of the group and when the community applies social control it makes a statement about its boundaries. It declares how much variability and diversity can be tolerated within the group before losing its distinctiveness. The important point is that a group's boundaries are elastic such that at one point in time certain activities fall within those boundaries while at another they may not. In Salem, behaviours falling outside the boundaries included unusual behaviour and apparent fits among young girls who claimed that the fits were caused by witches. The people the girls identified as witches were already marginal members of the community, for example a West Indian slave, a beggar, and a woman who was lax in church attendance and lived with a man before marriage. In a sense, these individuals were the most dispensable to the community. But when the girls started to accuse respectable individuals doubts about their infallible judgement began to grow, and the incidence of witchcraft declined.

Within the functionalist perspective Talcott Parsons offers one of the most sophisticated accounts of deviance. According to Parsons, no behaviour is intrinsically deviant. It is only deviant insofar as it violates the norms of some social system. Ideally, social systems are integrated; actors are oriented to norms which ensures continuity in social interaction and equilibrium. In reality, deviance exists thereby raising problems of order and integration. According to Parsons, 'Deviance is the tendency on the part of one or more of the component actors to behave in such a way as to disturb the equilibrium of the interactive process' (1951b, p. 250).

Figure 2.1 Parsons' conception of deviance and social control

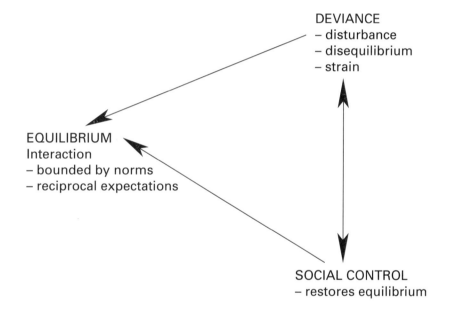

Deviance places strains on individuals as their expectations are not met and they must adapt or adjust to that situation. Parsons (1951b, p. 252) suggests three ways an individual can manage the strain:

1 *accommodate* the deviance by ignoring it or by changing the original expectations;
2 *transfer* attention to a new situation or relationship;
3 *renounce* or redefine the set of expectations which have been violated.

Social control, then, comprises those processes in the social system which tend to counteract the deviant tendencies. Figure 2.1 illustrates the central features of this theory of deviance. Parsons expresses less interest in the origin or causes of deviance than in the consequences of the disturbance for the social system and the processes involved in restoring equilibrium. As actual social systems are never integrated perfectly, deviance is always present. Because of the inevitability of deviance, social control cannot eliminate deviance, it can only limit its consequences and prevent the spread to others.

Merton's work seeks to move beyond the social relationship to provide a social structural account of the emergence of deviant behaviour. In an early essay 'Social Structure and Anomie' (1938), Merton sets out to identify the processes through which social structures generate the circumstances in which infringement of social codes constitutes a 'normal response'. He questions why it is that the frequency of deviant behaviour varies within different social structures and that deviations have different shapes and patterns in different social structures. Merton aims to discover 'how some social structures *exert a definite pressure* upon certain persons in the society to engage in nonconformist rather than conformist conduct' (1938, p. 672, emphasis in original).

Merton hypothesises that deviant behaviour results from a disjunction between culturally defined goals to which most members of society aspire; and institutionalised norms, that is, acceptable or legitimate (as defined by the relevant social system) means for achieving the goals. He terms this condition anomie,[1] or strain, which individuals must accommodate or manage. Figure 2.2 presents Merton's typology of the five possible adaptations to anomie:

Figure 2.2 A typology of modes of individual adaptation

	Modes of Adaptation	Culture Goals	Institutionalized Means
I	Conformity	+	+
II	Innovation	+	−
III	Ritualism	−	+
IV	Retreatism	−	−
V	Rebellion	±	±

Source: Merton, Robert K. 1968, *Social Theory and Social Structure*, The Free Press, New York, p. 194.

1 *conformity* prevails when goals are achievable through legitimate means. This response is the most prevalent, allowing the stability and continuity of the society to be maintained;
2 *innovation* results when the individual aspires to such cultural goals as financial success, but lacks access to institutional means, for example a post-secondary education. Merton suggests that higher rates of crime occur among working class and ethnic minorities who experience pressures toward deviance because of restricted access to the conventional means for success;

3 *ritualism* occurs when the means are followed but the cultural goals lose their relevance. For example, the bureaucrat who diligently follows organisational rules often loses sight of the purpose of those regulations and the overall goals of the agency;

4 *retreatism*, the least common adaptation, signifies rejection of both culturally prescribed goals and institutional norms by complete withdrawal from society. This category includes psychotics, vagabonds, chronic alcoholics and drug addicts;

5 *rebellion* involves envisaging and seeking a transformed social structure by replacing existing social goals and means.

Merton's deviants are people adapting to anomie stemming from socially structured problems of adjustment. Cohen (1965, pp. 10–12) suggests that in certain respects Merton's theory is atomistic and individualistic as each person seems to solve problems alone, unaware of others in the same situation. In contrast, Sutherland's *differential association theory* points to the importance of relationships and the learning process in understanding the emergence of deviance.

According to Sutherland, deviant behaviour is learned in the same way as any other behaviour (Sutherland 1983; Sutherland & Cressey 1978, pp. 80–2). He explains crime in terms of the learning process, not in terms of personality, poverty, stress, biological or psychological abnormality. He disagrees that crime is a working-class phenomenon and demonstrates that people in white-collar jobs are not immune from criminological influences (see chapter 8). In the process of interaction with others, usually in primary groups, individuals confront various definitions of behaviour, some of which are favourable to law violation. An excess of definitions favourable to law violation encourages deviance. This is the principle of *differential association*. Sutherland elaborates nine propositions regarding the learning process and the frequency, duration, priority and intensity of associations and the consequent exposure to definitions favourable to deviant behaviour. Sutherland theorises that associations, not general needs or values, explain criminal behaviour, and maintains that it is the job of empirical research, not theory, to explain the existence or distribution of those associations within the social structure. In a sense, there is no deviance in Sutherland's conception, because everybody conforms to some set of expectations. It is the expectations which conflict with the law.

Becoming deviant involves learning the techniques of deviance as well as the motives, attitudes and rationalisations (Sutherland & Cressey 1978, pp. 81–2). Sykes and Matza (1957, p. 664) develop this point and argue that much delinquent behaviour is based on justifications or rationalisations that the perpetrator sees as valid, thereby not defining his or her behaviour as deviant. Norm violation does not necessarily mean a rejection of norms, but may involve such rationalisations as denying responsibility, injury or the existence of a victim, or defining the condemners as deviant. Without damaging self-image, rationalisations neutralise or deflect disapproval arising from a discrepancy between internalised norms and behaviour.

While Sutherland and Sykes and Matza still operate within the normative conception of deviance, they clearly do not accept a model of normative consensus. They recognise a variety of norms and values not all of which are compatible with those codified in the legal system, especially the criminal law. These theorists recognise the importance of opportunity structures, but this aspect remains undeveloped as they emphasise learning processes. A student of both Sutherland and Merton, Albert K. Cohen combines Sutherland's emphasis on the learning process with Merton's anomie theory in a discussion of subcultures. In *Delinquent Boys* (1955), Cohen argues that individuals engage in criminal and delinquent activities by taking over the criminally oriented subcultures in their environment, but he later asks the Mertonian structuralist questions: 'Why are such subcultures there to be taken over; what is it about the society that accounts for the distribution of its subcultures?' (1968, p. 346).

According to Cohen, people in situations of strain frequently are not alone, as often several actors in close communication with one another share the same problems. If they collectively and simultaneously adopt a solution to their shared problems, including restricted access to achievement, a deviant or criminal subculture emerges with its own distinct norms, values and definitions of conformity and deviance. Cohen explains: 'The crucial condition for the emergence of new subcultural forms is the existence, in effective interaction with one another, of a number of actors with similar problems of adjustment' (1955, p. 59). He takes specific interest in the delinquent gang which he argues is primarily a male, lower-class phenomenon emerging in response to the denial of the material and cultural resources necessary to compete effectively with middle-class boys. The formation of a subculture establishes goals the lower-class boys can achieve and may make non-conformity with the expectations of outsiders a positive criterion of status within the group. Cohen describes the subcultural values of delinquent gangs as the inverse of the wider culture, namely short-term hedonism and irrational behaviour. Miller goes further and suggests that the distinctive cultural system and way of life of the lower-class community itself generates delinquency, rather than a 'delinquent subculture' which emerges through conflict with middle-class culture and emphasises the deliberate violation of middle-class norms. The focal concerns of lower-class culture are trouble, toughness, smartness, excitement, fate and autonomy which support, or at least do not inhibit, a range of illegal behaviour on the part of members of adolescent street corner groups (Miller 1958, pp. 5–7, 18).

Cohen and Short subsequently identify several types of male delinquent subculture, namely the parent–male subculture, the conflict-oriented subculture, the drug addict subculture, semi-professional theft and the middle-class delinquent and acknowledge that little is known about the numerous varieties of female delinquent subcultures, except that they exist (Cohen & Short 1958, pp. 24–8, 34–5). Similarly, Cloward and Ohlin (1960, pp. 20–7) elaborate Cohen's notion of delinquent subcultures by identifying three different types—the criminal, the conflict, and the retreatist—which reflect the influence of Merton's typology. Just as access to legitimate means for goal achievement is distributed unequally throughout society, so is access to the illegitimate opportunity structure, namely, the opportunity to learn, practice and to perform deviant and criminal roles. The opportunity to learn derives from associations with others who engage in and accept the law-breaking behaviour, and these associations are differentially distributed. Each type of subculture reflects the community characteristics that determine the illegitimate opportunity structure and thereby the form that delinquency will take. For example, in some neighbourhoods successful criminals interact and communicate with young people and provide them with opportunities to learn criminal attitudes and skills.

The writers discussed thus far take deviant behaviour as their point of departure. Another type of theory within the normative conception, *control theory*, posits that the task of theory is not to explain deviance but to account for conformity. The question becomes not why do people deviate but why do they conform to social norms. Hirschi, the major proponent of control theory writes: 'According to *control* or bond theories, a person is free to commit delinquent acts because his [sic] ties to the conventional order have somehow been broken' (1969, p. 3, emphasis in original). The absence of control increases delinquency. Essentially, this approach looks at Durkheimian concerns with collective consciousness and integration from the individual's point of view. Control theory proposes that individuals make rational choices, albeit unconsciously, regarding the comparative costs and benefits of conventional and deviant activities. It assumes that individuals pursue activities which maximise benefits and minimise costs. However, other factors like persuasion, loyalty, and power inequalities may affect individuals' decisions to engage in high risk activities. In a sense, it is rational for the individual to do so but then rational choice appears very much like rationalisation which occurs after the deviance rather than before.

Hirschi (1969, pp. 16–26) identifies four elements of the bond to conventional society:

1 *attachment* to others, including parents, school and peers. To lack these attachments frees an actor from moral restraints. However, this assumes that those social groups themselves are committed to conformity rather than deviance;

2 *commitment* to such conventional forms of action as education and occupational success which involve investments of time and energy, thus rendering deviance costly. Ambition and aspirations play important roles in producing conformity.[2]

3 *involvement* in conventional activities makes a person too busy to find time to engage in deviant behaviour. The opportunity to commit deviant acts rarely arises because the person is tied to appointments, deadlines, schedules and working hours;

4 *belief* in the norms prohibiting deviant activities.

These bonds inhibit deviance because they represent things of value which deviant activities may jeopardise. Their absence 'frees' individuals to maximise their own self-interest thereby increasing the probability of criminal deviance. The nature or existence of social bonds may change over the life course. After re-analysing the Gluecks' data on delinquent and non-delinquent males, Sampson and Laub conclude that the stronger an adult's links to work and family the lower the levels of crime and deviance regardless of delinquency as a child (1990, p. 625).

In their refinement of control theory, Gottfredson and Hirschi (1990) argue that the classical conception of human behaviour as pleasure-seeking and pain-avoiding explains crime and deviance which are distinguishable only by the sanctions attached. They conclude that most criminal acts are trivial, mundane incidents requiring little preparation or special skill which result in little loss and little gain. People likely to engage in criminal and analogous acts will tend to be impulsive, insensitive, physical (as opposed to mental), risk-taking, short-sighted, and nonverbal. In sum, such individuals lack self-control; there are few restraints on their behaviour. Gottfredson and Hirschi attribute low self-control to the absence of nurturance, discipline or training which results from ineffective child-rearing.

In another variant of control theory, Cohen and Felson argue that changes in the 'routine activities' of every day life influence deviant behaviour by altering opportunities and social control mechanisms. Specifically, norm-breaking requires a convergence in space and time of motivated offenders, suitable targets, and the absence of capable guardians against a violation (1979, p. 589). Changes in routine activities entailing a dispersion of activities away from households and families decrease social control. Cohen and Felson demonstrate that the decline in controls through routine activities has been accompanied by an increase in illegal predatory activities, especially residential burglaries. The rapid growth in high-value property which is easy to carry and easy to sell, for example video cameras, compact disc players and microwave ovens, plus the availability of such technological advances as the automobile, small power tools and telephones also increase the opportunities for criminal deviance. This 'routine activity approach' usefully integrates elements of anomie theory by paying attention to opportunity structures and bond theory by positing the centrality of social control in an explanation of deviance and conformity. It also contributes to theories of victimisation, specifically the proposition that individuals' personal lifestyles which are related to the differential exposure to dangerous places, times and others, affect the risk of criminal victimisation (Meier & Miethe 1993, pp. 466–74).

Braithwaite's theory of reintegrative shaming is another attempt to synthesise existing theories while retaining the view that most criminal laws, especially those dealing with predatory offences against persons and property, are the outcome of overwhelming consensus (1989, p. 3). He takes elements from labelling, subcultural, control, opportunity and learning theories in order to link societal pressures with individuals' choices to engage in criminal deviance or to conform. Hirschi's central proposition that deviance results when individuals' bonds to society are tenuous is a core assumption in Braithwaite's argument, however, he is more concerned with strengthening those ties than is Hirschi (Uggen 1993, p. 486).

The notion of reintegrative shaming is central to achieving conformity because it allows for social control without stigmatising or ostracising the offender from the community. Braithwaite maintains that: 'Reintegrative shaming means that expressions of community disapproval, which may range from mild rebuke to degradation ceremonies, are followed by gestures of reacceptance into the community of law-abiding citizens' (Braithwaite 1989, p. 55). The ideal type of shaming occurs within loving families where punishment is imposed within a framework of reconcilable and collective interests. Where family ties are strong and individualism is weak crime rates will be low. He concludes that crime is best controlled when members of the community actively participate in shaming and the subsequent reintegration of a norm breaker. Social control from this perspective has moral, denunciatory and educative dimensions and is not totally repressive or stigmatising. Braithwaite demonstrates the relevance of shaming, interdependency, communitarianism and apology to crime control by relying on the example of Japan, one of the few industrial nations to experience a decline in crime rates since the Second World War. However, the number and salience of male-dominated criminal or delinquent sub-cultures indicates that Japanese society is neither totally homogeneous nor integrated (Kersten 1993, p. 278). Japan has a higher rate of juvenile offending than the USA, but rates drop dramatically with age (Uggen 1993, p. 489).

Norm-breaking theories of deviance share a number of problems or limitations. First, these approaches start with conceptions of value consensus and normative integration, but recognise disintegration as more frequent and usual. Deviance signifies the incompleteness of normative integration and the existence of values and norms which conflict with dominant norms and laws. In this conception, social control follows deviance as the way to reinstate the social order. Indeed, Durkheim (1933, p. 70) makes social control, that is punishment, part of the definition of crime which renders his conception tautological.

Class bias constitutes another major problem with this approach. With the exceptions of Sutherland and Braithwaite, the theorists discussed above assume that deviant behaviour overwhelmingly is a lower-class phenomenon, because, in Merton's terms, that is where the gap between pressures to succeed and the reality of low achievement is the greatest. An alternative argument is that members of the lower class and minority groups are more likely to be detected and labelled as delinquent, criminal, alcoholic or mentally ill than are members of the middle and upper classes who may engage in the same norm-breaking activities. Studies of white-collar and corporate crime show that law violation and immoral activities also occur in the highest social stratum but perpetrators are less likely to be caught and identified as criminal. In other words, they are less likely to be labelled deviant. This indicates the importance of distinguishing rule-breaking behaviour from a deviant self-identity. The following section outlines the labelling perspective on deviance by discussing the work of key theorists as well as identifying some of its limitations.

The labelling perspective

Labelling theory, sometimes termed symbolic interactionism, focuses on the societal reaction, that is, the responses of others who identify and interpret activities or individuals as deviant, not on the person who violates norms (Becker 1963; Kitsuse 1962; Schur 1971). The reactions depend not only on the violation of a rule but on who breaks the rules, the time and place, and whether he or she is visible to others motivated and with the authority to invoke sanctions. The definition of behaviour as deviant depends on the social audience, not just on the norm-breaking activity. The forms of behaviour do not themselves activate the processes of social reaction. The application of deviant labels and rule infraction are logically distinct. The consequences of a deviant label for an actor's public image, self-identity and moral career contrast with the actor not so labelled, though both may break the same norms.

The labelling perspective reached its zenith in the 1960s and early 1970s. However, its intellectual roots derive from the interactionist tradition of George Herbert Mead. In this perspective deviance is not a static phenomenon but results from dynamic processes of social interaction which continuously shape its construction (Schur 1971, p. 7). Tannenbaum, an early theorist, describes the process of making someone criminal as a process of 'tagging, defining, identifying, segregating, describing, emphasising, making conscious and self conscious' (1938, pp. 19–20) to such a degree that a shift occurs from defining specific acts as evil to defining the individual as evil. He terms this 'the dramatization of evil'.

The central concern of labelling theorists is to distinguish rule-breaking behaviour from deviance, that is, to separate the objective acts from the identification of an individual or group as deviant and ultimately their subjective view of themselves as such. Becker formulates the most influential and oft-cited position of the labelling perspective. He writes: 'deviance is *not* a quality of the act the person commits, but rather a consequence of the application by others of rules and sanctions to an "offender". The deviant is one to whom the label has successfully been applied; deviant behaviour is behaviour that people so label' (1963, p. 9, emphasis in original). Becker suggests that the term 'deviant' be reserved for those labelled as deviant by some segment of society and concludes that 'whether a given act is deviant or not depends in part on the nature of the act (that is, whether or not it violates some rule) and in part what other people do about it' (1963, p. 33).

Even so, the distinction between rule-breaking and deviance is somewhat ambiguous. This is evident in Becker's typology of deviant behaviour, presented in figure 2.3, which cross-classifies kinds of behaviour and the responses they evoke, thus distinguishing four theoretical types of deviance (1963, pp. 19–22). This typology generates much criticism, particularly regarding the category of secret deviance, which Becker defines as an improper act to which no one reacts. The question immediately arises: 'How can a secret deviant exist?'. If deviance requires societal definition, then all a secret deviant can be is a secret norm-breaker. It is also incorrect to classify conformity, that is, obeying a rule and being perceived as doing so, as a type of deviance.

Figure 2.3 Becker's typology of deviant behaviour

	Obedient behavior	*Rule-breaking behavior*
Perceived as deviant	Falsely accused	Pure deviant
Not perceived as deviant	Conforming	Secret deviant

Source: Becker, Howard S. 1963, *Outsiders: Studies in the Sociology of Deviance*, The Free Press, New York, p. 20.

Labelling theorists stress that becoming deviant, or acquiring a deviant self-identity, is a process and does not automatically follow rule-breaking behaviour; it depends on a social audience's enforcement of a rule. A critical aspect of the process of building a stable pattern of deviant behaviour is the experience of being caught and labelled by official agents of social control. Garfinkel (1956, pp. 420–4) describes the degradation ceremony where an actor's public identity is destroyed ritually and replaced by another lower status with associated auxiliary traits, which becomes the most important component of an individual's identity (Hughes 1945, p. 353). For many people, 'homosexual' is a dominant status carrying such auxiliary attributes as effeminacy, potential AIDS carrier, weakness and passivity. 'Unemployed' is another example, with auxiliary attributes of laziness, indolence, lack of education or intelligence, and dole-bludger. Possession of one trait defined as deviant has a generalised symbolic value so that others automatically assume that the incumbent possesses the associated auxiliary traits. The labelled person's access to such legitimate activities as employment or housing may be restricted even though her or his 'deviance' does not affect conformity with other social norms. This is an important reason for homosexual people not to come 'out of the closet' despite decriminalisation. A final step in the deviant career is movement into an organised deviant subculture which enables the formation of identities in opposition to the wider or mainstream culture. The subculture provides self-justifying rationales and ideologies which generally repudiate conventional moral rules and institutions. Studies of male homosexuals indicate that participation in a homosexual subculture is important for participants' well-being, it involves learning subtle stereotypes of heterosexuals and how to manage homosexual identity. In short, subcultures provide an acceptable interpretive framework to counter mainstream definitions (Weinburg & Williams 1974, pp. 270–1).

Perhaps the most useful contribution within the labelling perspective is Lemert's distinction between primary and secondary deviation (1951, pp. 75–6; 1967, pp. 62–3). He recognises that initial norm-breaking acts can derive from various social, cultural and psychological factors. Primary deviation remains situational and is rationalised; it does not affect a person's self-conception or public identity as a conforming member of society. In contrast, secondary deviation involves an actor engaging in norm-breaking behaviour and assuming deviant roles and identities which are adaptations to the problems created by societal definitions and reactions to the initial deviance. Rule-breaking activity increases in response to sanctions and stigmatisation which results ultimately in the actor's acceptance of a deviant social status and conformity with the associated social expectations. Once defined as deviant, the person may be rewarded for playing the deviant role and punished or not believed for conforming to social norms (Tannenbaum 1938, p. 19; Scheff 1966, p.84).

For labelling theorists the focus must be on the social audience which determines whether certain activities are defined as deviation and whether an actor becomes deviant (Erikson 1962, p. 308; Kitsuse 1962, p. 253). The concern is not with what 'caused' the individual to engage in specific acts or behaviour but with the nature of the response and the subsequent definitions of the individual, that is, the processes that produce deviant outcomes.

The labelling process operates on at least three levels of social action, namely interpersonal relations, organisational processing and collective rule-making (Schur 1971). Everyday interaction, formal agencies of social control ranging from police departments, courts, hospitals to government bureaucracies and legislative bodies, constitute different audiences. They all stereotype, interpret activities retrospectively, bargain and negotiate, all of which are essential in producing deviant outcomes. A large body of research documents how official social agencies identify, classify and label individuals as deviant and the implications for their careers (Kitsuse & Cicourel 1963, p. 135). Sudnow's study (1965, pp. 259–64) of the public defender's office, for example, demonstrates that an image of the typical crime emerges during routine interaction with alleged offenders. It entails assumptions about the conditions of the crime and the suspected offender's social characteristics. These descriptions become 'normal crimes' attributable to all people accused of such acts. Questioning becomes not so much an attempt to assess the defendant's situation but a process of fitting that person into the stereotyped imagery of the criminal and the crime.

Similarly, Goffman (1961, pp. 117–56) examines the implications of organisational labelling processes for the moral career of the psychiatric patient. He argues that hospitalisation alters the private and public identity of the individual who becomes a patient. Organisational contingencies and the occupational values and assumptions about the appropriate or typical behaviour of psychiatric patients affect hospital staff's reactions. Goffman maintains that the 'sick' behaviour imputed to the patient stems from the labellers' social distance from the patients' situation, rather than deriving inevitably from the psychiatric illness.

Arranging for people who had never suffered psychiatric symptoms to be admitted to psychiatric hospitals enabled Rosenhan (1973, pp. 250–1) to investigate the labelling process within a mental hospital. Each of the eight pseudo-patients claimed to have been hearing voices but upon admission ceased simulating any signs of abnormality. Hospital staff never realised the deception. Except for one person, all were admitted with a diagnosis of schizophrenia and were discharged with a diagnosis of schizophrenia 'in remission'. This research shows that the label 'schizophrenic' profoundly affects others' perceptions of individuals and their behaviour. The label was so powerful that hospital staff ignored many of the pseudo-patients' normal actions or interpreted them in terms of the initial diagnosis and the medical model of mental illness.

The labelling perspective has been the subject of a range of criticisms, including proponents' greater attention to the successfully labelled deviants rather than to social audiences, their neglect of self-labelling processes, the lack of explanations regarding why some individuals are motivated to break rules, and the assumption that labelling only escalates deviance thereby ignoring the deterrent effects of sanctioning (Rotenberg 1974, p. 335). Liazos (1972, p. 104) criticises labelling theorists for not systematically relating 'deviance' or the organisation of social audiences to larger social, historical, political and economic contexts. Although labelling theorists emphasise social reaction, most of their research deals with how deviants manage their labels, particularly within subcultures. While they seek to humanise and normalise the 'deviant', their emphasis on the deviant undermines that aim. The concern is more with the subculture and identity of the deviants themselves than on their oppressors and persecutors, or on those who break norms but because of power and influence avoid negative labels. This indicates a tacit acceptance of the current successful definitions of deviance and further marginalisation of the successfully labelled. Avoiding such difficulties requires shifting attention from the processes of interaction to wider political and economic structures to show how power operates in the designation of deviance (Liazos 1972, p. 115). In a particularly scathing critique Gouldner (1968) claims that labelling theorists' pull to the underdog indicates an attraction to their exotic difference and easily takes the form of essays on 'quaintness'. He unequivocally proposes that Becker's theorisation of the deviant as the product of society, rather than as the rebel against it, paradoxically treats the deviant as a passive nonentity, as a victim responsible neither for the situation nor its alteration (1968, p. 106). Moreover, labelling theory's critical analysis of the deviance processing agencies, including the courts and psychiatric hospitals, diverts attention from the political economic structures and powerful interest groups that shape various definitions of deviance.

Discussion of white-collar or corporate crime is difficult from a labelling perspective as the destructive activities of many corporate actors are not publicly labelled deviant, and in many instances do not even break laws, because none prohibit their activities. The labelling perspective, then, is more applicable to certain kinds of behaviour where considerable disagreement prevails about the norms, for example homosexuality, drug abuse and mental illness, rather than such violent crimes against the person as murder or rape, where general consensus about their deviant status usually exists. Even so, the activities that constitute any form of norm-breaking or deviance involve a process of definition and classification.

A further limitation of the labelling approach is failure to account for why some persons are motivated to engage in activities which break norms or are likely to be labelled negatively. Gibbs suggests that the lack of concern with etiological factors indicates that the labelling theorists seek a theory about reactions to deviant behaviour not deviant behaviour *per se*, which makes their empirical investigations on deviants problematic (1966, p. 12). Moreover, proponents do not specify the kind of reactions essential for deviance designation or explain why reaction to behaviour is not purely random and idiosyncratic. One response would be that people label behaviour as deviant because it offends generally agreed upon social norms.

In his reconsideration of labelling theory, Becker argues that the original proponents do not offer solutions to the etiological question but aim to expand the study of deviance by including in it activities of others than the allegedly deviant actor. The principal theoretical contribution of the labelling perspective is distinguishing norm violation from social control and treating social rules as fluid and continually constructed in accordance with the convenience, interests, will and power of various groups (1973, p. 192). Attention to questions of power, socio-economic structures and the organisation of interest groups is explicit in political economy theories of crime and deviance which the following section outlines.

Political economy theories

In the 1970s, a surge of interest and theoretical development emphasised the importance of power and conflict in the content and application of criminal laws. These theories have been variously termed the 'new', 'radical', 'conflict', 'critical' or 'Marxist' criminology (Inciardi 1980, p. 7). Theories within this conflict orientation incorporate many of the principles of the labelling perspective but concentrate more on social structure than social interaction. They seek to demonstrate how the criminalisation of certain types of conduct and the differential enforcement of criminal laws reflect the interests of economically and politically powerful groups. These theories are less concerned with why individuals or groups are motivated to be criminally deviant and more concerned with why the behaviour is defined as criminal. Moreover, they do not approach the criminal law or the enforcement agencies as mechanisms of dispute resolution or social control, but as manifestations or outcomes of social conflict and diversity. Specifically, the activities of lower-class people are disproportionately defined in law as criminal and they are more likely to be arrested, charged, convicted and sentenced than are middle- and upper-class people. Many of these theories commence with the writings of Marx and focus on the influence of economic elites on legal change (Chambliss 1974, p. 16; Quinney 1974, pp. 138–9; 1977, pp. 26–9; 1978; Taylor, Walton & Young 1973, p. 270) while others have a more pluralist conception of society (Turk 1966, pp. 347–51; 1976a, pp. 279–80; 1976b, pp. 284–5).

Even though neither Marx nor Engels develop theories of law, crime or deviance, many of their writings form the basis of political economy theories of crime and deviance. In *The Debates on the Law on Thefts of Wood* (1975), Marx recognises that in capitalist society laws favour the interests of the bourgeoisie by being completely compatible with the goals and conditions of capitalism. Marx and Engels see crime as located in the lumpenproletariat, whom they disdain because of their unproductiveness and individualism which prevent the development of a revolutionary consciousness.

Given Marx's fragmentary remarks on crime, some critics argue that there cannot be a Marxist theory of crime or deviance (Hirst 1972, p. 28). Even so, *The New Criminology* by Taylor, Walton and Young (1973) proposes a Marxist theory of deviance which attempts to explain both the immediate circumstances and the structural conditions of deviance and social control. The authors explicate the ways in which particular historical periods give rise to economically and politically powerful groups which order society. They ask: 'Who makes rules and why?' (1973, p. 220). Their approach synthesises many earlier theories of crime and deviance.

The first requirement of the theory is to locate the act within the opportunity structure which is determined by power, wealth, and economic inequalities, that is, a political economy of crime. Secondly, it identifies the immediate origins of the act: the events, experiences and structural developments that precipitate the act. Thirdly, it requires analysis of the different ways actors interpret structural demands. Here, there is a need to acknowledge that some individuals may consciously choose to be deviant as a way of managing certain problems. The actual act is an outcome of both appropriate values and opportunities to violate norms. The other side of the theory deals with social control and encompasses the immediate origins of the social reaction, the wider origins and the outcome of the social reaction on deviants' further behaviour. In order to explain deviance, these formal requirements must all appear in the theory in dialectical relationships with one another.

Taylor, Walton and Young argue that the causes of crime are bound up with the kind of social arrangement existing at a particular point in time, thus for crime to be abolished the social arrangements must also undergo transformation. The authors hold a revolutionary vision of a future society in which no political, economic or social need exists to criminalise deviance. They acknowledge the Durkheimian observation that deviance is universal, yet their conception of deviance is unclear because criminalisation is only one form of social control.

Another key theorist in the political economy tradition is Quinney, whose work has become progressively more radical. His early writing reflects a pluralist conception of society where interest groups lobby to affect public policy, including the content and enforcement of criminal laws. He regards crime as a definition of conduct which authorised agents in a politically organised society formulate (1970, p. 15). Criminal definitions result from conflicts and unequal power between different segments of society. Powerful groups control activities which threaten the realisation of their interests by criminalising the activities. The extent of the criminal law reflects the amount of conflict in society. The criminal law does not represent consensus but conflict. Enforcement of the criminal law also depends on the extent to which the behaviours of the powerless conflict with the interests of the powerful. Individuals not represented in organisations that formulate and apply criminal laws are more likely to act in ways that will be defined as criminal compared with those segments that do formulate public policy.

Quinney (1977, pp. 78–85) subsequently develops a theory of crime in which the state and the ruling class become central to criminal definition and management. This instrumentalist view of the law has its origins in *The Communist Manifesto*, first published in 1848, where Marx and Engels state: 'The executive of the modern state is but a committee for managing the common affairs of the whole bourgeoisie' (Marx & Engels 1964, p. 5). Quinney maintains that the state, through the legal system, protects its interests and those of the capitalist ruling class. Crime control represents the coercive means of checking threats to the prevailing social and economic order. The contradictions of capitalism produce poverty, inequality and exploitation which lead to crime as a means of survival. According to Quinney, burglary and drug dealing, crimes against the person, and industrial sabotage and other predatory crimes are rational responses to the inequities of capitalist society. These activities may ultimately become conscious political action oriented to overthrowing the system. Compared with the activities the criminal law prohibits, the capitalist class and the state commit many social injuries including price fixing, discrimination, pollution and economic exploitation which are rarely criminalised or sanctioned as crime. Quinney calls these practices crimes of domination.

Viewing the state and the criminal law as instruments of the bourgeoisie seeking to preserve its dominance and the social order almost suggests a conspiracy and comes close to being tautological (Beirne 1979, pp. 378–9). On the other side, structuralist Marxists argue that the state enjoys relative autonomy and the capitalist class cannot manipulate state institutions at will. This is shown by the state's pursuit of policies contrary to the interests of certain segments of capital, for example welfare legislation, legal prohibitions on price fixing, monopolies, insider trading, and anti-discrimination and occupational health and safety laws. Even though the immediate impact of legislation is not always in the interests of capital their long run and overall interests are embodied in such laws (Chambliss & Seidman 1982, p. 143). For example, Hopkins (1983, p. 287) suggests that strong consumer protection legislation, such as the Trade Practices Act, only represents a symbolic defeat for business interests because of the difficulties in enforcement. While laws prohibit restrictive trade practices, in actuality such restrictive practices are pervasive. Empirical research is required to discover whether such deviance results from conscious or intentional business decisions to violate laws or because the absence of social control, due to disunity or dispersion among consumers, for example, leaves the practices unchecked.

During the 1980s a new critical perspective known as 'left realism' emerged, particularly in the United Kingdom with some resonances within Australian criminology (Brown & Hogg 1992, p. 195). Left realists criticise previous criminology for being offender-centred and argue that the Marxist criminologists of the 1970s ignore the victim of illegal behaviour and present the perpetrators as victims of capitalist economics, disadvantage, and unjust criminal law enforcement. They argue that crime is a real problem which is not reflected in officially collected data. In contrast, victim surveys which interview people about crimes which may have been committed against them indicate that a vast majority of people commit serious offences for which they are never arrested. Not only are people from poor or working-class areas more likely than the middle class to be engaged in or apprehended for alleged crimes against property, but they are also most likely to be victims of ordinary and corporate crime thus compounding social inequality and vulnerability. The task of theory, then, is to explain the interrelationships between offenders, victims and enforcement agencies (Brown & Hogg 1992, pp. 199–203; Matthews & Young 1986, p. 1; Hogg 1988, p. 28; Young 1986, pp. 20–3).

A number of writers investigate the ways in which various political and economic forces, including the interests of the ruling class, shape the legal definitions of crime. In an early paper Chambliss (1964) examines the emergence of vagrancy statutes in fourteenth-century England which were designed initially to coerce labourers to accept employment at a low wage, thereby ensuring landowners had an affordable labour supply. By the early sixteenth century the statutes emphasised the criminal aspects of vagrancy and were targeted at rogues, vagabonds and other criminal suspects. This change Chambliss attributes to the disintegration of feudalism, the increased emphasis on commerce and industry which increased the numbers of merchants and traders transporting goods. The vagrancy statutes were used to control persons preying upon the merchants carrying goods. Chambliss (1978) also analyses the development of laws outlawing opium. In order to stem Chinese immigration, the United States government passed the first anti-opium legislation in the world in 1886. Previously, opium was imported legally into the USA and was used mainly by Chinese immigrants who worked on the railroads and in the gold and silver mines. The opium constituted a palliative to their working conditions and was administered as medical treatment. By the late 1880s the need for cheap labour declined and the government was concerned by the growing numbers of immigrants who were rapidly becoming a burden rather than an asset. The new laws rendered opium trade illegal.

Chambliss argues (1979, p.153) that the process of law-making is dialectical, by suggesting that society manifests contradictory elements which stimulate social change. The most central contradiction within capitalism is between labour and capital and it, like all other contradictions, creates conflicts and dilemmas which people try to resolve. Within the constraints of the economic structure action is possible, but the resolution of some conflicts generates new dilemmas, indicating that the law and its enforcement can never be static, nor are they instruments of one class. Many interest groups may participate in the legislative process (Hagan & Leon 1977, pp. 595–7; Hagan 1980, pp. 622–5).

The various conflict theories of crime and deviance have difficulties. In many respects the 'new criminology' is not new as it incorporates such established sociological theories of crime and deviance as social pathology, functionalism and symbolic interactionism and rephrases them in political terms (Meier 1977, pp. 463–8). While dissensus exists regarding vagrancy, prostitution and the use of certain drugs, a high level of consensus regarding seriousness and the need for control attaches to offences like homicide, robbery and rape (Rossi et al. 1974, p. 227). Political economy theories generally present the violator of criminal laws as powerless and a victim of social inequality, thereby denying any responsibility to the actor. These arguments break down in a discussion of white-collar crimes, or crimes of domination, where possession of power and economic resources are the explanations of criminal, or at least deviant, behaviour by corporate actors. Ironically, conflict theories make some functionalist assumptions, for example, crime is functional for the ruling class; it is able to maintain social order and its dominance through coercion rather than consensus. Also, crime as defined by criminal law as a lower-class phenomenon is reminiscent of Merton's anomie theory.

A further important theorist interested in power is Michel Foucault, a French historian and philosopher, who identifies relationships between power, knowledge (or discourses) and forms of social control. Of particular relevance to the discussion of deviance is Foucault's analysis of prisons and punishment and the emergence of the hospital, especially the asylum. The central themes of his analysis are:

1 *reason*, or rationality, as it emerged in the West during the Enlightenment, which led to increasing segregation and individuation of punishment and treatment;
2 increasing *control* over consciousness and the mind rather than physical punishment;
3 *diffusion* of the power to punish and treat with the emergence of new experts, particularly psychiatrists.

Foucault argues that during the eighteenth century the community acquired an 'ethical power of segregation, which permitted it to eject, as into another world, all forms of social uselessness' (1988, p. 58). In this period, people deemed insane were confined rather than banished, or forced to labour with vagabonds, the undeserving poor or other 'deviants'. Under the guise of therapy and treatment in the asylum, judgements about individuals were made without appeal. This signifies the 'conversion of medicine into justice, of therapeutics into repression' (1988, p. 266).

Foucault develops the notion of the increasing subtlety and pervasiveness of social control in *Discipline and Punish* (1979), where he describes the disappearance of torture as a public spectacle and the increasing protests against public execution during the second half of the eighteenth century. As the law was the sovereign's will, breaking the law meant a personal attack on the monarch who thereby had the right to obtain vengeance. Growing opposition decried the barbarity and irregularity of the public execution and sought to end the sovereign's vengeance. Additionally, during this period the nature of crimes being committed changed from violence against the person to property crimes, reflecting economic change and a higher juridical and moral value placed on property relations (1979, p. 77). Foucault debunks the notion that the impetus for change in punishment stems from increasing humanitarianism, and argues it arose from a tendency towards a more finely tuned justice, 'towards a closer penal mapping of the social body' (1979, p. 78). In Foucault's terms:

> The reform of the criminal law must be read as a strategy for the rearrangement of the power to punish, according to modalities that render it more regular, more effective, more constant and more detailed in its effects ... In short, the power to judge should no longer depend on the innumerable, discontinuous, sometimes contradictory privileges of sovereignty, but on the continuously distributed effects of public power (1979, pp. 80–1).

The segregation and continuous surveillance of 'problematic populations', combined with an emphasis on discipline and correction, formed central goals of the reform movement. The goals were all met architecturally in Bentham's prototype control structure, the Panopticon, which was the perfect disciplinary apparatus, enabling a single gaze to see everything constantly. At the periphery was a ring-shaped building divided into cells, each of which had an outward- and an inward-facing window; in the middle was a watch tower with windows. The supervisor in the central tower could see everything, but the prisoners were never aware when they were being watched, so they had to behave all the time. They had no contact, even visual, with other residents (1979, pp. 200–3). Order and security were guaranteed.

Foucault identifies two dimensions of discipline:

1 the *discipline–blockade*, the enclosed institution established on the periphery of society turned inward towards negative functions such as controlling crime and eradicating criminal associations.
2 the *discipline–mechanism* which improves the exercise of power by making it lighter, more rapid, more effective—a design of subtle coercion. Increasing regimentation, regularity, routinisation and regulation result in the disciplinary society (Foucault 1979, p. 209).

This sounds very much like Weber's conception of bureaucratic rationality. The disciplinary practices, once concentrated in the prison and the asylum, diffuse throughout society and the power to punish becomes fragmented and less identifiable. The punitive and juridical functions of the sovereign are visibly obvious, unlike those of the psychiatrist, the probation officer, the psychologist, the teacher, the social worker, the doctor and the counsellor. This results in punishment becoming the most hidden part of the penal process.

Stanley Cohen elaborates this argument in a critique of community control (1979, 1985). He maintains that the apparent changes in the formal social control apparatus, specifically the movement away from imprisonment to alternative, community-based forms of punishment, results in a blurring of the boundaries between inside/outside, guilty/innocent, freedom/captivity, punishment/treatment and imprisoned/released (1979, p. 344). The recent emphasis on community corrections and diversion of most people from the formal justice system increases the amount of official intervention and increases the total number of people who come into contact with the criminal justice system, thus 'thinning the mesh' and 'widening the net'. The proliferation of community-based programs adds to the quantum of social control, albeit in a more diverse, diffuse and less visible guise (see chapter 5).

In numerous ways, Foucault makes a unique contribution to the analysis of social control and deviance. Nevertheless, many of his ideas parallel Weber's discussion of rationality and Durkheim's notion of penal evolution. In Foucault's work reason appears inexorable; there is little room for individual action or for resistance. Moreover, he expects reason and discipline to unfold in a linear fashion, or run like ink on blotting paper. This view cannot account for such practices or policies as the increasing emphasis on punishment for an offence rather than treatment or rehabilitation of the convicted offender. One of Foucault's main contributions is to highlight the fact that reform movements propounding the inhumanity of certain punishments or treatments may actually result in more subtle interventionist and totalitarian forms of control. Finally, Foucault does not clarify why retributive punishments are less insidious than surveillance of the mind.

Theories of female deviance and feminist theories

A common theme of feminist critiques of sociological theories of deviance is their neglect of women (Chesney-Lind 1986; Heidensohn 1968, 1985; Klein 1973; Millman 1975; Naffine 1987; Smart 1976). All argue that what purport to be general theories of deviance—including functionalist, strain, differential association, labelling and critical theories—are biased because they mainly address and study deviant men, thus marginalising the analysis of women. Where research on female deviance exists it tends to rely heavily on assumptions about women's nature and to centralise marital and reproductive roles—actual and anticipated—in explaining deviant activities. Feminist critics also argue that such theories adopt a deterministic view of women's and girls' behaviour by claiming that supposedly essential or natural female qualities—emotionalism, deceit, irrationality, sexuality and the tendency for promiscuity among single women and girls—constitute key factors in female deviation. Women and girls are depicted as engaging in such sex-specific and gender-related deviance as shoplifting, prostitution and transgressing motherhood norms. As Brown sums up 'the crime of the deviant woman is first and foremost a crime against her nature as a woman and only secondly against the state' (1986, p. 360).

In contrast, male deviance is explained in terms of social, economic and political conditions and normal learning processes. Millman (1975, p. 253) observes that news stories and the sociological literature tend to identify with male deviants and portray them as active, taking initiative, managing limited alternatives and committed to their group or subculture while women are depicted as fragmented, individualistic and disorganised. This male bias results in the underinvestigation of such topics as domestic violence, rape and sexual harassment, everyday deviance and social control, particularly within the family and the interpersonal regulation of women by men. The focus on deviant men also largely ignores the consequences of that deviance for others, especially their often female victims. The following section discusses some early theories of female deviance, then assesses the attempts to generate feminist theories of crime and deviance.

Even though few theorists subscribe to Lombroso's atavistic theory, at least with regard to men, beliefs in biological determinism, implicit acceptance of double moral standards and a failure to incorporate social, economic, political and legal factors still appear in analyses of female deviance and crime (Brown 1986; Smart 1976). Lombroso and Ferrero's *The Female Offender* (1895) specifically studies female criminals and claims that women are less criminal than men because their lack of intelligence, passion and sedentary lifestyle restrain them. Feminine and criminal, according to these researchers, are contradictions. Women involved in crime possess masculine characteristics which indicate degeneration rather than evolutionary advancement. They argue that the born female criminal, the prototype being the prostitute, possesses all the criminal qualities of men combined with women's worst characteristics, namely cunning, spite and deceitfulness (Lombroso & Ferrero 1979, pp. 10–13). While many authors accept that Lombroso and Ferrero adopt a biologically determinist account of female crime, Brown points out that this conclusion is unwarranted as they focus on women's conformity as the object of analysis and view women's biological nature as antithetical to crime. Women's law-breaking cannot be caused biologically because their biology causes conformity, thus external, non-biological antecedents to explain women's criminal deviance must be identified (Brown 1990, pp. 50–1).

Other theories explain women's deviation from sex roles as the major cause of crime and delinquency. W. I. Thomas, for example, observes that poverty might prevent a woman from marrying whereby she would resort to prostitution as an alternative to marriage but as enabling her to continue in a feminine service role (Smart 1976, pp. 37–45). Davis (1937, p. 746) also sees women generally as using sex to obtain the economic and social status men supply, and describes prostitutes as being paid not for their services but as compensation for loss of social status. He views prostitution as mercenary, promiscuous and emotionally indifferent; the antithesis of female gender roles. The prostitute violates the moral code which prohibits the commercialisation of sex. But that moral code is applied only to one half of the relationship, the supply side. Men are not accused or convicted of promiscuity, or adultery. Neither Thomas nor Davis consider the dual moral code and fail to explain why men's promiscuity and extra marital sexual activities are not deviantised. Nor did they consider economic factors in their explanations.

Another theorist of women's deviance writing in the 1950s, Otto Pollak, proposes that with the exception of prostitution, men's and women's deviance is similar (1979, pp. 37–44). He argues that official crime statistics fail to reflect the scale of women's deviation because of under-reporting of their offences, the police and courts' lenient treatment, and women's ability to conceal information through manipulation, deceit, cunning and mendacity. While acknowledging the importance of social contexts, Pollak claims that women's criminality reflects their biological nature in a specific cultural setting which distinguishes their behaviour from that of men. He identifies the critical factors in female crime as the so-called generative phases—menstruation, pregnancy and menopause—which result in psychological disturbances with a crime-promoting influence. Menstruation can result in thefts, shoplifting, and homicide; menopause, in perjury, insults and breaches of the peace; and pregnancy in infanticide. Two major factors have a crime-inducing influence on women. The first is a repressive sexual morality juxtaposed by advertising focusing on women as consumers, which provides them with many temptations. The second factor is the special opportunities which female roles offer for the commission of crimes. He argues that the opportunities for women to commit crime are great while the chances of detection are low, thereby deflating official crime data. Like other theorists, Pollak specifies women's hormones, reproductive roles and capacities as determining their emotionality, impulsiveness, unreliability and deviousness, which lead to crime (Heidensohn 1985, p. 112).

Debate regarding the status of conventional theories of deviance questions whether they are so laden with male bias as to be totally inadequate for analyses of female deviance, or whether they are general theories of deviance. Some authors maintain that many traditional theories need refinement and that male bias stems from the fact that most research on deviance has been conducted with male samples therefore their applicability to women is unknown. Because most theories were developed to account for male deviance does not mean that they cannot account for female deviance. Schur, for example, applies the labelling perspective to explain the differential application of norms and definitions of deviance to men and women (1984, pp. 22–30). As the norm is male, to be female is to be deviant. Women do not have to engage in specific acts to be labelled deviant; the gender system routinely devalues and subordinates them. The range of marital, occupational, sexuality and appearance norms applied to women but not to men underscores this point. The gender system makes certain kinds of deviance, for example mental illness, hysteria, obesity, and shoplifting, more appropriate for or expected from women than men. Women thus face a double bind. Gender norms make women deviant but deviation from those norms invokes more deviant labels.

While much of the feminist literature is devoted to identifying male bias and gender-based assumptions in theories of deviance and crime, there are attempts to develop new theories to explain women's deviance and crime. Different strands of feminism—liberal, socialist, radical and postmodern— have problematised traditional assumptions about crime, victimisation and the justice process. Feminist theories encompass concerns with the origins of women's deviance, the structure and content of the criminal law, the activities of official agents of social control, women's experiences as victims of crime and gender inequality in the criminal justice system (Daly & Chesney-Lind 1988, p. 497; Simpson 1989, p. 606). Even so, attempts to generate a feminist criminology have not advanced much further beyond criticism of existing theories. Gender specific theories raise the further problem of separatism, that is, perpetuating dualistic theories: one set to explain men's deviance, the other to explain women's deviance (Brown 1986,

p. 372). Moreover, Brown warns against the temptation to replace theories accused of being biologically determinist with social determinism (Brown 1990, p. 45).

From a liberal feminist perspective, Freda Adler (1975, pp. 5–30), proposes a theory of female crime to account for the tremendous increase of serious crimes committed by women, as measured by arrest data. She argues that a new breed of women criminals involved in violent offences is emerging. She interprets the female arrest rates in the USA, which surpassed those for men in robbery, fraud, larceny and burglary but not murder or aggravated assault, as signifying that both men and women are concerned with financial gain. Adler identifies the women's liberation movement as the major contributor to these trends. As opportunities expand for women in the occupational structure, accompanied by women's heightened aspirations, so do illegitimate opportunities and their aspirations in regard to criminal and illegal activities. She describes this apparent narrowing of the gap between men and women in the criminal world as the dark side of the women's liberation movement. Women endeavouring to gain status in the criminal as well as the civil spheres are beginning to emulate men's pattern of offending, made easier by technological advancement in firearms, and electronic devices rendering physical strength and size less important. As women enter the paid labour force they experience the same temptations, stresses and frustrations as men thus increasing their motivation for crime.

The women's liberation thesis has been largely discredited and positive relationships between female emancipation and crime have been refuted (Box 1983, pp. 189–92; Chesney-Lind 1986, pp. 79–80; Naffine 1987, pp. 92–100; Smart 1979, p. 58). That increasing involvement in property offences parallels growing opportunities for women in the labour market is a strange argument, given many theories' emphasis on poverty, economic disadvantage and associations as significant causes of law-breaking behaviour. More significantly, there is not much evidence that a high degree of equality prevails between men and women. Women generally enter lower-paid jobs with less security and fewer opportunities for promotion than men. Adler's use of arrest rates also presents problems, as percentage increases when numbers are small distort the overall picture. Changed arrest rates for women may be more indicative of changes in police department policy than of alterations in women's actual behaviour. Subsequent research indicates that only a few types of female criminality are increasing, in particular petty property offences. Chapter 6 elaborates the scope and dimensions of women's deviance and criminal behaviour.

More recently, feminist theorists have turned from comparing male and female deviance and crime to asking questions about the impact of gender on deviance (Allen 1988, 1989; Cain 1990, p. 3; Edwards 1989, p. 166). Traditional theorists failed to analyse the most central finding of research on criminal deviance, namely its masculinity. Even though conventional deviance research studied men and boys, neither maleness nor masculinity were addressed as significant explanatory variables. In other words, 'the role of men's membership of a *sex* is never investigated as it is for women, by non-feminists and feminists alike' (Allen 1988, p. 16, emphasis in original; see also Harris 1977, p. 14). Allen suggests that feminist inquiry should examine the contributions that forms of masculinity make to the construction of criminality as a masculine resort, to the policing or non-policing of offences and to the criminal justice responses to women offenders. Rather than asking why women do not offend, theories should explain how the social construction of maleness connects with the universal finding that most criminals have always been and are men. Such an approach may necessitate rejecting the notion of 'crime' as a sexually neutral category and acknowledging its sex specificity (Allen 1989, p. 36; Cain 1990, p. 11).

Radical feminist criminology places women's experiences as victims of crime and the criminal justice system's treatment of female victims at the centre of inquiry (Simpson 1989, p. 611). For example, radical feminists redefine the crime of rape from a sex crime to one which emphasises male power, control and domination which also infuse rape trials. Moreover, feminist theories and feminism as a social movement have been instrumental in expanding official conceptions of violence and changing the criminal law.

Summary

This chapter addresses the central sociological ideas about deviance and demonstrates the lack of consensus regarding the causes and definitions of deviance. Because the concept is so 'polymorphous' different theories are useful to explain certain deviant activities, or to analyse why some people respond to particular acts or people by labelling them deviant. All theorists agree that deviance is a social product, that norms or definitions have to be applied or constructed before deviance exists, but they disagree as to whether the focus should be on the actor who has broken particular norms, on the mechanisms of social control, or on the processes of defining activities as deviant. The following chapter examines a range of activities often defined as deviant and sometimes criminalised. In Western societies, social control of such behaviours as abortion, pornography and homosexuality was initially the domain of religious institutions, then the criminal law, and most recently the medical profession.

Notes

1 Merton uses the term 'anomie' differently from Durkheim for whom it means normlessness, that is, many norms which are incompatible thus signifying deregulation and social disorder.

2 Recent incidents of insider trading, that is, the exchange of confidential price sensitive information about the share market, seem to contradict this point. The motivation for insider trading among lawyers, stock brokers and investment bankers is ambition and achievement in the conventional world. This issue is discussed further in chapter 8.

Key terms

Normative theories	Pathological and normal
Repressive and restitutive sanctions	Anomie
Functionalism	Differential association
Techniques of neutralisation	Subcultures
Control theory	Reintegrative shaming
Symbolic interactionism	Labelling
Primary and secondary deviation	Discipline
Political economy theory	Degradation ceremony
Conflict criminology	Feminism
Feminist criminology	Societal reaction

Main points

1 Normative theorists view deviance as behaviour which violates social norms. They examine the factors—opportunities, social background and social environment—which motivate individuals to break norms. Merton, a major proponent of this tradition, sees deviance as resulting from a disjunction between culturally defined goals and institutionalised means.

2 Differential association theory focuses on the learning process and maintains that deviant behaviour is learned in the same way as any other behaviour. Sutherland suggests that the frequency, duration, priority and intensity of contact with definitions of behaviour favourable to norm violation encourage deviance. Conceptually, then, deviant behaviour is not concentrated among people in poverty with few opportunities and resources.

3 Labelling theorists emphasise societal reaction in order to explain the development of a deviant self-identity. They distinguish between rule-breaking behaviour and individuals' adoption of deviant roles. Primary deviation refers to the initial norm-breaking acts which are not recognised as deviance or are explained away. Secondary deviation occurs after negative sanctioning and the norm-breaker's entry into a new social status, that of the deviant.

4 Political economy theorists argue that laws, in particular the criminal law, do not reflect societal consensus, but the values and interests of the powerful. Rather than resolving disputes or maintaining social order the

law is a source of conflict and repression. Moreover, because of inequalities certain groups are more likely to engage in criminal behaviour.

5 Michel Foucault is less concerned with deviant behaviour than with forms of social control or discipline. He and his followers argue that social control is becoming less visible, more subtle and dispersed.

6 Feminist writers criticise conventional theories of deviance because of their neglect of women and their assumptions about women's nature and gender-specific types of deviance. So far, however, an integrated and comprehensive feminist theory of deviance has not emerged.

Further reading

Becker, Howard S. 1963, *Outsiders: Studies in the Sociology of Deviance*, The Free Press, New York.

Braithwaite, John 1989, *Crime, Shame and Reintegration*, Cambridge University Press, Cambridge.

Brown, David & Russell Hogg 1992, 'Essentialism, Radical Criminology and Left Realism', *Australian & New Zealand Journal of Criminology*, vol. 25, pp. 195–230.

Chambliss, William & Robert Seidman 1982, *Law, Order and Power*, 2nd edn, Addison-Wesley, Reading, Massachusetts.

Cohen, Albert K. 1983, 'Crime Causation: Sociological Theories', *Encyclopedia of Crime and Justice*, vol. 1, ed. Sanford Kadish, The Free Press, New York.

Gelsthorpe, Loraine & Allison Morris eds 1990, *Feminist Perspectives in Criminology*, Open University Press, Milton Keynes.

Gottfredson, Michael R. & Travis Hirschi 1990, *A General Theory of Crime*, Stanford University Press, Stanford.

Heidensohn, Frances 1985, *Women and Crime*, Macmillan, London.

Smart, Carol 1976, *Women, Crime and Criminology: A Feminist Critique*, Routledge & Kegan Paul, London.

Sutherland, Edwin & Donald Cressey 1978, *Criminology*, 10th edn, Lippincott, New York.

CHAPTER

3

Criminalisation and decriminalisation

The boundary between deviance and conformity is subject to contest, negotiation and change, especially where little consensus exists on the status of certain activities, behaviour or actors. Deviantisation or criminalisation are processes by which moral boundaries are drawn and segments of the population controlled. This chapter reviews a number of practices and behaviours variously defined as sin, crime and illness and usually seen by at least some members of society as deviant, immoral, or as violating religious or natural law. Morality refers to conceptions of right and wrong usually legitimated by a generally considered unique source of all morality, for example God or Nature (Kallen 1963, p. 643). While morality is usually associated with religious precepts, economic circumstances also shape the content of morals, for example particular groups' arguments about morals can reflect members' concern to preserve their own social status or economic interests. Appeals to morality often underpin attempts to control segments of the population defined as problematic by criminalising them or at least by restricting their access to social resources, including education, employment and housing. The criminal law usually becomes an arena in which social movements and political actors attempt to have their conceptions of deviance and morality legitimated. The first part of this chapter examines the concept of morality and the role of religious organisations (especially in the Judeo-Christian tradition) and moral entrepreneurs in designating such widespread practices as homosexuality, abortion, pornography, prostitution and drug and alcohol abuse as sinful, immoral and deviant. The second part looks at each of those activities individually.

Morality and religious values

In pre-industrial society morality or value consensus was essential for social integration, according to Durkheim, and the law reflected morality. Morality was shared among members of the society and little or no conflict existed between it and the law. Moral rules were absolute. Durkheim holds the view that: 'Morality lacks all basis if it does not rest upon religion, or at the very least, on a rational theology; that is to say, if the categorical imperative does not emanate from some transcendent being' (1973, p. 304). Durkheim also maintains that criminal law reflects a shared morality or conscience collective in complex societies.

In most pre-industrial societies law, morality and religion were indistinguishable. The Hebraic world view, for example, equated law with morality which derived from God or developed through divinely inspired individuals, or 'conduits'. Law and morality were one and no recognition could be granted to any laws lacking in divine inspiration.

Durkheim focuses on linkages, analogies and parallels between legal and moral rules and conceptualises law as derivative from and expressive of a society's morality (Lukes & Scull 1983, p. 3). Whereas the state—an external constraint or social fact—exercises the law, morality is exercised by the whole society in the form of public opinion. Indeed, without the support of morality laws cannot be effective (Durkheim 1986, pp. 352–4). In contrast, social constructionists or labelling theorists argue that conceptions of morality are neither collective nor consensual but socially constructed through the enterprise of certain groups—moral entrepreneurs—seeking to obtain general societal acceptance of their particular values and world views (Becker 1963, pp. 147–63). Certainly, the concept of 'morality' is nebulous, with various behaviours being immoral and moral at different points in time, and their designation as one or the other is often the outcome of social movements' political action. Identifying the processes whereby certain behaviour becomes immoral and/or illegal involves analysing the distribution of power in society and the social conditions under which such definitions become codified into law.

Religious institutions have had a central role in defining morality. Despite secularisation, many kinds of behaviour previously defined as sin and as immoral, including homosexuality, abortion and prostitution, have come under the jurisdictions of law and medicine and are now defined as criminal or as illness. Religion distinguishes between the sacred and the profane and practices falling within the latter are defined as sins. Only religious leaders have the authority and responsibility for social control. In Islam, for example, special religious judges or *kadi* (in Malaysia they are called *mufti*) assign penalties for such religious sins as adultery. Asceticism and renunciation are central Christian values and the early church specified asceticism as requiring sexual celibacy. Sexual self-restraint became a key virtue and tenet of the faith indicating the first and indispensable condition of righteousness and avoidance of earthly or human temptation and weakness. St Augustine equated original sin with concupiscence and venereal emotion (Bullough & Bullough 1987, p. 70). Early ascetic literature emphasised that secular sources of happiness are inevitably transitory and deliverance is attainable only through renunciation of the world and oneself.

Although virginity and celibacy were the highest ideals, marriage was designed to moderate desire by diverting it to the task of procreation, the only acceptable purpose of sex. Procreation was the only purpose of marriage and the quality of the marriage depended on conception and the number of children (Bullough & Bullough 1987, pp. 62–70; Foucault 1981, pp. 36–9). These values persist in contemporary society where being childfree by choice or involuntarily childless incur negative stigma (Miall 1986, p. 268).

Christian morality frequently defines homosexuality, masturbation, contraception, abortion, assisted reproduction, adultery and prostitution as deviant, immoral and hedonistic. The Roman Catholic Church strongly opposes abortion, perceiving it as murder of the innocent, which violates natural, divinely given rights. It also opposes *in vitro* fertilisation and other procreative technologies because they interfere with the marital relationship, involve masturbation and, where gametes are donated, constitute adultery.

These values treat as immoral other practices, for example drug or alcohol consumption and pornography, which may reduce self-control, increase temptation or stimulate extramarital or non-procreative sexual relations. Even though contemporary society is secular and the church is not the dominant institution of social control, moral proscriptions against these activities and the people who engage in them prevail. Conrad and Schneider (1980, p. 172) suggest historical complementarity and continuity between religious, legal and medical definitions and explanations of deviance. These three institutions of social control typically reinforce each other in the general moral definitions and prescriptions they advocate. In addition, the Christian confession as a form of social control has been taken on by legal and medical personnel.

The confessional

Since the Middle Ages, Western societies have established the confession as one of the main rituals for producing the truth, and sex has always been a privileged theme of the confession. Only Christianity appears to have an institution of private guilt and confession and an obligation to confess controlled by religious elites who monopolise the power of absolution and reconciliation (Hepworth & Turner 1982, p. 9). In contemporary, secular society, forms of the confession occur in the police station, courtroom, the doctor's surgery, psychiatrist's office, and even the advice columns of the tabloid press and television programs such as the Oprah Winfrey and Phil Donahue talk-shows. In each of these settings deviance is absolved through a conviction, a prescription, or advice. The confession operates on an individualised conception of deviance and guilt and a power imbalance where the one who listens manifests authority and represents the collective religious, legal or medical consciousness (Foucault 1981, pp. 20–1, 60–5; Hepworth & Turner 1982, pp. 66–7).

The socially constructed need to confess parallels social pressures on people who violate social norms to provide accounts. Accounts are excuses or justifications made to explain untoward behaviour and bridge the gap between actions and expectations thus neutralising questionable acts. Excuses are legitimate ways of relieving responsibility for deviance, and include appealing to accidents, duress or coercion, biological necessity and scapegoating, whereas justifications involve accepting responsibility for certain actions but denying their deviant status (Scott & Lyman 1968, pp. 46–51). Confessions, accounts, rationalisations, and 'techniques of neutralisation' all explain deviance away and reaffirm conformity. A converse process involves locating, identifying and designating culturally legitimate activities as deviant. This is known as 'moral entrepreneurship' which aims to establish and create categories of deviance through legal and attitudinal change.

Moral entrepreneurs and social movements

Studies of moral entrepreneurs examine the impact of groups or social movements espousing a particular set of values on the emergence of new laws. Many moral crusades manifest strong humanitarian overtones and are couched in terms of protecting basic human rights, for example those of the innocent, children and the unborn. Moral entrepreneurs appeal to higher loyalties, including natural law, Christian or traditional values, or the sanctity of human life in their attempts to change laws. Moral indignation is a central attribute of this form of social protest (Pakulski 1991, chapter 1). Many laws, especially those prohibiting practices deemed acceptable by some segments of society, are not automatic but result from the enterprise and collective action of groups seeking to have their world views and conceptions of morality codified in law. Examples include legislative change relating to drugs (Becker 1963; Duster 1970), pornography (Zurcher et al. 1971), and abortion (Luker 1984).

Gusfield demonstrates how the Prohibition campaign in the USA developed into a symbolic crusade which provided an opportunity for status discontents to engage in status politics (1963, pp. 12–30, 166–83). With increasing urbanisation, secularisation, ethnic diversification and industrialisation in the small rural towns, the Protestant middle class sensed a threat to its status position and lifestyle. Drink and abstinence became symbols of status group membership, with religious dedication and sobriety becoming hallmarks of middle-class respectability and routes to self-improvement and social mobility. Gusfield argues that members of the Women's Christian Temperance Union sought legislative change more to reaffirm publicly their values, morality and lifestyle than to regulate drinking (1963, p. 111). The temperance movement was a means for a formerly acknowledged status elite to regain some lost status by winning a legislative victory and symbolically reaffirming a lifestyle. Pixley focuses on the gender dimensions rather than the class politics of the temperance movement and argues that temperance constituted resistance to the form of patriarchy, especially regarding male drinking and sexual habits, prevalent during late nineteenth-century Australia. The temperance movement also initiated and popularised women's demand for voting rights (1991, pp. 293–8).

More generally, the affirmation of a norm through law and government action indicates the public worth and power of one subculture or viewpoint over others (Gusfield 1967, pp. 176–8). Gusfield specifies two orientations to moral reform:

1 *assimilative*—campaigners see themselves as expressing values and options which have the full agreement of the majority of the population. They perceive their primary task as one of converting the norm violator or deviant to a style of life they consider morally and socially superior;
2 *coercive*—when reformers consider they no longer have the support of the majority their strategies involve attempts to compel the moral dissenter to conform.

Anti-pornography campaigns also have symbolic value in status politics when their accomplishments reaffirm a lifestyle or set of basic values in the face of social change (Zurcher et al. 1971, pp. 222–5). However, social groups engaged in forms of moral protest may be more likely to share a common culture than a similar status position. For example, right-wing groups seek to reinstate what they perceive or have experienced as healthy traditional values emphasising communal or family life and Christian morality to counter what they see as increasing disorder, permissiveness, family breakdown and irresponsibility (Coleman 1988, p. 88; Dworkin 1983, pp. 100–4; Platt 1969, chapter 5). Additionally, occupational groups in the pursuit of professional goals are instrumental in designating certain behaviours as deviant, and extending the criminal law. The initiative of a low status segment of the medical profession, pediatric radiographers, led to the emergence of the battered child syndrome and child abuse as a social problem (Pfohl 1977, pp. 315–8). The criminalisation of abortion was associated directly with the professional claims of medical practitioners, especially their asserted superior expertise in saving lives (Luker 1984, p. 31; Mohr 1978).

The tactics and arguments of moral reform groups depend upon the motives protesters assign to those they define as immoral. For example, anti-abortionists project the women seeking abortion and those individuals campaigning for free abortion on demand as selfish, unconcerned with the rights of the unborn, pragmatic and unfeminine (Clarke 1987a, pp. 135–7; 1987b, pp. 241–5). Research on the small, personal and frequent meetings of a pro-life organisation in a rural United States community finds that:

> Abortion is fused metaphorically with the imagery of decadence and destructive, usually male, sexuality, in this case 'a decline in the culture' and 'the rape of motherhood'. By contrast abortion is opposed to female experiences of pregnancy, birth and maternity. The latter are cast as the domain of creation, innocence, pure motive and nurturance ... In this logic, women who advocate legal abortion are misguided, if not immoral, because they violate boundaries between these domains and in that sense are not appropriately female in their actions (Ginsburg 1989, p. 99).

Anti-pornography crusaders often associate pornography with sexual and violent crime, sexual aberration, self-abasement and self-abuse, juvenile delinquency, marriage failure, drug addiction, venereal disease and rejection of religion (Zurcher et al. 1971, pp. 223–5).

Moral entrepreneurs, then, focus on certain kinds of activity on which there is little consensus regarding its deviant status. Ben-Yehuda (1992) suggests that when two or more symbolic–moral universes meet, compete, negotiate and clash, deviantisation and criminalisation become major strategies for members of one universe to assert their dominance over members of other universes. The ability of different symbolic–moral universes to generate and use power and to legitimate their claims determines who will deviantise and criminalise who, where and when (Ben-Yehuda 1992, p. 76). Forms of behaviour designated as crime may not be threatening or dangerous *per se*, but are significant as battlegrounds for the supremacy of value commitments and world views. Struggles over criminal definitions entail generating and manipulating cultural symbols and attempting to produce moral panics with the aim of transforming public attitudes, policy and the law (Cohen 1980, p. 10). The emergence of legislation, especially a criminal statute, indicates a symbolic victory even if the law has negligible deterrent effects or is rarely enforced. Many of the so-called crimes against morality are often termed 'victimless crimes'.

Victimless crimes

The theorist most closely associated with the concept of 'victimless' crime is Edwin Schur who defines crimes without victims as: 'Situations where one person obtains from another in a direct exchange a commodity or personal service which is socially disapproved and legally proscribed. The combination of the exchange transaction combined with lack of apparent harm to others constitutes the core of a victimless crime' (1965, p. 170).

Victimless crimes are created when criminal legislation attempts to prohibit the exchange between willing partners of strongly desired goods and services. Abortion, the sale of illicit drugs, homosexual acts, gambling, the sale of pornography, prostitution and any proscribed sexual behaviour between consenting partners are major examples (Schur & Bedau 1974, p. 6). The argument is that these practices are personal concerns and not matters for public policy or the criminal law. Morris and Hawkins argue that the 'overreach' of the criminal law into areas of private morality and social welfare is 'expensive, ineffective, and criminogenic' (1970, p. 2). They maintain that public drunkenness, gambling, disorderly conduct, vagrancy and juvenile delinquency should also be decriminalised. Adopting a liberal viewpoint, the British (Wolfenden) Committee on Homosexual Offences and Prostitution Report states:

> Unless a deliberate attempt is to be made by society, acting through the agency of the law, to equate the sphere of crime with that of sin, there must remain a realm of private morality and immorality which is ... not the law's business. To say this is not to condone or encourage private immorality (Wolfenden 1957, p. 24).

The general unenforceability of laws banning victimless crimes stems in part from the absence of a complainant and the consequent problems in obtaining evidence. The criminalisation of these activities provides a monopoly profit for entrepreneurs, specifically illegal abortionists, drug traffickers and brothel owners, willing to break the law. It also encourages the formation of deviant subcultures as well as establishing the economic basis for black market operations, organised crime and police corruption. Many of the laws create 'secondary' crime, other than the proscribed behaviour itself, and create new criminals, many of whom are otherwise law-abiding individuals. For example, it is often argued that increases in property offences, especially theft, are directly related to the high cost of illegal drugs.

The concept of victimless crime has received extensive criticism, the major contention being that no crime is without victims, even though the direct participants may not consider themselves victimised. Some, for example, argue that the victim of an abortion is neither the doctor nor the pregnant woman, but the unborn child (Schur & Bedau 1974, pp. 67–8). Schur subsequently narrows the concept to accommodate these arguments by de-emphasising the lack of harm component. He indicates that the concept is applicable to situations where the proscribed activity involves a willing exchange of goods and services that does not often generate a directly involved complaining victim who initiates enforcement activity. A better description, then, is that these are complaintless crimes. The participants do not perceive themselves as being victimised immediately by the desired exchanges regardless of others' assessments (1984, pp. 183–5; 1988, p. 107). However, 'complaintless' and 'victimless' are not equivalent. Victims, for example children, of such crimes as rape or incest often do not report the offence to the police. Despite difficulties with the notion of victimless crime, it is often argued that homosexuality, abortion, pornography, prostitution and drugs and alcohol use are not crimes in the same sense as theft, homicide, or fraud, and that their status as crime reflects a specific morality rather than general consensus. The remainder of this chapter examines each of these activities and the role of moral entrepreneurs in their criminalisation.

Homosexuality

Homosexuality has variously been interpreted as sinful, criminal, sick, and, most recently, a lifestyle decision. Legislation decriminalising sexual relations between consenting adults, anti-discrimination laws and increases in people 'coming out' suggest that homosexuality is becoming more accepted and homosexual people more integrated into society. However, the so-called AIDS 'epidemic' and the focus on gay men as the major risk group indicates that their integration is far from realisation.

Popular definitions of homosexuality focus on overt appearance and mannerisms, in particular the assumption that homosexual people think and act like members of the opposite sex (Schur 1965, p. 69). Connell observes that: 'To many people [male] homosexuality is a *negation* of masculinity, and homosexual men must be effeminate' (Connell 1992, p. 736, emphasis in original). Moreover, people who deviate from gender norms, for example if a woman remains unmarried and childfree, or a man exhibits sensitivity or dresses in a certain manner, are often assumed to be homosexual. 'Homosexual' becomes a generalised and derogatory term signifying anything less than masculine or feminine ideals. Homosexuality can be a stigma which tends to homogenise every one so labelled. Sexual orientation becomes the dominant characteristic of a person identified as homosexual, and such other attributes as education, occupation or experience become irrelevant (Simon & Gagnon 1967, p. 179).

However, there are many homosexualities distinguished by a variety of lifestyles, personality characteristics, motivations and sex behaviour patterns: some people are lifelong exclusive homosexuals, others experience episodes of homosexuality and heterosexuality, and there are many gradations in between (Karlen 1978, p. 225). Sociologists challenge the validity of categorising people according to their sexual orientation and focus on variations in gay subculture, homosexual roles and careers and the management of a homosexual identity (McIntosh 1968, p. 184; Risman & Schwartz 1988, pp. 136–9).

Anthropological research demonstrates that homosexual conduct is an institutionalised aspect of social life in many pre-industrial societies, including ancient Greece, the Azande in Africa, the Moslem Middle East, the Germanic tribes and the Americas, even though no conception of a homosexual person or homosexual roles existed (Greenberg & Bystryn 1982, pp. 517–9; McIntosh 1968, pp. 185–7). Among the Aranda of Australia and the Koraki of New Guinea, for example, older men engage in anal intercourse as part of initiation rights. In late antiquity the general acceptance of homosexuality in the Mediterranean basin ended with the spread of asceticism promulgating hostility toward all forms of sexual pleasure. A period of tolerance followed this ascetic denunciation, but during the thirteenth century the Christian Church again became preoccupied with homosexuality. This preoccupation stemmed from attempts to increase social control of the clergy by establishing sarcerdotal celibacy which severed family ties and prevented the dispersal of church wealth through inheritance (Greenberg & Bystryn 1982, p. 534).

The emergence of homosexuality, as distinct from heterosexuality, and the development of homosexual roles and expectations are historically specific rather than natural phenomena. During the first half of this century medical researchers took a great interest in the identification and treatment of sexual problems (Greenberg 1988). Their overwhelming focus was on male homosexuality. An analysis of all the professional medical, psychiatric and psychological journal articles on homosexuality between 1900 and 1950 discerns two dominant themes (Martin 1993, p. 248). Most of the articles dealing with homosexuality in women were published between 1903 and 1925. They argued that lesbianism led to masturbation, nymphomania, feeling superior to men, or being a suffragist, thereby prescribing both correct sexual and correct gender behaviour. Between 1934 and 1942, the predominant medical concern was to determine who was homosexual by devising numerous tests and scales which tended to define homosexual people as deviant less in terms of their sexual behaviour than in their gender behaviour. 'Lesbians were not only failed heterosexuals but failed women. Gay men were not just homosexual but, more important, were not masculine' (Martin 1993, p. 254).

Alfred Kinsey and his colleagues at the Institute for Sex Research (Indiana University) undertook the first major study of human sexuality which marked a watershed in sex research. Resulting publications, *Sexual Behavior in the Human Male* (1948) and *Sexual Behavior in the Human Female* (1953) were landmark efforts in the large-scale surveying of sexuality through personal interviews. Their research methodology relied on volunteers, which raises questions about the validity of findings based on an unrepresentative sample. Nevertheless, the Kinsey reports offer considerable information on human sexuality and dispel many myths about the pervasiveness of homosexuality, which they conclude is not rare but perfectly natural (Schur 1988, pp. 53–5). Kinsey and his colleagues suggest that 37 per cent of the adult white male population had at least one homosexual experience compared with 13 per cent of women. They argue that 50 per cent of people unmarried at age thirty-five had such an experience, and 4 per cent were exclusively homosexual. Kinsey devised a seven-step continuum of human sexual preferences, ranging from no overt homosexual practice to exclusive homosexuality.

In the USA, the definition of homosexuality as pathology derives from the American Psychiatric Association's official classification of psychiatric disorders in its *Diagnostic and Statistical Manual of Mental Disorder* (DSM), also widely used in Australia. The first edition, in 1952, specifies homosexuality as one of the several forms of sexual deviance within the general 'sociopathic personality disorder' category. During the 1960s pressures for legislative reform and the decriminalisation of homosexuality emerged. In 1957, the British Wolfenden Committee recommended legislation decriminalising homosexual acts in private between consenting adults and concluded that homosexuality was not a disease. It was decriminalised in 1968. However, the decriminalisation of homosexuality has not altered the many institutional arrangements defining homosexuality as mental illness or psychiatric disorder (Spector 1977, p. 52).

Following the organisation of the Gay Liberation Movement in the USA, the term 'gay' came to signify a lifestyle rather than a condition. Inconclusive and contradictory scientific evidence for the disease theory of homosexuality and the lack of any notably effective treatment contributed to the success of legal reform in this area. The 1973 DSM indicates that homosexuality does not itself constitute a psychiatric disorder, but an association with sickness and deviance persists as there is a category of 'homosexual conflict disorder' but no equivalent heterosexual category.

In Australia, a strong prejudice prevails against homosexuality among men and women which is reflected in the stereotypes and language used to describe homosexual people. Unlike the USA, there is less of a tradition of equal rights, as no Bill of Rights is constitutionally entrenched. Homosexuality between males has been a criminal offence in most jurisdictions with penalties including imprisonment. South Australia was the first state to decriminalise homosexuality in 1975, and it came about not because of pressure from a gay lobby but from the liberal reformist Parliament (Sinclair & Ross 1986, p. 121).

Tasmania remains the only Australian state where, although rarely prosecuted, homosexuality remains illegal. The Criminal Code Act 1924 (as amended) prohibits 'sexual intercourse against the order of nature' (s 122a), interpreted as any non-vaginal sex act, and provides that: 'Any male person who, whether in public or private, commits any indecent assault upon, or other act of gross indecency with, another male person, or procures another male person to commit any act of gross indecency with himself or any other male person, is guilty of a crime' (s 123). In April 1994, the United Nations Human Rights Committee found this law to be in breach of the International Covenant on Civil and Political Rights, a treaty to which Australia is a signatory. While this ruling can have no direct effect on the legal situation in

Tasmania it is an important symbolic victory for the Gay and Lesbian Rights Group and the Federal government is able to use its external affairs power to override state legislation in order to fulfil international treaty obligations. The quest to reaffirm the criminal status of homosexuality seems to be motivated, or at least rationalised, by both religious and secular ideals. For example, the state Attorney-General told a press conference: 'Tasmania is a nice, quiet place, a Christian-based society, whose people believe in the Bible' (Montgomery 1994, p. 11). In contrast, Tas-Alert, a group formed to oppose reform of the laws, publicly emphasises that gay sexuality is a public health issue (Adams 1994, p. 2).

While medical and psychological studies and theories aim to identify the biological factors or types of family relationships resulting in homosexuality, sociologists are as interested in the subsequent 'career' of individuals who engage in homosexual relations or who become publicly labelled as such. Concern is with how social situations and social definitions of homosexuality affect individual behaviour and self-identity. Homosexuality is conceptualised in terms of social statuses and role expectations rather than as a condition (McIntosh 1968, p. 184).

In a study of homosexual males' relations to the heterosexual and to the homosexual worlds and to potential psychological problems in three societies—the USA, the Netherlands and Denmark—Weinburg and Williams (1974, pp. 12–13) identify two major adaptations: overt acceptance of a homosexual role; and covert homosexuality.[1] They specify three processes whereby a person accepts the label of 'homosexual', and establishes a meaningful sense of identity:

1 acculturation refers to the extent to which one is socialised into common homosexual practices;
2 *normalisation* involves seeing homosexuality as normal, not as deviant or as evidence of personality disorder;
3 commitment, demonstrating a reluctance to give up homosexuality (1974, pp. 160–1).

Covert homosexuality entails public denial but private acceptance, where the individual conceals his or her homosexuality and 'passes' as heterosexual. Covert homosexuals sometimes go to extremes to publicly denounce homosexuality in order to divert attention from their own sexual orientation. 'Passing' reflects a concern about exposure and potential sanctions such as rejection by family and friends and discrimination at work (Weinburg & Williams 1974, pp. 177–80). The concern about being overt is reflected in the term 'coming out of the closet'.

Research on 'coming out' often adopts a unidirectional, unfolding developmental model of the processes involved in homosexual identity formation which is viewed as replacing a heterosexual identity. Coming out is presented as a process of discovery and recognition of one's true essence as homosexual. In contrast, symbolic interactionists view sexual identity formation as an active process of identity creation and re-creation in the light of available social constructs and social relationships (Rust 1993, pp. 68–70). An examination of 346 lesbian-identified and 60 bisexual-identified women indicates that most do not progress through stages of identity formation sequentially. The women often switched back and forth between sexual identities, experienced phases of ambivalence and periods of having no particular sexual identity. Because bisexuality is not considered an authentic form of sexuality in popular discourse, identity-seeking individuals focus on heterosexual and homosexual, albeit unequally due to the dominance of norms reinforcing heterosexuality, and do not perceive bisexual identity as a valid, permanent option (Rust 1993, pp. 69–71).

Connell suggests that a focus on identity and subculture shifts attention from structural questions about gender (1992, p. 738). His primary concern is with gay men and masculinity, specifically 'the construction of masculinity in the lives of gay men; the construction of sexuality and its relationship to identity and subculture; the interplay between heterosexual and homosexual masculinities; and the experience of change in gender relations' (Connell 1992, p. 738). By investigating the life histories of eight men recruited from an urban gay community in Sydney, Connell details the construction of a homosexual masculinity via multilateral negotiations around emotional relations in the home, among friends and in the sexual marketplace and negotiations of economic, workplace and authority relations. Despite differences in personal experiences, the narratives revealed three common elements in the process of homosexual masculinity construction: an engagement with hegemonic masculinity; a closure of sexuality around relationships with men; and participation in the collective life of the gay community (Connell 1992, p. 747). This last element, however, has a class dimension. Working-class men do not often seek a 'gay identity', but draw on conventional working-class masculinities and as such are more committed to informal networks than to urban, gay communities (Connell, Davis & Dowsett 1993, pp. 112–13, 125–6).

Arguments for the decriminalisation of homosexuality emphasise individuals' rights and freedoms to make choices about their sexuality. The notion of choice carries with it a conception that individuals are rational and responsible. That rationality and responsibility assume new dimensions in the current medical, public and political controversies surrounding Acquired Immune Deficiency Syndrome (AIDS), seen largely as a male homosexual disease. Even though over four-fifths of all AIDS cases reported in Australia between 1982 and 1987 were identified as resulting from homosexual transmission, it is not an inherently male homosexual disease. Table 3.1 shows the increasing prevalence of AIDS in Australia and the mode of transmission. Up to 30 September 1992, 3518 cases of AIDS and 2322 known deaths from AIDS deaths had been reported. In 86 per cent of all known deaths from AIDS, the virus was transmitted via male homosexual and bisexual contact, blood transfusion accounted for 2.6 per cent of deaths and

Table 3.1 Aids cases reported and related deaths [1], Australia, by transmission category and year of diagnosis, 1982 to end of 1987

	1982	1983	1984	1985	1986	1987	Total
Homosexual transmission							
AIDS cases reported	1	4	30	99	195	302	631
Related deaths	1	4	30	84	149	136	404
Needle sharing drug use							
AIDS cases reported			1		2	1	4
Related deaths					2		2
Homosexual transmission and/or needle-sharing drug use							
AIDS cases reported		2	1		12	7	22
Related deaths		2	1		9	2	14
Blood transfusion							
AIDS cases reported			7	9	13	12	41
Related deaths			7	9	13	12	41
Clotting factor							
AIDS cases reported			2	1	1	5	9
Related deaths			2	1	1	3	7
Heterosexual transmission							
AIDS cases reported				2		7	9
Related deaths				1		1	2
Transmission category other or pending							
AIDS cases reported			1	2	1	11	15
Related deaths			1	1		6	8
Total all categories							
AIDS cases reported	1	6	42	113	224	345	731
Related deaths	1	6	41	96	174	160	478
Cumulative Total							
AIDS cases reported	1	7	49	162	386	731	
Related deaths	1	7	48	144	318	478	

1 By October 1988.

Source: Department of Community Services and Health 1988, *AIDS: A Time to Care a Time to Act: Towards a Strategy for Australians*, AGPS, Canberra, table 1, p. 45.

intravenous drug use accounted for 4.6 per cent (Australian Bureau of Statistics 1993b, pp. 279–80).

Much paranoia surrounds AIDS. Many people view it as a plague, a moral problem, a result of promiscuity and violation of 'natural' monogamy, divine retribution for sodomy and other unnatural practices (Matthews 1988, p. 119). Sontag observes: 'Plagues are invariably regarded as judgements on society, and the metaphoric inflation of AIDS into such a judgement also accustoms people to the inevitability of global spread. This is a traditional use of sexually transmitted diseases: to be described as punishments not just of individuals but of a group' (1990, p. 54). The idea prevails that as gay men chose their so-called lifestyle they have elected a hazardous way of life and are solely responsible for the result (Patton 1988). Discussion focuses on risk groups rather than risk behaviour which stigmatises gay men as being responsible for AIDS. Increases in 'casual' sexual exchanges over the past twenty-five years and in the number of sexual contacts reflects heightened opportunity to be exposed to or to infect others with the Human Immunodeficiency Virus (HIV), rather than homosexual behaviour (Kaplan et al. 1987, p. 142).

An Australian government discussion paper indicates that homosexual and bisexual men remain a priority for AIDS prevention and education programs. A problem with the focus on gay communities is that many men who have sex with other men do not define themselves as homosexual or bisexual and may have no contact with the gay community. The report recommends the specific targeting of other social groups for AIDS prevention and education programs, specifically women, needle-sharing drug users, prostitutes, prisoners, adolescents, Aborigines, and recipients of blood transfusions (Department of Community Services and Health 1988a, pp. 128–50). The only group not listed is healthy, law-abiding, adult white men. The assumption seems to be that people already deemed to be deviant are by virtue of that status more susceptible to AIDS.

The assumption that gay men with AIDS are responsible for contracting and spreading the virus is underscored by the sympathy for other people who contract the virus, namely children, hospital workers, blood transfusion recipients and haemophiliacs. The notion of the accidental contraction of AIDS by non-homosexual people suggests that gay men are responsible and perhaps criminally responsible for knowingly transmitting the disease (Department of Community Services and Health 1988a, p. 126). The AIDS crisis has brought with it a plethora of new discriminatory practices on the part of hospitals, insurance companies and employers against gay men. The Australian Medical Association has called for compulsory HIV testing before any surgical operation as a means of reducing transmission of the virus through needle-stick injuries which seem to occur frequently in hospitals (Ragg 1994, p. 20).

Religious world views and morals remain central to the re-emergence and reinforcement of negative labelling of homosexuality and 'deviantisation' of homosexuals. Similarly, abortion, the target of reform movements and calls for decriminalisation in the 1970s, has returned recently to the political agenda.

Abortion

Abortion has not always been a controversial moral issue or a social problem. Rather, the controversy results from interest groups defining abortion in various ways and seeking legal reform which reflects their definitions and values. Fifty years ago abortion existed as a private dilemma; in contemporary society it is a public issue engendering bitter debate. Opponents of abortion claim that since the embryo is an unborn child abortion is morally equivalent to murder. No doubt medical technology which makes viewing the foetus in the uterus possible and enables premature babies to survive contributes to the conception of a foetus as a human rather than a potentiality (Petchesky 1986, chapter 9; 1987, p. 271). In most jurisdictions the criminal law only protects a born child, or sometimes a viable foetus. The development of a concept of foetal rights presumably will change this and extend the criminal law (Gallagher 1987, p. 31). Indeed, the Irish constitution declares that the: 'State acknowledges the right to life of the unborn and, with due regard to the equal right to life of the mother, guarantees in its laws to respect, and, as far as practicable, by its laws to defend and vindicate that right' (Gearty 1992, p. 442). This provision received world-wide attention when a judicial order prevented a fourteen-year-old girl, whose pregnancy was result of her rape, from leaving Ireland to have an abortion in Britain.

On the other side, pro-choice activists emphasise women's right to make choices about their own bodies and to control reproduction. Maintaining that abortions will occur regardless of legal status, they argue that safe, clean, affordable abortions performed by publicly accountable personnel are essential for women's health. Like any moral issue the abortion controversy is not about facts but about the interpretation of those facts according to some set of values and the assignment of meaning to the practice and the participants (Luker 1984, p. 5).

Abortion is nothing new. While the early Christian Church denounced abortion and contraception, it was often ignored legally. In the English common law tradition abortion undertaken before 'quickening' (foetal movement, usually occurring between the sixteenth and eighteenth week of pregnancy) was at worst a misdemeanour. Melbourne Women's Hospital figures from 1900–1935 (probably underestimates) suggest that abortion was widespread among Australian women of all classes (Finch & Stratton 1988, p. 52). Neighbourhood networks provided knowledge of chemical and other abortificants. Until about 1910 almost all working-class abortionists were women—midwives, fortune tellers and other agents.

Lord Ellenborough's Act of 1803 in England was the first criminal abortion statute. It appears to have been a response to the increased visibility of abortion and the perceived inadequacy of the common law, however, it did not specifically forbid a woman from procuring her own abortion. The subsequent *Offences Against the Persons Act* 1861 became the model for comparable legislation throughout the world, including the Australian states. This legislation made it an offence for a pregnant woman to attempt to procure her own miscarriage unlawfully and made it an offence for any person to attempt to procure the unlawful miscarriage of any women, whether or not she was pregnant (Petersen 1993, pp. 19–21). Despite similar legislation everywhere in the USA during the nineteenth century, both legislatures and courts remained ambivalent towards women seeking abortions. Even though abortion was not condoned publicly, it certainly was not a moral crisis (Williams 1991, p. 1573).

The emerging medical profession was the single most important influence in the criminalisation of abortion in the late nineteenth century, especially in the USA (Davis 1986, pp. 376–9; Larson 1977, pp. 19–25; Luker 1984, pp. 27–35). By taking an anti-abortion stand physicians could make claims to superior scientific knowledge, based on the latest medical theory and research which buttressed their arguments that pregnancy was continuous and that any non-medical intervention was immoral (Mohr 1978, pp. 147–70). The fledgling medical profession sought to enhance its professional status and eradicate competition from unlicensed practitioners, specifically midwives (Ehrenreich & English 1978, pp. 39–40). This involved the abnormalisation of childbirth which middle-class women especially came to view as dangerous and requiring medical skill (Petersen 1993, chapter 1). Abortion gave physicians the opportunity to claim to be saving human lives by asserting both the embryo's right to life as well as the need for some abortions, for example to save the life of the pregnant woman. As abortion decision-making was defined as technical, women, clergy and lawyers did not have the skills or credentials to challenge doctors. Once medical control of therapeutic abortion was complete all other abortions by definition were criminal.

Like their campaign against 'quacks' and midwives in general, the medical profession's move against traditional abortionists was effected through strategic legislation and judicial decision. In Australia and Britain, however, as the law did not specifically provide for legal abortion, the legal status of those performed for therapeutic indications remained uncertain. This uncertainty culminated in the first test case on therapeutic abortion— the English decision of *R v. Bourne* (1939) 1 KB 687—where the trial judge was at pains to distinguish the allegations against Dr Bourne from those against professional abortionists, thus viewing them as mutually exclusive categories. Justice MacNaghten summed up to the jury:

> [T]his is a case of great importance to the public and, more especially, to the medical profession; but you will observe that *it has nothing to do with the ordinary case of procuring abortion.* In those cases the operation is performed by a person of no skill, with no medical qualifications, and there is no pretence that it is done for the preservation of the mother's life ((1939) 1 KB 687 at 691–2, emphasis added).

Under this system of illegality the quality and safety of abortion services a woman obtained depended largely on ability to pay.

By the 1950s, the legal criterion for abortion, namely preservation of the woman's life, was no longer meaningful as medical developments reduced life-threatening conditions during pregnancy. The criteria for abortion were widened to include psychiatric and social factors. Fewer abortions were performed to preserve physical life, but to preserve mental health and the quality of life. Such a shift meant that medical practitioners' claims to be the only ones who could legitimately determine the conditions for abortion became more tenuous. Nevertheless, conflicts surrounding this development were contained within the profession and the moral issues remained latent. Abortions for married women, or those who had been raped or whose embryos had some physical problem—those that did not raise questions of sexual morality—were often performed (Luker 1984, p. 89).

In the late 1960s such social changes as women's greater access to paid work and increasing criticism of traditional gender roles and women's relegation to the domestic sphere strengthened arguments that women should control their fertility and have the right to choose whether or not to continue a pregnancy. Despite isolated, individual efforts in the 1960s, discussion of abortion in Australia was barely broached publicly until the British Parliament's liberalisation of abortion law in 1967. From then, abortion achieved accelerating momentum as a woman's, rather than a technical, medical issue and became a hallmark of the emergent women's movement (Coleman 1988, p. 76). Even so, physicians have been able to construct and dominate a market in abortion provision (Goldstein 1984, p. 527).

In the late 1960s and early 1970s abortion became legal, either by legislation, as in Britain, South Australia and the Northern Territory, or through judicial decision as in New South Wales, Victoria, Queensland and the USA. The United States Supreme Court's 1973 decision in *Roe v. Wade* (1973) 410 US 113 gave women limited rights to abortion by holding that all state laws with respect to abortion were an infringement of privacy rights and therefore unconstitutional. The Court held:

> This right of privacy ... is broad enough to encompass a woman's decision whether or not to terminate her pregnancy. The detriment that the State would impose upon the pregnant women by denying this choice is altogether apparent. [The Court then listed a variety of harms] ... All these are factors the woman and her responsible physician necessarily consider in consultation ((1973) 410 US 113 at 153).

Decriminalisation did not provide women with rights to abortion in either Australia or the UK but allows medical practitioners to perform abortions under certain circumstances, specifically when there is a danger to the woman's physical or mental health, including economic and social considerations. Abortion remains regulated by the criminal law (Gibson 1990, p. 181). Rather than quelling the debate, liberalisation of abortion laws heightened polarisation between the pro-life and the pro-choice activists

(Clarke 1987a, p. 123; Coleman 1988, pp. 75–6; Schur 1984, p. 104). The emergence and shape of debates about abortion reflect the interests and specific values of various interest groups who often use similar tactics. A favourite tactic of anti-abortionists is the screening of the film *The Silent Scream*, which allegedly records the scream of a foetus as it is being aborted. On the other side, pro-abortionists carry banners illustrating coat-hangers to convey the serious health consequences to women of illegal abortions. The polarisation of the debate provides both pro- and anti-abortionists with a clearly defined antagonist: for right-to-life groups the pro-choice lobby represents the destruction of family life, marriage, increasing irresponsibility and women's rejection of motherhood which conservative groups value; while for pro-choice groups the right-to-life movement indicates the attempt to undermine the achievements of women's liberation by seeking women's return to traditional gender roles and limiting their choices. Debates about human rights, morality and personal autonomy also emerge in the discussion of pornography, which, like abortion, is an arena in which various groups—moral entrepreneurs—seek to stake claims and have their values translated into law. Nonetheless, the nature of the abortion debates varies in different societies.

In Australia, the first Right to Life group was formed in Queensland in 1970, and had strong links to religious theology and the Catholic Church. The group split in 1979 with the formation of Right to Life Australia. Despite the secular nature of Australian society and the widespread acceptance of abortion, right-to-life movements are well organised and adopt a high media profile. While not undoing the legal reforms of the 1970s, the efforts of anti-abortion groups have contributed to their erosion by placing abortion on the political agenda again. Numerous attempts have been made to restrict the availability of abortion, for example lessening the number of available facilities, and hospitals' refusal to perform abortions during the second trimester, as is the case in South Australia even though the law allows these terminations. Additionally, the idea has been mooted for the national health insurance scheme, Medibank, to exclude coverage of abortions (Warhurst & Merrill 1982, p. 123). The NSW Supreme Court in April 1994 reaffirmed the illegality of abortion unless the physical or mental health of the woman is in danger. Finding that the pregnancy would not have endangered her health, Justice Newman rejected a woman's claims against doctors' failure to diagnose her pregnancy sufficiently early to enable a termination. This ruling demonstrates the tenuous legal status of abortion when it rests on judicial decisions not binding on superior courts. Right-to-life activists welcome the decision as supporting their viewpoint (McAsey 1994, p. 9; Neill 1994a, p. 23).

In the USA, abortion is a salient, political issue because it raises constitutional questions; rights discourse dominates the political–legal culture so that the debates often become a contest between women's rights and those of the unborn: overturning *Roe v. Wade* became the single unifying goal of the right-to-life movement. In 1981, the Reagan administration in the USA cut funding for abortions for low-income women and a series of Supreme Court decisions have narrowed the right to choose an abortion, ironically using the language of the *Roe* decision to limit its applicability (Eisenstein 1991, p. 106). While not overruling the 1973 decision, the court in 1989 upheld a state's decision not to fund abortions in public hospitals, arguing that a woman's 'right to choose' remains unaffected (*Webster v. Reproductive Health Services* (1989) 109 S. Ct. 3040). Three years later the court decided that:

> Though the woman has a right to choose to terminate or continue her pregnancy before viability, it does not at all follow that the State is prohibited from taking steps to ensure that this choice is thoughtful and informed ... The State may enact rules and regulations designed to encourage her to know that there are philosophic and social arguments of great weight that can be brought to bear in favour of continuing the pregnancy to full term and that there are procedures and institutions to allow adoption of unwanted children as well as a certain degree of state assistance if the mother chooses to raise the child herself (*Planned Parenthood of Southeastern Pennsylvania v. Casey* (1992) 120 L Ed, 674 at 711–2).

Political change in Eastern Europe has galvanised nascent women's movements around the right to abortion which was readily available under the previous regimes. Before unification, East German women had greater access to legal abortion, paid work and state-funded child care programs than did their West German counterparts (Rosenberg 1991, p. 129). In Poland, new laws restricting abortion have followed increased pressure from the Roman Catholic Church (Fuszara 1991, p. 117; Zielinska 1993, pp. 69–85).

Pornography

No consensus exists regarding the definition of pornography. The word derives from the Greek 'pornográphos'—the writing of harlots (*Macquarie Dictionary* 1987, p. 1325)—and usually conveys the graphic depiction of erotic behaviour intended to cause sexual arousal. A related concept is 'obscenity' which usually refers to sexual morality or immorality. The Latin root *obscenus* means foul, repulsive, filthy, morally impure or indecent (Special Committee on Pornography and Prostitution [Canada] 1985, p. 47). The emphasis on sexual immorality is central to much legal theory of obscenity. The United States Supreme Court provides an oft-quoted definition of obscenity comprising three central elements:

> (a) whether the average person, applying the contemporary community standards, would find that work, taken as a whole, appeals to the prurient interest, (b) whether the work depicts or describes, in a patently offensive way, sexual conduct specifically defined by the applicable state law, and (c) whether the work, taken as a whole, lacks serious literary, artistic, political or scientific value (*Miller v. State of California* (1973) 37 United States Supreme Court Reports, Lawyers' Edition, 419 at 422).

Australian courts define obscenity as whether the material in question offends the sensibilities of the citizen by violating the contemporary standards of decency in the community. In a 1968 case dealing with indecent magazines entitled *Obscenity* Barwick, the then Chief Justice of the High Court, says:

> In my opinion, a picture, printed or written matter which, on being seen or read by him or her, in the circumstances in which, and having regard to the manner in which, it is presented to him or her to be seen or read, would offend the modesty of the average man or woman in sexual matters is indecent (*Crowe v. Graham* (1968) 121 CLR 375 at 379).

Rather than clarifying the matter, these conceptions beg questions regarding values over which there is little consensus. For example, who defines 'prurient interest', 'patently offensive', 'lacks serious literary, artistic, political or scientific value', 'contemporary standards of decency', or the 'modesty of the average man or woman', and how are the definitions made? Recourse to the 'average person' is a legal abstraction which is of little practical assistance, except perhaps for the courts to shroud their perceptions with reference to public interest and morality. Nevertheless, when discussing the alleged harm or effects of pornography the focus is on potential consumers and the community in general, not the sex industry workers. Most discussion of pornography has been at pains not to develop a definition which encompasses what is often deemed to be literature or art such as Shakespeare's plays, D.H. Lawrence's and James Joyce's novels or Picasso's and Rubens' paintings.

Traditional opposition to pornography deplores the offences against public morals and encouragement of elicit sexual practice that contravenes religious mores and family values. It is also linked to class reproduction. The overwhelming elite support for campaigns against vice in Boston, New York City and Philadelphia during the late nineteenth century was related to three aspects of upper-class formation and reproduction. Specifically, the loss of political control to immigrants, the attempt to control upper-class children's education by sending them to elite boarding schools, and the construction of a high culture which distinguished the upper class from social inferiors were central to elite anti-vice mobilisation (Beisel 1990, p. 46; 1993, pp. 149–50). The social class of the viewer became a primary determinant of whether a painting or a photograph was deemed art or obscenity. This became apparent when the New York upper class failed to support Comstock's (a vigilant anti-vice crusader) arrest of a leading art dealer because the incident questioned their own purity, taste and refinement (Beisel 1993, pp. 157–8).

On the other side, civil libertarians argue for protecting the value of freedom of speech which entails allowing all forms of expression. This liberal position gets most fully articulated in the USA where the Constitution protects the right to freedom of expression. Since 1945, censorship reforms in Australia increasingly protect the freedom of adults to consume pornography or censored material in private. The reforms also reflect concerns to protect the moral development of children by restricting their exposure to pornography (Sullivan 1991, pp. 11–13).

Recent opponents of pornography emphasise the commodification and objectification of women; power differences between men and women; and argue that pornography presents women as objects to be purchased and consumed by men (Diamond 1980, p. 689). Feminist campaigns against pornography emerged in the USA, the UK and Australia in the late 1970s and early 1980s. They focus on the relationship between violence and images of women in the media, and target films, books, magazines and billboards that display women as 'bound, gagged, beaten, whipped and chained' (Eckersley 1987, p. 150). In many ways their tactics are very similar to anti-abortionist campaigners, in the use of dramatic imagery and the most extreme cases to make a general point. These feminist critics interpret pornography not merely as the reflection of men's sexual fantasies but primarily as one of the mechanisms sustaining men's systematic and historical domination of women. They maintain that pornography, rather than being an example of freedom of speech, is a form of censorship and control silencing women (Diamond 1980, p. 686; Griffin 1981, p. 201; MacKinnon 1986, p. 71). This critique emphasises that the debates about pornography are not about community values but about political practice (MacKinnon 1986, p. 64). From this feminist viewpoint, pornography is a form of forced sex, a practice of sexual politics, an institution of gender inequality. According to MacKinnon, with the rape and prostitution in which it participates, pornography institutionalises the sexuality of dominance and submission with the social construction of male and female (1987, pp. 8–17). The notion of freedom of expression can never be realised where institutionalised inequality prevails. This feminist perspective sees pornography as dehumanising women, and as the ideology of a culture which promotes and condones rape, woman-battering and other violent crimes against women. According to Brownmiller (1975), pornography is the philosophy of rape.

Ironically, the anti-pornography feminists have found themselves allied with the moralistic New Right whose traditional concern has not been with the rights of women. Among right-wing groups, pornography symbolises a variety of moral wrongs, including the erosion of traditional values, extramarital sex, marital and family dissolution, homosexuality and adultery; their concern is not with discrimination or the rights of minority groups (Baron 1987, p. 6). Some feminists argue that the feminist anti-pornography position presents a very narrow and stereotypical view of women's sexuality and parallels historical attempts to 'protect' women's chastity through laws which perpetuate gender inequality (Duggan, Hunter & Vance 1984, p. 142; Hunter & Law 1987–88, p. 105–8; Roach Anleu 1992, pp. 429–31).

In the USA, a new type of municipal ordinance proposed in Minneapolis in 1983 and Indianapolis in 1984 sought to enable women to bring civil actions against those responsible for the production, sale, exhibition or distribution of pornography, and also for being coerced into pornographic performances. The drafters of these by-laws define pornography as:

> The graphic sexually explicit subordination of women through pictures or words that also includes women dehumanized as sexual objects, things, or commodities; enjoying pain or humiliation or rape; being tied up, cut up, mutilated, bruised, or physically hurt; in postures of sexual submission or servility or display; reduced to body parts, penetrated by objects or animals, or presented in scenarios of degradation, injury, torture; shown as filthy or inferior; bleeding, bruised, or hurt in a context that makes these conditions sexual (MacKinnon 1987, p. 176).

The emphasis is on subordination and inequality, thus defining pornography as discrimination on the basis of sex—a civil rights violation—not a moral issue (MacKinnon 1986, p. 63, fn 1). Although the definition is framed in terms of depictions of women, both by-laws provided that the use of men, children or transsexuals in the place of women in these depictions also constitutes pornography. Both ordinances failed because of the wide definition of pornography and the implications for freedom of speech. The Court decided that:

> The [Indianapolis] ordinance discriminates on the ground of the content of speech ... [It provides that] Speech treating women in the disapproved way—as submissive in matters sexual or as enjoying humiliation—is unlawful no matter how significant the literary, artistic, or political qualities of the work taken as a whole ... The Constitution forbids the state to declare one perspective right and silence opponents (*American Booksellers v. Hudnut* (1985) 774 F 2d 323 at 325).

Despite this failure it appears that the legal discourse around pornography is changing. For example, in 1992 the Canadian Supreme Court upheld an anti-obscenity law by focusing on the violence, degradation and dehumanisation in pornography. It decided that the aim of the law was not moral disapprobation but the avoidance of harm to society, especially violence against women, which warrants a restriction on freedom of expression. The court specified that the harm takes the form of violations of the principles of human equality and dignity (*R v. Butler* (1992) 1 SCR 452 at 455–7).

A major problem with all attempts to outlaw pornography is the lack of unequivocal empirical evidence for a direct relationship between exposure to pornography and sexual violence or family breakdown. One of the terms of reference of a 1988 Australian report on pornography was to ascertain the likely effects upon people, especially children, of exposure to violent, pornographic or otherwise obscene material (Australia 1988, p. xix). On the evidence before it the Inquiry concludes that excessive exposure to violent material can have negative effects upon some people, especially children and those predisposed to aggression (1988, p. 229). Experimental research shows that exposure to pornography increases men's willingness to be aggressive against women; makes both women and men substantially less able to perceive accounts of rape as accounts of rape; makes normal men more closely resemble convicted rapists psychologically; increases hostility toward women, propensity to rape or force sex on a woman if one knew one would not get caught; and produces other attitude changes in men such as increasing the extent of the trivialisation, dehumanisation and objectification of women (Donnerstein 1984, pp. 78–80; Malamuth 1984, pp. 40–7).

Numerous problems exist with laboratory research and the assumed relationship between attitudes and behaviour. Even though participants exposed to pornography under experimental conditions express more aggression against women, and take on some of the values presented by the material, a causal connection between measures of laboratory aggression and acts of rape has not been established. Experimental research shows at most that pornography facilitates the expression of anger if anger already exists, rather than causing the anger (Gray 1982, p. 390). Moreover, the long-term effects of exposure to pornography are unknown, which also raises some ethical questions about this kind of research. The validity of the scientific data is probably less important than its existence, for feminist critiques of pornography. The appeal to research findings enables them to distinguish their arguments from those of the traditional, conservative opponents of pornography.

Prostitution

As with homosexuality and pornography, prostitution is difficult to define and is a general label often applied to women who deviate from gender norms of monogamy, virginity, marriage and etiquette. Most definitions of prostitution mention promiscuity, multiple sexual partners, continuous sexual offences, payment and an element of notoriety, but people not defining themselves as prostitutes may possess some of these characteristics (Bullough & Bullough 1987, p. xi). Historical and cross-cultural evidence demonstrates that institutionalised prostitution has been aimed at a male clientele and the overwhelming majority of prostitutes have been women. The clients of male prostitutes also appear to be predominantly men (van der Poel 1992, p. 264).

Prostitution *per se* is not a criminal offence in any of the Australian jurisdictions, but such activities as permitting premises to be used for the purposes of prostitution, soliciting in a public place or living on the earnings of a prostitute are subject to criminal sanctions (Waller & Williams 1993, p. 129). Generally, these laws criminalise the sex worker and not the customer and most prosecutions have been against the former (Egger & Harcourt 1993, p. 115). Everyday discussion and research views prostitution as a form of female deviance. For example, parliamentary debates at the turn of the nineteenth century projected an image of the female prostitute as deviant, diseased and dangerous whereas clients were viewed as ordinary men seeking fulfilment of their natural desires (Sullivan 1991, p. 5).

Following decriminalisation, the position of the female providers has become less deviant, however the clients of prostitutes are now more likely to be viewed as deviant, that is, as men unable to sustain 'normal' heterosexual relationships. Sullivan quotes one Victorian parliamentarian's statement that: 'Anyone who uses a brothel in this age must have either a deep physical need, be desperately lonely or have some sort of psychological hang-up' (1991, p. 15). Nevertheless, recent comments in the legal context suggest that prostitutes are perceived as less harmed by rape compared with other women. In the case of *Hakopian* a trial judge in Victoria argued that prostitutes as a group were less likely to be psychologically affected by rape than either 'chaste' or 'happily married' women (Cass 1992, p. 202).

Many theorists seek to distinguish prostitution from marriage. Kingsley Davis (1937, p. 746), for example, rejects the notion of prostitution as the use of sexual responses for an ulterior purpose as this would include marriage where, he argues, women trade their sexual favours for the economic and social status men supply. In contrast, Engels (1972, p. 134) asserts that bourgeois marriage often becomes crass prostitution where the woman only differs from the ordinary courtesan in that she does not contract her body on piecework as a wage worker, but sells it once and for all into slavery. Prostitutes frequently insist they are not selling their sexuality any more than married women, only they are doing it more openly and less hypocritically.

Early sociological literature focuses on the contractual nature of the relations between the client and the prostitute as distinct from personal, familial and emotional relationships (Davis 1937, pp. 745–6; Simmel 1971, pp. 122–3). It characterises prostitution as comprising elements of hire, lack of commitment, promiscuity and emotional indifference which are incompatible with primary or gemeinschaft associations. Moreover, they deviate from gender norms specifying that women should be loving, emotional and altruistic. Prostitution provides an outlet for male sexual expression which would be illegitimate in courtship leading to marriage which is oriented to reproduction. In commercial prostitution sex is an end in itself and the payment constitutes a reward for loss of status rather compensation for work (Davis 1937, p. 750).

Despite the contractual relationship between two people, it is the prostitute whose behaviour, respectability and legal status become treated as problematic. In general, prostitutes' clients are not defined or prosecuted as criminally deviant. According to Davis (1937, p. 752), prostitution is a difficult crime to deal with as one of the wilful parties is the ordinary law-abiding citizen who participates in such vital institutional relationships as family, business, church and state. This citizen cannot be held guilty because of the impracticability of punishing half the population for a crime! Davis misses the point that the decriminalising or legalising of prostitution would make prostitutes law-abiding citizens.

Common assumptions about prostitutes include that they are primary sources of sexually transmitted diseases and that they deviate from marital and maternal norms. The presumed association between prostitution and disease has a long history. In the 1860s the British Parliament enacted Contagious Diseases Prevention Acts to provide that, in the designated naval and military cities, any woman believed to be a 'common' prostitute by the police or by any informer could be ordered by a magistrate to undergo a physical examination at a certified hospital. The impetus for this legislation came from the military (Bullough & Bullough 1987, pp. 195–6; Daly 1988, pp. 175–6). In 1989 a moral panic emerged over a prostitute with AIDS who was detained against her will under the New South Wales Public Health Act (Hicks 1989, p. 71). The effect of the sensational media attention is to reinforce the association between prostitution and disease and to blame prostitutes for contagion, even though it is often the customer who refuses to wear a condom. Indeed, an investigation in Victoria found that the rate of infection among prostitutes was low and the sexual contacts with non-prostitutes accounted for the majority of infections of men attending a communicable diseases clinic (Neave 1985b, pp. 73–84). It would seem that sex workers have a particular interest in remaining healthy as their occupation entails no compensation for ill-health.

Conceptualising prostitution as an occupation enables analyses of recruitment, career paths, job-related skills, division of labour, occupational values, opportunity structures, working conditions and earnings. The Victorian Inquiry into Prostitution (Neave 1985a, pp. 48–58) identifies three main types of prostitution:

1 Street prostitutes are at the bottom of the prostitution hierarchy, a minor segment of the business, which attracts considerable media attention and conforms most closely to the stereotypical prostitute. They tend to come from a disrupted family background, be drug abusers, more likely to be ignorant about contraception and the long-term effects of disease. This form of prostitution is most vulnerable to the attention of city planners, local residents and business owners who seek to 'clean up' areas where street prostitution occurs. Streetworking prostitutes routinely face the threat and reality of violence in their work and must develop strategies to establish and maintain client compliance throughout the commercial sexual encounter (Barnard 1993, p. 683). These prostitutes are highly visible to police and are frequently arrested. Selective enforcement has led to a reduction in the numbers of street prostitutes combined with an increase in brothel and escort agency prostitution (Neave 1988, p. 206). This development increases social control as concentrating prostitution in brothels provides police with clear targets during 'crackdowns'. Brothels and escort agencies are also a source of graft for police who offer extra protection.

2 *Brothel prostitution* often occurs under the guise of massage parlours or health studios. Operators of brothels and brothel prostitutes are more informed about sexually transmitted diseases than street prostitutes and some establishments require regular medical checks for workers.
3 Escort agencies ostensibly provide only paid companionship but in practice they offer prostitution services. This form of prostitution is higher paid than brothels, but may be more dangerous since the worker goes to the client's meeting place. Escort work carries the highest status in the industry and prostitutes working for busy agencies have high earnings. Escort agency operators require the women to have regular medical checks and avoid employing workers who are narcotic addicts since they tend to be unreliable with money.

Following this inquiry, the Victorian government decriminalised bro hel prostitution which became regulated through a licensing system. New South Wales decriminalised brothel-keeping and soliciting for prostitution outside residential areas in 1979. However, as a result of successful campaig.,s by the NSW Police Association and the residents of Darlinghurst, an amendment to the legislation outlawed soliciting in a public street, near a dwelling, school, church or hospital (Egger & Harcourt 1993, p. 116).

Becoming a prostitute entails a process of recruitment and socialisation. Research on call-girls indicates that occupational entry depends on a personal contact involved in call-girl activities. The second phase involves an apprenticeship where the new recruit learns occupational norms and techniques regarding how to converse with the customer and obtain the fee. Most importantly, during the training period the novice obtains information on building a clientele (Bryan 1965, pp. 290–4). Heyl observes that professional socialisation involving the acquisition of knowledge about hustling, managing clients, sexual practices, physical skills and personal hygiene is especially critical among house prostitutes for two reasons. First, most madams only hire trained prostitutes; and second, the close interaction of prostitutes operating within the confines of a house requires a common set of work standards and practices (1977, pp. 551–4).

The drift into prostitution involves the internalisation of a deviant self-identity in response to informal labelling, public reaction and stigma, and comprises three main stages: first, casual sexual encounters leading to a second, transitional phase characterised by an on-the-job learning period where the women postpone self-definition of the deviant status and vacillate between conventionality and deviance. Finally, the professionalisation stage involves an unequivocal perception of the self as deviant. Behaviour becomes regularised and the self-conception revolves around sex as a vocation which also provides rationalisations and a legitimating ideology[2] (Davis 1978, pp. 198–215).

The organisation of male prostitution seems very similar. An investigation of men working as prostitutes in Amsterdam identifies four types:

1 *Pseudo-prostitutes* are men posing as prostitutes for some purpose other than prostitution, including defrauding or gay-bashing;
2 *Hustlers* earn their living from a range of illegal activities only one of which is prostitution;
3 *Occasionals* lead an otherwise 'conventional' life and participate occasionally in the prostitution market;
4 *Professionals* actively participate in prostitution as a career, adhere to codes of behaviour and may work as street prostitutes, in brothels, be independent call-boys or innovative entrepreneurs (van der Poel 1992, pp. 263–72).

Poverty, lack of education, unemployment, minority group membership and labour market exploitation are significant factors accounting for recruitment into prostitution. An Australian study found that of twenty-three male and ninety female prostitutes, the main reasons for beginning to work as a prostitute were financial, specifically to pay for food and rent, and prostitution provides better money than other available jobs. Little education, limited job skills and options are common among prostitutes and many women working as prostitutes with dependent children find social security funds insufficient (Neave 1985a, p. 84).

Many feminists decry prostitution as the commercialisation and objectification of women whose value is measured only in terms of sexual pleasure which is bought and controlled by the male purchaser. On the other side, prostitutes seek to affirm the dignity of people who work as prostitutes and have lobbied to decriminalise prostitution and remove its stigma. Others argue that prostitution cannot be just another occupation because it is doubtful whether many people would opt for this work if other better-paying jobs were available. Prostitution is a highly stratified occupation where male clients, businessmen who refer clients, pimps and police largely determine work conditions which vary by type of prostitution (Heyl 1977, p. 545; Schur 1988, p. 105).

Some writers argue that as a result of the so-called sexual revolution and the development of effective contraception, prostitution is declining (Bullough & Bullough 1987, p. 297). Increasing public awareness of child prostitution counters this argument, yet little is known about its incidence and the relationship to rising rates of homelessness among young people. Davis describes the descent into homelessness for girls as possibly comprising a domestic crisis, then departure from home, followed by geographic dislocation then chronic homelessness, that is, full-time street involvement. In this fourth stage most activity focuses on prostitution, drug sales, theft and, for a few, assault and armed robbery (Davis 1993, pp. 28–9).

Drugs and alcohol use

Consuming drugs, including alcohol and cigarette smoking, can be conforming, normal, even expected behaviour. However, as with all forms of deviance it is the situation—the norms constructed and applied—which renders some forms of alcohol and drug use deviant. Alcohol and drug use are subject to religious, legal and medical controls. Their consumption is often seen as evidence of weakness, immorality, a lack of discipline or little self-restraint. Laws prohibit drunkenness, under-age drinking, drink driving and cigarette smoking in airports and workplaces, and the medical model views alcoholism and drug addiction as diseases requiring treatment and rehabilitation.

Most discussion about drug abuse and addiction focuses on illegal drugs, specifically cannabis, such opiates as heroin and opium, and cocaine. All of these substances have been available for centuries and used for both medicinal and recreational purposes, but it is only during the twentieth century that they have become illegal and defined as criminal. The processes whereby certain drugs become illegal, others controlled by the medical and pharmaceutical professions, and others available 'over-the-counter' do not reflect the physiological effect of the drug but are the result of political–economic factors, the activities of interest groups, and moral entrepreneurs. There is no evidence that marijuana is addictive, unlike alcohol and tobacco, and heroin and morphine have similar effects and compositions yet the former is viewed as a dangerous drug while the latter a necessary painkiller. Neither natural nor intrinsic differences exist between legal and prohibited drugs; the differences stem from the successful application of specific social definitions.

The USA first sought to define opiate use as an international problem and initiated the crusade to control consumption of these drugs. Opiates, especially as part of many patent medicines, were widely available during the nineteenth century, and the majority of the people dependent on them were white middle-class women. Another significant user group were the Chinese who migrated to work on the Californian railroads. The Chinese workers became the scapegoats for economic difficulties and unemployment after the railroads' completion in 1880. The first opium laws in the USA and Australia, in part, aimed to control the activities of the Chinese. Attention pivoted on the alleged vice and immorality among the Chinese, and concern for the protection of white women and girls from these corrupting influences. Strong pressure from the USA resulted in Britain's passage of legislation regulating the importation, exportation, manufacture, sale and use of opium and other 'dangerous' drugs. Britain had previously been actively involved in opium trade between India and China (Chambliss 1978, pp. 118–20; Ward & Dobinson 1988, pp. 129–41). Domestic politics, especially the emergence of the Quaker-based Society for the Suppression of the Opium Trade (SSOT) in 1874, and the emerging pharmaceutical profession which sought to control the supply of opiates were also instrumental in the criminalisation of opiate use. During the first half of the nineteenth century opium dependence was generally viewed as a habit and by the turn of the century the SSOT viewed it as an addiction. Moreover, the opium addict was cast, not as a victim of the physiological effects of opium, but as an 'irresponsible individual wilfully adopting a course of self-destruction ... [whose] addition was a symptom of a pathological breakdown or impairment of normal moral functioning' (Harding 1986, p. 82). This interpretation enabled criminalising the individual user of opium.

Becoming a drug user involves a number of phases. The 'novice' must learn and identify the effects and attach meaning to them, which may involve a career path from a beginner, to an occasional user and, ultimately, to a regular user (Becker 1963, p. 61). Becker argues that using marijuana requires:

1 *learning to smoke* the drug in a way which will produce real effects;
2 *learning to identify* the effects and associate them with drug use, that is, learning to get high;
3 *learning to enjoy* the sensations perceived which are not automatically pleasurable (Becker 1953, p. 242; 1963, p. 58).

Learning to enjoy a drug is necessary but not sufficient for a person to develop a stable pattern of drug use. The person must deal with social control mechanisms, rationalise the 'deviant' behaviour, and have access to a supply of the drug. These conditions are usually met by participating in a sub-culture where drug-use is normal.

Drug use is seen as contributing to two types of crime:

1 *acquisitive crime* on the part of users who, because of the high cost of illegal heroin and cocaine, inevitably resort to theft in order to pay for the drugs. Research in south London reveals that most heroin users committed burglaries and/or shoplifted with a few involved in cheque and credit card frauds. The rapid spread of heroin use in that neighbourhood was facilitated by the ease with which stolen goods could be exchanged for money and heroin (Burr 1987, pp. 338, 343). Interviews with thirty-two 'hard-core' heroin addicts indicate that the situation is far more complex and dynamic than simply drug use causing crime. Crime seems to facilitate drug use for most heroin users, except for 'street junkies' who closely approximate the stereotype of the heroin user (Faupel & Klockars 1987, p. 64).

   Ethnographic fieldwork in relation to women who use crack cocaine in New York City suggests that the widespread use of crack in many poor, urban, minority neighbourhoods has increased the number of women participating in street-level sex markets, often the only income source available to them. Conditions of extreme competition have deflated prices and increased levels of violence and robbery. An effect of the Reagan administration's 'war on drugs' during the 1980s has been to increase the victimisation of women crack smokers and street-level sex workers by male dates, male smokers, police and local youth (Maher & Curtis 1992, pp. 225, 238–42, 245, 248). Another aspect of the 'war on drugs' is the attempt to criminalise women who abuse drugs, including alcohol, during pregnancy (Note 1990, p. 1325).

2 *trafficking and importation* offences by the suppliers of illegal drugs which. is a form of organised crime. The media give widespread and regular attention to customs and police seizures of large quantities of heroin or cocaine and marijuana crops. Law enforcers seek to uncover international syndicates, cartels or drug rings responsible for the illicit drug trade. In 1984 the federal government established the National Crime Authority (NCA) to investigate and counter organised crime (see the discussion on organised crime in chapter 8).

Various myths surround the use of prohibited drugs: people who consume them are addicts; addiction results from 'experimenting' with these drugs which is often encouraged by 'pushers'; and their consumption leads to death and destruction. However, a parliamentary inquiry into drug use in Australia suggests: 'The typical drug user is not the stereotype of the "junkie" in the gutters of Kings Cross' (Australia 1989, p. ix). It indicates that young people are most likely to try illegal drugs in the company of friends, rather than due to the influence of 'pushers', and the majority of drug users do not become physically dependent (1989, p. 24). In the USA the most recent 'drug scare' revolves around the use of crack cocaine which public discourse and media attention tie to the problems of urban decay and to the lives of inner-city Blacks, Hispanics and young people (Reinarman & Levine 1989, pp. 115–16).

The most commonly used illicit drug in Australia is cannabis and its use appears to be on the increase. Taking into account age, the proportions reporting that they had tried the drug are higher in the twenty to twenty-nine age group. The 1991 National Household Survey conducted on behalf of the National Campaign Against Drug Abuse (NCADA), launched in 1986, found that 20 per cent of females as compared with 39 per cent of males reported having tried marijuana (Makkai & McAllister 1993, p. 34). Most cannabis is produced domestically and controlled by Italian organised crime groups.

Heroin and cocaine are used by smaller numbers of people, however illegal amphetamine production and use appear to be on the increase. In 1991 3 per cent of the respondents in the NCADA household survey reported that they had tried cocaine and 2 per cent indicated that they had ever tried heroin, and these patterns have remained consistent over time. Despite the public concern and media attention around such 'hard' drugs, it appears that frequent users are a very small minority of the general population (Makkai & McAllister 1993, pp. 45–8). Ethnic Chinese criminals dominate international heroin trafficking and are responsible for 80 per cent of heroin annually imported into Australia, most cocaine derives from South America and motor cycle gangs appear to control illicit amphetamine distribution (Dobinson 1993, p. 373; Makkai, McAllister & Moore 1994, pp. 122–7). McAllister and Makkai suggest that the anticipated upsurge in cocaine use in Australia has not occurred because of its relative expense and the negative imagery and fatal consequences associated with crack cocaine, especially among the urban under-class in the USA (1991, pp. 117–18).

Recent concern surrounding illicit drugs focuses on their contribution to HIV transmission through the sharing of needles. Sharing injecting equipment is high risk behaviour for infection with the HIV virus. Many intravenous drug users share needles for a variety of situational and economic reasons (Department of Community Services and Health 1988a, p. 131). The very illegality of high-demand drugs increases the probability of crime and medical problems because of the development of a 'black market' which inflates prices and encourages the practice of 'cutting' (that is, mixing heroin with other substances) which can be very dangerous. Under conditions of short supply, injection becomes the most efficient mode of consumption as the effects are immediate and direct and require the least amount of the drug.

Controlling illegal drug use in Australia is the responsibility of both federal and state governments. The general policy is total prohibition of illegal drugs. Broadly, Commonwealth laws and enforcement agencies deal with importation and trafficking offences, as well as organised crime, while the states criminalise cultivation, manufacture, possession, use, and supply of prohibited or restricted substances. During the 1980s, law enforcement efforts in some jurisdictions were directed away from users and toward large-scale drug importation, trafficking and organised crime. For example, in 1987 an expiation system for possession, cultivation or personal use of small amounts (less than 100 grams or 20 grams of resin) of cannabis by adults came into effect in South Australia. Adults found committing the offences are issued with a Cannabis Expiation Notice (CEN)—similar to a traffic fine—by the police. Paying the fine avoids the possibility of a court appearance and record of conviction. On the other side, those deemed to be large-scale operators are subject to large fines and lengthy imprisonment (Sarre, Sutton & Pulsford 1989, pp. 1–3). The ACT followed this approach in 1992. Except for these two jurisdictions, it appears that legislation aimed at reducing illicit drug use has become more draconian (Makkai, McAllister & Moore 1994, p. 135). In the USA, the reform movement to remove criminal penalties for possession of marijuana was fragile, brief and limited to a few states during the 1970s. Di Chiara and Galliher (1994, pp. 47–50) suggest that during this period a narrow 'policy window' was created by political leaders' explicit disquiet regarding the effect of arrest on high-status youths coupled with the support of law enforcement agencies keen to use limited resources efficiently.

In terms of the public health problems, legal drugs clearly outweigh the illegal drugs, largely because more people use them. In 1986 tobacco caused 17070 deaths, alcohol 3465 (including 1494 road accidents where alcohol was involved) and opiates (including legal drugs) 249 deaths (Australia 1989, p. 4). Seventy-one per cent of all drug-related deaths were attributable to tobacco use in 1990 with cancer and ischaemic heart disease accounting for around 60 per cent of all tobacco-related deaths. Tobacco use declined among males, but, until 1989, increased among females. However, passive smoking is increasingly becoming defined as a major cause of tobacco-related mortality with some courts awarding damages to victims of passive smoking (Department of Health, Housing and Community Services 1992, p. 21). Cigarette smoking is being re-defined from desirable and expected behaviour to that which is deviant, unhealthy and harmful (Markle & Troyer 1979, p. 622).

Over-the-counter and medically prescribed drugs are highly used. The 1989–90 National Health Survey found that 70 per cent of the population took some form of medication in the two weeks prior to interview. The proportion of persons using all medications (excluding vitamin and mineral supplements) increased from 47.7 per cent in 1983 to 64.1 per cent in 1989–90 (Australian Bureau of Statistics 1991b, p. 4). Both men's and women's use of these drugs increased with age; 40 per cent of women in the sample reported recent use of medically prescribed drugs (excluding oral contraceptives) compared with 33 per cent of the men. Women were more likely to use over-the-counter drugs, while men reported greater use of such licit social drugs as tobacco and alcohol (Department of Health, Housing and Community Services 1992, p. 41).

The interpretation of alcohol consumption is ambivalent: it can be socially integrative as well as socially and personally destructive and deviant (O'Connor 1984, pp. 177–9; Room 1976, p. 1050). As the consumption of alcohol by adults is legal, except for some prohibitions in public areas, it is less associated with the criminal law than is drug consumption. Repeated alcohol intoxication is likely to be defined as disease or illness, the idea is that the combination of some biophysiological flaw with alcohol produces the disease of alcoholism (Conrad & Schneider 1980, p. 75; Schneider 1978, pp. 363–4). Although the medical model provides information on the effects of alcohol within the body it ignores the entire cultural meaning and social definitions of alcohol use. Consuming large quantities of alcohol is only deviant and problematic under certain conditions.

Alcohol is the most widely used drug in Australia; more than nine in ten adults have tried alcohol, however, only around five in ten adults consume alcohol weekly (Makkai & McAllister 1993, p. 26). Alcohol is the second major cause of drug-related mortality, but this is declining due to the reduction in deaths cause by alcohol-related motor vehicle accidents. In 1981, 44 per cent of drivers and motorcycle riders killed had a blood alcohol reading over the legal limit; this had dropped to 31 per cent in 1991 (Department of Health, Housing and Community Services 1992, pp. 7, 68). Alcohol use among Aboriginal people has been identified as a major social problem and public drunkenness is a major route through which they come into contact with the police (McDonald & Biles 1991, p. 196; Moore 1992, p. 174).

The first systematic attempts to characterise chronic and disruptive intoxication as a sickness emerged at the end of the eighteenth century in the USA and Britain. While drinking in the American and Australian colonies was the norm (for adult men), drunkenness was frequent and arrests for drunkenness common. Temperance movements guided by religious morals sought to prohibit alcohol consumption. In the USA the Eighteenth (or Prohibition) Amendment of 1919 rendered illegal but did not eradicate drinking, drunkenness, and habitual drunkenness. The end of the nineteenth century in New South Wales was the high point of prohibitionist activity, dominated by Anglicans calling attention to the wave of drunkenness apparently engulfing Sydney. However, a Commission of Inquiry presented findings unfavourable to their cause (Grabosky 1977, p. 93).

Developments in medicine supported the social movement for temperance, specifically the clinical descriptions of physiological effects of alcohol and the suggestion that repeated drinking is itself a disease (Conrad & Schneider 1980, p. 82). The self-help group Alcoholics Anonymous (AA), formed in the USA in 1935, adopts the view that alcoholism is a disease rooted in an allergy to alcohol. AA is an example of a mutual aid organisation aiming to encourage conformity and the cessation of disruptive and deviant drinking. This involves a process of 'delabelling', whereby the stigmatised label is replaced by an acceptable one emphasising repentance and reform (Trice & Roman 1970, pp. 538–9). Although a secular organisation, AA retains strong links with religious imagery, specifically the emphasis on confession, repentance, correction of moral lapse, and 'being born again'.

The criminal law also reflects the notion of excessive alcohol consumption as illness, therefore reducing responsibility and rationality but requiring treatment or rehabilitation. Judges can order a defendant participate in an alcohol or drug rehabilitation program as part of a criminal sentence. Additionally, judges view intoxication as reducing culpability for a criminal offence if the consumption of alcohol or other drugs displaced a person's self-control or knowledge of his or her actions (Waller & Williams 1993, p. 803).

Summary

In conclusion, the designation of certain activities or individuals as immoral reflects the process whereby particular groups seek to maintain their status and have their values translated into law. Homosexuality, prostitution, abortion, pornography and drugs and alcohol abuse constitute contested terrains in which various moral entrepreneurs seek to enforce their views of the world. Indeed, the very conception of these activities results from the application of specific norms, yet little consensus prevails over their 'deviantness'. At various points in time these activities have been, and still are in some jurisdictions, prohibited or at least regulated by the criminal law. The next chapter addresses the question of crime in general.

Notes

1 Their method of recruiting respondents through homosexual organisations and at 'gay' social events or bars limits the representativeness and generalisability of this study as it excludes people not participating in gay subcultures or networks, or who do not define themselves as gay and therefore would not enlist in a gay organisation. However, obtaining a representative, random sample of gay men would be highly difficult given the stigma associated with admitting to homosexuality.
2 These findings are somewhat constrained by the data source, namely a jail sample of thirty streetwalkers legally defined as 'common' prostitutes.

Key terms

Morality
Moral entrepreneurs
Victimless crime
Decriminalisation
Right-to-life
Prostitution

Confessional
Symbolic crusade
Homosexuality
Abortion
Pornography
Drug and alcohol abuse

Main Points

1 Despite secularisation, religious conceptions of deviance and immorality still prevail in discussions of homosexuality, abortion, pornography and prostitution.
2 Moral entrepreneurs have organised to have their views of the world translated into law. The impetus for moral crusades may derive from proponents' concern to maintain their social status or reinforce particular cultural values rather than rejection of the specific activities, *per se.*
3 The concept of 'victimless' crime refers to activities which are prohibited by law but which usually lack a complaining victim. Examples include abortion, homosexuality, prostitution and drug use, and it is often argued that these activities are the concern of private individuals rather than the criminal law.
4 During the 1960s pressures, in particular the activities of such movements as Gay Liberation, emerged for the decriminalisation of homosexuality. Currently, homosexuality is on the political agenda as gay men are seen as the primary cause of AIDS. This focus has resulted in renewed discrimination and stigmatisation of gay men.
5 Discussion of abortion and pornography are examples of symbolic crusades with both proponents and opponents representing a particular set of values. Pro-choice activists argue for the right of women to decide about their own bodies, whereas anti-abortionists see a need to reinstate family values and a concern with the rights of the unborn child.

6 Many people tend to blame the individual when explaining why people become prostitutes or abuse drugs or alcohol without paying attention to economic factors or the processes of recruitment.
7 Consuming drugs and drinking alcohol can be conforming, normal, even expected behaviour. The most widely used illegal drug in Australia is marijuana which has been subject to considerable debate regarding the removal of criminal penalties for personal use. Both the legal and the medical systems attempt to control and regulate the consumption of drugs and alcohol.

Further reading

Becker, Howard S. 1963, *Outsiders: Studies in the Sociology of Deviance*, The Free Press, New York, chapter 8.

Best, Joel ed. 1989, *Images of Issues: Typifying Contemporary Social Problems*, Aldine de Gruyter, New York.

Greenberg, David 1988, *The Construction of Homosexuality*, University of Chicago Press, Chicago.

Gusfield, Joseph 1963, *Symbolic Crusade: Status Politics and the American Temperance Movement*, University of Illinois Press, Urbana.

Luker, Kristin 1984, *Abortion and the Politics of Motherhood*, University of California Press, Berkeley.

McAllister, Ian, Rhonda Moore & Toni Makkai 1991, *Drugs in Australian Society: Patterns, Attitudes and Policy*, Longman Cheshire, Melbourne.

Schur, Edwin M. 1988, *The Americanization of Sex*, Temple University Press, Philadelphia.

CHAPTER

4

The 'crime problem'

Crime rates and expenditure on crime prevention or control are central and highly contentious aspects of public policy. There are always claims that governments are not doing enough to counter crime as continually rising crime statistics suggest escalating crime. Others assert that governments are doing too much for convicted offenders with reports of luxurious prisons and lenient penalties. This chapter examines the so-called crime problem in Australia, as measured by officially collected statistics. It identifies the many problems in using such data to make claims about the amount of crime in Australia. National crime figures in Australia are especially problematic given jurisdictional differences in criminal laws and data collection practices. Nevertheless, officially collected information provides insights into the types of people who come into contact with the criminal justice system. The chapter also investigates the media's portrayal of crime, the generation of moral panics and 'crime waves', and the relationship between victimisation and the fear of crime.

Crime data

Police data are a major source of public information about crime and the most frequently used data on crime, in part because they are readily available and accessible. The usual measure is offences becoming known or reported to the police, a statistic which has not been subject to the extensive filtering process of the criminal justice system. At each decision point—arrest, laying of charges, prosecution, conviction, sentencing—discretion is exercised and decisions may not be based entirely on the severity or nature of the offence. As Sellin recognises: 'The value of a crime rate for index purposes decreases as the distance from the crime itself in terms of procedure increases. In other words, police statistics, particularly those of "crimes known to the police", are most likely to furnish a good basis for a crime index' (1931, p. 346, emphasis omitted). No officially recorded offence data accurately measures the total amount of crime, that is, activities which violate the criminal law, in a society and prison statistics are useless as indexes of crime. In contrast, Tappan suggests that only convicted offenders should be viewed as constituting the amount of crime. He argues that until a case is proven beyond a reasonable doubt and a person is convicted (or pleads guilty) he or she has not violated a criminal law and therefore should not contribute to the crime statistics. People suspected, arrested or charged cannot be known as law violators and to include them in studies of crime or criminals is inaccurate (1947, pp. 100–1). Nonetheless, police, court and prison statistics are useful as indicators of the types of people and offences coming into contact with various aspects of the criminal justice system.

It is never clear to what extent such officially collected statistics actually measure crime. In a sense, crime data are products of police and other rate-generating departments. Organisational policies, procedures, resources, skills and priorities all affect the production of crime rates. These data inevitably contain distortions and biases because only a proportion of offenders become known to the police and are incorporated into official records (Cicourel 1968 pp. 58–69; Kitsuse & Cicourel 1963, p. 133). Phenomenologists and ethnomethodologists maintain that the goal of theorising is to explain the emergence, construction, organisation and the meaning of crime statistics produced in organisations where informal norms, values, interpretive paradigms and practical contingencies including the volume of work and resources inform decisions. Kitsuse and Cicourel suggest shifting attention from investigating how and why individuals are motivated to engage in behaviour defined as deviant to the societal reactions, specifically within the criminal justice system, which define various forms of behaviour as crime. Thus, *'rates of deviant behaviour* are produced by the *actions taken by persons in the social system* which define, classify and record certain behaviours as deviant' (Kitsuse & Cicourel 1963, p. 135, emphasis in original). The question becomes not the extent to which official crime statistics measure crime but the nature of the definitions incorporated into the categories used by personnel in the criminal justice system to identify, classify and record behaviour as an offence. Organisational constraints, administrative discretion, informal norms, everyday practices, personal idiosyncrasies, ambiguities in legal definitions and evidentiary problems all affect whether an incident will be classified as a crime and whether a person will be identified as an offender. 'To reject these [officially collected] statistics as "unreliable" because they fail to record the "actual" rate of deviant behaviour assumes that certain behaviour is always deviant independent of social actions which define it as deviant' (Kitsuse & Cicourel 1963, p. 136). Crime statistics, then, are useful sources of information, but what they indicate must be carefully interpreted; they may tell us more about police activities and recording practices than about the amount of crime.

Offences becoming known to the police depend on police witnessing an offence and an offender, or on a victim (if one exists) deciding to report the incident and being prepared to press charges and provide evidence which will be cross-examined in court. Large differences exist between the reporting of larceny, robbery, assault, break and enter, car theft and such crimes as embezzlement, fraud, forgery, tax evasion and corporate crime, partly because the former are highly visible and have identifiable victims and consequences, and the latter do not. Only about half of all victims report a crime to the police and the likelihood of reporting varies with type of offence.

Figure 4.1 Victims of crime by type of offence in the last twelve months, Australia, 1983 and 1993

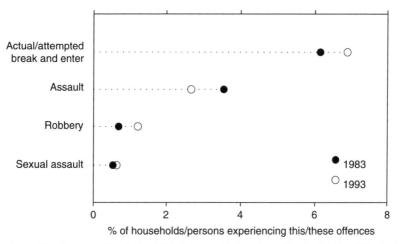

Source: Australian Bureau of Statistics 1994, *Crime and Safety Australia, April 1993*, ABS, Canberra, Cat. no. 4509.0, p. 1.

The 1993 Australia-wide crime and safety survey in which approximately 52 300 persons aged fifteen years and over finds that 94 per cent of the victims of motor vehicle theft, 79 per cent of break and enter victims but only 25 per cent of sexual assault victims reported the incident(s) to the police. Fifty-two per cent of robbery victims and 32 per cent of both assault and attempted break and enter victims told the police (Australian Bureau of Statistics 1994a, p. 12, table 3.1).[1] Figure 4.1 illustrates changes in the pattern of reporting between 1983 and 1993. The likelihood of reporting sexual assault has increased only slightly. With the exception of sexual assault, most victims not informing police gave as their reason that the crime was too trivial or unimportant or that they felt that the police could not or would not do anything. The major reasons given for not reporting sexual assault were that it was a private matter and the victims feared reprisal or revenge (Australian Bureau of Statistics 1994a, p. 12, tables 3.2 & 3.3). These findings accord with overseas studies. In the USA, victimisation surveys rival official data for the attention of criminological research and generally show that non-reporting has more to do with the type and seriousness of the offence than with the characteristics of the victim (Gottfredson 1986, pp. 253–7).

A major problem in Australia is obtaining uniform national crime statistics. In contrast to the USA and Britain, where victim surveys are standard aspects of social policy research, national victims of crime surveys have only been conducted in Australia in 1975, 1983 and 1993. Australia participated in an international crime victim survey in 1992 but the sample comprised only 2006 respondents (Walker & Dagger 1993, p. 34). Most information about crime, then, comes from police data which makes comparison between jurisdictions and the generation of national data difficult. This situation will improve following the establishment of the National Crime Statistics Unit (NCSU) in September 1990. It is funded by state and territory police departments, the Commonwealth Attorney-General's department and the Australian Bureau of Statistics (ABS) to compile Australia-wide statistics of crimes reported to police. The NCSU has developed standards for the collection and production of national crime statistics and its first uniform report of national crime statistics, to be updated every six months, was released on 31 May 1993 (Australian Bureau of Statistics 1994c, pp. 5–9; Dusevic & Carruthers 1994, p. 3). Additionally, the Standing Committee of Attorneys-General resolved to financially support the establishment of a National Court Statistics Unit to produce statistics on cases heard and sentencing, and consultation is occurring between the jurisdictions to reach greater similarity in criminal laws (Walker 1994, pp. 1–2). Currently, lack of comparability between state police departments which collect and collate crime statistics stems from:

1 *differences in legislation*. Some offences have no equivalent in other jurisdictions, alternatively, the same offence may be differently defined as is the case, for example, with rape, sexual assault, and break and enter (Murphy 1988, pp. 5–9). Four Australian jurisdictions have replaced the crime of rape with the crime of sexual assault, defined by some in terms of the magnitude of violence or threat of violence, others define the crime 'aggravated sexual assault' (Mukherjee & Dagger 1990, p. 1). Changes to legislation within jurisdictions, for example broadening the legal definition of rape or re-classifying domestic violence as criminal assault, will increase crime rates even though the actual incidence of the behaviour remains unchanged. Alternatively, decriminalisation of such offences as personal cannabis use and public drunkenness decreases the number of offences being reported or becoming known to police;

2 *differences in recording*. South Australian police statistics include all alleged offenders regardless of whether or not they were arrested or subsequently proceeded against. Offender statistics for other states are significantly lower because they exclude persons who are not arrested or who receive a formal police warning (Office of Crime Statistics 1986b, pp. 11–12). The collection and classification of crime data within one police department must be taken into account when interpreting the data. A sudden rise or fall in crime statistics may not indicate a real change in the incidence of criminal activity, but may reflect differences in the mode of collecting and categorising information that comes to the police. Steffensmeier and Cobb (1981, pp. 45–6), for example, find that the declining differentials in the arrest rates of men and women between 1934 and 1979 result from changes in police policy and improvements in recording, not an increase in female offending.

3 *changes in the intensity of policing* affect the recorded incidence of some crimes. Traffic offences rise whenever there is a police crackdown and figures on vagrancy, gambling, under-age drinking, prostitution, and illegal drug use change with policing policy and practice. Drug offences statistics increased by more than 1000 per cent between 1975–85 in South Australia, but about 95 per cent of recorded offences still relate to the use or consumption of cannabis. Rather than indicating an escalation in illegal drug trafficking, the dramatic rise reflects a shift in police enforcement practices for minor drug offences from the drug squad to regional criminal investigation units and uniformed personnel. The tendency for multiple charges, for both possession and use, to be laid against alleged offenders, with each charge being counted separately, further inflates arrest data (Office of Crime Statistics 1986b, p. 10). Moreover, police decisions to actively enforce certain laws may result in increased reporting and recording of other alleged offences. A case study of an anti-heroin campaign in one United States city shows an escalation of arrests for marijuana-related offences despite the absence of public and police sentiments against marijuana use (Sheley & Hanlon 1978, p. 273).

While the incidence of recorded crime generates considerable fear in our society, especially among certain groups like the elderly, most arrests and subsequent convictions are for such relatively minor offences as traffic violations and theft. Figure 4.2 shows that violent offences constitute a very small proportion of the total offences becoming known to the police. Most recorded crime relates to property offences, notably theft. Homicide rates remain relatively stable and have a high clearance rate, which means that murder cases are likely to be solved by a conviction or a not guilty finding. Table 4.1 indicates the overall growth in a number of offences reported and becoming known to the police in each state and territory combined to provide an Australia-wide overview. The information in the table should be read as indicating general trends rather than definitive numbers because of the problems in compiling national data. With the exception of homicide, crime rates have increased roughly threefold over the past twenty years, although there are jurisdictional differences. Controlling for population changes, between 1973/4 and 1991/2 the greatest increase in reports to police were for serious assaults which rose by more than 500 per cent. Reports of robbery, drug offences and fraud increased threefold. While these offences represent the greatest increases in reporting they are not the most voluminous. Reports of stealing and break, enter and steal doubled over the time period, yet these two offence categories account for 70 per cent of all offences reported to police; a small increase in rate means a large increase in actual numbers. The National Crime Statistics show that the most frequently reported crime in 1993 was unlawful entry with intent, of which there were 2161 incidents per 100 000 population, followed by motor vehicle theft at a rate of 637 per 100 000 population. The most common type of violent crime reported to the police was robbery which occurred at a rate of 72 per 100 000, then sexual assault, representing a rate of 70 per 100 000, while murder occurred at a rate of 1.6 per 100 000 population. Most violent offences against the person—murder, attempted murder and sexual assaults—took place in private dwellings (Australian Bureau of Statistics 1994b, p. 1).

Figure 4.2 Number of offences reported/becoming known to the police

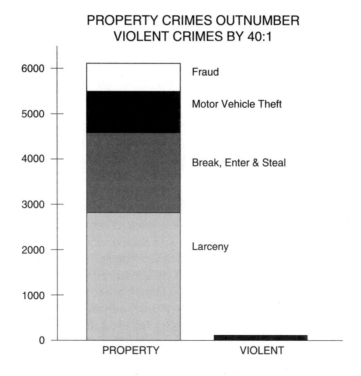

Source: Mukherjee et al. 1989, *Source Book of Australian Criminal and Social Statistics 1904–88*, Australian Institute of Criminology, Canberra, p. 161.

Table 4.1 Selected offences reported to police, 1973–74 to 1991–92 (rate per 100 000 population and total numbers), Australia

Type of offence	1973–74	1978–79	Year 1983–84 (per 100 000 population)	1988–89	1989–90	1990–91	1991–92
Homicide	2	2	2	2	2	2	2
Serious assault	21	33	54	101	105	114	115
Robbery	23	24	43	50	54	64	67
Break, enter and steal	880	1131	1773	1961	2002	2142	2069
Motor vehicle theft	375	477	636	756	798	866	803
Fraud	234	294	411	734	581	705	716
Stealing	1478	1896	2283	2701	2779	3047	2993
Drugs	n/a	137	331	379	355	425	491
Total N of offences	391 744	575 975	862 180	1 122 839	1 137 672	1 271 361	1 268 616

Source: Mukherjee, Satyanshu K. & Dagger, Dianne 1993, *Size of the Crime Problem in Australia*, *Updates*, Australian Institute of Criminology, Canberra, tables 2.2, 2.3, 2.4, 2.5, 2.7, 2.8, 2.9 and 6.2.

Table 4.1 excludes information on rape and sexual assault because of the recent legislative and jurisdictional differences in defining these offences. However, it appears that in most Australian jurisdictions reports of sexual assaults are increasing (Mukherjee & Dagger 1990, p. 121). Figure 4.3 illustrates the reporting of selected sexual offences to the South Australian police between 1982 and 1992. Reports of rape increased five fold and reports of indecent assault quadrupled during the decade. This information is capable of at least three interpretations:

1 a real increase in the incidence of rape and sexual assaults;
2 the increased likelihood of reporting as a result of reforms in police and court procedures thereby reducing trauma for the victim in making a report or giving evidence;
3 changes in the definitions of the offences and the fact that a single report can contain several counts of the same offence (Office of Crime Statistics 1993, p. 8).

Figure 4.3 Selected sexual offences becoming known to police, 1982–92, South Australia

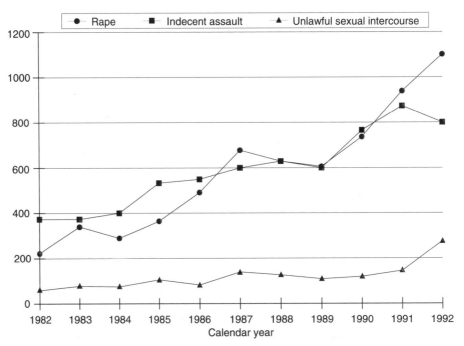

Source: Office of Crime Statistics 1993, *Crime and Justice in South Australia 1992*, Attorney-General's Department, Adelaide, figure 1.3.

Victims of crime data for South Australia suggest a real increase in the incidence of sexual assault. The number of victims of sexual assault (rape, attempted rape, indecent assault, assault with the intent to sexually assault) increased from 1500 in 1983 to 4200 in 1993 which represents an increase in the victimisation rate from 0.3 per cent to 0.8 per cent of the female population. Most of these victims will not have reported the incident to the police (Australian Bureau of Statistics 1994a, p. 22, tables 4.13 & 4.14). The National Crime Statistics also indicate that South Australia has the highest rate among the states of reported or detected sexual assault at 54.64 per 100 000 population, with Tasmania experiencing the lowest rate of 11.44 per 100 000. The Northern Territory is the jurisdiction with the highest incidence of reported sexual assault (Australian Bureau of Statistics 1994b, p. 8, table 3).

Even though crimes reported to the police is the statistic least contaminated by decision-making and processing in the criminal justice system, only about two in five of all offences are cleared. An offence can be solved or cleared when a person is charged with committing the crime (by far the most common mode of clearance), when it is discovered that no offence occurred, when the offender is below the age of criminal responsibility (usually ten years old), or has been committed to a psychiatric hospital (Mukherjee & Dagger 1990, p. 37). Table 4.2 demonstrates the clearance rates for major categories of crime in the period 1973–74 to 1991–92. Serious crimes against the person are much more likely to be cleared than are property offences; the most frequent offences—break, enter and steal and stealing—are the least likely to be cleared, and clearance rates are on the decline overall.

Table 4.2 Clearance rate and total number of selected offences cleared by police, 1973–74 to 1991–92, Australia

Offence	Year		
	1973–74	*1982–83*	*1991–92*
Homicide	93	86	74
Serious assault	73	74	65
Robbery	28	26	26
Break, enter and steal	19	13	11
Motor vehicle theft	14	14	11
Fraud	81	74	57
Stealing	28	23	18
Total N of selected offences	109 853	164 277	230 861

Source: Mukherjee, Satyanshu K. & Dagger, Dianne 1993, *Size of the Crime Problem in Australia*, Updates, Australian Institute of Criminology, Canberra, tables 3.1, 3.2, 3.3, 3.4, 3.6, 3.7 and 3.8.

Another change over the past twenty years is the expanding number of women coming into contact with the police as offenders. Increases are greatest for property crimes, especially fraud and forgery, where women constituted almost one-third of all offenders in 1990–91. Despite numerical increases women constitute a small proportion of offenders becoming known to the police. For example, while their involvement in robbery more than doubled between 1973–74 and 1990–91, only 129 women were involved in robberies cleared for 1990–91 compared with 1019 men (see table 4.3).

Age, gender and race are associated strongly with court appearances. In South Australia, 26 225 male and 4563 female defendants appeared before magistrates courts (which deal with the large majority of criminal cases) in

Table 4.3 Women as percentage of (adult) persons involved in selected crimes cleared by police,[1] 1973–74 to 1990–91[2], Australia

Year	Serious Assault		Robbery		Break, enter & steal		Motor vehicle theft		Fraud	
	% women	Total N	% women	Total N	% women	Total N	% women	Total N	% women	Total N
1973–74	7.0	1816	4.8	942	3.4	6933	2.2	5146	16.6	6196
1978–79	5.6	3074	6.6	1023	4.7	9104	2.8	5501	23.6	7470
1983–84	6.8	5358	8.8	1640	6.8	14 459	5.2	7251	28.7	10 719
1988–89	8.2	3811	9.9	951	8.7	19 562	6.5	8336	32.8	14 949
1989–90	6.9	3380	11.8	1980	9.3	19 758	7.0	9871	29.5	13 505
1990–91	8.0	3476	11.2	1148	8.3	14 563	6.1	6394	31.2	11 825

1 'Crimes cleared' usually means that the police have charged (including arrest) a person for the reported crime.
2 This table should be read as indicating general trends and directions; the actual numbers are unreliable due to changes in various states' recording practices over the time period. Refer to the 1993 edition of the updates to *The Size of the Crime Problem in Australia* (reference below) for statistical information relating to each state.

Source: Mukherjee, Satyanshu, K & Dianne Dagger, 1993, *Size of the Crime Problem in Australia, Updates*, Australian Institute of Criminology, Canberra, tables 5.1–5.5.

1992. There were 1850 male and 185 female defendants before the supreme and district courts. Women constituted 14.8 per cent of all magistrates court appearances and 10 per cent of higher court appearances. Almost half (46 per cent) of male and two in five (38.3 per cent) female defendants in the magistrates court were between 18 and 24 years of age. More than seven in ten men (78.5 per cent) and women (74.1 per cent) were below the age of 35 (Office of Crime Statistics 1993, tables 3.28a & 3.28b). The largest proportion of men were defending charges for driving offences (19.5 per cent), followed by offences against good order (17.8 per cent), drug offences (17.5 per cent) and larceny and receiving (14.9 per cent). In contrast, the largest proportion of women were defending charges for larceny and receiving (33.6 per cent), drug offences (15.3 per cent) and driving offences (14.1 per cent) (see table 4.4). In the supreme and district courts in 1992, men were most likely to be defending drug charges (19.3 per cent), offences against the person (18.4 per cent), and sexual offences (17 per cent) while women were also most likely to be defending drug charges (25.9 per cent), then fraud, forgery and false pretences (16.2 per cent), and offences against the person (14.1 per cent) (Office of Crime Statistics 1993, tables 4.25a & 4.25b).

Table 4.4 Magistrates court appearances: sex, average age and offence charged, 1992[1], South Australia

Major charge	Males	Females	Average age of all defendants
	(%)	(%)	(%)
Offences against the person	11.7	9.0	30.4
Sexual offences	1.2	0.2	34.5
Robbery & extortion	0.8	0.5	24.7
Burglary, break & enter	4.5	2.4	25.0
Fraud & misappropriation	2.3	5.1	31.7
Larceny & receiving	14.9	33.6	31.2
Property damage	4.7	2.2	26.6
Offences against good order	17.8	13.8	28.1
Drug offences	17.5	15.3	26.0
Driving offences	19.5	14.1	30.3
Other offences	1.5	1.7	33.4
Non-offence matters	3.6	2.1	33.0
TOTAL %	100	100	
	(N = 26 225)	(N = 4563)	

1 Each appearance by a defendant has a separate entry. Age is determined at the time of arrest.

Source: Office of Crime Statistics 1993, *Crime and Justice in South Australia 1992*, Attorney-General's Department, Adelaide, tables 3.28a, 3.28b and 3.28c.

Aboriginal people are ten times more likely to appear before a magistrates court as compared with other Australian-born defendants. They are most likely to appear for offences against good order and offences against the person; nearly one-third (30 per cent) of all Aboriginal defendants compared with 16.5 per cent of all other defendants faced charges regarding offences

Table 4.5 Changes in characteristics of prison population 1983–92, Australia

Prisoner characteristics (%)	Year					
	1983	1985	1987	1989	1991	1992
Under 25	39.4	38.8	35.7	33.0	33.0	32.1
Female	3.9	4.6	4.7	5.2	4.8	4.9
Aboriginal[1]	13.4	13.4	14.7/14.8	14.3	14.9	14.3
Overseas born	19.1	19.3	18.9	20.7	19.9	19.1
Unemployed[2]	50.9	57.0	59.8	60.8	64.6	65.8
Known prior imprisonment	61.1	62.8	60.6	56.3	56.9	58.2
Homicide	10.2	10.7	10.9	10.4	10.1	9.7
Other violence	30.6	30.3	30.1	31.6	32.4	33.4
Property offences	34.6	33.6	33.7	32.3	32.1	28.7
Good order	5.4	5.6	6.0	7.3	7.3	7.6
Drug offences	7.9	10.3	10.4	10.0	9.0	9.8
Driving offences	9.8	9.0	7.7	5.6	6.8	6.5
Remandees	11.4	13.7	13.2	13.0	13.1	11.9
Fine defaulters	2.6	2.6	2.2	1.4	1.7	2.3
Sentenced < 1 year	26.9	23.1	26.5	24.9	30.7	25.6
Sentenced > 5 years	37.4	40.6	38.3	39.7	30.9	31.2
Sentenced Life G.P.	7.0	6.8	6.7	7.0	5.6	5.3

1 Percentages exclude prisoners whose status is unknown. Where two figures are given for 1987 the first figure excludes Queensland data, and is therefore comparable to years 1983–85. The second figure includes Queensland data and is therefore comparable to years 1989 and onwards.

2 Percentages exclude New South Wales prisoners, for whom data on unemployment status prior to imprisonment have not been supplied.

Source: Walker, John assisted by Sue Salloom 1993, *Australian Prisoners 1992*, Australian Institute of Criminology, Canberra, table D10.

against good order in 1992. Non-Aboriginal people are most likely to appear for driving offences, then larceny and receiving. Most people who appear in the magistrates court are unemployed (49 per cent in 1992); the next largest category are employed (37 per cent) and the remainder are pensioners, students or performing home duties. Sixty per cent of defendants have never married and 17 per cent are currently married (Office of Crime Statistics 1993, p. 17, tables 3.29, 3.30 and 3.31).

Prison Data

The daily average number of prisoners in the year ending 30 June 1992 was 15 559, 88 per cent of whom had been sentenced, the remainder being remanded in custody. Table 4.5 presents overall changes in the prison population between 1983 and 1992. The table suggests that prison populations are getting older and despite the Royal Commission into Aboriginal Deaths in Custody the proportion of Aboriginal people in prison actually increased slightly. Women constitute a small—in the 1992 prison census 760 prisoners were female—but increasing proportion of all prisoners. There were slight increases in the percentage of prisoners who were serving sentences for drug offences, good order offences and offences of violence but decreases for property offences and driving offences. Rates of imprisonment vary by jurisdiction; the highest rates are in the Northern Territory, South Australia and Western Australia with Victoria having the lowest. Jurisdictions with high reception rates have relatively low sentence lengths, suggesting a revolving door effect. For example, in 1991–2 the Western Australian imprisonment rate was 31.4 persons per 100 000 adults who served an average of 4.38 months whereas the rate of imprisonment in Victoria was 3.8 persons per 100 000 who served an average of 15.05 months in prison (Walker 1994, pp. 27–31).

Table 4.6 indicates that around one-third of offenders sentenced to prison are property offenders; four in ten women as compared with three in ten men were incarcerated for all property crimes, including fraud. More men (32 per cent) than women (18 per cent) were serving sentences for homicide or other offences against the person and women were slightly more likely to be in prison for a drug offence and men were more likely to be imprisoned for driving offences. Persons aged twenty-four and below account for one-third (32 per cent) of the prison population, and those aged thirty-four and below account for more than two-thirds (72 per cent). Young prisoners are more likely to be property offenders; break and enter represented the most serious offence for almost one-quarter (23 per cent) of all male prisoners twenty-four years old and under and this was true for 18 per cent of their female counterparts. The most serious offence of one-fifth of male prisoners aged thirty-five years and above was a sex offence, the next largest sub-group (14 per cent) were convicted of homicide, followed by drug trafficking (12.5 per cent). Older female prisoners were more likely to be imprisoned for fraud and misappropriation, homicide and drug offences as compared with younger women in prison (Walker & Salloom 1993, tables 20a & 20b).

Table 4.6 Total number of prisoners, sex by most serious offence/charge, 30 June 1992, Australia

Offence	Males (%)	Females (%)
Homicide	9.8	8.9
Other offences against the person[1]	22.2	9.4
Robbery and extortion	12.1	9.4
Property offences[2]	26.7	33.1
Fraud and misappropriation	3.3	8.2
Drug offences	9.5	14.1
Driving offences	6.7	2.7
All other	9.6	14.3
TOTAL N	14 799	760

1 Includes assault and sex offences.
2 Includes break and enter, receiving, property damage and other theft.

Source: John Walker assisted by Sue Salloom 1993, *Australian Prisoners 1992*, Australian Institute of Criminology, Canberra, table 12.

Aboriginal people (including Torres Strait Islanders) are over eighteen times more likely to be in prison and over twenty-six times more likely to be in police custody than are non-Aboriginal people (Walker 1994, p. 32). For example, in South Australia the 0.8 per cent of Aborigines in the general population comprise 16 per cent of the prison population (Biles 1986, p. 247). The 1988 National Police Custody Survey shows that Aboriginal people constituted almost 29 per cent of those in police custody indicating that they are apprehended and placed in police cells some twenty-seven times more than non-Aboriginal people. Aboriginal women made up 49 per cent of all women in custody, although they constitute around 1 per cent of the national adult female population. Public drunkenness and offences against good order were the most frequent reasons for Aboriginal people's placement in police custody (McDonald & Biles 1991, pp. 192–6). Overall, Aboriginal and Torres Strait Islander men constitute 14 per cent of the male prison population while women make up 18 per cent of all female prisoners (see table 4.7). Research conducted for the Royal Commission on Aboriginal Deaths in Custody finds that Aboriginal people are nearly 13 times more likely to die in prison than are non-Aboriginal people, explicable by the over-representation of Aboriginal people in prisons (Biles, McDonald & Fleming 1989b, p. 23).

The mass media

Most everyday knowledge about crime comes from the media, which rely on police data, although there is some investigative journalism. An uneasy alliance ensues between police departments and reporters. If reporters react too strongly against police interpretations of certain events they will be

Table 4.7 Total prison population by jurisdiction, sex and Aboriginality [1], Australia

	NSW	VIC	QLD	WA	SA	TAS	NT	ACT	AUST
Males (%)									
Aboriginal & Torres Strait Islander	8.5	4.4	18.0	29.6	16.2	4.9	72.2	17.6	14.1
Other	90.2	95.6	82.0	70.4	83.2	95.1	27.8	82.4	85.2
Unknown	1.4	0.0	0.0	0.0	0.0	0.6	0.0	0.0	0.7
Total N	7087	2163	1941	1799	1089	264	439	17	14 799
Females (%)									
Aboriginal & Torres Strait Islander	12.3	8.8	26.3	44.7	17.5	0.0	62.5	0.0	18.0
Other	87.7	91.2	73.7	55.3	82.5	100.0	37.5	100.0	82.0
Total N	398	114	76	94	63	5	8	2	760
Total Persons (%)									
Aboriginal & Torres Strait Islander	8.7	4.7	18.3	30.3	16.2	4.8	72.0	15.8	14.3
Other	90.0	95.3	81.7	69.7	83.2	95.2	28.0	84.2	85.0
Unknown	1.3	0.0	0.0	0.0	0.6	0.0	0.0	0.0	0.7
Total N	7485	2277	2017	1893	1152	269	447	19	15 559

1 The Census regarded prisoners as Aboriginal or Torres Strait Islanders if they so identify themselves, and if they are accepted as such by other Aboriginal and Islander people.

Source: Walker, John assisted by Sue Salloom 1993, *Australian Prisoners 1992*, Australian Institute of Criminology, Canberra, table 3.

excluded from both official and unofficial sources of information (Grabosky & Wilson 1989, p. 131). The public views crime as a working-class phenomenon because the police only deal with everyday or ordinary crimes. The perusal of any daily newspaper supports this observation, with regular reporting of the proceedings of the local criminal courts which deal with such offences as break and enter, dangerous driving, robbery, assault, homicide and rape. According to one Melbourne television news editor, crime stories are 'very important. They would rank in the top two or three stories for our bulletin' (Grabosky & Wilson 1989, p. 9). Moreover, police are more likely to provide information on armed robbery, shootings, stabbings and other violent crimes because they perceive them as newsworthy, and editors seek out stories which tend to outrage or threaten members of the community. There are no comparable statistics on white-collar crime or corporate violations of tax, securities, equal employment, occupational health and safety, or trade practices legislation and regulations. The media reproduce the common image of crime and in Durkheimian/Foucauldian terms serve the function of the public hanging by reinforcing the collective consciousness through moral outrage.

News organisations further interpret and distort the information the police submit (Chibnall 1975, pp. 52–6; 1977, pp. 22–45; Humphries 1981, p. 204; Molotoch & Lester 1974, p. 101). The media emphasise violent and dramatic crimes which are more closely linked to a sense of personal threat, obscuring the fact that most crimes are overwhelmingly property offences. Such distortions may not be conscious or intentional as the organisational structure of news work requires raw materials or unexpected events to be typified and routinised, to be presented as a news story. Rather than distorting reality the process of news reporting reconstitutes the everyday world (Tuchman 1973, p. 117). This entails the construction of crime 'waves' and the dramatisation of police work which contribute to the general assumptions about crime. Developing news themes requires journalists to link together often-unrelated incidents, the underlying premise being that a big news item in the form of a crime wave is more newsworthy than several unrelated incidents. The notion of news themes enables journalists to portray an incident as an element of a larger whole (Fishman 1978, p. 540).

The media reproduce a common image that 'real' crime is crime on the streets, crime occurring between strangers, crime which brutalises the weak and defenceless and crime perpetrated by vicious young men, and the imagery is of war. It is not unusual to see such headlines as 'war on crime', 'outbreak of crime' and 'police as defenders of public safety'. After describing a number of brutal murders, a special *Time Magazine* report alleges that the widespread community perceives that 'throughout Australia, crime is out of control. That we are no longer safe. In the war between good and evil, between the law-abiding and the lawless, the bad guys are winning' (Gawenda 1988, p. 12). These crimes exist, but this imagery becomes the only reality of crime which people will take seriously because it is the dominant reality the media provide. However, the media do not present a homogeneous image of crime, nor does it necessarily have a monolithic, unidirectional impact on individuals' view of crime. It is over-deterministic to assert that the public automatically and uncritically accepts the image of crime presented by the mass media. Knowledge about crime derives from a variety of sources—the experience of being a victim or a witness of crime, discussions with acquaintances or friends who have been victimised, direct knowledge of the operation of the criminal justice system—which shapes the ways in which different people interpret the information newspapers and television provide. Moreover, the media are diverse and have several functions, not only to stimulate moral outrage. It offers direct assistance to the police through the broadcasting of emergency information, for example, presents information on corporate crime, may participate directly in law reform, and provides opportunities for citizens to redress grievances and achieve justice through letters to the editor or such consumer oriented television programs as 'The Investigators' (Ericson 1991, pp. 223–30).

Direct telecasting of court cases which may replace fictional television crime stories blurs the distinction between the reality and the imagery of crime. In the USA, Court TV, a cable television station which started in 1992, broadcasts only court cases and has over fourteen million subscribers. Considerable attention has been given to a series of court cases involving such high profile people as Michael Jackson and allegations of child sexual abuse, Heidi Fleiss defending prostitution charges and Tonya Harding regarding the assault on a rival Olympic ice-skater (Lyons 1994, p. 12). The broadcasting of the entire William Kennedy Smith rape trial on the Cable News Network (CNN) medium had considerable impact on the representation of the parties involved; ironically, the purple smudge used to protect the identity of the witness/victim left an impression of her as diffuse and sloppy in contrast with Smith's clean cut self-presentation (Freeman 1993, p. 536). Courts around Australia are considering the televising of some court proceedings. While it might be suggested that this would increase the accuracy and reality of crime reporting, the mass media are not a neutral conveyer of facts but offer selective representations of events within the court bolstered by interviews with the lawyers (who are not impartial, and are not supposed to be) for the parties during the trial. The televising of court actions raises numerous questions about the relationship between entertainment and justice; sensational media attention and commentary can reduce the possibility of a fair trial. Even though news reporters are careful to indicate that the defendant has been accused, not found guilty, of an offence, the nature of the reporting may reduce the significance of that distinction to the viewing public, including members of the jury.

Moral panics and youth offending

Since the early 1990s there has been considerable public discussion on youth offending, especially regarding such minor property offences as graffiti, motor vehicle theft and street activities which have led to calls for curfews and reduced hotel trading hours. As one commentator observes: 'The notion that a juvenile crime wave has, or is about to, engulf the community seems to have wide popular currency' (Freiberg 1993, p. 242). The former Minister for Family and Community Services in South Australia maintains that:

> There is a widespread public perception that the current system of juvenile justice does not deal effectively with young offenders, especially those who commit serious offences or who are long-term recidivists ... [I]t is believed that the system fails to deter young people from re-offending and fails to adequately protect the community from such criminal behaviour (South Australia 1993, p. 2849).

Moral panics surrounding young people and crime are nothing new. Cohen defines a moral panic as 'a condition, episode, person or group of persons [which] emerges to become defined as a threat to societal values and interests; its nature is presented in a stylized and stereotypical fashion by the mass media' (Cohen 1980, p. 9). He demonstrates the ways in which moral panic in Britain has been associated with the emergence of various forms of youth culture, participants of which are engaged in deviant or delinquent behaviour. They are identifiable by a distinctive dress code and become social types, for example the mod, the rocker, the greaser, the vandal, the soccer hooligan, the skinhead and the hippy. The media are instrumental in portraying these young people as 'folk devils' by exaggerating and distorting the seriousness, numbers of people and the degree of damage or violence involved in particular incidents and confrontations with the police. Hall and his associates document a moral panic about 'mugging' in Britain in 1972–73 which entailed the conversion of weak statistical evidence into widely publicised 'hard facts', thus creating the impression that violent crime, especially mugging, was rising dramatically (Hall et al. 1978, p. 17). Subsequently, media representations associated the 'crime' problem with such broader social problems as racial conflict, poverty and inner city decay. However, 'rather than trace the complex links between the deteriorated physical environment, patterns of cultural organisation and individual acts of crime, the inference is that a derelict and neglected house or street infects the inhabitants with a kind of moral pollution. The litter in the streets becomes the sign of incipient criminality' (Hall et al. 1978, p. 115).

Recent media reports in Australia have focused on several serious and/or violent offences committed by repeat offenders which justify arguments that the juvenile justice system requires reform and that young offenders should be punished more severely. In Western Australia a number of high speed car chases between police and juveniles in stolen cars, often resulting in fatal outcomes, was the catalyst for legal change in 1992 (Wilkie 1992, p. 187). Thus far, the high watermark of moral panic around youth crime is the global media attention on two ten-year-old boys who kidnapped and murdered a two-year-old child in England (Smith 1994). The tenor of the reports reflects contemporary Western societies' ambivalence about young people: on the one side there is incredulity that children could be capable of extremely cruel criminal acts; on the other, the view exists that where they do commit such crimes, then they deserve retribution and penal sanctions. Young people become a symbol of such wider social issues as the nature of the family, the relationship between families and the state, the apparent lack of morality and responsibility, unemployment, concerns about crime and personal safety, the kinds of penalties that should be adopted and the meaning of citizenship.

While some young people do commit serious and violent offences they constitute a very small minority of a small percentage of young people coming into contact with the justice system. There is little evidence that juvenile crime is out of control (Wundersitz 1993, pp. 33–4). Despite the difficulties comparing crime statistics across jurisdictions, table 4.8 indicates that the large majority of young people involved in official interventions face charges for property offences. Except for New South Wales, less than one in ten of all young persons appears for offences against the person, but this appears to be on the increase. South Australian data indicate an overall decline in the numbers of young people coming before the former Children's Court or Aid Panel in the period 1985–92 but show an increase—from 6 per cent in 1988 to almost 10 per cent in 1992—in those appearing for an offence against the person (see table 4.9). Five per cent (N=338) of total appearances in 1992 involved a serious crime of violence as compared with 2.6 per cent (N=201) in the previous year (Office of Crime Statistics 1992, p. 29; 1993, p. 26). Interestingly, the proportion of young people involved in official interventions for driving/traffic offences is extraordinarily high in Western Australia. While serious offences constitute a minority of the overall volume of young offenders they are sufficient to incite a moral panic and calls for tougher measures to control juvenile crime.

Table 4.8 Type of offences involved in official juvenile justice interventions: cautions, panels, courts

Offence	SA (1990–91) (%)	Vic (1988–89) (%)	NSW (1989–90) (%)	Tas (1990) (%)	WA (1988–89) (%)
Against person	7.9	2.0	14.8	4.5	3.3
Against property	57.2	65.6	53.2	46.5	45.0
Fraud	1.3	0.8	2.6	0.5	2.0
Break and enter	14.0	15.4	14.0	18.3[1]	43.0[2]
Vehicle theft	8.7	7.2	10.2	—	—
Other theft	31.5	42.6	21.2	25.8	—
Unlawful possession	1.7	—	5.2	1.9	—
Damage property	9.4	6.1	7.7	3.4	5.4
Driving/traffic	2.2	7.6	3.0	1.4	21.8
Drug	8.2	1.2	3.8	0.8	3.7
Against good order	11.2	10.6	8.1	33.4	13.4
Other	4.0	6.5	9.4	10.1	7.4
TOTAL N	8688	13 695	18 445	1661	34 530

For SA, Vic., NSW and Tas., the most serious offence finalised per case is detailed. For WA, all finalised offences are listed. Queensland was omitted because no offence data were provided for cautioned matters.
1 Break and enter, and vehicle theft combined.
2 Break and enter, vehicle theft, other theft, receive/unlawful possession combined.

Source: Wundersitz, Joy 1993, 'Some statistics on youth offending: and interjurisdictional comparison', in *Juvenile Justice: Debating the Issues*, eds Fay Gale, Ngaire Naffine and Joy Wundersitz, Allen & Unwin, Sydney, p. 31.

Table 4.9 Juvenile offenders: court and panel appearances by offence[1]

Offence	1988 %	1989 %	1990 %	1991 %	1992[2] %
Offences against the person	6.0	5.7	6.4	7.5	9.7
Robbery	0.4	0.3	0.6	1.0	1.0
Sexual offences	0.6	0.7	0.5	0.7	0.6
Drugs	7.3	8.8	8.6	8.8	10.4
Break and enter	13.0	13.1	13.9	13.4	21.8
Other property	51.2	51.0	51.9	53.7	38.3
Driving and traffic	3.5	3.6	2.9	2.2	n/a
Offences against good order	14.1	12.7	11.4	8.7	13.2
Other	4.0	4.1	3.8	4.0	4.8
TOTAL N	8327	7251	8163	7764	6586

1 Aid panels (abolished in SA from 1994) aim to divert young people from court. After a child admitted the allegations the panel could warn or counsel him/her or could refer the case to the Children's Court.
2 The offence categories changed in 1992 which may account for some percentage increases. For example 'other property' was replaced by 'larceny and receiving', 'property damage' and 'fraud, forgery and false pretences'.

Source: Office of Crime Statistics 1990–93, *Crime and Justice in South Australia 1988–92*, Attorney-General's Department, Adelaide.

Fear of crime

Not only are crime rates a source of concern to policy makers and members of the public, but the fear of crime has become defined as a discrete social issue and topic of research. Fear of crime usually is defined as 'the amount of anxiety and concern that persons have of being a victim' (Yin 1980, p. 495). An overriding concern of researchers is to examine the relationship between the incidence of crime and the fear of crime, specifically: 'Is fear of crime a response to the underlying crime rate as reflected in personal victimisation and the victimisation of friends and associates (communicated through interpersonal ties) or to the reported crime rate as reflected in the victimisation of strangers (communicated through the media)?' (Liska & Warner 1991, p. 1448).

Sociological research on the fear of crime addresses three central issues: the relationship between victimisation and fear of crime; the social, demographic, geographical and individual factors which increase the likelihood of fear; and how fear affects people's activities and precautions regarding personal security.

1 The relationship between victimisation and fear of crime
One of the earliest findings is that the elderly and women (not mutually exclusive categories) express the highest levels of fear, yet paradoxically they have the lowest rates of actual victimisation. Recent victimisation appears to increase concern about crime, but its effect declines because victims take more precautions, thus becoming less fearful, others neutralise the effects of being victimised and some allow the experience to abate with time. However, in decaying and deteriorating inner-city neighbourhoods the effect of victimisation is to increase fear (Box, Hale & Andrews 1988, p. 352; Skogan

1987, p. 151). The 1993 Australian Crime and Safety Survey (of victims) demonstrates that in the year to April 1993, 8 per cent of people in the 15–24 age range were the victim of a personal crime (robbery, assault or sexual assault) compared with 0.7 per cent of those aged sixty-five years or over. Males aged between fifteen and twenty-four years are most at risk of victimisation. Except in the sixty-five years and above category more men report being the victim of a crime than do women (see table 4.10). Regarding employment status, 7.9 per cent of unemployed people indicated that they had been a victim compared with 3.9 per cent of employed people and 2.5 per cent of those not in the labour force. The survey reveals that households are at greater risk of victimisation than are individuals; 8.3 per cent of Australian households were the victims of at least one actual or attempted break and enter or motor vehicle theft, while 3.7 per cent of persons were victims of a crime against the person. Households consisting of a single parent/guardian with unmarried children are most at risk of victimisation, followed by a person living alone, whereas the lowest risk is for married couples (Australian Bureau of Statistics 1994a, pp. 3–4). This last finding qualifies the conclusion that women have a lower risk of victimisation than do men because the single adult in households with children is more likely to be female than male. A small-scale study of reported 'break and enter' dwelling offences in suburban Adelaide supports the proposition that all-female households are more vulnerable to 'break-ins' than is the general population. It finds that almost one-third of the 256 victims interviewed lived in all-female households, either one woman living alone, two or more adult women sharing a house or a single mother and her children (West 1994, pp. 28–9).

Table 4.10 Victims of personal crime[1] in the twelve months prior to April 1993: age by sex

| | Victims (victimisation rate, %[2]) | | |
Age (years)	Males	Females	Persons
15–24	9.3	6.5	7.9
25–34	5.4	3.6	4.5
35–44	3.6	2.9	3.2
45–54	2.6	1.7	2.2
55–64	1.5	0.9	1.2
65+	0.6	0.8	0.7
Total	4.4	3.0	3.7

1 robbery, assault or sexual assault.
2 of persons.

Source: Australian Bureau of Statistics 1994, *Crime and Safety Australia, April 1993*, ABS, Canberra, Cat. no. 4509.0, table 2.3.

Explanations of gender differences in the fear of crime emphasise the peculiar characteristics of such crimes as rape which affect women disproportionately (Gardner, Carol 1990, p. 313). Nevertheless, survey data suggest that women exhibit higher fear than men for every offence type. Fear of rape declines with age but that is due, in part, to increasing fear of other offences among older women, not simply to an absolute decline in fear of rape. The high fear associated with rape stems from the seriousness of the crime and the perception that it is relatively likely (Box, Hale & Andrews 1988, p. 344; Warr 1984, p. 687; 1985, pp. 241–3). Greater fear among the elderly despite a relatively low risk of victimisation may stem from the media's tendency to sensationalise crimes against the elderly. Moreover, the elderly are more likely to discuss crimes, they have less extensive support networks and are less involved in their neighbourhoods and thus confront more strangers than young people, all of which contribute to a heightened sense of fear (Yin 1980, p. 499; 1982, p. 244).

2 Factors which increase the likelihood of fear

Perceived vulnerability, neighbourhood conditions, personal knowledge of crime and victimisation, confidence in the police and criminal justice systems, perceptions of personal risk and seriousness of various offences all contribute to fear (Box, Hale & Andrews 1988, p. 341; Yin 1980, p. 493). Fear increases when people consider their immediate neighbourhood to be threatening because it is populated by strangers whom they perceive as engaging in such 'anti-social' activities as late-night parties with loud music, or by young people hanging around street corners, or by homeless people (Taylor & Covington 1993, pp. 374–6). Most research indicates that the effect of crime rates on fear is weak and the effect of official crime rates is mediated through the newspaper coverage of crime. Stories about homicide occurring locally have the strongest relationship to fear, whereas newspaper coverage of crime in other cities makes people feel safe by comparison (Liska & Baccaglini 1990, pp. 366–71).

3 How fear affects people's activities

Substantial gender differences exist in the precautions individuals adopt to manage fear of crime, especially with respect to social or lifestyle precautions. Compared with men, women are more likely to avoid going out alone, are less likely to go out at night and are more likely to avoid certain parts of the city. An Adelaide survey shows that 54 per cent of women interviewed feel somewhat or very unsafe when walking alone at night as compared to 13 per cent of the men interviewed and a Queensland study indicates that 47 per cent of women as compared with 86 per cent of men feel reasonably or very safe walking alone at night. Women feel less safe being alone at home both at night and during the day and very few men or women feel unsafe walking alone during the day (Mukherjee & Dagger 1990, pp. 55–7). Carol Gardner examines the ways in which women's experiences of public places and their fear of crime affects their behaviour. Her interviews uncovered the strategies that women use to convey the impression that they are not alone, for example by placing items of men's clothing in their cars or affecting the presence of a male companion (1990, pp. 316–20).

Fear of crime studies suggest that the fear constrains individuals' activities; they are more likely to remain at home during the evenings and are more likely to keep their fears and concerns private rather than discuss them with others. The fear itself, then, becomes a form of social control which reduces social interaction, especially among strangers. This runs counter to Durkheim's arguments that crime, or the reaction to it, enhances social solidarity and increases social interaction. In contemporary urban societies, the reaction to crime seems to keep people apart instead of integrating them. Liska and Warner suggest that, paradoxically, this tendency may reduce crime as opportunities for crime decline as more routine activities are constrained to the home (Liska & Warner 1991, p. 1445).

Summary

This chapter documents the major sources of information about crime in Australia. While offences becoming known or reported to the police are the most often used statistic because it is least contaminated by the decision-making processes in the criminal justice system, it is incorrect to conclude that such information is an accurate measure of the volume of crime. Not all criminal offences come to the attention of the police, in part because, for various reasons, victims or witnesses do not report crime incidents to the police. Nevertheless, such statistics can provide an insight into police department priorities and recording practices. As the federal, state and territory governments are separately responsible for the content and administration of the criminal law, obtaining national crime data in Australia is especially problematic; this is changing with Australian Bureau of Statistics' six-monthly publication of uniform crime data. Victim surveys are also an important source of information about crime and indicate that some crimes are more likely to be reported to the police than are others, thus attesting to the inaccuracies inherent in police data. Overall, officially collected statistics indicate that the volume of crime in Australia is on the increase, the proportion of women coming into contact with the criminal justice system is expanding, especially for fraud and forgery and other property offences, and Aboriginal people are disproportionately represented in the criminal justice system as accused and convicted offenders, mostly for public order offences. Probably the major source of everyday knowledge about crime comes from the mass media. News organisations tend to sensationalise stories about crime thus perpetuating the image of crime as involving personal victimisation, even though crimes against the person are less frequent than crimes against property. Recent research focuses on the role of the media in inciting moral panics about crime and on the relationship between victimisation and fear of crime. The following chapter examines the organisation and operation of the criminal justice system.

Note

1 The survey defined victim as a person or household reporting at least one of the offences listed, that is, assault, actual and attempted break and enter, motor vehicle theft and sexual assault (questions only asked of women). Data was not collected for crimes without specific victims, for example trafficking in narcotics or for crimes against commercial establishments (Australian Bureau of Statistics 1994a, pp. 1, 33).

Key terms

Criminal justice system   Crime rate
Victims of crime surveys   Victims
Crime wave   Moral panic
Fear of crime
Offences becoming known/reported to police

Main points

1 The criminal justice system involves a series of crime-processing stages: suspicion or report of illegal activities; apprehension, prosecution, conviction and sentencing.
2 While offences reported or becoming known to the police are the main source of information about crime in society they must be treated with extreme caution. This is especially true in Australia where uniform, national crime statistics are only just becoming available. Police departmental policy and mode of data collection affect crime statistics as well as the fact that not all law violators come into contact with the criminal justice system.
3 Victims surveys are an alternative source of information about crime, however only three have been conducted in Australia, the most recent being in 1993. These surveys indicate that victims of motor vehicle theft and break and enter offences are most likely whereas victims of sexual assault are least likely to report the incident to the police.
4 A symbiotic relationship exists between the media and the police. The police provide accounts of unusual crimes because they think this is what people want to know and the media's reporting of these events reinforces the view that most crime is serious, brutal and occurs between strangers.
5 Moral panics are conditions, episodes, persons or groups of persons which emerge to become defined as a threat to societal values. The mass media are instrumental in generating moral panics, particularly surrounding the illegal or delinquent activities of young people.
6 Research suggests that women and the elderly are the least likely sub-groups to be at risk of victimisation yet they indicate a greater of fear of crime. Fear of crime among the elderly is exacerbated by sensational media coverage of crimes where the victim is elderly and lacks support networks, and women's fear probably stems from fear of rape, a crime for which women are disproportionately at risk.

Further reading

Australian Bureau of Statistics 1994, *Crime and Safety Australia April 1993*, Cat no. 4509.0, ABS, Canberra.

Australian Bureau of Statistics 1994, *National Crime Statistics, January–December 1993*, Cat no. 4510.0, ABS, Canberra.

Cohen, Stanley 1980, *Folk Devils & Moral Panics: The Creation of the Mods and Rockers*, Basil Blackwell, Oxford.

Ericson, Richard V., Patricia M. Baranek & Janet B.L. Chan 1989, *Negotiating Control: A Study of News Sources*, University of Toronto Press, Toronto.

Kitsuse, John I. & Aaron V. Cicourel 1963, 'A Note on the Uses of Official Crime Statistics', *Social Problems* vol. 11, pp. 131–9.

Liska, Allen E. & Barbara D. Warner 1991, 'Functions of Crime: A Paradoxical Process', *American Journal of Sociology*, vol. 96, pp. 1441–63.

Mukherjee, Satyanshu K. & Dianne Dagger 1990, *The Size of the Crime Problem in Australia*, Australian Institute of Criminology, Canberra.

CHAPTER

5

Crime control

As outlined in the introduction, social control involves all the actions oriented to eradicating deviant behaviour by modifying an actor's conduct (or thoughts) to bring him or her in line with others' expectations. This chapter concentrates on the criminal justice system which formally seeks to control criminal deviance. Of course, such informal control mechanisms as parental sanctioning, operate to counter criminal deviance but the activities of police, the courts and correctional facilities are the most visible and powerful means of controlling behaviour violating the criminal law.[1] Most people view the criminal justice system as responding to crime. In contrast, critics of the police, courts and prisons maintain that they escalate crime and have little deterrent effect.

The criminal justice system

In Australia, the responsibility for crime control lies with the state and federal governments, the former having more to do with everyday crimes, like offences against the person and property, whereas the latter deals with illegal immigration and importation, terrorism, deviation from social security regulations, and organised crime. All states have statutory or common law criminal codes, and state governments administer police forces and such sanctions as probation, parole and the prisons.

Crime control as a key policy area and responsibility of central governments funded through general tax revenues is a relatively recent phenomenon. Currently, many governments are attempting to reduce public expenditure on crime management and delegate some social control functions by decriminalising selected offences, developing such community programs as community work orders and neighbourhood watch, and instigating the 'privatisation' of prisons.

The criminal justice system involves a series of crime-processing stages, namely:

1 suspicion, report or investigation of law breaking activities;
2 arrest and charge of suspected offender;
3 prosecution;
4 conviction;
5 sentencing—prison, fine, community corrections.

At each stage decisions are made and discretion exercised; some people continue to the next stage, whereas others leave the system. The number of people receiving sentences is much lower than the number of people suspected of deviating from the criminal law, thus suggesting a 'funnel effect'. The following sections deal with the various stages of the criminal justice system.

Crime investigation

State police departments are primarily responsible for crime investigation, the laying of initial charges and, in some cases, for conducting prosecutions. Additionally, the states and the federal government have established a number of special investigatory agencies, for example the Independent Commission Against Corruption (ICAC) in New South Wales and the National Crime Authority (NCA). Other agencies such as the Australian Tax Office (ATO) and the Australian Securities Commission (ASC) also have wide investigatory powers.

Organised police forces developed in Europe, the USA and Australia during the nineteenth century. Earlier, citizens rotating in local offices— sheriffs, constables and magistrates—or members of the militia, yeomanry corps or watch and ward committees maintained legal order. In England, crime control moved from general community responsibility to a specialised office with the establishment of the constabulary in the late thirteenth century. The constabulary also became part of the system of control in the North American and Australian colonies (O'Malley 1983, pp. 52–7; Parks 1970, p. 76). Officials were unpaid; their duties to be performed from civic rather than pecuniary motives. Responsibilities encompassed general security, providing assistance to citizens, looking out for fires, and enforcing vagrancy laws and curfews (Parks 1970, pp. 77–8). Gradually, the constabulary took on pecuniary potential as citizens paid deputies to avoid their turn, and constables demanded rewards for special protection or investigation. In Australia, especially in rural areas, local power holders controlled constables and their organisation remained decentralised. Police duties became paramilitary in scope as police officers often discharged duties similar to those of the United States Army on the American frontier (Foley 1984, p. 161; O'Malley 1983, p. 53).

The tasks of the first police force, the Metropolitan Police, established in London in 1829, included the prevention of crime by regular patrols and control of the 'dangerous classes' when they formed mobs and riots. The police regularly patrolled beats and operated under strict rules which allowed some individual discretion. The peaceful and propertied classes appreciated the fact that the modern police relieved them of the obligation to discharge police functions and reduced the possibility of a resort to the military for internal peace-keeping purposes (Silver 1967, pp. 7–9). The emergence of a centralised police force was part of the broader shift toward a laissez-faire capitalist democratic order. This involved the demise of the rural elite and its replacement by an urban bourgeoisie advocating an ideology of equality and legal and political rights. In such a climate the establishment of an overtly partisan police force identified with the militia became repugnant. The police came to be seen as an independent force concerned to enforce the law impartially and maintain order (O'Malley 1983, pp. 54–5). However, problems of order denote some conflict of interest and antagonism in society. Apparently the reorganisation of police in Sydney, as in London, was far more closely related to civil strife and crises of public order, especially in the gold fields, than to the increasing size of the towns or to criminal predation on the rising middle classes (Gurr 1976, pp. 131–4; Robinson & Scaglion 1987, p. 113). By the end of the nineteenth century the organisational philosophy and structure of the police forces in each Australian state was based broadly on the English model, with crime prevention as the central function (Corns 1988, p. 34).

For most citizens the police force is a highly visible form of formal social control; police are the gatekeepers of the criminal justice system. Usually, people coming into contact with the criminal justice system as complainants, victims or as suspects deal with the police. The role of the police involves prevention and detection of criminal activities, and public order maintenance. Formally, the police are politically independent and enforce laws impartially, regardless of government pressure and intervention. This situation is often far from reality. Policing has been described as 'Janus-headed' and as having a double and contradictory origin and function because it simultaneously expresses social divisions as well as universal communal interest (Reiner 1985, p. 3; Robinson & Scaglion 1987, pp. 109–10). While police have peace-keeping and controlling responsibilities, their activities generate criticism and conflict because they enforce dominant conceptions of social order and protect private property. Much police work involves regulating public space—the streets, parks, shopping malls. As working-class people are more likely to use public space for their leisure activities than are the middle class they are more likely to be policed. This is especially true for Aboriginal people whose settlements are often declared as public places and are thereby subject to a degree of policing which would not be tolerated in suburban areas (Cunneen 1988, p. 201).

Each Australian state and the Commonwealth has its own police force established legislatively, bureaucratically organised, financed by government revenues and staffed by state employees. Police administrations are organised into departments and special units including the Criminal Investigation Bureau (CIB), the Licensing Branch and Traffic Police. Private forms of crime control and detection, including private detectives and security guards, also exist. By the end of the 1960s private security agents in most capitalist democracies considerably outnumbered public police personnel (Spitzer & Scull 1977, pp. 24–7).

In the British, North American and Australian legal systems, a strong tradition of the independence of the police exists encapsulated in the separation of powers doctrine, specifying that political leaders should not determine or influence police work, and that police should not, or at least should not be seen to, bolster an unpopular political regime (Bittner 1967, p. 700; Corns 1988, pp. 41–2). In Australia, the Police Commissioner is responsible for superintendence of the force, subject to direction from the Minister of Police. However, a number of judicial decisions have maintained that the Commissioner is independent of the Executive and is not subject to any directions in the enforcement of the law. This situation has led to virtual police immunity from external scrutiny; an uneasy tension prevails between the notions of legal autonomy and accountability, that is, the obligation to answer for a responsibility that has been conferred (Freckelton & Selby 1988, p. 225).

The common view is that police arrest persons who have committed an offence. However, making arrests constitutes only a small component of everyday police activities. The so-called crime function of police may constitute between 10 and 20 per cent of daily activities (Blumberg 1985, p. 6). In Victoria, for example, more than five hundred distinct duties exist within policing (Corns 1988, p. 39). Police work includes maintaining social order, detection and prevention of criminal activities, providing assistance to members of the public, dealing with various complaints, and clerical activities. Not only is police work heterogeneous—so are the skills, functions, organisations, jurisdictions and expertise. Often the tasks of police personnel are ambiguous and vague, with actual activities reflecting the demands of particular situations rather than a codified duty statement. Divisions recur between administrators and police on the beat; between police whose knowledge derives from experience and those who have obtained credentials and aspire to professional status; and between specialist branches and general police work. Two themes predominate in the literature on police and policing:

1 *Police discretion* and accountability, in particular the scope and use or abuse of coercive powers;

2 *Police deviance*, especially corruption, and the effects of organisational socialisation on police activities.

Police discretion

Discretion is an integral part of police work. Discretion can be defined as a situation where a police officer can choose between two or more task-relevant alternative interpretations of suspected, observed or reported events (Sykes, Fox & Clark 1985, p. 172). Discretion can have both just and unjust consequences; decisions can be based on an array of legal and non-legal considerations. On one side, flexibility is important because general and abstract laws must be interpreted in relation to particular circumstances. The negative side of discretion is that it can result in discrimination and selective policing of certain groups who are more visible and powerless, but more easily convicted.

Given limited resources, discretion is important for decision-making about the types of offences which require policing. Law is only one resource or alternative that police apply in circumstances where an arrest is technically possible. Police personnel often employ such alternative sanctions as a warning or 'keeping an eye' on certain persons. The exigencies of actual situations, rather than legal mandates, often determine peace-keeping procedures. Police work on 'skid row', for example, requires obtaining personal knowledge about the residents, making arrests on the basis of risk not culpability, and being concerned to reduce the aggregate total of troubles in the area rather than dealing with individual cases (Bittner 1967, p. 714).

In their encounters with citizens police have a wide latitude of discretion. They might:

1 ignore the commission of an offence;
2 ignore a complaint from a victim or observer;
3 identify an offender then issue a caution, summons, ticket or make an arrest;
4 incriminate a citizen by planting evidence or make an arrest based upon slight evidence.

Police officers exhibit reluctance to expose certain people to the stigma associated with official police action. With respect to young people, departmental policy might specify that age, attitude and prior criminal record be taken into account in determining action. A study of police–juvenile encounters shows that for nearly all young people suspected of minor offences and for some suspected serious delinquents the assessment of character and the following sanctions are based on the youth's personal characteristics, not on the alleged offences. The researchers identify demeanour as a major determinant of decisions in half of the juvenile cases police process and conclude that a few readily observable criteria—the youth's prior offence record, race, grooming and demeanour—affect the exercise of police discretion (Piliavin & Briar 1964, pp. 208–10).

A large-scale study involving systematic observation of police–citizen transactions in three United States cities specifies the social conditions under which police make arrests in routine encounters (Black 1970, p. 735; 1971, p. 1088; Black & Reiss 1970, p. 65). Sanctioning probabilities depend upon social situations, not just the rule-breaking activity. The police rely on citizens for information about suspected law-breaking activities and respond to a complainant's (observer or victim) report. With the exception of such special units as the licensing branch, traffic police or vice squad, most police work is reactive not proactive, which means that most criminal cases pass through a moral filter in the citizen population before police involvement.

The decision to arrest reflects the citizen's preference, which is affected by the relational distance between a complainant and suspect. The greater the relational distance, the greater the likelihood of arrest. Australian research on the enforcement activities of regulatory agencies extends this finding to white-collar or corporate crime (Grabosky & Braithwaite 1986). Likelihood of arrest decreases if the complainant is a friend, neighbour or acquaintance and is negligible if the complainant is a family member. The probability of arrest increases if the situational evidence is strong and if the offence is legally serious. Nonetheless, the complainant's preference is more significant than evidence; the more serious a complainant perceives the offence, the greater the chance of an arrest. The highest probability of an official response occurs when the crime is serious and the adversaries are strangers, and the lowest is for misdemeanours when the adversaries are friends, neighbours or acquaintances. The police are the instrument of the complainant in two ways: they handle what the complainant wants them to handle, and they handle the matter in the way the complainant prescribes (Black 1971, pp. 1104–9).

This research finds no evidence of racial discrimination in police encounters, but explains the higher arrest rate among blacks as resulting from the greater rate at which blacks show disrespect for the police (Black 1971, p. 1109). However, it does not examine the extent to which police action or provocation contributes to suspects' disrespect. South Australian data show that Aboriginal people are more likely than are non-Aborigines to be arrested, not because of direct and overt discrimination, but because police are more likely to arrest unemployed people and Aborigines are more likely than others to be unemployed. Moreover, the kinds of offences for which Aborigines are likely to be arrested, specifically those relating to public order and alcohol use, have high arrest rates, whereas the opposite is the case for the kinds of offences for which non-Aboriginal people get arrested, for example shop-lifting and break and enter (Gale & Wundersitz 1987, pp. 90–2).

Australia-wide research on young people's perceptions and experiences of police contact suggests that the police are more likely to be 'heavy-handed' in their interactions with young men, Aboriginal youth and marginal youth, i.e. those not in full-time education or work. Such young people were most likely to be stopped by police, taken to a police station, strip searched or to report being 'roughed up'. At the police station boys, Aboriginal and marginal youths are more likely to report being yelled at or physically pushed around by the police. Those stopped by the police indicate that they were just 'hanging out', walking or drinking when approached. Young people who experienced police-initiated contacts are less likely than others to express positive perceptions of the police (Alder 1992, pp. 20–6). Police-youth clashes are most likely to occur in the commercial areas of a city where police are called in to protect public safety and private property from street crimes, perceived to be the motivation for young people to congregate in central business districts. White suggests that in policing public spaces many police officers employ a conceptual shorthand to anticipate potential troublemakers and troublespots (White 1993, p. 210). This results in selective policing.

Recently, there has been a shift in police work from crime prevention to crime detection, and a breakdown in community or consensus policing. The idea of community policing indicates that neighbourhoods or communities accept, or at least tolerate, police intervention in order to prevent crime and maintain order. Police depend on citizens for information and the latter seek police assistance, thus indicating an interdependent relationship. British research describes a crisis in policing signified by increasing alienation of people from the police and marginalisation of the latter, ultimately resulting in military-style policing operating on conflict and antagonism between police and the public (Kinsey, Lea & Young 1986, pp. 11–36). The introduction of patrol cars, the implementation of 'unit beat policing' in the 1960s, and mergers between police forces in response to rising crime rates, coupled with the 'technological revolution' of the 1970s increasing the reliance on computers and police intelligence, resulted in heavy reliance upon specialist squads and on the tactics of stop-and-search. This situation, known as 'fire brigade policing', weakens the contact between the police and the community. Where information flow declines, the police become proactive and act according to their own suspicions. If the police stop and search in the street 'likely' candidates for a particular offence, they will undoubtedly approach a large number of innocent people, which increases distrust and lowers the community's acceptance and provision of information to the police. This vicious circle indicates a drift away from consensus policing towards military policing (Kinsey, Lea & Young 1986, p. 39). Proactive policing tends to recruit certain types of people, specifically those who congregate in public places and spend much time in city streets and parks.

In the UK, considerable debate has centred on police malpractice, particularly racism. The Scarman Report in 1981, which followed race riots in Brixton (a suburb of London), finds that the hostility and suspicion of blacks towards the police was fanned by harassment, misconduct, racial prejudice, and the stop-and-search tactics which antagonised innocent people (Cain & Sadigh 1982, pp. 92–3; Reiner 1985, p. 200). Being young, male, Afro-Caribbean, unemployed or in low-paid irregular work all are related to a greater probability of being stopped and searched, arrested and charged by the police (Reiner 1992, p. 478). West Indian blacks are charged more often than whites as a result of proactive policing which focuses on motoring offences, drunkenness, being a suspicious person or obstructing the police (Cain & Sadigh 1982, p. 88). The Police and Criminal Evidence Act 1984 (PACE) aims to formalise, clarify and specify police powers and suspect's rights. It represents a shift from policing by law to policing by consent; the exercise of police powers are delineated and require an environment of consent (Dixon, Coleman & Bottomley 1990, p. 358).

Recently, unprecedented attention has focused on police powers in Australia. A central concern is police use of lethal weapons which has resulted in a number of fatal shootings, especially in Victoria. Police departments have been subject to a number of inquiries regarding procedures of criminal investigation and the standard of police behaviour in the exercise of criminal investigation (Sallmann 1986, pp. 199–200). Police abuse of discretion and selective non-enforcement of certain offences can seriously undermine the public perception of the law's effectiveness which strengthens police claims for additional resources in order to protect people on the streets. In New South Wales, police responded to the decriminalisation of such street offences as offensive behaviour and drunkenness by selectively enforcing the law thereby creating an impression that it was not workable and claiming that the maintenance of public order requires legislation giving police more powers. The Greiner government reintroduced the original law (Egger & Findlay 1988, pp. 211–15). The discretion to make an arrest and to use often lethal physical force stimulates concern about police discriminatory treatment and coercion of certain groups, especially young people, lower classes, ethnic minorities, Aboriginal people and homeless people.

An apposite example of selective enforcement relates to police–Aboriginal relations in Australia which have always been antagonistic resulting from language and cultural differences and discrimination (Foley 1984, pp. 168–72). Pre-dawn police raids on homes in Redfern, a Sydney suburb, where many Aboriginal people live, have fuelled antagonism and indignation among blacks toward the police (Rintoul 1990, pp. 4–5). Police–Aboriginal relations have assumed violent proportions in some rural towns, for example Bewarrina and Wilcannia in New South Wales. However, most Aboriginal people come into contact with the police because of public order offences, most notably drunkenness. Aborigines are approximately twenty times more likely than non-Aborigines to be held in police custody (Biles, McDonald & Fleming 1989a, p. 1). While policy changes to decriminalise drunkenness emphasise welfare and rehabilitation, the police always retain power to detain intoxicated people. In South Australia, the Public Intoxication Act 1984 decriminalises drunkenness.[2] It empowers police officers to apprehend people found intoxicated in public places and take them to their home, a police station or a hostel. Detainees are to be released as soon as sober, and no-one is to be held for more than ten hours in a police cell or eighteen hours in a hostel. The legislation also authorises non-government authorities to provide pick-up and sobering-up facilities. However, an Office of Crime Statistics report comparing apprehensions for drunkenness during six-month periods before and after decriminalisation indicates that the introduction of the new law increases the rate at which people come into contact with law enforcement agencies (but not the courts as there is no prosecution). Detentions were 46 per cent higher in the first six months of the act's operation than total apprehensions when drunkenness was a criminal offence. At least 94 per cent of detainees spent the entire sobering-up period in police cells. Decriminalisation of drunkenness aimed at decreasing the number of detentions for drunkenness actually led to greater police contact in South Australia, particularly for young men and women and for Aboriginal people (Office of Crime Statistics 1986a, pp. 12–17).

Another topic of concern is the number of Aboriginal deaths in police custody. Research for the Royal Commission into Aboriginal Deaths in Custody shows that for the period 1980–88 the fifty-nine Aboriginal deaths in police custody are equivalent to nearly twenty-six per 100 000 Aborigines in the community whereas the 123 non-Aboriginal deaths are equivalent to less then one per 100 000. Around half (53 per cent) of all people in prison cells who died were being detained for drunkenness (Biles, McDonald & Fleming 1989a, pp. 4–5).

In contrast to 'crime control policing' the concept of 'community policing' developed which entails attempts to re-establish police–community links and to involve the community more in crime control and crime prevention (Goldstein 1987, pp. 8–9). Such programs as Neighbourhood Watch, and the spin-off programs of School Watch, Hospital Watch and Business Watch, as well as special initiatives, including Operation Noah (to encourage citizens to report drug-related crimes), Operation Paradox (to facilitate reporting of child abuse) and Operation Thunderbolt (to encourage ethnic Chinese residents, particularly in western Sydney, to provide information on heroin importation from the Golden Triangle), underscore police dependence on the citizenry and their attempts to increase contact with the community as a source of information about crime. The aim of Neighbourhood Watch is to 'keep an eye' on neighbours' property and inform them or the police of any suspicious situations. The other 'Watches' adopt the same principle of encouraging individuals and communities to act as carefully circumscribed adjuncts to police work (Sutton 1994, pp. 223–4). In a sense, these programs extend police surveillance and represent privatisation of some police patrol activities. These police practices widen the net and extend the operation of the law. For example, in South Australia, three-quarters of the charges made as a result of the 1989 Operation Noah 'phone-in' were for cannabis possession or cultivation; none were for major drug offences (South Australian Police Department 1989). Other developments in community policing include Blue Light discos aimed at improving relations with young people, and Operation Ethnos in Victoria to improve links with ethnic communities.

Despite its popularity, the term 'community policing' remains amorphous with many police departments viewing it as public relations or treating it as ancillary and secondary to the 'real' police work of crime control. However, Bayley (1989, pp. 64–76) identifies four recurrent elements:

1 *Community-based crime prevention.* In Australia, Neighbourhood Watch programs, first established in the early 1980s, are the most visible and substantial effort by police to develop community based crime prevention. United States research suggests that while residential burglaries decline substantially with Neighbourhood Watch, the effects begin to disappear after a year and return to previous levels after two years. Moreover, little evidence suggests that neighbourhood meetings reduce fear of crime or cause local residents to exercise greater informal social control by engaging in neighbourhood surveillance (Rosenbaum 1986, pp. 127–8). A study of reported 'break-in' offences in two Adelaide suburbs suggests that living in a Neighbourhood Watch area has little impact, if any, on a household's risk of victimisation. Indeed, more homes in the Neighbourhood Watch areas were the subject of 'break and enters' than the non-Neighbourhood Watch areas between 1 November 1993 and 31 January 1994 (West 1994, pp. 49–51).

2 *Patrol deployment for non-emergency interaction with the public,* an aim of which is to reduce levels of fear of crime. Foot patrols are gradually being reintroduced in a number of places and 'shopfront' police stations located in city areas and suburbs to encourage walk-in enquiries have been set up in Melbourne and Adelaide.

3 *Active solicitation of requests for service not involving criminal matters.* Research shows that people bring all sorts of problems to the police that have nothing to do with law violations or crime control; what is new is the police response to such requests. 'Problem-oriented' policing suggests that law enforcement, rather than an end in itself, is only one of several means by which the police manage various problems, and in seeking solutions they seek input from residents, businesspeople, offenders, government public servants and anyone else who might know something (Eck & Spelman 1986, pp. 38–9; Goldstein 1987, pp. 16–17).

4 *Creation of mechanisms for grass-roots feedback from the community,* which in Australia occurs most often through the Neighbourhood Watch network.

A number of problems beset the implementation of community policing. At the most general level, it is unclear who or what is 'the community'.

Discussions of community involvement in crime prevention and dispute resolution are tinged with utopian visions of the *gemeinshaft*-type society Tönnies describes, which seems incongruous with contemporary, urban neighbourhoods. The prevailing image is of an over-riding moral community to which all members of society—victims, residents, offenders and police—subscribe (see Braithwaite 1989). At a practical level, limited resources make it impossible for police to simultaneously respond to inquiries, to solve crimes and to engage in the crime-preventive and fear-reducing strategies associated with community policing (Moore 1992, pp. 148–50). Additionally, police culture and hierarchical administrations which prioritise crime control and accountability to the police organisation rather than to the community constitute inertia in the face of innovation.

The relationship between police culture and allegations and evidence of police corruption and other law-breaking activities is another dimension of the recent 'crisis in policing'.

Police deviance

Police deviance attracts a large degree of media attention, demonstrated most clearly by the allegations of corruption in the Queensland Police Force and the findings of the Fitzgerald Inquiry. However, there is nothing new about police corruption and it is not confined to certain police departments. Police corruption varies in degree and type but is inherent in the nature and organisation of police work, rather than stemming from the type of people who become police officers. Departures from correct procedures in exchange for goods, services or money denote corruption (Box 1983, p. 91). There have been recent corruption allegations and scandals in Queensland, New South Wales, South Australia, London, New York and Amsterdam. The apparent upsurge in police corruption, or at least public awareness of it, does not warrant a conclusion that we are witnessing increasing numbers of bad men or women involved in dubious activities. Informal occupational and organisational culture, norms and expectations impose rights and obligations which are just as binding as those of the formal system.

Corruption includes accepting bribes for not enforcing the law, fabricating or ignoring evidence, planning or executing crimes, and acquiring the proceeds of illegal activity. In Amsterdam, a corruption scandal that surfaced in 1976 focused on such practices as entrapment, escorting drug deals, planting evidence on suspects, passing illegal firearms and receiving gifts or payments from people involved in criminal activities. The New York Police Department has a corruption scandal roughly once every twenty years, suggesting that corruption is ingrained in police and criminal practices and that previous investigations merely displace rather than eradicate the problem (Punch 1985, pp. 22–3).

Employee deviance, including work avoidance, pilfering, circumvention of formal procedures, and acceptance of and offering favours, occurs in most occupations. These activities are relatively trivial and to a certain degree are tolerated by employers. Corruption is a more serious form of employee deviance, often involving criminal activities, which the public perceives as more serious when committed by police whose role is law enforcement. When exposed, police corruption incites moral outrage because of the essential trust relationship that is violated, and the power of the police. Punch (1985, pp. 13–14) identifies four types of police corruption:

1 straightforward corruption: or bribery, where police accept rewards of some kind in payment for doing or not doing something. The Knapp Commission which investigated corruption among New York City police in the 1970s found that the most frequent form of gratuity was free meals and drinks and other gifts in exchange for extra protection (Knapp Commission 1984, pp. 431–7);
2 *predatory corruption*: the police encourage crime, forgo prosecution for information, extort money and actively organise graft;
3 *combative corruption*: involves planting evidence, 'verbals' where unsworn statements are made verbally, and paying informants with illegally obtained drugs;
4 corruption as perversion of justice: lying under oath and intimidating witnesses.

Several aspects of police work and its organisation facilitate corruption. Firstly, the police organisation is not a harmonious, integrated entity governed by consensus, but is divided deeply by semi-autonomous and often conflicting units. Conflict occurs between upper and lower ranks, between patrol officers and administrators, and between the professionally and traditionally oriented. Competition for resources and fragmentation leads to intra-occupational suspicion, distrust and conflict.

Secondly, a strong occupational culture defines the norms surrounding work in terms of the reality of working in the streets, which conflicts with administrative and legal requirements. The code of secrecy covers colleagues' involvement in deviant or corrupt behaviour; protects their involvement in work avoidance; protects illicit practices from internal supervision and external authority; and provides an informal reward system. The secrets shared among police contribute to internal cohesion, act as a buffer to citizens' complaints and mystify police work, thereby sustaining public respect and awe (Manning 1971, pp. 177–8). Van Maanen (1975, p. 220) describes police socialisation as the gradual development of an 'in the same boat' collective consciousness stressing a 'don't make waves' occupational philosophy. This involves the normalisation of deviant and corrupt practices, making them part of everyday work. Lies, deception and falsification may simply become part of the job and perceived as normal and legitimate, even essential to the maintenance of public order. The pressure for results, ambiguous legislation, vulnerability to legal sanctions, and precarious bargaining with criminals, informants and lawyers can lead to short cut methods, lies, covering up, falsification of evidence and intimidation of suspects.

The Fitzgerald Inquiry into vice and police corruption, established in 1987, reports that the police culture in Queensland incorporates and nurtures corruption, misconduct inefficiency and contempt for the criminal justice system (1989, pp. 362–3). Under the unwritten police code, loyalty to colleagues is paramount, police cannot be criticised, key activities including contact with informants remain unscrutinised and police do not monitor other police or enforce the law against them. The Inquiry also finds that officers are presented with constant temptations for malpractice, and general knowledge among police insists that 'the code' will protect them if they engage in misconduct. Punishments such as ostracism follow violations of the informal police culture. The Report indicates:

> The code's operation has meant that honest police have often not reported knowledge of corruption, either because of loyalty to the corrupt, or because they were unsure whether the senior officers who denied problems existed were themselves involved in corruption. Police suspected of misconduct, or even those charged and acquitted, have not been impeded in their careers, while those making allegations have been punished and held back. The operation of the code means that police reject criticism and external supervision (Fitzgerald 1989, p. 363).

The two main types of misconduct supported by police culture are *verballing* and *corruption*. Verballing refers to the recording of unsworn verbal 'confessions' which allows opportunities for fabricating and tampering with evidence or intimidating alleged offenders. The widespread use of 'verbals' stems from frustration with and contempt for the operation of the criminal justice system, and a perception that successful prosecutions are one of the few positive aspects of police work. Corruption involves taking advantage of opportunities which arise in the course of their duties to obtain personal benefits. Opportunities may involve theft of seized or forfeited property, use of informants to dispose of illegally acquired property, and accepting bribes or other illicitly earned money (1989, pp. 206–8). A central tenet of the police code requires the assumption that whatever a police officer does occurs legitimately in the course of duty.

Thirdly, police work is a matter of negotiation based on social contexts where the law is sometimes invoked to solve situational dilemmas. The high level of autonomy and discretion in practical police work means that police policy is carried out directly by occupants of the lowest position in the organisational hierarchy. The field officer exercises greater actual authority and independence than more senior police officers. Moreover, field officers' activities are not highly visible to senior administrators. An analysis of the corruption scandals in New York, London and Amsterdam describes a major schism between the work cultures of the upper and lower ranks, while attempts at imposing accountability have largely failed to penetrate the informal practices of street level police work (Punch 1985, pp. 151–85).

Generally, police corruption relates to the so-called victimless crimes—gambling, vice and drugs—where large profits are at stake, involving an illegal but high demand service, and where police work is proactive, as officers must actively locate suspects and make arrests. In Queensland, the Fitzgerald Inquiry uncovered a police protection racket that took money in the form of graft and kickbacks from illegal gambling, Starting Price (SP) bookmaking, heroin dealing and prostitution. By 1983, the system was receiving so much graft money that it could afford to pay pensions to members who left the force or who were transferred (*The Advertiser* 1988, p. 4; Nolan & Lynch 1988, pp. 1–2). After 12 000 pages of oral testimony, 1000 public and 50 confidential exhibits and more than 250 witnesses, the Commissioner of the Inquiry limited the investigations as it was impossible to even identify most of the corruption. Members of the then Commonwealth Police (now the Australian Federal Police), and the Australian Bureau of Criminal Intelligence (ABCI) knew of police corruption, massage parlour owners, and drug dealers years before the Fitzgerald Enquiry but were unable to do anything about it (Harbutt & Hogarth 1988, p. 6). Interestingly, the media ignited the scandals in New York, London and Queensland, thereby underlining the importance of investigative journalism in uncovering corruption.

Most inquiries into police corruption advise institutional reforms and the prosecution of key individuals, thus relying on structural as well as the 'bad apple' conceptions of corruption. The Fitzgerald Inquiry recommends restructuring the Queensland Police Force to achieve an emphasis on crime prevention, increasing community involvement, 'flattening' the hierarchy, clarifying lines of communication, specifying responsibility and decentralising authority. The Report also suggests two commissions, one to review and evaluate electoral and administrative laws, the other to monitor the administration of criminal justice conduct (Fitzgerald 1989, pp. 364–72). Reforms in New York and London involved lateral recruitment of chiefs, decentralisation of authority, increased accountability for senior officers, new measures to investigate deviance, a diminution of autonomy for the detective branch, and rotation of personnel. These measures seem to be reducing corruption or at least making it more difficult. The most likely outcome, however, is a cycle of deviance, scandal, reform and repression, gradual relaxation and relapse into former patterns of deviance, followed by a new scandal. The nature of the work, which may appear impossible without short cuts and rule bending, an occupational culture condoning illicit practices, secrecy and deception, an organisation that implicitly stimulates deviance as a solution to getting results, and public and governmental demands that police tackle crime, all generate police deviance.

Sentencing and corrections

The formal goal of the criminal justice system is crime control and prevention through punishment, deterrence and rehabilitation. Punishment focuses on past activities whereas deterrence and rehabilitation are oriented to modifying future behaviour. Similar acts may incur different penalties depending on criminal justice policies and the prevailing sentencing ideology, for example if the courts emphasise punishment over rehabilitation a different sanction will be applied.

Beccaria, an early proponent of the punishment or retributive model of justice, maintains that a penalty must fit the crime and formal sanctions must be proportional to the extent of the damage the law-breaking activities cause (Monachesi 1960, p. 43). If sanctions contain other aims, including reformation, then the individual's rights are encroached upon, signifying injustice and power abuse. In recent years, there has been renewed support for this model of corrections (von Hirsch 1976, pp. 66–76). The American Friends, a Quaker organisation, maintain that justice and equity require punishments to be deserved and to correspond with the gravity of the offences. They recommend sentencing standards specifying the penalties attached to different crimes. The central idea of the 'back to justice' movement is that punishment constitutes 'just deserts'. However, when this model of sentencing is applied to white-collar or corporate offenders special problems arise, such as the large volume and complexity of offences which 'deserve' to be punished, difficulties in assigning guilt and culpability and determining the amount of harm done (Braithwaite 1982, pp. 750–6).

In contrast, advocates of deterrence argue that sanctions, or the threat of them, must be sufficiently burdensome or painful so as to prevent future law violation either by the individual convicted or potential offenders in the general population. Public hangings, warnings that all shoplifters will be prosecuted and police uniforms are general deterrents if they induce some people to conform to laws which they had contemplated breaking. There is little conclusive evidence of the 'success' of deterrence in reducing crime. Beccaria maintains that certainty of punishment yields higher deterrent returns than increasing its severity (von Hirsch 1976, p. 61). More precisely, where commitment to crime is low and the act is instrumental, for example occasional shoplifting, white-collar crime or traffic law violations, both general and specific deterrence operate. Conversely, where a high commitment to crime as a way of life exists, for example drug addiction, or where the act is expressive such as homicide, the threat of punishment, including capital punishment, will have little deterrent effect (Chambliss 1967, p. 713).

Even if a change in the crime rate follows a change in penalty it cannot be concluded that the penalty deters the crime unless other possible influences on the crime rate, such as police reporting and detecting procedures or opportunities for law-breaking, are controlled. Research into drink-driving in Connecticut, for example, indicates that a decline in the number of recorded offences after the passage of legislation carrying stringent penalties, suggesting a deterrent effect, actually resulted from police officers' failure to enforce the law which they considered too severe (Campbell & Ross 1968, pp. 52–3).

Rehabilitation, a dominant concept in sentencing ideology, is now unpopular because rehabilitation programs in prisons do not reduce re-offending and rehabilitation is seen as unjust and leading to inconsistency (Brody 1976, p. 37; Martinson 1974, p. 25). Rehabilitation focuses on the individual's needs and requirements for behaviour modification with the aim of reducing the probability of re-offending. A medical view of the offender as sick, as less responsible and therefore requiring psychiatric or psychological treatment and re-education underpins the concept of rehabilitation.

The sentencing court is supposed to take into account which penalty—imprisonment, probation, bond, fine, community work order or a combination of these—and how much will best promote rehabilitation. As a corollary, the sentencing court has a wide latitude of discretion to select the sanctions and thereby tailor the sentence to the individual's needs rather than punish the offender for breaking the law. Regarding imprisonment, the judge sets a maximum and minimum term but a parole board determines the actual release date. The sentence is indeterminate; at the point of sentencing, neither the court nor the convicted offender knows the actual length of the prison term. A prisoner becomes eligible for parole after about one-third of the sentence, but there is no guarantee of release. The parole board's decision takes into account prison reports, parole officers' and perhaps psychiatrists' or social workers' assessments and recommendations. These reports may have little bearing on the particular offence but be more concerned with the offender's employment opportunities, family life and attitudes. Release on parole is conditional and imprisonment can be reactivated if the parolee re-offends or ignores a parole officer's requests.

Considerable debate focuses on the inequalities and inconsistencies of parole board decisions. In the case of parole, the courts do not make the final judgement about punishment yet prisoners have no right of appeal or legal representation *vis-à-vis* parole boards. Foucault describes this as the 'fragmentation of the legal power to punish' (1979, p. 21). Juridical decision-making becomes divided among psychiatric or psychological experts, social workers and correctional services officers thereby extending punitive powers beyond the court. In some Australian states, for example South Australia and New South Wales, the role of parole boards has been curtailed in an attempt to make sentencing more determinate and to reduce prison populations. In 1983, a South Australian law removed the parole board's power to decide whether or not a person sentenced to at least a year in prison would be released at the end of the non-parole period and enabled parole release dates to be brought forward through a system of remissions for good behaviour. Ironically, after these changes, judges tended to increase the length of non-parole periods in anticipation that prisoners would earn full remissions; many did not and therefore the length of prison sentences increased (Department of Correctional Services and Office of Crime Statistics

1989, pp. 57–8; Weatherburn 1985, p. 281). The High Court subsequently declared these judicial practices to be invalid.

Current concerns about the scope of discretion in sentencing and the consequent disparities point to frequent unequal outcomes for members of disadvantaged groups—the poor, women, and racial and ethnic minorities. Inappropriate disparity or sentencing decisions based on extra-legal factors can result from intentional discrimination arising from personal idiosyncrasies and inconsistencies. Alternatively, discrimination might be institutionalised as members of minority groups are less likely to be able to afford good lawyers, more likely to be scrutinised and to be observed in any law violation, more likely to be arrested and to be on remand, more likely to be found guilty, and more likely to receive harsher treatments than other people (Chambliss 1969, p. 86). Considerable literature documents widespread disparities in sentencing practice in relation to similar cases, and the general concern is that equity and fairness demand that the criminal justice system administers similar punishment to similar cases (Ashworth 1992, pp. 183–96; Lizotte 1978, pp. 565–70; Sarri 1986, p. 89). Discrepancies also arise from plea bargaining where the accused person agrees to plead guilty to a lesser offence in exchange for some benefit, in particular a judicially sanctioned lesser penalty, than if she/he were convicted on the original charges. Unlike the situation in the USA, plea bargaining is not an institutionalised aspect of the judicial process in Australia. Nevertheless, negotiations about the charges to be laid and the facts of a case occur between the prosecution and the defence, but not the sentencing judge, with the view of obtaining a guilty plea at the earliest opportunity (Zdenkowski 1994, pp. 171–2, 175–6).

Numerous proposals have been advanced, including sentencing guidelines or a sentencing commission, as ways of decreasing disparities in sentencing and the unjust inconsistencies in the treatment of like cases. The terms of reference of an inquiry into sentencing federal offenders which reported in 1980 included an examination of the need for greater uniformity in sentencing and the need for sentencing guidelines and principles. The inquiry involved a national survey of the judiciary which showed that they favour conferences, discussion, consultation but not legislation, sentencing guidelines or mandatory penalties to promote sentencing uniformity (Australian Law Reform Commission 1980, Appendix B). The central idea behind calls for more determinate sentencing and for the 'back to justice' movement is that convicted offenders deserve punishment for past offences and the punishment should fit the gravity of the illegal behaviour, with some flexibility for extenuating circumstances.

A further reform involves an increased role for the victim in the sentencing process. As the conflict in criminal cases is between the prosecution (representing the conscience collective) and the alleged offender, until recently, the victim's sole input was as a witness for the prosecution and the only compensation he/she received was the satisfaction of seeing the perpetrator convicted, if that was the outcome. Victims' groups argued that the judicial system's overwhelming emphasis on the rights of the accused person marginalised their needs and concerns. Activists from the women's movement identified the lack of support services for victims of sexual assault and their traumatic experiences during the trial. Victims' rights organisations—for example the Victims of Crime Service (VOCS) formed in South Australia in 1979 and the Victims of Crimes Assistance League (VOCAL) in Victoria—emerged to provide information and emotional support to victims and to lobby for criminal justice reforms, in particular for courts to have direct information on the impact of the crime on the victim. Governments have established funds from which a victim can apply for compensation for loss or harm as a result of an offence and in some jurisdictions courts can order the offender make restitution to the victim as part of the sentence (Sumner 1987, pp. 197, 201).

In 1985, the United Nations approved the Declaration of Victims Rights, article 14 of which provides that the victim of crime has the right to 'have the full effects of the crime upon him or her made known to the sentencing court either by the prosecutor or by information contained in a pre-sentence report; including any financial, social, psychological and physical harm done to or suffered by the victim' (SA Attorney-General's Department n.d., p. 9). South Australia was the first state to provide for Victim Impact Statements which allow prosecutors to provide the court with details of any injury, loss or damage to the victim of the crime. Previously, such information might not have come to the attention of the sentencing court. Victim Impact Statements have been the subject of much debate regarding whether this kind of information should be taken into account when sentencing, and whether the reform will lead to harsher sentences. However, it seems that victims are not particularly vengeful or punitive in the sentence they wish a convicted offender to receive, but want more contact from justice authorities, to be kept informed about case developments, and want more information on support services (Gardner, Julie 1990, pp. 28–9).

The prison

The central penalty in the criminal justice system, the prison, emerged in the USA in the 1820s. Previously, the prison was a holding station before hanging or transportation. Humanitarian ideology guided the development of the prison, with early proponents arguing that isolating the prisoner, establishing disciplined routine and removing the offender from all temptations and bad influences would be reformative and less cruel than torture or the scaffold (Rothman 1971, chapter 4). The underlying religious ideology emphasised a commitment to daily hard labour as well as periods in isolated separate cells which gave time for reflection and moral reform. A close correspondence prevailed between ideas on the causes of crime and the structure of the penitentiary. Reformers saw idleness as part symptom and part cause of deviant behaviour. Those unwilling to work were prone to commit all kinds of offences; idleness gave time for the corrupted to encourage and instruct one another in a life of crime.

The organisation of most prisons has had deleterious effects on the achievement of its official goals. As a formal organisation the prison has two sets of goals: one relating to the prevention of crime; and the other deriving from bureaucratic imperatives, including achieving prisoners' compliance and ensuring internal order and the completion of routine tasks (Blau & Scott 1962, pp. 2–8). A major criterion for evaluating prison officers' performance is the extent to which prison rules are enforced and stability maintained. Because prisoners are not motivated through financial incentives or value commitments to conform to organisational rules, prison officers frequently rely on prisoners for the successful performance of daily tasks and the maintenance of order. Prisoners' compliance often depends on prison officers ignoring minor rule infractions, expanding access to information, possessions or privileges, and by tolerating abuse, corruption, exploitation and inequality. Achievement of internal order requires the corruption of prison officers' authority and the violation of prison rules (Cressey 1958, p. 48; Sykes 1956, pp. 259–62; 1958, pp. 63–83).

Prisons have always sparked heated public debate and political conflict. Currently, considerable disillusionment surrounds imprisonment as a sentencing option. Media reports detail the use of drugs and the spread of AIDS in prisons, and the number of Aboriginal deaths in custody culminated in a Royal Commission. Most Australian governments have taken legislative or administrative steps to reduce or prevent increases in the number of prisoners by utilising prison as a last resort and developing such alternative community-based sanctions as probation and community work orders. However, there is considerable debate regarding whether decreasing the length of prison sentences, diverting offenders from gaol, or providing early release schemes effectively reduce prison populations and problems of over-crowding (Harding 1987, pp. 23–5; Weatherburn 1988, p. 119).

A major criticism of the prison as a sentencing option is cost. The maintenance of one prisoner costs almost $40 000 per year with a total annual expenditure amounting to $440 million (Mukherjee et al. 1989, p. 598). Many writers argue that the movement toward community corrections, sometimes called 'decarceration' or 'deinstitutionalisation', is related more to the fiscal crisis of the capitalist state than to humanitarian concerns (Scull 1977a, pp. 24–7). Even though non-custodial or community-based corrections are far less expensive than imprisonment, the policy changes have not brought about any reduction in public expenditure on corrections as the new measures are often used in addition to, not in place of, imprisonment (Chan & Zdenkowski 1986b, pp. 137–8).

A dominant theme in arguments for diverting convicted offenders from imprisonment is that total deprivation of liberty is too harsh for many offenders, it is an undue trespass on civil liberties and personal autonomy, and is detrimental to a prisoner's family and employment therefore inhibiting chances of re-integration and the pursuit of a law-abiding career upon release (Scutt 1979, p. 61; Greenberg 1975, pp. 7–11; Morris 1974, p. 1162). Incidents of brutality, inhumanity and harsh treatment by custodial staff in prisons flavour this argument. Numerous inquiries in Australia document the use of illegal force by prison personnel to coerce prisoners and this, combined with over-crowding, initiated several highly publicised riots during the 1970s (Zdenkowski & Brown 1982, pp. 235–43). Accordingly, it is argued, prisons should deal principally with certain types of offenders for whom community-based measures or other alternatives have been considered and rejected, namely dangerous offenders convicted of a serious crime against persons or property, or the offenders involved in organised crime. The prison's failure to prevent crime forms another source of discontent. Moreover, the prison has been accused of inducing rather than reducing criminal activity, of generating corruption and encouraging hostility to the society.

Decarceration and privatisation

The broadest definition of decarceration involves a continuum of practices which aim to divert people from the criminal justice system, especially the prison. Non-custodial penalties, notably capital and corporal punishment and the fine, have a long history. From the mid-1970s in Australia (and earlier in the USA and the UK) a variety of community-based corrections were implemented, including:

1 *probation*: the convicted offender meets regularly with a probation officer for a period of time specified by the court;
2 *community work orders*: convicted offenders must perform various tasks on community projects, for example constructing playgrounds, clearing weeds or rubbish. Often volunteers supervise the performance of this work;
3 *parole*: similar to probation, except that the offender has spent a period of time in jail;
4 *periodic detention*: convicted offenders are incarcerated during evenings or weekends, thereby enabling them to lead relatively 'normal' lives;
5 *good behaviour bonds, suspended sentences*: the court specifies certain conditions to which the convicted offender should conform. Subsequent deviance could activate the suspended sentence.

These penalties all vary in the extent to which they deprive liberty and the courts can combine them in a number of ways thereby expanding the availability of sentencing options. Following the implementation of community-based corrections, imprisonment rates for Australia fell dramatically in the mid-1970s, remaining relatively stable until the mid-1980s when they began to rise to the levels of the early 1960s (Walker 1994, p. 23). There have been slight increases in parole, large increases in the rate of probation and community work orders which suggest the increasing popularity of community-based measures which have had little effect on the use of imprisonment (Chan & Zdenkowski 1986a, p. 81). While official ideology emphasises the humaneness of such alternatives, the connection with imprisonment has never been completely broken. The penalty for breaching a community work order, a suspended sentence or for failing to pay a fine is often a prison sentence.

A recent development is the privatisation of prisons, which many governments view as the solution to problems of prison over-crowding and associated deterioration and fiscal constraints. The idea is to remove the operation (and sometimes ownership) of an institution from the state and delegate it to a private concern. While 'privatisation' connotes a general shift away from the public sector, it can entail various initiatives: the complete sale of existing prison buildings and assets to private corporations who lease them back to the state or the contracting out of services related to the everyday running of prisons, including catering, gardening, laundry, even security. Privatisation may or may not mean a shift of functions to profit-making entities; charitable and other volunteer or community organisations historically have performed numerous tasks delegated by the state. Queensland opened Australia's privately operated maximum security prison, the Borallon Correctional Centre, and its Corrective Services Commission allocates a daily sum for each of the gaol's 240 prisoners. There are now three private prisons in Australia—two in Queensland and one in New South Wales—and other states are also considering this possibility. In the USA most private prisons are minimum-security while the state continues to administer maximum-security prisons. By the late 1980s, of the approximately 5000 adult correctional institutions in the USA, between twenty to thirty were privately run, however hundreds of juvenile detention centres are administered by private interests (Chan 1992, p. 228). The major criticism of privatising the prisons is the effect of the profit motive which could provide few incentives to maintain standards or reduce overcrowding. Public scrutiny and political accountability also would be reduced (Robbins 1986, p. 326). Interestingly, the rhetoric of decarceration and of privatisation is very similar, despite the fact that the former seeks to reduce prison populations while the latter attempts to accommodate them. Both movements focus on the failure, inefficiency and costs of mprisonment as it currently exists and seek to reduce the role of the state in crime control by attracting more input from the community, in the form of volunteers or community resources and private businesses (Chan 1992, p. 241).

On a smaller scale, privatisation is occurring in Australia with the development of home detention or house arrest schemes which represent a move toward 'offender pays' (George 1988, p. 211). Generally, those given home detention are non-violent and low-risk offenders without drug problems. Such a scheme places the behaviour of other members of the household and friends under the surveillance and potential control of the state. In the home detention scheme in South Australia, a computer automatically rings the telephone several times a day and the detainee is required to clock in. He or she must telephone the home detention centre to obtain permission to take children to school, and the home detention supervisor can come at any time of day and administer random breath and drug tests. The prisoner is able to obtain a job but it must be approved by the authorities (Brice 1988, p. 4).

As these innovations are relatively recent it is too early to gauge their ultimate success or failure. Even so, a large body of literature suggests that decarceration, including the introduction of non-custodial sentencing options, has not reduced the use of imprisonment in the UK, the USA, Canada or Australia. The Australian imprisonment rate has remained relatively stable from 1960 to 1980 with the most notable change being a fall since the early 1970s and a slow upward trend in the 1980s. Alternatives to imprisonment frequently are used for offenders who would not have been incarcerated, so they are not genuine alternatives.

Some suggest that the emphasis on informality and community involvement masks the widening of discretionary power. Community-based correctional programs are attractive precisely because they are informal and hence economical, but the blurring of the boundaries creates uncertainties regarding notions of voluntary or coercive, formal or informal. Rather than limiting social control and preserving individual liberty and autonomy, the community corrections movement represents a widening of the net, a dispersion of social control, an extension and diffusion of juridical functions and a blurring of the boundaries between the community and imprisonment (Cohen 1979, pp. 346–50; 1985, p. 57; Foucault 1979, pp. 22–3). Cohen argues that the segregated and insulated institution rendered the business of crime control invisible, but it made its boundaries obvious; clear and meaningful distinctions remained between inside and outside, guilty and innocent, freedom and captivity and imprisonment and released (1979, p. 344). The proliferation of community corrections increases categorisation of types of control and types of offenders. More and more actors participate within the criminal justice system and make decisions and judgements, thus dispersing surveillance and disguising social control (Chan & Zdenkowski 1986b, p. 141; Cohen 1985, pp. 40–4). Probation officers and volunteers are less visible than judges, and with home detention the controllers are even less open to public scrutiny. The social control or discipline functions of the prison are dispersed throughout society, but identifying the functional equivalents of the prison officer becomes more difficult.

Juvenile justice systems

By the 1920s, most Western societies had implemented distinct juvenile justice systems, reflecting the view that children, as compared with adult offenders, are less culpable, are more malleable and have greater potential for rehabilitation, thereby breaking the supposed career path from juvenile delinquent to adult recidivist. Consequently, reformers viewed adult courts and corrections as unduly coercive, stigmatising and inappropriate for young offenders. Separation of the juvenile from the adult justice system reflects different conceptions of the causes of offending; the causes of delinquency do not stem from the individual child, but from their allegedly pathological family circumstances. The argument, then, is that taking the child away from those conditions or injecting expert advice into family relations will eradicate juvenile delinquency (see chapter 9). One reformer during the Progressive Era in the USA asks:

> Why is not the duty of the state, instead of asking merely whether a boy or a girl has committed a specific offence, to find out what he [sic] is, physically, mentally, morally, and then if it learns that he [sic] is treading the path that leads to criminality, to take him [sic] in charge, not so much to punish as to reform, not to degrade but to uplift, not to crush but develop, not to make him [sic] a criminal but a worthy citizen (Mack 1907, p. 107).

The benevolent state should intervene where parents have failed to provide a supportive, educative environment which will provide children with guidance and socialisation to be responsible, law-abiding citizens.

Juvenile justice systems are constituted by children's courts with distinct, less formal, confidential procedures and relaxed rules of evidence; input from social workers, educationalists and child psychologists who assess a child's physical or social development and family background, then make recommendations to the court; and institutions of social control emphasising welfare and rehabilitation rather than punishment. Additionally, special categories of offence emerged, sometimes termed status offences, for example under-age drinking and smoking, being ungovernable, at risk, or truant. As family background and social circumstances became more important than the commission of an offence, distinctions between children deemed to be in need of care and protection or neglected and those identified as offenders became blurred. As Carrington indicates, for policy makers: 'the delinquent and neglected child are symptomatic of the same problem—a dysfunctional family, which has failed to adequately rear, care and educate their offspring' (1993, p. 122). The original children's courts dealt with both delinquency and child welfare cases and often did not differentiate between them. In the name of rehabilitation, guardianship of both categories of children could be transferred to the Minister of Community Welfare (or the equivalent) until the age of majority.

By the 1960s in the USA and the 1970s in Australia disenchantment grew with the juvenile justice system. Among the concerns were the lack of due process or procedural protection for young people within the juvenile court; in the name of welfare some young people were receiving harsher 'penalties' than would their adult counterparts. An early critic of the children's courts' welfare orientation proposes that:

> their greatest fault is in failing to give to the defendant some of the most basic protections of due process which inhere in our modern legal system ... The best and

safest criterion justifying court action is the commission of an act in violation of a rule of law specifically defining the conduct to be avoided. Such a criminal act expresses— as no vague standard of recalcitrance or 'moral depravity' can—a clear, definite and relevant foundation for court action (Tappan 1946, pp. 309, 310).

Second, many viewed the intervention in the life a young person and their family as unjust, especially given the usual gap between the official treatment aims of a program and the experiences of the young people (Carrington 1993, chapter 7). Third, critics pointed out the lack of evidence that intervention and treatment actually reformed the individuals or reduced juvenile offending. In response, numerous programs diverting young people accused of non-serious matters from the children's court and separating them from children in need of care and protection were established. For example, in South Australia, screening panels (now abolished) considered most allegations against a child and determined whether the case went to an aid panel or to the court. After a child had admitted the allegations, aid panels (also established in Western Australia and now abolished in South Australia) could warn or counsel a child and her/his guardians and request them to follow its directions, including to participate in a rehabilitative or training program. Normally, then, only the very serious cases went to the children's court. These panels were staffed by members of the police force and the social welfare department (Children's Protection and Young Offenders Act 1979). Additionally, deinstitutionalisation policies sought to remove most young offenders from secure detention centres or state institutions into community settings (Klein 1979, pp. 150–4). Nevertheless, researchers demonstrate the ways in which such programs and polices may actually enhance the quantum of state control and result in the unequal treatment of certain young offenders (Alder 1984, p. 400; Bullington et al. 1978, pp. 59–71; Lerman 1980, pp. 281–98; Wundersitz 1992, p. 116; Wundersitz & Gale 1988). Net-widening is not necessarily automatic or persistent. Wundersitz indicates that the implementation of aid panels in South Australia did extend social control, but was limited to the second and third year of their operation, after which the numbers of youths coming into contact with the panels stabilised and since the late 1980s has been declining (1992, p. 129).

The current moral panic surrounding youth offending, which overwhelmingly focuses on the small number of young people convicted of repeat, violent and serious crimes, has stimulated major reforms in juvenile justice systems in contemporary societies. These reforms displace concerns with welfare and rehabilitation and seek to make young offenders responsible for their actions. They provide more scope for victims' participation and view community protection and safety as an important goal of the juvenile justice system. In the USA, greater numbers of juveniles are dealt with by adult criminal courts than previously and juvenile courts increasingly emphasise punishment for an offence rather than rehabilitation of the offender (Fagan & Deschenes 1990, pp. 322–5; Feld 1993, pp. 233–54).

In 1992, the Western Australian government announced its intention to pass 'the toughest laws in Australia' aimed at 'hard-core juvenile criminals' (Wilkie 1993, p. 187). The resulting Crime (Serious and Repeat Offenders) Sentencing Act applies to serious repeat offenders and those committing various violent offences in the course of motor vehicle theft. The sentencing court must balance rehabilitation with the protection of the community by taking into account the circumstances of the offence and the victim, any harm or damage done, and the offenders' past record, age and remorse. Rehabilitation and the interests or needs of the young person are no longer the primary concern, indeed those convicted of serious, repeat or violent crimes are less deserving of re-education or welfare measures than are others.

South Australian reforms encapsulated in the Young Offenders Act 1993 aim to make young people accountable for their behaviour, increase the range, severity and deterrent value of penalties, enhance the role of the police, protect the rights of victims to restitution and allow victims to confront the young offenders and make them aware of the harm they caused (South Australia 1993, pp. 2849–50). The legislation abolishes screening and children's aid panels, reduces the role of the welfare department and the input of social workers in court decisions, and implements a system of police cautioning and family conferences to deal with minor offences. Family conferences aim to bring together a young person (who has admitted the allegations), members of his/her family and the victim in an informal setting which is mediated by a youth justice co-ordinator. These conferences implement Braithwaite's notion of reintegrative shaming (1989, pp. 177–82). The assumption is that when a young person directly confronts the victims he/she will feel remorse, embarrassment and guilt, with the conference providing the opportunity to make amends: to apologise, compensate the victim or remedy the damage. Family conferences are supposed to re-integrate the young person into the community, re-establish family bonds and offer an educative experience in order to promote conformity and a sense of responsibility (O'Connell & Moore 1992, pp. 16–19; Roach Anleu 1995). The tenor of all these juvenile justice reforms is to separate the management of young people admitting minor offences from those accused of serious crimes. The underlying rationale seems to be that most young offenders can be re-integrated into society and make amends for their offences, whereas those accused of more serious or repeat offences must confront the adversarial court system and be punished upon conviction.

Summary

The criminal justice system is just one type of social control, albeit the most visible. Discussion about crime often becomes highly reified as attention focuses on what to do about 'criminals', as though they are easily identifiable and distinct. This discussion demonstrates that coming into contact with police and the courts does not depend solely on law-breaking activities but is determined by citizens' reports to the police, the alleged offender's personal characteristics and relationship with the victim, as well as criminal justice policies, priorities, resources and ideologies. The following chapter examines the role of the medical profession in delineating deviant or sick behaviour rather than responding to pre-existing illness.

Notes

1   According to Weber:
An order will be called law if it is externally guaranteed by the probability that coercion (physical or psychological) to bring about conformity or avenge violation, will be applied by a staff of people holding themselves specially ready for that purpose (Weber 1954, p .5).

   On this definition societies without a special enforcement apparatus existing independently of the incidence of deviance cannot have law. They will have social control but it will not be legal.
2   Since 1976, South Australian law specifies that intoxication should not be treated as an offence and that people found drunk in public places should be dealt with on a health and welfare basis, but lack of funding prevented the establishment of sobering up places and legislation decriminalising drunkenness was not proclaimed until 1984 (Office of Crime Statistics 1986a, p. 1).

Key terms

Police discretion
Community policing
Proactive and reactive policing
Sentencing disparity
Prison
Deterrence
'Back to justice' movement
Deinstitutionalisation
Probation
Parole
Declaration of Victims Rights
Welfare orientation

Corruption
Neighbourhood Watch
Verballing
Corrections
Rehabilitation
'Just deserts'
Decarceration
Privatisation
Community work orders
Reintegrative shaming
Juvenile justice system

Main points

1   Most police work is reactive, that is, it relies on reports from members of the community, and police personnel have a wide deal of discretion in making arrest decisions. Police reliance on the community is underscored by such programs as Neighbourhood Watch and its spin-offs and special strategies to encourage the reporting of particular types of crime.

2 Recently, police powers and deviance have been subject to widespread discussion and governmental investigations. Pervasive corruption has been uncovered, which relates more to the organisation of police work and the occupational culture than the presence of 'bad' individuals.

3 Most Western societies currently emphasise using imprisonment as a last resort and have developed or expanded such community-based programs as probation and community work orders. While the rationale is to reduce the stigmatising and debilitating effects of imprisonment for most convicted offenders, many critics argue that the 'decarceration' movement actually increases social control and contact with the criminal justice system. Some jurisdictions have established private prisons.

4 Since the 1970s, criminal justice systems pay greater attention to the interests and concerns of victims than previously. In 1985, the United Nations approved the Declaration of Victims Rights, article 14 of which provides that the victim of crime has the right to 'have the full effects of the crime upon him or her made known to the sentencing court either by the prosecutor or by information contained in a pre-sentence report; including any financial, social, psychological and physical harm done to or suffered by the victim'.

5 Juvenile justice systems are separate and distinct from the processing of adult crime. For most of this century the juvenile system emphasised the welfare and needs of the offender rather than the criminal nature of the alleged offence. Social workers, educationalists and child psychologists usually have considerable input into the decisions of children's courts.

6 Widespread dissatisfaction with the welfare model and a concern to hold young people responsible for their illegal activities has led to reforms in contemporary juvenile justice systems, in particular a movement away from the welfare orientation, at least for some young offenders, especially those convicted of serious, repeat or violent offences.

Further reading

Ashworth, Andrew 1992, 'Sentencing Reform Structures', *Crime & Justice: An Annual Review of Research*, vol. 16, pp. 181–241.

Chappell, Duncan & Paul Wilson eds 1994, *The Australian Criminal Justice System: The Mid 1990s*, Butterworths, Sydney.

Cohen, Stanley 1985, *Visions of Social Control: Crime, Punishment and Classification*, Polity Press, Cambridge.

Foucault, Michel 1979, *Discipline and Punish: The Birth of the Prison*, Vintage Books, New York.

Gale, Fay, Ngaire Naffine & Joy Wundersitz 1993, *Juvenile Justice: Debating the Issues*, Allen & Unwin, Sydney.

Punch, Maurice 1985, *Conduct Unbecoming: The Social Construction of Police Deviance and Social Control*, Tavistock Publications, London.

CHAPTER

6

Medicine, illness and deviance

Sick people are not usually perceived as deviant. Sick behaviour is seen as involuntary, resulting from a physical condition or illness over which there is no control; people are not responsible for acting in the ways that they do. In contrast, deviance is seen as motivated or wilful behaviour, either on the part of the actor who breaks the rules, or on the part of the social audience which defines certain activities or individuals as deviant. Additionally, the medical profession is perceived usually as oriented to the treatment and cure of illness, unlike professions in the criminal justice system who are agents of social control. This chapter questions these everyday assumptions about illness and the medical profession and investigates the proposition that illness is a type of deviant behaviour. It argues that in many respects illness is socially constructed, reflects social norms and values, and entails social control.

The chapter first examines the sick role concept and the process of medicalisation, that is, the increasing application of medicine and notions of health and illness to everyday life. It then discusses medical personnel as social control agents by arguing that their work and knowledge is not limited to treating physiological or mental illness with scientific therapeutic techniques, but involves returning patients to their usual social roles. Finally, the chapter discusses the distribution of health and illness, especially mental illness, in Australian society.

The sick role

Talcott Parsons (1951a, 1951b) first pointed out that illness is not just a physiological condition but a special type of deviant behaviour. The sick role is one alternative available to an individual facing strain; it is one way of avoiding social responsibilities (1951b, p. 431). While not denying the organic causes of illness, Parsons rejects the notion that illness is purely physiological. The test for whether being sick constitutes a social role is the existence of institutionalised expectations with corresponding sentiments and sanctions. The sick role has four dimensions:

1 the sick person is exempt from the performance of certain normal social obligations. The degree of exemption depends on the nature and severity of the illness, and it usually requires legitimation by a physician. A person with the flu, for example, is exempt from occupational obligations for a period of time, but not indefinitely;
2 people defined as ill are not held responsible for their condition. In this sense illness differs from criminal deviance. Illness is seen as something occurring in nature and therefore not subject to human choices or decisions;
3 the legitimacy of the sick role rests upon the individual seeking specialised, usually medical, assistance. The sick person is under an obligation to get well and stigmatising illness as undesirable reaffirms the value of health, thus paralleling Durkheim's view of crime. An employer's requirement of a medical certificate as evidence of an employee's illness illustrates the partial legitimacy of the sick role;
4 by entering a relationship with institutionalised medicine, the sick person acquires the additional role of patient, thereby incurring specific obligations, especially that of co-operating with the physician in the process of trying to get well (Parsons 1951b, pp. 455–6). Lorber (1975, pp. 217–8) finds that most hospital patients feel they should be obedient, co-operative and undemanding. Deviance from the good-patient norms can result in medical neglect or a stigmatising label.

This characterisation of the sick role fails to include many illness types (Levine & Kozloff 1978, p. 317). It is most applicable to acute illness, such as pneumonia and appendicitis, and to operable conditions, rather than to such chronic illness as diabetes or disability (Gallagher 1976, p. 209; Haber & Smith 1971). While the notion of conditional and temporary legitimacy differentiates the sick from the criminal, the legitimacy of chronic or incurable illness cannot be conditional (Freidson 1988, p. 229). This is because the conditionality of the sick role is based on returning to a healthy or normal state. Entry to the sick role is not available to sufferers of certain illness who are deemed responsible for their condition. For instance, patients with AIDS, sexually transmitted diseases or cancer are not always held to be exempt from either blame or responsibility for their condition. The opposite is true, making the interpretation of their condition more akin to crime, that is, a result of wilful, motivated and intentional activities. There is also a growing tendency to blame individuals who allegedly precipitate their own illness by pursuing lifestyles involving cigarette smoking, alcohol consumption, poor diet or lack of exercise. Insurance premiums, for example, are higher for people who smoke cigarettes. In everyday language 'fitness' and 'health' have become synonymous, and fitness is portrayed as a means of protection from such characteristic ills of modern culture as drug abuse, depression and eating disorders (Glassner 1989, pp. 181–2).

In a later piece of work, Parsons allows that the concept of social deviance does not cover the whole range of phenomena associated with the sick role (1975, p. 269). In the case of relatively acute illness, the physician's obligation is to reinforce the patient's motivations to recover, whereas in chronic illness cases the corresponding obligation is to reinforce the patient's motivation to minimise incapacity, to conform with normal social roles. The social control aspects of the physician's role are more important than treatment in chronic illness. Parsons (1979, p. 132) changes the emphasis from illness as *deviance* to illness as an individual's *incapacity* to perform effectively the roles and tasks for which she or he has been socialised. Consequently, two models of illness exist within Parsons' discussion—a structural model focusing on illness as incapacity for role performance, and a psychodynamic model emphasising illness as motivated deviance (Gerhardt 1979, p. 230).

Despite these modifications, the sick role concept remains crucial for identifying and linking the cultural and social with the physiological dimensions of health and illness. Other authors have gone beyond Parsons' view of the physician as responding to and diagnosing illness and emphasise medicine's active role in seeking out and defining physiological conditions as illness. This is the social constructionist view of medicine, which the next section discusses.

The social construction of illness

The social constructionist critique of medicine parallels the symbolic interactionist critique of deviance. Within this view, physical conditions do not by their nature constitute illness but require identification and classification which are not value-neutral or objective processes. The success of the medical profession in monopolising definitions of health and illness provides it with considerable authority and scope for social control. Empirical research within this perspective identifies the social conditions under which certain illness emerge and analyses the effect of claims made by medical practitioners on the development of conceptions of illness.

A major proponent of the view of medical practice and knowledge as socially constructed is Freidson (1988), who argues that medicine actively and exclusively constructs illness and therefore determines how people must act in order to be treated. Rather than disinterestedly detecting symptoms and physiological causes and administering objective therapeutic techniques, medical practice involves interpretation and judgement about what is normal and abnormal, which circumstances are suitable for medical intervention and which are not. The symptoms do not speak for themselves, and their interpretation and categorisation are informed by social values and assumptions about what constitutes health (normal) and illness (deviant). Illness and disease are human constructions: they do not exist without someone proposing, describing and recognising them; they are neither self-evident nor naturally occurring. Social constructionists ask how it is that certain areas of human life come to be defined, or not, as medical issues under certain conditions (Freidson 1988, pp. 30–1; Wright & Treacher 1982, p. 9).

The development of determinist theories of causation and medicine's association with the natural sciences encouraged a perception of medical practice as scientific, objective, and morally neutral, which was central to its achievement of professional status, power and domination (Conrad & Schneider 1980; Freidson 1986; Larson 1977). In Australia, state patronage in the form of legislation in the first third of the twentieth century provided for self-government and market control. The compatibility of medical knowledge taught in universities with the dominant class identities of most medical students were important factors in explaining medicine's success (Willis 1989, p. 81).

Like the symbolic interactionists who focus on societal reaction rather than on the etiology of the offensive behaviour, social constructionists pay little attention to the physiological aspects of illness. They are concerned primarily with the medical interpretation of those events. Freidson suggests that as illness gets defined as something bad to be eradicated, medicine plays the role of moral entrepreneur, creating new rules to define deviance and attracting and treating the newly defined sick (1988, p. 252). The moral judgements implicit in the designation of illness as such, are frequently overlooked because of the virtually universal consensus about the undesirability of illness.

Different types of medical moral entrepreneur exist:

1 *specialist medical associations*, such as the Australian College of Obstetricians and Gynaecologists, seek to influence government health policy by issuing statements to the media and submitting position papers to government inquiries;

2 *general associations*, for example, the Australian Medical Association, frequently make statements endorsing such health measures as physical fitness, bans on smoking and the quarantining of AIDS sufferers; expound public policy positions, for example the decriminalisation of the personal use of marijuana; or publicly advocate specific reforms to the health care and insurance systems;

3 *individual practitioners* may assume roles as crusaders in health matters, by becoming spokespeople and experts on particular diseases or questions of health. The current discussions surrounding AIDS and euthanasia provide examples of individual medical practitioners who espouse certain treatments or policies;

4 *physicians* in their capacity as medical personnel may be prominent in other interest groups which crusade against specific diseases or such medical procedures as abortion.

The moral entrepreneurial activities of medicine as an occupation are not unique. Other professions and members of occupations also attempt to influence public policy and have their definitions and values translated into legislation. The point that the social constructionists make is that these moral and political activities run counter to medicine's professional ideology of objectivity, value neutrality, universalism and reliance on science.

An extension of the social constructionist view of medicine is the notion of medicalisation, that is, the almost imperialist expansion of medicine into new areas of social life. One example of this is the increasing use of medical terms as metaphors for social analysis. Rising crime rates become evidence of a 'sick' society; like disease, high rates of inflation or unemployment 'strike' national economies; we talk of 'saving the lives' of whales, forests and the ecosystem; governments make 'painful' expenditure 'cuts'; industries are 'unhealthy'; and physical exercise is 'therapeutic'. The appeal of the medical model rests in part on its assumed moral neutrality and the view that illness connotes something painful and undesirable which can and should be eliminated (Sontag 1977, p. 3; Zola 1972, p. 489; 1977, p. 63).

One theme of the medicalisation thesis is that medicine is displacing religion and the law as the major institution of social control. Behaviour previously defined as immoral, sinful or criminal has been given medical meanings and designated as illness requiring treatment and rehabilitation (Conrad & Schneider 1980, chapter 10). Bittner argues that the structure and force of one medical specialty, psychiatry, is located in the distribution, relevance and use of psychiatric expressions, evaluations and patterns of influence in society at large. He says: 'It can be seen in the ways mothers deal with children, judges deal with offenders, managers deal with personnel, teachers deal with students, welfare workers deal with the poor, and so forth' (1968, p. 430). Medicalisation exemplifies the rationalisation of social life which encourages scientific explanations for a wider range of problems (Zola 1972, p. 487). Foucault emphasises the role of medical discourse and knowledge as the basis of social control or surveillance through the exercise of discipline over the body and whole populations (1975, 1981, 1988). The clinical gaze provides medicine with widespread social power to define reality and to control deviance and disorder. Medical practice goes beyond the application of techniques for curing ills to embrace conceptions of the healthy or model person, which involves dictating normative standards for physical and moral relations of the individual and of the whole society (1975, p. 34). Morrow suggests that medicine provided the scientific model sexologists (often physicians or psychologists) followed, yet their conceptualisations of sexual dysfunctions 'represent negatively valued deviations from certain taken for granted norms of human sexual functioning', which reflect the dominance of a heterosexual, reproductive model of sexuality (1994, pp. 20–1).

The medicalisation of crime and other social issues, including alcoholism, drug abuse, eating disorders, unemployment, infertility and mental illness results in individualistic and ahistorical explanations. The individual becomes the location of a disorder's cause and the focus for intervention and treatment, thereby diverting attention from broader social and economic conditions and definitions of deviance. Two examples of 'deviance' which have become defined as pathological and therefore in the domain of medicine are abortion and certain types of crime, including homicide. The liberalisation of abortion laws gives the medical profession a monopoly on the performance of the procedure and provides for psychiatric assessments, which are often a criterion for access to abortion. Chapter 3 describes the links between the status of abortion, medical claims-making and professionalisation.

Violators of the criminal law may be defined as requiring treatment or rehabilitation, indicating a view of them as sick and less responsible for their actions. The starkest example is the insanity defence to murder formulated in the trial of Daniel M'Naghten found guilty of murdering the British Prime Minister's secretary in 1840. The court stated that:

> to establish a defence on the ground of insanity, it must be clearly proved that, at the time of the committing of the act, the party accused was labouring under such a defect of reason, from disease of the mind, as not to know the nature and quality of the act he [sic] was doing; or, if he [sic] did know it, that he [sic] did not know he [sic] was doing what was wrong (cited in Waller & Williams 1993, p. 762).

A successful insanity defence results in acquittal of murder, but mental hospitalisation 'at the Governor's pleasure', the actual length of time in an institution, being determined usually by psychiatrists. As Foucault observes: 'the gravity of the act was not altered by the fact that its author was insane, nor the punishment reduced as a consequence; the crime itself disappeared. It was impossible, therefore, to declare that someone was both guilty and mad' (1977, pp. 19–20). Additionally, courts may order participation in a drug or alcohol rehabilitation program as part of the sentence. The focus is not just on the legal status of the alleged offences but on the defendant's personality, nature or level of danger (as determined by psychiatrists) that he or she poses to society at large or to him or herself. The shift is from the criminal offences to an individual's criminality to be assessed by non-legal personnel. According to Foucault: 'The purpose of the sanction will therefore not be to punish a legal subject who has voluntarily broken the law; its role will be to reduce as much as possible—either by elimination, or by exclusion or by various restrictions, or by therapeutic measures—the risk of criminality represented by the individual in question' (1978, p. 16). The treatment becomes the penalty and the penalty the treatment. This may represent more rather than less social control.

Increasing reliance on medical conditions or syndromes in defending criminal accusations expands the way for medical practitioners and other professionals to provide expert evidence to the court. Use of the insanity defence, for example, requires a psychiatrist's opinion to determine whether or not the accused person was insane at the time; the psychiatrist does not determine whether or not the defendant's actions violated the law. The increasing role of non-legal professionals in court proceedings and decision-making exemplifies the fragmentation of the legal power to punish and the shift away from penalising the act to making judgements about the accused person, which encompasses predictions about his or her future behaviour, including the likelihood of dangerousness or repeat offending. Foucault explains that 'the practice of calling on psychiatric expertise, which is widespread in the assize courts,[1] ... means that the sentence, even if it is always formulated in terms of legal punishment, implies, more or less obscurely, judgements of normality, attributions of causality, assessments of possible changes, anticipations as to the offender's future' (1979, p. 20). Despite claims to be providing evidence of an objective medical condition, sceptical legal commentators question the expertise of the experts and indicate that 'experts can always be found to give a diagnosis or prognosis which will favour one side rather than another' (Ligertwood 1993, p. 374). Freckelton argues that such newly created psychological syndromes as the battered woman syndrome and the rape trauma syndrome do not constitute areas of expert knowledge because they lack sufficient scientific validation; they belong in the therapeutic not the forensic context (1994, p. 31). It is not correct to assert, then, that the legal system provides no resistance to the increasing medicalisation of definitions of crime and medical intervention into court proceedings.

The conceptualisation of deviance as a medical problem and the construction of new types of illness are not automatic, but depend on broader social relations and processes of negotiation. The relationship of the medical profession to the class structure, competition with other occupational groups or between segments of the medical profession all affect definitions of health and illness (Bucher 1962, p. 40; Bucher & Strauss 1961, p. 326). Navarro, a historical materialist, suggests that due to its position within the social division of labour, medicine reproduces capitalist class relations. He maintains that bourgeois ideology legitimates and facilitates the reproduction of the power relations of capitalism through medicine based on a science/ideology dichotomy which generates an expert/layperson dichotomy. These dichotomies reflect the dominant/dominated relations of capitalist society (1980, p. 541). Specifically, the post-Second World War expansion of state medical expenditures constitutes an aspect of the control of the working class rather than concern for their health and welfare. The individualised mode of treatment directs concern away from the causes of diseases, including unhealthy and dangerous workplaces maintained by the overriding profit motive (1983, pp. 185–6).

Figlio (1978, p. 589) further elaborates the way medicine and illness mediate social relations. He argues that the perceived explosion of female diseases during the nineteenth century represented a strain on bourgeois values more than an increase in clear physical pathology. He examines chlorosis, a kind of anaemia, which occurred typically among adolescent middle-class girls. This pattern of 'illness' served two functions: the middle-class clientele aided the emerging medical profession's status claims; and the disease differentiated middle-class, non-labouring from lower-class working girls. The characteristics of the former were exaggerated by defining adolescence as a new child-like stage corresponding to the age of intensive labouring in the working class and by throwing into sharper relief the image of asexual, non-working delicate femininity (Figlio 1978, p. 609).

The discovery of new illness and treatment practices also reflects the professional aims of segments of the medical profession, rather than arising from an unfolding corpus of scientific knowledge. Paediatric radiologists, a marginal medical specialty, increased their status by identifying and naming a new medical problem as child-abuse, or the 'battered child syndrome'. Other medical personnel had not identified this problem because they saw isolated individual cases and usually dealt with the parents rather than the child, whereas radiographers consistently saw X-rays of children's broken bones and were not exposed to parents' explanations of their child's injuries (Pfohl 1977, pp. 316–19). This example shows that medical technology, the social organisation of professional–client relations, and claims-making on the part of professional segments are important components of the emergence and identification of a medical problem.

The emergence of new illness designations also results from negotiation and contest between interest groups. This is especially true in work-related illness and disease. A number of studies document the processes whereby symptoms became recognised as occupational diseases (Figlio 1982, pp. 190–7; Smith 1981). The 1968 miners' movement in West Virginia, for example, aimed to extend workers' compensation coverage to victims of 'black-lung', a variety of respiratory trouble which miners contract in the workplace (Smith 1981, pp. 343–4). Factors external to science, specifically mechanisation which contributed to unemployment, miners' powerlessness, and higher dust levels, shaped and changed the definition of the illness. The controversy represented a movement by miners and their families to reclaim political and economic bargaining power, and the goal of obtaining compensation for black-lung represented a demand for retribution from the industry for the destructive human consequences of its economic transformation. In a study of the Broken Hill mining industry, Couch (1988, p. 75) concludes that the contest between labour and management about workers' health and safety reflects conflicting frames of reference, and involves disagreement about the apportionment of risk and the disbursement of the costs of unsafe and unhealthy work practices and sites. A further example is the emergence of tenosynovitis or Repetitive Strain Injury (RSI) in the 1980s. This 'condition' became problematic among office workers using computer technology and has been described as the 'new' industrial epidemic of Australia (Ferguson 1984, p. 318). However, little medical consensus exists over its causes, nature and treatment, or even its existence. While the symptoms have existed for a long time, RSI's emergence represents a political struggle between management, unions and insurance companies (Willis 1986, p. 213). According to Willis: 'Occupational injury or illness mediates the social relations of work in that it provides a means of resisting "managerial prerogative" by arguments about the consequences of a particular form of work organisation for the health and safety of workers' (1986, p. 215).

The medicalisation of reproduction, notably pregnancy and childbirth, has been well-documented and critiqued (Ehrenreich & English 1978). Research demonstrates increasing medical intervention and diagnostic testing during pregnancy, the movement from home to hospital births, and male physicians' progressive exclusion of female midwives from the birthing process (Rothman 1986, pp. 86–115; Sullivan & Weitz 1988). Most recently, medical researchers and practitioners have been instrumental in the designation of infertility as a medical condition requiring medical treatment and intervention (Becker & Nachtigall 1992, pp. 457–8; Strickler 1992, pp. 113–15). Biomedical interventions aimed at alleviating (rather than treating) infertility by producing a pregnancy have expanded rapidly since the birth of the first baby conceived through IVF in 1978 (Blank 1990, pp. 11–16; Scritchfield 1989, p. 99). United States data show that despite no increase in the overall incidence of infertility, visits to physicians for infertility services more than doubled between 1968 and 1984 (Office of Technology Assessment 1988, p. 5). A study of forty-three couples undergoing a medical evaluation for infertility finds that the treatment heightened their sense of deviance from cultural norms and abnormality in terms of body function and image (Becker & Nachtigall 1992, pp. 463–5). Greil argues that infertility is similar to chronic illness as it is long-term in nature, it becomes the focal point in sufferers' lives and the 'illness' trajectory is unknown (1991, pp. 23–4). Others suggest that involuntary childlessness can be conceptualised as a form of physical disability, however, it is invisible and usually remains undiagnosed or unrecognised until a conception is sought. It is inferred from the absence of a pregnancy and children rather than demonstrated by the presence of a disease (Sandelowski, Holditch-Davis & Harris 1990, p. 198).

The medicalisation of infertility is incomplete given the low success rates and many critics contest its status as an illness arguing instead that the real 'problem' is deviation from social norms, specifically pervasive pro-natalist and motherhood norms (Lorber 1988, p. 117; Roach Anleu 1993, p. 17). Women who are physically infertile and those who are fertile but involuntarily childless experience considerable stigma and deviantisation during everyday life which have profound effects on their social identity and behaviour (Miall 1986). The norms applied to women make deviation from family roles more serious for them than for men. A study of twenty-two married infertile couples shows that women are more likely to seek medical intervention and to view infertility as a devastating experience or a cataclysmic role failure spoiling their ability to live normal lives (Greil,

Leitko & Porter 1988, p. 181). Men perceive infertility as disappointing but not devastating, so long as it remains assumed that the cause of the problem is the female partner. The authors suggest that possibly because the expectation to be a father is not as important a part of male identity as the expectation to be a mother is of female identity, few husbands speak in terms indicating that they experience infertility as a role failure. Even where there was clearly a male reproductive impairment wives still tend to view the situation as their problem. Regardless of who is biologically 'at fault', it is the woman who is unable to display the visible signs of an expected and desired change in status and thus deviates from the pervasive norms surrounding motherhood (Greil 1992, p. 32).

A Canadian study also demonstrates how involuntarily childless women perceive their own and their partner's 'problem' and how they manage its potentially stigmatising implications in social interaction. There was an overwhelming sense of stigma and perception that involuntary childlessness entailed very negative consequences. Nearly all the women who themselves were infertile experience feelings of anxiety, isolation, and conflict as they explored the possibility of personal infertility. Most express concern that an awareness of their infertility problems would cause others to view them differently and negatively. However, fertile women (married to men with documented infertility) took on a courtesy stigma allowing others to believe that the origin of the problem was their own biology and not that of their male partner, thus permitting the social audience to view them negatively. The personal and social experiences of the involuntarily childless women reflect self-labelling, a relatively under-examined concept within the sociology of deviance (Miall 1986, pp. 271–8).

The social constructionist view of medicine has considerable value in identifying the variability and historicity of medical knowledge, the relationship between illness and social conditions, and medical personnel's active role in seeking out, identifying and classifying symptoms or conditions as disease and pathology. However, a number of problems exist, the most important of which is the relativist trap. Claiming a central, if not privileged, position for social accounts of medical knowledge and concepts poses questions about the critics' own knowledge and theories. The charge that medical knowledge, like all knowledge, is socially constructed means that no external criteria of evaluation exist. Medical knowledge is just as valid (or invalid) as that of the critics; they are just different perspectives. Demonstrating the values inherent in medical categories does not necessarily undermine their legitimacy or consequences (Bury 1986, p. 165). Defining symptoms as illness gives people's conditions and complaints legitimacy and reality. For instance, on the one hand, assumptions about the nature of women and hormones inform the medical definition of menopause as a 'deficiency' disease but on the other, medical definitions legitimate, explain and relieve the symptoms which are not dismissed as figments of the imagination (Bell 1987, p. 540). Arguing that illness categories are socially constructed does not help a person suffering the consequences of a broken leg, acute appendicitis or a massive heart attack. Arguing that medical dominance is complete and unidirectional and medicalisation is 'unnatural' further deviantises consumers or patients who are presented as duped by medical science, victims of medical intervention and lacking agency, unlike those who do not seek medical solutions to their problems.

Social constructionists seem to assume that the medical profession's control over definitions of health and illness is complete and its dominance unquestioned. Nevertheless, many people do not rely totally on technical and medical explanations of illness or its management. There is evidence of a growing disenchantment with conventional medicine, including the development of discerning medical consumers who are able to evaluate medical services, demand the right to make informed decisions and seek a range of alternative or complementary health care options (Easthope 1993, pp. 290–3). This medical consumer is very different from the dependent, helpless patient Parsons describes in his model of the sick role. Moreover, experiencing illness does not result automatically and unequivocally in a person seeking medical attention. Of the persons who took health-related action during the two weeks prior to participation in the National Health Survey, 26 per cent went to a doctor, 12 per cent consulted with other health professionals but most people took vitamins and various medications (Australian Bureau of Statistics 1991b, p. 26, table 15). Health-related decisions are outcomes of socially constrained choices and individuals' participation in networks which provide information and strategies for managing health and illness (Pescosolido 1992, pp. 1096–9). Greater consumer awareness and education, combined with the routinisation of many aspects of physicians' work in large bureaucratic hospitals, suggest that medicine's autonomy and monopoly status is declining, or becoming deprofessionalised and proletarianised (Haug 1973, p. 197; 1975, p. 211). Even so, medical dominance and autonomy remain largely intact, especially as one of the profession's responses to competition from complementary health practitioners is to incorporate elements of non-medical, social welfare or holistic health care into its own practice while simultaneously excluding alternative practitioners (Easthope 1993, pp. 295–6; Freidson 1986, pp. 109–33; Willis 1989, pp. 216–20). The social constructionist critique is most valuable in explaining mental illness where identifiable physiological symptoms or causes often do not exist.

Mental illness

In the Middle Ages, the dominant conception of madness was theological. Disease was God's punishment for sin, especially the sin of unfaithfulness. Around the fourteenth century mad persons were considered witches and subject to persecution. The guidebook for the Inquisition—the *Malleus Maleficarum* (Hammer of Witches)—published in 1487, depicted most dissidents, mad people and other deviants as witches who had made a compact with the Devil and were therefore his agents. In the following two centuries, those considered insane were deemed witches and often burned at the stake. Over eighty-five per cent of these people were women, who still constitute the majority of those designated mentally ill (Ben-Yehuda 1980, pp. 20–1).

Between the sixteenth and eighteenth centuries in Western Europe a number of significant changes occurred regarding the management of madness. By the end of this period the medical model became the dominant way of identifying people with mental illness, and physicians gained legitimacy and authority for their treatment. Before the seventeenth century some people designated as deviant were ejected periodically from towns and were free to travel around the countryside. Early management of insanity is exemplified by the Ship of Fools which sailed the Rhine embarking and disembarking mad people who had been expelled from towns. In the seventeenth century enormous houses of confinement opened, for example the Hôpital Général in Paris, to accommodate mad people, criminals, libertines, beggars, vagabonds, prostitutes, the unemployed and the poor. The Hôpital combined the characteristics of an asylum, a work house, and a prison, but no medical treatment was administered. Confinement was a seventeenth-century solution to an economic crisis involving reduced wages, unemployment and coin shortages affecting the Western world (Foucault 1988, p. 49). The society exercised segregative powers which enabled it to render as outcasts all people deemed to be useless (1988, p. 58).

As the importance of the labour force increased, the next step was separation of the able-bodied poor from the mad to protect them from the contagion of madness for social and economic, not medical reasons. This involved the emergence of separate institutions: the almshouse, the workhouse, the insane asylum and the prison. Increasing homogeneity of populations within each setting enhances and facilitates social control. Despite the lack of medical treatments or explanatory theories of madness, physicians assumed a small but central role as gatekeepers of the asylums. In England, in 1774, a physician's certificate was required for commitment to an asylum. Most of the therapies, ranging from bloodletting, purgation and dunking, to rotation in a suspended chair, were more akin to punishment than treatment. Foucault makes the central point: 'It is not as a scientist that *homo medicus* has authority in the asylum, but as a wise man. If the medical profession is required, it is as a juridical and moral guarantee, not in the name of science' (1988, p. 270).

By the end of the eighteenth century two reformers—Philippe Pinel in France and William Tuke in England—sought to eliminate the physically punitive aspects of life in the insane asylum and reinforce the benefits of moral treatment with an emphasis on training, obedience, work and the value of property. Pinel developed one of the first typologies of madness by distinguishing between melancholia, mania, dementia and idiocy.

Physicians argued that as both moral and medical responses were appropriate they should have a monopoly on dispensing both. Their successful claim to provide moral assistance was especially central to their autonomy in the area of mental illness because they were unable to show the physiological causes and had not demonstrated any cures. The decline of the Church, the new scientific discoveries of the Englightenment, and the humanitarianism of the Renaissance all aided physicians' achievement of 'professional dominance' in this area and the emergence of a unitary conception of mental illness.

The separation of deviants was an essential pre-condition for the development of a medical specialty (the forerunner of psychiatry) claiming to possess a specific expertise to deal with madness. This, in turn, further enhanced the legitimacy of the concept of mental illness as a distinguishable entity reflecting and caused by an underlying pathology, rather than an amorphous cultural view of insanity indicating demonological and non-human influences (Scull 1975, pp. 241–5; 1977b, p. 344). Nevertheless, the concept of mental illness remained closer to an ideology than a scientific achievement. The causes of mental illness that psychiatrists identified during the nineteenth century included ill health, religious anxiety, disappointed love, pecuniary embarrassment, acid inhalation, suppressed menstruation and general poor health. In the post-Civil War period in the USA, medical practitioners linked the origins of insanity with the radical social transformations and dislocation that were occurring; social chaos and uncertainty were reflected in mental chaos and uncertainty (Rothman 1971, chapter 5). Sutton summarises psychiatrists' classificatory schemes during the nineteenth century as 'crude nosologies, eclectic arrays of behavioral symptoms loosely organised in terms of prevailing moral judgements ... [and] too often prevailing "moral" therapies practiced in asylums consisted only of the work and disciplinary routines that contributed to administrative efficiency' (1991, p. 668).

During the Progressive period in the USA, asylums grew faster than other institutions of social control such as prisons, juvenile reformatories and almshouses. The population of mental hospital patients increased more than six fold between 1880 and the mid-1920s, making them the largest of all custodial institutions. Although psychiatrists during the nineteenth century had successfully monopolised the official definition of insanity as a medical condition with identifiable causes, moral judgements and lay concerns influenced the diagnosis of insanity. Psychiatry was not approved as a medical specialty until 1934 (Neff, McFall & Cleaveland 1987, p. 45). Madness was an elastic concept—a category of residual deviance—which could be applied to a variety of individuals whose deviance stemmed from poverty, homelessness or physical disability. Unlike the other custodial institutions, commitment to an insane asylum entailed neither a trial, a fixed term of internment nor the legal protections associated with criminal proceedings. The United States government's incapacity to systematically address and solve the problem of poverty, especially among the aged, the closure of the almshouses combined with flexibility in the medical concept of insanity and the relatively simple commitment procedures contributed to the enormous expansion in asylum populations (Sutton 1991, pp. 667–8, 675–6).

Psychiatry continues to be one of the most contested areas of medical work. Discussion on the causes of mental illness—genetic, physiological, psychological, social—is far from conclusive and psychiatrists' ability to predict potential dangerousness in patients is highly questionable (Cocozza & Steadman 1978, p. 265; McLean 1990, pp. 979–81). Critics, especially proponents of the labelling perspective, stress the social control rather than the treatment dimensions of the medical model and psychiatry, and reject a unitary concept of mental illness. Szasz, for example, maintains that the replacement of the Church by medicine as the institution of social control merely redefines and relabels deviance with medical terminology (1961, pp. 204–20; 1973, pp. 69–78). Thus, the concept of mental illness serves the same social control function in the contemporary world as did witchcraft in the late Middle Ages. Both are imprecise and all-encompassing concepts freely adaptable to whatever the priest or physician wishes.

Social reaction rather than physiological symptoms is the most important determinant of entry into chronic mental illness as a social role. A range of behaviour may be interpreted as evidence of mental illness but the behaviour itself is not sufficient. Most people act in 'strange', 'odd', 'crazy' or 'uncharacteristic' manners, but are not labelled mentally ill. Scheff defines the variety of norm-breaking behaviour not fitting into the categories of crime, alcoholism, or illness, as 'residual rule-breaking' (1966, pp. 31–54). After exhausting cultural classifications of such norm-breaking behaviour as drunkenness, a residue of diverse violations, for which the culture provides no explicit label, always remains. This residue of diverse violations which are not explicitly defined includes witchcraft, spirit possession and mental illness and arises from fundamentally diverse sources—organic, psychological, external stress, or volitional acts of innovation or defiance. However, this behaviour is usually transitory, albeit pervasive, and is explained away by rationalisations. Social audiences may interpret aberrant acts as resulting from work pressure, family stress or a recent disappointment. This means that most people do not become 'mentally ill', because they are not perceived and labelled as such. Rationalisations may no longer be invoked if the behaviour persistently occurs without a reasonable 'account', thereby placing a strain on social relationships, or if others consider a person to be a likely candidate for mental illness, for example an alcoholic, an unemployed person, or someone who does not speak English. Indeed, Szasz (1960, p. 113) argues that non-organic mental illness would best be termed 'problems in living'. He indicates that the term 'mental illness' is widely used to describe something which is very different from a disease of the brain and suggests that problems in living derive not so much from a struggle for biological survival as from the stresses and strains inherent in social interaction between complex human personalities. Mental illness is a myth which obscures difficulties located in social relations.

When this deviant behaviour cannot be rationalised the label of mentally ill is likely to be applied and the labelled person may be rewarded for conforming to the stereotyped conception of insanity. Secondary deviance emerges when the individual's own self-conception is in line with the deviant label and his or her actions conform to others' expectations. Being identified and labelled for breaking residual rules is the key to recruitment into the role of a mentally ill person. The assignment of the label 'mentally ill', especially by a psychiatrist, is very difficult to remove (Scheff 1966, pp. 80–3).

The social constructionist, or labelling perspective on mental illness has received much criticism for ignoring the organic bases of mental illness, for treating mental illness purely as a social or ideological definition, and for attributing too much power to societal reaction whose impact is viewed in a highly deterministic manner. The vast majority of persons who enter the role of the mentally ill do so voluntarily (Gove 1975, p. 42). Given the stigma attached to being mentally ill, it is difficult to comprehend why persons would voluntarily seek psychiatric treatment, particularly in-patient care, unless they were experiencing behavioural problems or emotional disturbance. For the two most serious forms of mental illness—schizophrenia and manic depressive psychoses—evidence suggests a very strong genetic component, which appears to run counter to the labelling perspective. Persons in psychiatric treatment are more likely to manifest such symptoms of mental illness as a critical life event prior to hospitalisation, than those not in treatment (Gove 1975, p. 51).

The labelling perspective implies that the application of mentally ill labels is relatively unproblematic and automatic, that once labelled a deviant career is inevitable. However, designating someone as mentally ill often follows extended efforts at tolerance and re-integration rather than immediate exclusion. The societal reaction approach cannot account for the ways in which mental patients and persons experiencing 'symptoms' of mental illness interpret their own 'problematic' feelings and behaviours. They tend to view their own 'symptoms' far more positively in the moral dimension than would be expected had they been completely resocialised into a mentally ill role based on the community's cultural definitions (Meile & Whitt 1981, p. 241; Whitt & Meile 1985, p. 683). People who confront symptomatic behaviour in themselves or in family members go to great lengths to avoid using mental illness as an explanation; it is a last resort interpretation.

Yarrow and her associates (1955), for example, describe the processes whereby women reorganise their perceptions of their husbands from a well person to one who is mentally sick or in need of psychiatric intervention in a mental hospital. At first, wives do not interpret unusual behaviour, which psychiatrists would identify as symptoms of mental disorder, as manifestations of mental illness or emotional disorder. Wives use various forms of defense against recognition. Some tend to normalise the behaviour, by seeing the husband's neurotic and psychotic symptoms in other people. Others attenuate the seriousness of the behaviour by adopting an alternative explanation relating to work pressure, for example, or balance the husband's bizarre episodes with instances of normal behaviour. Finally, some women deny that the problematic behaviour can be interpreted in a mental illness framework. The following quotation illustrates their reticence to resort to mental illness interpretations of unusual behaviour: 'I put it out of my mind—I didn't want to face it—anything but a mental illness' (Yarrow et al. 1955, p. 22). The shift in definition from 'no problem' to the realisation that a problem of some sort exists results from an eventual piling up or accumulation of events rather than from a single strange or bizarre episode.

Part of this disagreement about the status of mental illness—whether it is a social construct emerging in social interaction or a psychiatric disease with discrete symptoms—arises because of the variety of behaviours ranging from schizophrenia, psychoses, neuroses and emotional and personality disorders to depression falling within the category of mental illness. The lack of agreement about what constitutes the physiological or social causes and symptoms of mental illness necessarily results in judgements and interpretation informed by cultural values and social norms regarding appropriate behaviour. In different societies, the same behaviour, for example 'hearing voices' or 'seeing visions', might be defined as indicating high social status or divinity, not negative stigmatisation.

The labelling theorists' main contribution to the study of mental illness is the analysis of the variability of the process of definition and the consequences of being identified as mentally ill. On the other side, mental illness does involve real symptoms requiring medical treatment, which has become more apparent with the deinstitutionalisation of mental health facilities in most Western societies. The problems of minimising individuals' contact with mental hospitals will be discussed below.

The distribution of health and illness

Epidemiological studies demonstrate the distribution of various types of illness, especially mental illness, along class, ethnic, race and gender dimensions, and across different societies (Elling 1981, pp. 28–40; Graham & Reeder 1979, pp. 75–83). Frequently used health indicators are mortality or death rates, rates of morbidity or sickness and rates of chronic conditions. The most comprehensive source of information on the distribution of health and illness in Australia is the National Health Survey (NHS) which was first implemented between October 1989 and September 1990 by the Australian Bureau of Statistics. The Australian Health Surveys, carried out in 1977–78 and 1983, are the forerunners of the NHS which will be conducted every five years. It contains details on recent and long-term illness conditions experienced by respondents, their health-related actions, for example visiting a medical practitioner or taking medication, and such lifestyle characteristics as alcohol consumption, diet, exercise and smoking, which may affect health. Important independent variables include age, sex, occupation, employment and birthplace (Australian Bureau of Statistics 1991a). The NHS and previous surveys and studies all point to significant differences in the distribution of health and illness among occupational, gender, race and ethnic groups in Australia.

Generally, an inverse relationship exists between socio-economic status and mortality. An examination of the relation between mortality and occupational prestige (the measure of social class used) among Australian men aged between fifteen and sixty-four in the 1970s indicates that those in the lowest prestige grouping, including workers in primary industries, labourers and domestic service workers, have nearly double the death rates from all causes combined compared with those in professional occupations. With the exception of endocrine diseases, men in the lowest social class have the highest premature death rates, especially with regard to mental disorders, diseases of the nervous system and sensory organs, diseases of the respiratory system, and accidents (McMichael 1985, p. 224). Even though mortality rates from coronary heart disease declined by around 25 per cent from 1969 to 1978, the greatest declines were among people in professional occupations. Australian-born men in low-status occupations manifest higher blood pressures compared with professional or technical workers (Dobson et al. 1985, p. 283; Opit, Oliver & Salzberg 1984, pp. 763–4). The NHS indicates that of employed persons, managers and administrators followed by clerks and labourers have the highest prevalence of cardiovascular conditions, in particular heart disease, with the lowest prevalence occurring in professional and para-professional occupations (Australian Bureau of Statistics 1991c, p. 5, table 4).

Using occupation as a crude measure of social class table 6.1 shows higher death rates among men in blue-collar and unskilled occupations. Of the 18 271 deaths among males aged between fifteen and sixty-four in 1992, 46 per cent (8406) were employed as tradespersons, plant and machine operators, drivers and labourers and related workers. In contrast, almost 20 per cent (3608) were employed in managerial, administrative and professional occupations and 11.5 per cent were para-professionals, clerks or sales and personal service workers. The relationship between occupation and death is the complete reverse for females, in part because fewer women than men participate in the labour force and most women are employed in clerical and 'pink-collar' occupations. Of the 9386 deaths among females aged between fifteen and sixty-four in 1992, 15.8 per cent (1487) were employed as para-professionals, clerks and sales and personal service workers, 9.1 per cent (850) were in professional or managerial occupations and 7.1 per cent (669) were in blue-collar work. The most frequent illness condition involving absence from work that all occupational groups report is respiratory problems, including common colds, influenza, hayfever and asthma, but blue-collar workers are more likely to be absent from work due to injury than are professional, managerial and clerical workers (see table 6.2). Clerks, tradespersons and labourers report taking the most days and managers and para-professionals report taking the fewest from work due to an illness condition (Australian Bureau of Statistics 1992b, p. 44, table 35).

Table 6.1 Deaths: occupation, age group and sex, Australia, 1992

Occupation	Age group (years)		
	15–34	*35–54*	*55–64*
		MALES (%)	
Managers & administrators	4.9	13.5	13.9
Professionals	4.3	9.7	7.4
Para-professionals	3.6	3.8	3.9
Clerks	2.9	3.2	3.5
Salespersons & personal service workers	5.1	4.5	4.1
Tradespersons	20.5	17.7	18.8
Plant & machine operators & drivers	6.5	10.0	11.1
Labourers	17.9	16.1	18.1
Other & not stated	19.5	15.8	15.7
Persons not in workforce	14.9	5.7	3.5
TOTAL N	3283	6241	8747
		FEMALES (%)	
Managers & administrators	1.8	5.2	2.5
Professionals	6.3	7.5	4.0
Para-professionals	4.3	4.1	3.1
Clerks	10.4	9.9	6.0
Salespersons & personal service workers	8.1	4.1	3.2
Tradespersons	2.8	1.9	2.2
Plant & machine operators & drivers	.49	1.0	1.0
Labourers	4.3	4.9	3.2
Other & not stated	24.1	25.0	22.0
Persons not in workforce	37.1	36.5	52.7
TOTAL N	1218	3521	4647

Source: Australian Bureau of Statistics 1993, *Deaths, Australia 1992*, ABS, Canberra, Cat. no. 3302–0, table 14.

A study of Brisbane suburbs ranked according to socio-economic status indicates that mortality (including infant mortality) rates are higher in lower-ranking areas, and deaths from circulatory and respiratory diseases, accidents and lung cancer are greater than those in higher status suburbs (Siskind, Najman & Copeman 1987a, p. 15; 1987b, p. 24). Explanations for these patterns include the fact that people of lower socio-economic status tend to live and work in toxic environments, in industrial areas where the levels of pollution are relatively high because housing prices and rents are relatively low. Differential mortality rates also relate to lifestyle factors and access to quality medical care.

Table 6.2 Employed persons taking days away from work: selected illness condition[1] by occupation[2]

Illness condition	OCCUPATION (%)							
	Managers and administrators	Professionals	Para-professionals	Trades-persons	Clerks	Salespersons	Machine operators	Labourers
Nervous system	3.9	7.0	3.7	4.0	6.4	4.9	3.9	2.5
Respiratory system	32.5	41.7	38.0	32.2	37.6	44.4	28.1	28.7
Digestive system	9.3	12.3	11.9	9.4	8.5	11.0	16.8	12.8
Musculoskeletal system	15.4	4.0	7.0	11.3	9.6	9.7	15.2	17.8
Symptoms, ill-defined conditions[3]	11.7	16.4	9.0	15.2	15.6	11.6	11.7	14.8
Injury and poisoning	11.9	5.2	12.4	21.2	5.6	7.7	12.3	14.8
Genitourinary system	3.0	3.7	2.9	3.1	6.1	5.7	—	3.4
Total persons taking days away ('000)[4]	46.1	80.3	48.9	122.8	127.8	79.1	48.7	102.6

1 The most frequent illness conditions reported are included in this table.
2 Occupation in main job held at the time of interview.
3 Includes allergy, insomnia, various pains, heartburn, headache and hangover.
4 Each person may have reported more than one reason for days away from work.

Source: Australian Bureau of Statistics 1991, *1989–90 National Health Survey: Summary of Results, Australia*, ABS, Canberra, Cat. no. 4364.0, table 23.

Table 6.3   Recent illness conditions experienced: type of condition by sex, Australia, 1989–90

Type of condition	Males	Females	Persons
		(Rate per 1000 population)	
Infectious & parasitic diseases	25.0	27.9	26.5
Neoplasms[1]	10.9	10.6	10.8
Endocrine, nutritional & metabolic diseases	35.7	50.2	43.0
Mental disorders	24.9	45.7	35.3
Nervous system & sense organs	53.2	72.4	62.8
Circulatory system	98.1	137.9	118.1
Respiratory system	230.2	237.6	233.9
Digestive system	114.8	144.9	129.9
Genitourinary system	8.1	68.0	38.1
Skin & subcutaneous tissue	117.5	136.5	127.0
Musculoskeletal system	112.9	150.4	131.7
Symptoms, & ill-defined conditions[2]	195.1	279.5	237.4
Total persons who reported a recent illness[3]	675.6	782.9	729.4

1 Includes endocrine, nutritional and metabolic diseases and immunity disorders.
2 Includes insomnia, heartburn, headache, hangover, various pains.
3 Each person may have reported more than one type of illness and therefore components do not add to totals.

Source: Australian Bureau of Statistics 1991, *1989–90 National Health Survey: Summary of Results, Australia*, ABS, Canberra, Cat. no. 4364.0, table 7.

Despite lower female mortality rates than male, women report more illness and use health services more frequently than do men. Such obstetric and gynaecological conditions as pregnancy, child birth and menopause do not alone account for this higher utilisation. Table 6.3 shows that women report experiencing every type of illness condition at a greater rate than do men. The biggest gender differences are for diseases of the circulatory system, genitourinary problems, mental disorder and symptoms and ill-defined conditions, including headache, insomnia, heartburn and various pain. Women are also more likely to take health-related action than are men, in particular by using medication and vitamins or by seeing a medical practitioner (table 6.4). Four in five females and seven in ten males took health-related action in the two weeks prior to participating in the NHS; 23 per cent of the former and 17 per cent of the latter consulted with a doctor (Australian Bureau of Statistics 1992b, p. 8, table 4).

Differences in health also prevail among ethnic and race groups. Diet usually is identified as the major factor contributing to lower incidences of cancer among people of Southern European cultural heritage as compared with Anglo-Celtic culture and food traditions (Dunt 1982, p. 222; McMichael & Bonett 1981, p. 231). However, migrants from Southern Europe seem to have more mental health problems than other groups and work in occupations with high rates of industrial accident (Bates & Linder-Pelz 1990, pp. 36–8). Unlike most other Australians, Aboriginal people have not benefited from improved health care as measured by increases in life expectancy at birth. The life expectancy for Aborigines in Western Australia and the Northern Territory is between fifteen and twenty years less than for Australians as a whole (Department of Community Services and Health 1988b, p. 86). In New South Wales, Aboriginal mortality is more than four times that of the total state population, and among young and middle-aged adults mortality rates are up to twelve times higher. The principle causes of death among Aboriginal people include diseases of the circulatory system and injuries, with alcohol having a substantial effect in the thirty-five to forty-four age group (Thomson & Smith 1985, p. S49).

Table 6.4 Persons who took health-related action during the two weeks prior to interview: type of action by sex, Australia, 1989–90

Type of Action	Males	Females	Persons
		(rate per 1000 population)	
Took no action	300.2	190.0	245.0
Hospital inpatient	7.6	10.8	9.2
Visit to casualty	25.3	24.8	25.7
Doctor consultation	168.4	231.8	200.1
Dental consultation	47.9	58.2	53.1
Consultation with other health professional	81.4	107.3	94.4
Took vitamins	190.7	275.3	233.1
Used other medication	585.0	679.9	641.4
Days away from work/school	70.5	67.1	68.8
Other days of reduced activity	87.3	112.1	99.7
Total persons taking action[1]	699.8	810.0	755.0

1   Each person may have taken more than one type of action during the two weeks prior to interview and therefore components do not add to totals.

Source: Australian Bureau of Statistics 1991, *1989–90 National Health Survey: Summary of Results, Australia*, ABS, Canberra, Cat. no. 4364.0, table 15.

Australia is not the only society in which vast inequalities in health persist despite increased government expenditure, a national health scheme, and continuing developments in medical science and treatments. A 1980 United Kingdom health report shows that despite a dramatic reduction in nineteenth-century common causes of death the association between social or occupational class and health persists (Townsend & Davidson 1982, chapter 6). It documents an extensive and unequal distribution of ill-health and death among the British population which is widening due to inequalities in income, work (or lack of it), environment, education, housing, transport and conditions of work. For both men and women aged between fifteen and sixty-four the risk of death before retirement is two-and-a-half times greater in the unskilled class than in the professional occupational group. A relatively low death rate exists among tertiary sector employees, professions, teachers, managers and public servants in contrast to the high death rate for coal miners, labourers and participants in the manufacturing sector. Infant mortality is almost three times more likely in the unskilled category than in the professional (Townsend & Davidson 1982, chapter 2).

Three explanations exist for the unequal distribution of health and illness:

1 members of the middle class are more likely than others to come into contact with medical treatment. They can afford private health insurance and better health care and are not placed on long waiting lists for public hospitals;

2 the causes of disease and illness, including toxic wastes, hazardous work environments, lack of nutrition and inadequate medical attention, are distributed unequally throughout society;

3 instead of social or environmental conditions causing illness, ill people may gravitate to certain geographical areas. Because of sickness some people will be unable to remain in the labour force. If sickness benefits or invalid pensions are the only source of their income, they will seek low-cost housing, which tends to be in the most dilapidated and polluted areas of the city. Illness may then become the most important factor in downward mobility rather than social class causing health status.

The relationship between mental illness and social class and, more recently, gender, has occupied many sociologists' attention. Faris and Dunham's early study (1939, pp. 160–77) finds that centrally located areas in metropolitan Chicago, often the loci of poverty, were associated with the highest rates of first admissions to psychiatric hospitals for schizophrenia. However, this does not indicate whether a greater actual incidence of mental disorder occurs in those areas or whether residents of them are more likely to be labelled mentally ill. Hollingshead and Redlich's (1958, pp. 220–49) data on treated cases of mental illness indicate that individuals in lower classes are more likely to be diagnosed psychotic and given custodial care, whereas individuals in higher classes are diagnosed more commonly as neurotic and treated with psychotherapy.

The existence of a relationship between class and mental illness is unequivocal, unlike its interpretation. On the one hand, it has been interpreted as evidence of social causation with low status, social disorganisation, migration and social isolation producing the psychopathology. Alternatively, others accept mental illness as genetically caused, which in turn leads to downward social mobility. A central unsolved problem of psychiatric epidemiology is the measurement of untreated psychological disorder (Dohrenwend 1966, p. 33).

The relationship between individual psychological disorder and wider aspects of the social structure, including employment opportunities, socialisation and family roles is a recurring dilemma (Liem & Liem 1978, p. 139). Stress, which may have its origins in the community, neighbourhood, family or work life, provides a connecting factor between the individual and the social structure. Interpersonal relationships, ties to the community, familial supports or material resources may diffuse the effect of stress, or a significant life event. The unequal distribution of stress, then, must account for the relation of social class to mental disorder (Liem & Liem 1978, p. 142). Unemployment and homelessness may be significant stressors among the working class increasing the likelihood of mental illness. Indeed, the most frequently studied aspect of homelessness is mental illness (Wright 1988, p. 182). Generally, it seems that negative labels act as a magnetic force attracting additional stigmas. Homeless people are more likely to be defined as mentally ill, HIV carriers or alcoholics than are other members of the community.

A positive relationship also exists between gender and mental illness, but again, its interpretation is ambiguous (Nathanson 1975, p. 59). For example, women constitute almost two-thirds (63 per cent) of the 92 800 people consulting with a doctor for mental disorders in the two weeks prior to participating in the NHS in 1989–90 (Australian Bureau of Statistics 1992b, p. 23, table 18). Women are more likely than men to report experiencing emotional problems, nerves and depression, whereas men are slightly more likely to experience psychoses and other mental disorders. Table 6.5 presents NHS data on the number of employed persons reporting a mental disorder by occupation and by sex. It is often argued that women report more illness than men not because of real sex differences in the frequency of illness but because it is more acceptable for them to be ill. Phillips and Segal (1969, pp. 69–71) suggest that in Western societies it is culturally acceptable and appropriate for women to be expressive about their difficulties whereas men are more reluctant to admit certain unpleasurable feelings and sensations. Women conform more to the sick role and its requirements of helplessness, passivity and compliance than do men whose deviance is more likely to be identified as crime. Illness is less stigmatising for women than for men and women's mental illness has, historically, been linked with their reproductive capacity and organs. In other words, women's behaviour whether conforming to or deviating from gender norms of emotionalism, passivity and dependency, is especially liable to be labelled mentally disturbed (Barker-Benfield 1975, pp. 283–6; Busfield 1988, pp. 530–6; 1989 p. 344; Ehrenreich 1974, pp. 618–19; Schur 1984, pp. 197–201).

An alternative explanation is that as women's assigned roles are more stressful than those of men they experience more illness. In particular, women's oppression leads to mental illness; it is a social product rather than a social construct (Chesler 1971, pp. 757–8; 1972, p. 118). Gove and Tudor (1972, pp. 814–15) indicate that women are more likely than men to experience emotional problems because they are restricted to a single major role, that of housewife, and if that role is unsatisfactory few alternative sources of gratification exist.[2] Many women find their major activities of raising children and keeping house frustrating, of low prestige, technically undemanding, unstructured and invisible. Even when a married woman has salaried employment she typically works in a less satisfactory position than the married man, and frequently her paid work in the labour force is secondary and additional to child care and household responsibilities. Gove and Tudor (1972, p. 828) attribute women's higher rates of mental illness to the role of married women, as single, divorced, or widowed women do not

Table 6.5 Employed persons who reported recent mental illness: occupation by sex, Australia, 1989–90 ('000)

Mental Disorder	Managers and administrators	Professionals	Para-professionals	Tradespersons	Clerks	Sales & personal service workers	Plant & machine operators & drivers	Labourers	Total
MALES									
Nerves, tension, emotional problems	11.6	10.6	6.6	11.8	3.0	5.3	5.6	8.7	63.4
Depression	3.4	1.5	1.0	1.9	0.3	1.4	1.7	1.5	12.8
Psychoses	—	0.8	0.3	0.2	0.4	—	0.3	0.9	3.0
Other mental disorders	1.7	2.7	—	0.9	0.7	0.2	—	1.6	7.8
FEMALES									
Nerves, tension, emotional problems	6.4	12.1	4.0	4.9	26.0	15.5	2.7	10.5	82.0
Depression	0.6	2.8	0.8	0.8	5.7	4.2	0.8	3.2	18.9
Psychoses	0.2	0.7	—	—	—	0.3	—	—	1.3
Other mental disorders	0.7	0.3	0.1	—	2.6	1.3	—	—	5.0

Source: Australian Bureau of Statistics 1992, *1989–90 National Health Survey: Health Status Indicators, Australia*, ABS, Canberra, Cat. no. 4370.0, table 14.

have rates of mental illness higher than those of their male counterparts. Sex differences in the rates of mental illness are related to social roles, specifically their sex and marital roles, rather than to women's biological susceptibility to mental illness (Gove 1972, p. 34; 1978, p. 187).

Comparisons between men and women on the subject of mental illness are problematic because of the cultural differences between men and women which affect their recognition of and willingness to admit to psychological problems and symptoms (Phillips & Segal 1969, p. 59; Mechanic 1978, pp. 187–8). Secondly, many explanations fail to disaggregate the category of mental illness and thereby ignore the differences between the types of disorders men and women experience. Some epidemiological surveys indicate that while lifetime and recent incidence rates for overall mental disorder are similar for men and women, depressive and some anxiety disorders are more frequent among women while anti-social personality and alcohol and drug abuse/dependence are more common among men (Aneshensel, Rutter & Lachenbruch 1991, pp. 171–2). Thirdly, specific types of mental illness are not, in practice, independent of gender as they relate to perceptions of 'normal' male and female behaviour (Busfield 1988, p. 534). If women are expected to act in feminine ways, that is, dependent, less ambitious, expressive and considerate, then women who show more independence and ambition may be considered disturbed. Conversely, men who do not conform to male gender norms by displaying emotionality, a symbol of weakness and incapacity, are likely to be identified as unstable or mentally ill.

The hospital

With the advancement of medical technology and increasing medical specialisation the hospital is the site, in contemporary societies, where unusual but routine cases are treated. Hospitals can be defined as institutions where patients or injured persons receive medical or surgical care. This excludes nursing homes, homes for the elderly, sanitaria, and other domiciliary institutions that may provide nominal health care but not regular medical attention (Freidson 1988, p. 111). The usual functions of hospitals are treatment of the sick, professional training and research. The division of labour in the hospital is complex and its organisation bureaucratic resulting in two types of authority—professional and administrative, or collegial and bureaucratic—which may conflict (Coe 1978, p. 297).

In contrast to the view that bureaucratic and professional principles of organisation are antithetical, Bucher and Stelling argue that organisations employing professionals are distinctive as bureaucratic authority does not feature among professionals (1969, p. 12). Instead, power affects the extent to which individuals and groups can control their working conditions and access to resources and patients. This involves role-creation and negotiation; internal differentiation within professions; competition and conflict for resources; integration through a political process involving democratic decision-making; and shifting power as professional employees move through the organisation or as new issues arise. Certainly, within the hospital, physicians have considerable power based on their expertise, either actual or assumed. Authority relations based on expertise make most hospitals predominantly collegiate organisations, that is, their organising principle relies mainly on consensus among various formally equal professions, each possessing specialised knowledge (Waters 1989a, pp. 955–6). Even though expertise and power are intimately linked in the hospital context, physicians usually exercise the most power even though their knowledge base may not be superior to or very different from that of other professionals, for example nurses, in the hospital. Competition between various professions—medicine, nursing, radiography, social work, pharmacy—means that the hospital is a 'negotiated order' where everyday activities and procedures depend on continuous compromise between professionals, administrators and patients (Abbott 1988, chapter 6; Strauss et al. 1963, pp. 154–6). While any social setting is a negotiated order, the fact that most hospitals employ a wide range of professionals means that various groups with distinctive claims to expertise constantly vie for resources and patients. This is not to deny that some professions will more often be 'losers' than will others, and inevitably accede to physicians' dominance. Factors affecting a medical specialty's success at dominating ancillary workers include its cognitive legitimacy, the relevance of its techniques to the general profession, sources of payment for services, the organisation of its work and the character of the settings where work takes place (Halpern 1992, p. 1015).

Many authors from widely different theoretical perspectives argue that the hospital represents the centralisation of medical power and is a dominant location of social control in contemporary society (Foucault 1975, pp. 82–5; Freidson 1988, p. 110). Like the Church in the Middle Ages, the hospital is the centre of all the major questions of birth, life and death. Freidson writes:

> The hospital is becoming such an archetypal institution largely through a process whereby human behaviour is being reinterpreted. Disapproved behaviour is more and more coming to be given the meaning of illness, requiring treatment rather than of crime requiring punishment, victimisation requiring compensation, or sin requiring patience and grace (1988, p. 248).

This view relates to the earlier discussion of medicalisation, whereby the medical profession, and the hospital in particular, increasingly become the sites for resolving events defined as illness. One example is the rapid increase in medical control of childbirth in the first half of the twentieth century. Not only did birthing move from midwives to physicians but also from home to the hospital which significantly changed the nature of the child birth experience (Sullivan & Weitz 1988, pp. 23–8; Rothman 1983, pp. 263–9).

As complex organisations hospitals manifest informal as well as formal social structure (Blau & Scott 1962, pp. 6–7). Ethnographies undertaken in hospitals demonstrate the presence of a distinct social world created by patients, complex inter-relationships between patients and staff, with the health outcomes of hospitalisation often depending on these relations (Zussman 1993, p. 168). Informal obligations and expectations relate to patient roles which differ depending on the condition or illness type. For example, medical personnel refer to 'terminal patients', 'maternity patients', 'pediatric patients' and 'psychiatric patients'. Each of these patients will have a different relationship with the medical practitioner which also will be affected by whether the hospital is a public or private institution. However, a number of key differences exist between patients in general hospitals and those in mental hospitals, or nursing homes, for example.

Numerous studies examine the effect of informal organisation within the mental hospital on patients' situation (Goffman 1961; Perucci & Targ 1982, pp. 129–40; Stanton & Schwartz 1954, pp. 244–94). The classic study is Goffman's examination of the effect of hospitalisation on the career and identity of a mental patient. Goffman describes the mental hospital, like prisons, monasteries, and schools, as a total institution where the distinctions between sleep, leisure and work disappear. Daily activities are highly routinised and all aspects of life occur in one place separated from the outside world (1961, p. 17). A constant conflict prevails between humane standards and institutional efficiency, with the latter affecting the forms of treatment. The interpretive scheme of the total institution—the medical frame of reference—operates as soon as the patient enters, the staff perceiving entry as prima facie evidence that one must be the kind of person with whom the institution deals. The medical frame of reference legitimates any decision, including meal times, the residents' daily activities, and the mode of their performance. Although the tasks derive from the hospital's working needs the claim presented to the patient is that these tasks will assist reintegration into the community (1961, pp. 81–6). Goffman suggests that: 'the craziness or "sick behaviour" claimed for the mental patient is by and large a product of the claimant's social distance from the situation that the patient is in, and is not primarily a product of mental illness' (1961, p. 121). Goffman describes the moral career of the mental patient as consisting of the period prior to hospitalisation or the pre-patient phase, the inpatient phase during which the self is transformed in terms of the dominant therapeutic model, and the ex-patient phase. Inpatients actively construct a social existence for themselves which entails improvisation to substitute for aspects of their pre-hospital lives and subtly resisting, sabotaging and co-opting medical authority and the hospital regime. However, the number of days spent in psychiatric institutions has been declining over the past two decades and many of the large state-run facilities are being closed down, thus inhibiting the emergence of this hospital underlife which Goffman elaborates.

A different situation pertains in the general hospital as most patients are resident for only a short period of time, therefore peer networks and sub-cultures cannot develop. Social control, from the doctor's viewpoint, is less problematic, especially as many patients will be immobile. The special unit, in particular the intensive care unit—a characteristic of the contemporary hospital—fragments the ward experience by transferring longer-term patients who potentially play a critical role in the construction of patient culture (Zussman 1993, p. 172). Social control in the general hospital is further enhanced by the fact that most patients accept the norm of compliance largely because they agree with the medical view of their illness (Lorber 1975, p. 223). In contrast, mental hospital patients might be less likely to accept medical definitions of their condition, especially if their admission is not voluntary. Finally, social control or compliance will be increased as a result of patients' greater input into medical decision-making due to legal requirements regarding informed consent.

The next section examines the process of deinstitutionalisation which, as in the criminal justice and welfare systems, is occurring within the health and illness sector.

Deinstitutionalisation and community health care

Criticism of the hospital's, especially the mental hospital's, routinisation and dehumanising nature, combined with economic arguments, has stimulated a policy of deinstitutionalisation, or decarceration, of certain patients. The home-birth movement, for example, reflects a growing recognition of childbirth as a natural non-pathological event, an attempt to demedicalise its definition and to move the process out of the hospital where the physicians retain control. The self-help movement, health promotion campaigns, alternative therapies, the community health movement and women's health centres all emphasise less dependence on institutionalised medicine. Community health centres were established during the 1970s and seek to develop consumer participation in the planning, management and delivery of health services within communities (Bates & Linder-Pelz 1990, pp. 173–4).

Psychiatric patients also are being transferred to the community. From the mid-1950s in England, the USA and, more recently, Australia, following a period of continuous increase, the number of patients resident in psychiatric hospitals declined every year reflecting a policy which has gathered momentum over the past two decades of 'treating' the mentally disordered in the community (Scull 1977a, p. 67). Despite these decreases, overall admission rates increased, suggesting that residents spend less time in hospitals but may be readmitted several times, indicating a revolving-door phenomenon. In 1981, 13 per cent of all in-patients were in psychiatric hospitals or institutions which declined to 8.5 per cent in 1986. This decline occurred in every Australian state and the ACT (see table 6.6).

The development and marketing of psychotropic drugs during the 1950s apparently constituted a major impetus for deinstitutionalisation. However, the extent of their contribution to declining mental hospital populations is not entirely clear (Scull 1977a, pp. 83–4). Nevertheless, a dominant argument for decarceration is that community treatment is more humane and beneficial to reintegration than isolation in a total institution. The 1983 *Inquiry into Health Services for the Psychiatrically Ill and Developmentally Disabled* in New South Wales recommends that community-based care and rehabilitation of the mentally ill should be the government's highest priority and that a proportion of welfare housing should be set aside as hostel and group home accommodation for the mentally ill (Cousens & Crawford 1988, p. 196).

Deinstitutionalisation policies have resulted in such unintended consequences as an increase in homelessness and difficulties for the police, who are neither equipped nor trained to deal with the mentally ill. One major problem is that deinstitutionalisation programs assume (often erroneously) that family members exist who are prepared and have adequate resources to care for the mentally ill. Additionally, these programs do not take into account community acceptance. A New South Wales study shows that simple contact with neighbourhood residents cannot be relied on to produce subsequent acceptance or integration. Such attitude-changing measures as public education programs need to accompany community mental health facilities (Cousens & Crawford 1988, p. 205). Community mental health centres often discriminate against ex-mental hospital patients, refusing to treat them and seek out patients with milder and more treatable disorders, thus increasing their 'success' rates (Scull 1986, p. 388). Instead of representing an alternative to traditional psychiatric treatment, community mental health centres and programs retain the medical model by focusing on the individual, but widen the net to include alcoholism, drug addiction, children's school and behaviour problems, pre-delinquency, bad marriages, job losses and ageing, in addition to traditional mental illness. By defining more people in the jurisdiction of psychiatry and providing treatment for such people, psychiatry extends its social control functions.

A stronger criticism of the community mental health movement is inadequate funding, especially in the area of housing and care which, many argue, increases the problem of homelessness (Bassuk & Gerson 1978, pp. 48–9; Wright 1988, p. 187). A study of a shelter for the homeless in Boston shows a 90 per cent incidence of diagnosable mental illness (Bassuk 1984, p. 30). The definition of mental illness used is very broad including psychoses, personality disorders and chronic alcoholism. In contrast, a study of 164 homeless people living in or passing through Austin (Texas) finds that only 16 per cent had some contact with the mental health system and only 10 per cent had ever been institutionalised. Moreover, most of the contacts were for substance (especially alcohol) abuse rather than for psychiatric disorders *per se* (Snow et al. 1986, p. 407). Thus, the relationship between deinstitutionalisation and homelessness is unclear, in part due to the dearth of empirical studies and the fact that homeless people might be more susceptible to being labelled mentally ill than other people.

Table 6.6   In-patients of health institutions by type of institution, states and territories, 30 June 1986 and 1981 (%)

Type of Institution	NSW	VIC	QLD	SA	WA	TAS	NT	ACT	AUST
1986									
Hospitals[1]	37.9	40.4	36.6	35.8	38.1	35.3	73.2	63.8	38.4
Psychiatric hospitals or institutions	7.8	11.4	7.1	6.3	8.1	13.5	—	5.4	8.5
Nursing homes	48.7	44.8	51.5	49.6	49.5	47.3	24.4	28.4	48.1
Other health institutions[2]	5.6	3.4	4.8	8.4	4.3	3.9	2.4	2.3	5.0
TOTAL N	59 480	41 530	27 000	18 000	16 750	5400	760	1420	171 140
1981									
Hospitals[1]	41.6	44.6	41.9	41.9	47.9	37.7	78.2	65.6	43.2
Psychiatric hospitals or institutions	10.7	16.7	11.7	17.0	10.9	17.7	—	8.1	13.1
Nursing homes	45.9	35.9	45.2	39.5	47.9	42.4	21.8	24.5	41.7
Other health institutions[3]	1.8	2.8	1.1	1.6	2.1	2.1	—	1.8	2.0
TOTAL N	60 610	39 950	26 110	15 710	13 120	5240	720	1290	162 750

1 includes public and private hospitals.
2 hostels for the disabled.
3 includes institutions for the physically handicapped and other health institutions.

Source: Australian Bureau of Statistics 1989, *Characteristics of In-patients of Health Institutions, Australia*, AGPS, Canberra, Cat. no. 4347.0, tables 1 and 2.

Summary

This chapter demonstrates the contingent nature of conceptions of disease and illness. Rather than being a clear physiological phenomenon, illness designation requires the identification and interpretation of symptoms which rely on social norms and values regarding the healthy person. Being sick and being a patient involve specific role expectations and obligations which structure behaviour, which is thereby not determined wholly by physiological conditions. Access to the sick and patient roles is also structured according to perceptions of individual responsibility for the illness conditions. The more individuals are held responsible for their illness, the more societal reaction becomes overtly punitive rather than primarily treatment-oriented.

The following chapter deals with the topic of women and deviance, both as victims and perpetrators of deviant activities.

Notes

1 Assize courts were the former periodical sessions of the superior courts in English counties which heard criminal and civil matters.

2 Gove and Tudor (1972, p. 812) treat mental illness as a specific phenomenon; a disorder involving such personal discomfort as distress, anxiety, and/or mental disorganisation indicated by confusion, and at worst delusions and hallucinations. It is not caused by an organic or toxic condition. The two diagnostic categories which fit this definition are neurotic disorders and functional psychoses. Dohrenwend and Dohrenwend (1976, p. 1448) criticise this 'highly idiosyncratic definition' where disparate types of diagnosed psychiatric disorder, psychoses and neuroses, are included together, and reject Gove and Tudor's reliance on treatment statistics.

Key terms

Sick role	Medicalisation
National Health Survey	Social constructionism
Insanity defence	Mental illness
Expert evidence	The hospital
The asylum	Total institution
Bureaucratic	Deinstitutionalisation
Community health movement	Professional

Main points

1 Parsons' formulation of the sick role has four central elements: exemption from performing usual social roles; the sick person is not held responsible

for the condition; its legitimacy depends upon seeking medical assistance; and the sick person may acquire an additional role, that of the patient.

2 Rather than being value-neutral and scientific, medical knowledge and the designation of physiological conditions as illness reflect social values and interpretations regarding deviance and conformity.

3 The social aspects of illness definition are most clearly evident in the emergence of mental illness. Despite an inability to identify unambiguous causes and specify treatment, the medical profession retains control over defining, identifying and managing mental illness.

4 Becoming mentally ill involves a process of labelling and the associated stigma is almost impossible to remove.

5 As in the criminal justice system, recent developments emphasise a movement away from treatment in psychiatric hospitals to community-based facilities. Many speculate that the deinstitutionalisation process has increased the numbers of homeless people.

6 Epidemiological studies indicate that health and illness are distributed unequally among different occupational, gender, class and ethnic groups. In part, this pattern stems from the fact that different groups are exposed to environmental or occupational hazards and lack access to sufficient medical care.

Further reading

Aubert, Vilhelm & Sheldon L. Messinger 1958, 'The Criminal and the Sick', *Inquiry*, vol. 1, pp. 137–60.

Bates, Erica & Susie Linder-Pelz 1990, *Health Care Issues*, 2nd edn, Allen & Unwin, Sydney.

Freidson, Eliot 1988, *Profession of Medicine: A Study of the Sociology of Applied Knowledge*, University of Chicago Press, Chicago.

Scheff, Thomas 1966, *Being Mentally Ill: A Sociological Theory*, Aldine Publishing, Chicago.

Turner, Bryan S. 1987, *Medical Power and Social Knowledge*, London, Sage.

Willis, Evan 1989, *Medical Dominance: The Division of Labour in Australian Health Care*, Allen & Unwin, Sydney.

Wright, Peter & Andrew Treacher eds 1982, *The Problem of Medical Knowledge: Examining the Social Construction of Medicine*, Edinburgh University Press, Edinburgh.

CHAPTER

7

Women and criminal deviance

In the past twenty years or so, there has been an upsurge of interest in the topics of women and deviance, in particular women and crime, both as victims of criminal law violations and as perpetrators. New and expanded laws in the areas of rape, sexual harassment, equal employment opportunity, sex discrimination, and domestic violence, for example, indicate greater criminalisation of, or prohibitions on, certain kinds of behaviour. Previously, some individuals may have identified actions as unacceptable and deviant, but they remained private issues. Now domestic violence, harassment in the workplace and rape have become public concerns. Where new laws exist widespread debate focuses on the extent to which they are enforced. Despite explicit and unambiguous legislation the police and the courts, indeed segments of the population, may not agree that such proscribed behaviour as rape, domestic violence or sexual harassment, is really criminal, or deviant.

Considerable discussion and research also exists on the involvement of women in criminal activities and their treatment by the criminal justice system. Until recently, these were relatively unresearched issues. It is well established that women and girl's participation in criminal deviance is much lower than that of men and boys. For example, in Australia in 1990–91 females (adult and juvenile) constituted only 8 per cent of all break, enter and steal offences and 9 per cent of serious assaults cleared by the police (Mukherjee & Dagger 1993, tables 5.1, 5.3; see also table 4.3 in chapter 4). Women's lesser participation in criminal deviance does not justify their exclusion from the criminological literature, nor does it mean that women are not deemed deviant. Women are subject to a wide range of informal norms relating to appearance, reproduction and maternity, and sexuality which are not applied as rigorously to men (Schur 1984, pp. 51–132).

This chapter first discusses crimes and deviance where mostly women are victims, specifically rape, domestic violence and sexual harassment. Second, women's involvement in crime and their treatment by the criminal justice system is investigated. While the focus of this chapter is women and criminal deviance, it is not exhaustive; chapter 3 discusses prostitution, pornography and abortion, chapter 6 deals with gender and medical definitions of deviance and chapter 9 analyses the welfare system and implications for the status and social control of women.

Rape

In recent years rape laws have undergone a number of changes, the legal definition of rape is more inclusive than previously. This means that more activities are now defined as crime, at least according to the legislation. In Anglo-Australian law (as well as in other common law systems, like Canada) the crime of rape traditionally was defined as 'the carnal knowledge of any woman above the age of ten years against her will, and of a woman-child under the age of ten years with or against her will' (Hale 1971, p. 628). In effect, the insertion by a man of his penis into the vagina of a woman without her consent, where he knew or believed she was not consenting but went ahead regardless, constituted the common law crime of rape (Law Reform Commission of Victoria 1986, pp. 6–7). This conception received much criticism because it reflects one view of violation whereas for the victim there are other kinds. Brownmiller asks: 'Who is to say that the sexual humiliation suffered through forced oral or rectal penetration is a lesser violation of the personal private inner space, a lesser injury to mind, spirit and sense of self?' (1975, p. 378). The traditional definition meant that only women could be raped and only men could rape. The common law did not recognise rape in marriage; a man could not rape his wife, the justification being that entry into marriage implied the wife's irrevocable consent to all acts of intercourse with her husband (Waller & Williams 1993, p. 85). In 1976, South Australia, followed by Victoria in 1981, amended the criminal law to make the crime of rape non-gender, non-orifice and non-instrument specific while New South Wales abolished the crime of rape replacing it with three categories of sexual assault based on the harm done to the victim. Some jurisdictions have removed spousal immunity for rape charges, however the few successful prosecutions for marital rape suggest that a 'spousal exception' clause still operates (Naffine 1992, p. 747; Stubbs & Wallace 1988, p. 55). Additionally, rules of evidence in relation to rape trials have been modified, in particular the defense counsel can no longer cross-examine the victim about her/his previous sexual relations in an attempt to demonstrate lack of credibility. Nevertheless, the court may allow such cross-examination if it is of sufficient relevance—a nebulous notion (Ligertwood 1993, pp. 140–1).

A consequence of extending the definition of rape is that differences in rape situations are ignored. Because most sexual offences are committed by men against women, to make the offence gender-neutral does not reflect social reality (Law Reform Commission of Victoria 1986, p. 20). In South Australia, around 90 per cent of rape victims who report to the police are female (Weekley 1986, p. 10). It is useful, therefore, to distinguish between types of rape which differ in terms of the perpetrator's motive, the type of coercion employed, or the relationship between the victim and the perpetrator. Box (1983, pp. 127–8) suggests five types of rape. At the most extreme is sadistic rape where sexuality and aggression underlie a series of violent, mutilating acts, followed by anger rape, domination rape, seduction-turned-into-rape, and exploitation rape, where a man takes advantage of a woman's vulnerability based on her economic, social or emotional dependence on him, as in the case of the marriage relationship.

Change in the definition of rape is an example of how social movements, here the women's movement, particularly the Women's Electoral Lobby in Australia, affect the construction of deviance (Rose 1977, p. 75; Scott 1993, pp. 347–51). In the 1960s and 1970s, various groups, but most particularly the women's movement, articulated two long-term goals: substantial revision of rape laws and changes to traditional attitudes about rape. Major achievements of the anti-rape movement include the development of rape crisis centres and shelters (or refuges), telephone 'hot-lines' providing information, reform of some police practices, and a proliferation of self-defence classes for women. Proponents of the anti-rape movement criticise the police, the courts and the medical profession (all of whom are predominantly men) for their insensitive treatment of rape victims (Mills 1982, p. 53). Many women who have been sexually assaulted experience the rape trial, even the pre-trial discussions and procedures, as traumatic and humiliating (Smart 1989, p. 34). MacKinnon unequivocally states: 'Women who charge rape say they were raped twice, the second time in court' (1983, p. 651). Despite legal change judges' comments often reinforce assumptions about rape and rape victims (Soothill, Walby & Bagguley 1990, pp. 218–27). Judges have suggested that the harm and trauma to the victim is lessened if she is sexually experienced, works as a prostitute, or is unconscious at the time of the attack. Of late, some comments have received widespread media attention and public discussion followed by suggestions to reform and re-educate the judiciary. Justice Bollen's comments in a rape-in-marriage case in South Australia sparked considerable controversy in 1992–93, especially his assertion that: 'There is, of course, nothing wrong with a husband, faced with his wife's initial refusal to engage in intercourse, in attempting, in an acceptable way, to persuade her to change her mind, and that may involve a measure of rougher than usual handling' (*R v. Johns* (26 August 1992) unreported). The implicit suggestion that a some rough 'handling' of women was usual and acceptable led to calls for the judge's sacking and an inquiry into gender bias and the judiciary (Senate Standing Committee on Legal and Constitutional Affairs 1994; Sullivan 1994, pp. 1–2).

Rape is a crime around which hang many myths and assumptions regarding the kind of person who rapes and the kind of person who gets raped. Most people consider rape as a sudden, violent attack by a stranger in a deserted public place, after which the victim is expected to pro-vide evidence of the attack and of her active resistance (Weis & Borges 1973, pp. 71–2). Another rape situation which receives widespread media attention is the gang rape, such as the brutal Anita Cobby rape–murder case in New South Wales in 1986. Indeed, three of the five men found guilty of her murder appealed to the High Court arguing that the media attention adversely affected the outcome of the jury's decision (*Murphy v. The Queen* (1989) 63 ALJR 422). These characteristics constitute the 'classic rape', or 'ideal type' (in Weberian terms) against which all other incidents are measured. Police are most likely to make an arrest for sexual assault when the victim is able to identify a suspect, the victim is willing to testify, the incident included sexual penetration, and involved a weapon (La Free 1981, p. 582). Yet the 'classic rape' is atypical. A South Australian study of reported rapes during 1980 and 1984 shows that 58 per cent of the victims were acquainted with the perpetrator, while 40 per cent were strangers. These statistics are likely to be conservative as a victim will be less likely to report a rape when he or she knows or is related to the perpetrator. Victims were more likely to be raped in their own or the offender's home than in a public place, and usually the only coercion is verbal or 'roughness', not physical violence (Weekley 1986, pp. 11, 16–18, 19–21).

Rape is also a crime where victims sometimes are perceived or blamed for causing the crime, especially in circumstances differing from the 'classic rape'. In the culture of contemporary societies, much ambiguity surrounds sexual relations. In heterosexual relations men are expected to initiate relations but women are held responsible for the outcome, even if it is rape (Weis & Borges 1973, p. 85). Such women as prostitutes, hitchhikers, the sexually experienced or divorced women, are deemed ineligible or not credible rape victims (Box 1983, p. 122; Nelson & Amir 1975, p. 49; Schur 1984, pp. 152–3). Clark and Lewis suggest that women 'who voluntarily give up that which makes them desirable as objects of an exclusive sexual relationship are seen as "common property", to be appropriated without penalty for the use, however temporary, of any man who desires their services' (1977, p. 121). However, a married women may be rejected as an acceptable rape victim, if the perpetrator is her husband.

A comparison of legal discourse and media portrayals of rape during the Mike Tyson and William Kennedy Smith trials in 1992 demonstrates the representation of rape as something only certain 'types' of men do to certain 'types' of women (Freeman 1993, p. 527). Tyson was described as aggressive, unintelligent, brutal and rapacious, thus echoing long-held stereotypes about black men, whereas the victim—Desiree Washington—was portrayed as innocent, sexually inexperienced, naive and trusting, indeed the epitome of an 'all-American *girl*', thus enabling her to overcome the stereotype of black women as always sexual and consenting. She was portrayed as 'rapable' and credible, unlike the accuser in the Kennedy Smith trial whose single-motherhood status (evidence of sexual experience), age, extroverted social behaviour and presence in a bar late at night made her appear promiscuous, unreliable, desperate and a 'social-climber'. Moreover, Smith's family background, education, social class and race quash conclusions that he is the kind of man who rapes. Freeman concludes that: 'white women are prima facie rapable if they are either very young or of a higher class than the defendant; white women who are sexual (that is, anything other than very young or another man's property) are unrapable. Black women are prima facie unrapable (presumed to be sexually available) unless they are either childlike or of a higher class *and* are relatively assimilated within white culture' (1993, p. 533, emphasis in original).

One question of widespread sociological interest is why rape victims do not report the crime. Sociologists and psychologists have been concerned by what motivates or causes individuals to rape and legal theorists have been at pains to define what is rape, especially how to determine whether the victim consented and what kinds of evidence are appropriate.

Reporting rape

Rape is one of the least likely crimes to be reported to the police, and few reports lead to successful prosecutions and a conviction. Only 25 per cent of all sexual assault (including rape, attempted rape, indecent assault, assault with the intent to sexually assault) victims in Australia inform the police, and this rate of reporting has not changed over the past decade (Australian Bureau of Statistics 1994a, pp. 9, 12). Data for Canada and the USA indicate that between 25 and 50 per cent of actual and attempted rapes get reported (Williams 1984, p. 459). Rape is so underreported because:

1 the victim may fear retaliation from the perpetrator, especially if he/she is a family member, employer or acquaintance of the victim;
2 the victim may wish to avoid the trauma or stigma attached to a prosecution;
3 many victims blame themselves for being raped, or fear they will be blamed or not believed by family and friends, the police and the courts;
4 a successful prosecution will be difficult.

The main reason victims of sexual assaults give for not reporting is a perception that the incident is a private matter. One in five victims who did not inform the police indicate that they did not for fear of reprisal and revenge and 15 per cent failed to inform police because they feel that the police could not or would not do any thing about it (Australian Bureau of

Statistics 1994a, p. 12). Moreover, conviction rates for sexual offences are generally low. In the South Australian Supreme and District courts one-third of those charged for a sexual offence pleaded guilty, 11 per cent were found guilty and 13 per cent were acquitted in 1992. For all offences, 58 per cent of those charged pleaded guilty, 9 per cent were found guilty and 7 per cent were acquitted (Office of Crime Statistics 1993, tables 4.1, 4.3). Various aspects of the court procedure make prosecution difficult, although that is changing. Until recently, the victim in a rape case could be questioned about her sexual history and court rules required the trial judge to warn the jury of convicting the accused unless the victim's evidence was corroborated, for example by a witness (Law Reform Commission of Victoria 1988, p. 39). Gagnon's (1974, p. 261) discussion of the status degradation involved in sexual victimisation applies to the 'reliving' of the rape experience suffered by victims as their complaints are processed through the criminal justice system. Indeed, recognition of the victim's status degradation throughout the criminal justice process suggests that disincentives outweigh the temptation of making a false accusation (Le Grand 1973, p. 935; Law Reform Commission of Victoria 1988, p. 40). In South Australia from 1980 to 1984 less than 2 per cent of the 1096 rape reports to the police were unfounded (Weekley 1986, p. 44).

Before a report of rape can occur a victim must identify herself or himself as a victim of a crime and be confident that others will do so. A study of 246 female rape victims who had contacted a rape crisis centre (146 also reported to the police) finds that victims whose homes were broken into or who were attacked in their cars were most likely to report, followed by those who were attacked in public or abducted from a public place. Women raped in a social situation, such as on a date, were least likely to report and those raped by strangers or acquaintances reported more often than those raped by friends or relatives (Williams 1984, pp. 464–5). In other words, the closer the actual rape situation conforms to the 'classic rape' the more likely the victim is to report to the police. This supports Black's discussion of social distance (see chapter 4) as the central factor in determining whether a victim will do anything about a crime. As the social distance increases, the likelihood of reporting increases.

Causes of rape

Psychiatric approaches to rape focus on the perpetrator and tend to view rape as an individualistic, idiosyncratic symptom of a disordered personality. The notion of the 'irresistible impulse' (Glueck 1925, p. 323) suggests innate drives which have not been properly controlled through socialisation. Courts may attribute the cause of male sexual deviation to females who they perceive as initiating uncontrollable male emotions, passions, and unexplainable urges (Reiss 1960, p. 316). Ironically, some feminist writers seeking social, historical and cultural explanations of the prevalence of rape end up providing a biologically determinist account (Eisenstein 1984, pp. 27–34). Brownmiller (1975, pp. 16–30), for example, suggests that the meaning of rape is connected to the concept of women as property and from the Babylonian and Hebrew legal codes into the English common law tradition punishment for rape was an action brought by one man against another for damage to his property. It was a form of compensation for the loss incurred through the rape of a daughter or a wife, whose value either for exchange in marriage or as a possession, had been reduced or destroyed. Even though Brownmiller's account encompasses historical, social and cultural factors, the presence of rape is a constant and the ideology of rape plays a critical role in the social control of women. She says: 'rape is nothing more or less than a conscious process of intimidation by which *all* men keep *all* women in a state of fear' (1975, p. 15, emphasis in original). Like other violent crimes, when combined with widespread media sensationalism, rape instils fear in certain segments of the community and thereby operates as a form of social control. However, Brownmiller's claim that rape is a universal fact of human society enabling men to control women is ahistorical and collapses into a biologically determinist argument.

Other explanations focus on the contribution and therefore the responsibility of the victim. Amir's (1967, p. 496; 1971, pp. 259–78) study of police records concludes that around one in five rapes are victim-precipitated, that is, situations in which the victim actually (or so it was deemed) agreed to sexual relations but retracted before the actual act or did not react strongly enough when the suggestion was made by the perpetrator. Subsequent research on victim-precipitation indicates that female hitch-hikers accounted for 20 per cent of the total reported rapes in Berkeley (California) for the years 1968–70 (Nelson & Amir 1975, p. 51). This approach shifts blame from the offender to the victim and diminishes the importance of a range of other factors such as cultural ideals of masculinity, the structural subordination of women, and the low reporting and prosecution rates. As Box expounds: 'no bank robber has ever been found not guilty, or even pleaded in mitigation, that it was the bank's fault for not protecting itself better!' (1983, p. 134).

Sociological explanations focus on social learning theory and masculine sex-role socialisation, which designate men as the initiators and women as passive, as a cultural precondition of rape. The idealisation of femininity involves notions of dependence, submissiveness and mindlessness; women are taught to need men emotionally and depend on them economically. Rape behaviour is learned, rapists learn the attitudes and actions consistent with sexual aggression against women. Some men rape because they learn that sexual violence has rewards, not because they are irrational or 'sick' (Scully 1988, p. 201). As with other forms of deviance ranging from juvenile delinquency to white-collar crime, this learning process involves acquiring techniques of neutralisation. Scully and Marolla (1984, pp. 533–41) describe some convicted rapists' denials that what they did was rape through such justifications as women are 'seductresses'; when they say 'no' they really mean 'yes'; most women enjoy rape; and nice girls don't get raped. Alternatively, others admit the crime but attempt to excuse it or themselves by recourse to factors 'outside their control', like drug and alcohol use, or emotional problems. Convicted rapists who defined their behaviour as rape took satisfaction during the incident in the belief that their victim felt powerless, humiliated and degraded, however most expressed regret and sorrow for their victim subsequently. Men who denied that the sexual encounter was rape were either unaware of the victim's experience or assumed that she enjoyed it. For both admitters and deniers, victims had no importance outside of the roles they were forced to play during the rape, as a consequence the convicted rapists experienced no guilt, empathy or shame during the sexually violent behaviour (Scully 1988, pp. 210–1).

These rationalisations represent cultural values, internalised not only by perpetrators of rape. Indeed, some have suggested the concept of a 'rape culture' based on society's dominant patterns of socialisation and approved patterns of sexual interaction where male sexual aggression is seen as normal (Herman 1979, p. 43). In a sense, then, socialisation prepares women to be rape victims (Box 1983, p. 148). However, cultural explanations are insufficient. The notion of cultural determinism assumes that all individuals are passive recipients of dominant cultural norms, thus men are as much victims of cultural definitions as are women. This view cannot explain why some men do not commit rape when they participate in the same culture as those who do commit rape. Such other factors as economic inequalities need to be taken into account. It seems that rape is most likely to occur where women are economically dependent on men both in the home and in the workplace.

Consent

Consent, the lack of which is an essential element of the offence, is one of the most contentious issues in contemporary rape law reform discussions. The presence or absence of consent may be difficult to prove, especially where there is no visible evidence of physical injury or where the alleged offender argues that there was consent. The offender's belief (it only has to be honest, not reasonable) that the victim consented is one of the most common defences to a rape accusation (*Director of Public Prosecutions v. Morgan* (1976) AC 182 at 183; Law Reform Commission of Victoria 1986, pp. 9–12). Where a stranger leaps out from behind a bush in the middle of the night armed with a knife and sexually attacks another person it is easy to conclude that there was no consent. Even in this situation the victim may not be seen as totally blameless; walking alone at night may be considered inviting sexual attack. In 1986, in Central Park, New York, a woman jogging late at night was raped and newspaper reports asked 'what was she doing there anyway?'.

Much discussion about consent reflects a concern about false complainants and the conviction of an innocent person (Le Grand 1973, p. 931; Law Reform Commission of Victoria 1988, p. 39). The seventeenth-century English jurist, Sir Matthew Hale, warns: 'It is true rape is a most detestable crime, and therefore ought severely and impartially to be punished with death; but it must be remembered, that it is an accusation easily to be made and hard to be proved, and harder to be defended by the party accused, tho' never so innocent' (1971, p. 635). This influential statement suggests that women who make rape accusations are more likely to lie, be untrustworthy and lack credibility as compared with other witnesses (Mack 1993, pp. 329–35). Traditionally, judges automatically warned juries of the dangers of convicting a man on a rape charge where the complainant is the sole witness and where there is no corroboration of her evidence. This corroboration rule regarding women alleging rape conflicted with the usual common law rule that the jury was entitled to reach a guilty verdict on the unsupported testimony of one witness. Legislative reform in most jurisdictions abolishes any requirement to warn the jury that it is unsafe to convict a defendant on the uncorroborated evidence of the victim/witness (Ligertwood 1993, p. 168). Nevertheless, courts still allow corroboration warnings as part of judicial discretion to comment on evidence or to avoid a 'miscarriage of justice' (*Longman v. R* (1989) 168 CLR 79 at 86, 91). For example, in the South Australian Supreme Court, Justice Bollen, when directing the jury, stated:

> I must warn you to be especially careful in a case where sexual allegations are made. Experience has taught the judges that there have been cases where women have manufactured or invented false allegations of rape and sexual attack. It is a very easy allegation to make. It is often very hard to contradict (*R v. Johns* (26 August 1992) unreported).

However, it would not seem that rape is especially prone to false complainants, nor that a jury is any less capable of deciphering false accusations in rape trials than in any other (Wells 1985, p. 67).

Domestic violence

Crime data show that 'assault against the person' is a significant offence category, however, as with most crime statistics, recorded assaults only represent part of the picture. Most of the assaults becoming known to the police are 'public' incidents such as street brawls and muggings. What is excluded is domestic violence which often remains unreported to the police, or in which, when reported, police frequently fail to intervene, or charges are dropped. Much recent attention focuses on battered women or battered wives, but the term domestic violence is more inclusive and enables discussion of a range of abusive practices between spouses (both putative and legal) and abuse of and by children (Denzin 1984, p. 484). Two dominant social science perspectives on wife abuse have emerged. The family violence approach focuses on spouse abuse as part of a general pattern of violence occurring among all family members which has its origin in wider social norms and in the structure of the contemporary family. In contrast, the feminist approach emphasises gender inequality as the cause of violence which is one of a variety of controls men can exercise over women. Moreover, such dominant social institutions as the criminal justice system historically have condoned such violence as legitimate and private, and these ideas still persist (Kurz 1989, pp. 490–7).

Domestic violence, it is claimed, is one of the most common forms of assault. However, it is difficult to quantify as domestic violence, as such, is not a criminal offence. Nevertheless, in South Australia, 18 per cent of the 7492 violent crimes women reported to police could be classified as domestic violence. Crime survey data show that separated or divorced women were more likely than married or defacto women to have been assaulted by their ex-partner (Gardner 1994). Of all reported homicides in New South Wales from 1968–81, 42.5 per cent occurred within the family. Spouse killings accounted for almost one in four of all the killings, the majority of these (73 per cent) being committed by men (Stubbs & Wallace 1988, pp. 52–4). Wives are far more frequently the victims of spousal assaults than are husbands. National crime data based on police reports show that in 1993 for 64 per cent of sexual assault victims (N=12 390) and 36 per cent of homicide victims (N=39) the incident occurred in a residential location (Australian Bureau of Statistics 1994b, p. 16, table 11, p. 18, table 12). United States data on homicide patterns between 1976 and 1987 reveal that the homicide rate for married couples declined, but the decline was greater in the rate of wives killing husbands. The rate of unmarried women being killed by their male partners increased, while no pattern was discernible in the rate of unmarried women killing their male partners (Browne & Williams 1993, p. 78). Rather than being 'a haven in a heartless world' (Lasch 1977), the high incidence of domestic violence suggests that potentially the family is a very dangerous place.

The discussion of domestic violence parallels that of rape. Wife battering, particularly physical violence, and rape are very closely linked (Frieze 1983, p. 552). Violence against women and children in the family has a long history. Husbands have physically coerced their wives to perform activities they may have been unwilling or unable to undertake, to punish them for failing to meet marital demands and expectations, or simply as a prerogative of the husband's authority. Men have used violence in their attempts to maintain control over female family members far more than over the male members, to retain personal authority, and to gain personal service and domestic labour (Dobash & Dobash 1981, pp. 564–5).

In the Middle Ages, a man who beat his wife, children and servants was not usually subjected to community censure. Such violence was widely practised and legally acceptable, as long as the birch was no thicker than his thumb. Hence the term 'rule of thumb'. In the nineteenth century, the husband's legal right of chastisement began to erode and women were given some legal forms of redress, for example, cruelty became a ground for divorce, and punishment, including imprisonment, could be applied to aggravated assaults on women and children (Allen 1986, p. 123). However, not until the 1970s did wife battering become a social problem or a public issue. The emergence of wife beating as a social problem does not necessarily indicate any change in the actual incidence of violence, but resulted, in part, from social movements which mobilised resources to aid battered women (Breines & Gordon 1983, p. 491; Tierney 1982, p. 207). The first widely-publicised shelter for battered women was set up in London in 1971, followed by a very influential book *Scream Quietly or the Neighbours Will Hear* in 1974 written by Erin Pizzey, one of the founders. Many shelters for battered women seek to operate with a counter-bureaucratic organisational structure by having nonprofessional and volunteer staffs, adopting consensus decision making, and maximising residents' participation in administration (Rodriguez 1988, pp. 216–24). In Australia, state government initiatives in the form of task forces and reports to gather information, investigate police powers and assess the appropriateness of legislative change, a national conference on domestic violence sponsored by the Australian Institute of Criminology in 1985, and the establishment of the National Committee on Violence in 1988 have put violence in the home on the political agenda.

Domestic violence was the most common subject of submissions organisations made to the National Committee on Violence and they emphasised its private nature, that it is under-reported, that it occurs in all socio-economic groups and that there remains a high level of community acceptance of at least some forms of domestic violence (National Committee on Violence 1990, p. 34). The Committee reports that due to a failure to instil non-violent values in children families are the training grounds for aggression in general, not just against family members. It concludes that abusive parents tend to have been abused or neglected as children, but only one in three to five of abused or neglected children will mistreat their own children (National Committee on Violence 1990, p. 61). The report indicates that most homicides and assaults are committed by persons known to the victim and that men, especially those young, single and unemployed are at far greater risk of all forms of violence than are women, with the exception of sexual assault and domestic violence. The committee suggests that victims of violence tend to form two broad categories: men involved in altercations with other men; and women and children who experience violence from men with whom they live (National Committee on Violence 1990, p. 4). It points out that Aboriginal people have a much greater risk, possibly up to ten times, of being the victim of violence than the general Australian population. The issue of domestic violence within Aboriginal communities raises complex questions. Some victims and victim advocates maintain that reporting the incidents to the police further criminalises Aboriginal men and fragments the communities, while others point out that Aboriginal Legal Services are not an option because they are defendant, not victim, oriented (Neill 1994b, p. 1) .

Probably the most frequent question is: 'Why do battered women stay in abusive relationships?' (Ferraro & Johnson 1983, p. 325; Gelles 1976, p. 659). This question is based on the assumption that rational people would avoid physical pain and injury by leaving a situation where violence regularly occurs. A number of responses can be offered to the question. Most significant is economic dependence. Many women have little training and few job opportunities, and even if they could find jobs their standard of living, and that of their children, would decline considerably. Women, especially from an economically comfortable family, may opt for staying within the battering relationship rather than facing life reliant on the supporting parent benefit for income. Women who leave and receive social security benefits may be locked into a welfare cycle because of lack of access to the private housing market and child care (O'Donnell & Saville 1982, p. 61). An investigation of police and court records and in-depth interviews with battered women in Scotland shows that the principle factors determining the length of time women remain with spouses depend on their personal and material resources, and the responses of social institutions, in particular the availability of shelters (Dobash & Dobash 1979, pp. 220–1). Although the focus on external constraints to women's failure to leave acknowledges that staying is unreasonable, it relieves battered women of the responsibility of doing so; it makes them into passive victims (Loseke & Cahill 1984, p. 299).

Emotional or psychological dependence may explain why women remain in situations of domestic violence. The private sphere of the family is usually considered women's domain and many norms are applied to women as wives and mothers, the maintenance of emotional well-being and family relations are deemed women's responsibility. Consequently, many women's self-esteem and perceptions of success relate to being a good wife and mother, indicated by harmony in the family. When these perceptions are violated, women may blame themselves and feel they have failed to provide sufficient care and nurturance. The woman's degree of commitment to traditional ideology, perceptions that divorce is a stigma signalling failure as a wife and homemaker, and view that children need their father reduce the propensity to leave.

The perceived seriousness of the violence also needs to be considered in understanding why some women stay. The less severe and the less frequent the violence, the more a woman will remain with her partner and not seek outside aid. These perceptions may be affected by how much violence the woman experienced as a child. The more she was struck by her parents, the more she is not inclined to leave. Victimisation as a child raises the tolerance level of abuse (Gelles 1976, pp. 666–7). However, the longer the time period with the abuser may mediate the perceived severity by increasing tolerance levels. A sudden increase in the violence becomes an impetus to leave if women realise that the battering could be fatal. Moreover, women may balance the costs of the violent relationship with other positive aspects of the relationship, such as security or companionship.

A final important factor which mediates the violence, the economic and emotional dependencies and the failure to leave is the psychological adjustments which normalise the situation for the victim. Rationalising violence restores the status quo and battered women may not actively seek alternatives. Ferraro and Johnson (1983, pp. 328–31) identify six types of rationalisation which battered women employ:

1 *the appeal to the salvation ethic*: a common response to an alcohol- or drug-dependent abuser, the emphasis is on being of service and nurturing a 'sick' partner. Alcohol use is related to an increased probability of wife abuse (Kantor & Straus 1987, p. 224);
2 *the denial of the victimiser*: the violence is explained away by reference to some external event which is seen as atypical, such as loss of a job, or a crisis of some sort. Moreover, the socially acceptable 'time out' from normal rules which involves consuming alcohol permits men who reject the legitimacy of hitting their wives to disavow responsibility for their otherwise reprehensible behaviour (Kantor & Straus 1987, p. 225);
3 *the denial of injury*: the battered woman defines the injuries or pain as minimal or non-existent;
4 *the denial of victimisation*: victims often blame themselves for the violence thereby displacing their spouse's responsibility for the events. This is also often the view of professionals—police, lawyers, doctors—who perceive women as the cause of their own victimisation (Pagelow 1981, p. 20);
5 *the denial of options*: for various reasons some battered women do not take full advantage of the practical opportunities which are available, and some return to abusers voluntarily even after establishing an independent lifestyle;
6 *the appeal to higher loyalties*: commitment to children or belief in the sanctity of marriage may deter women from leaving an abusive relationship.

The discussion thus far has focused on women as victims and why they stay in abusive relationships. This focus, in a sense, reinforces the view of women as passive and subject and places them in the sick role suffering from the 'battered wife syndrome'. It also distinguishes them from other women, whom it is assumed stay in relationships where no abuse exists because they want to. This assumption is never explored. The portrayal as a victim becomes the person's major defining characteristic, the relationship becomes synonymous with violence, any other aspect of it is not investigated. By asking and answering 'why do they stay?' experts—academics, social workers, nurses, lawyers and women's groups—have constructed a new category of deviance: battered women who remain with their partners (Loseke & Cahill 1984, p. 297). In constructing their accounts, many experts automatically attribute to individual women sets of traits based on their sex. As females, battered women are assumed to be economically and emotionally dependent on their partners, to have low self esteem, and to hold traditional values and beliefs. This is partly a methodological problem as much of the research on battered women only includes women who have identified themselves as such and done something about it. Methodologies which might yield conflicting evidence are seldom used and when seemingly conflicting evidence is uncovered it is often explained away. For example, Walker implicitly argues that battered women have an inaccurate perception of themselves. She interprets the finding that battered women consider themselves to be in control of their own behaviour as a 'lack of acknowledgement that her batterer is really in control' (1983, p. 40). Many people remain in relationships that others may define inappropriate or as providing few benefits, thus battered women who remain in relationships which outsiders consider costly are not particularly unusual or deviant. The same factors—economic and emotional dependence, and feelings of guilt—may also may explain why other relationships where battering and abuse do not occur, are maintained.

Police and domestic violence

The role of the police in domestic violence incidents raises particular problems. Police practices represent the critical link to the prosecution process and to the provision of victim services in a community. Police are often reluctant to make arrests for domestic violence unless both disputants are present, victims demand an arrest and sign the arrest warrant, the victim alleges violence and male alcohol consumption, the neighbours complain, or the suspect contests or confronts police authority (Berk & Loseke 1981, pp. 341–2). Arrest is only one of the responses police might make. They may negotiate or 'talk out' the dispute, threaten the disputants by asking one of the parties to leave the premises, or make an arrest (Sherman & Berk 1984, p. 262). Arrest is a last resort and occurs only in the worst cases (McCulloch, Jude 1986, pp. 524–5). Police frequently inform battered women that nothing can be done unless the women themselves approach the court, yet the criminal law does not require the consent of the victim to make an arrest.

Police often explain their failure to intervene as based on the belief that the women would not prosecute, they do not want to aggravate the dispute, they seek to minimise the danger of injury to officers, or an arrest would result in family break-up (Gee 1983, p. 559). Non-intervention may be part of the formal organisational policy because of a perception that domestic violence differs from other assault offences. Specifically, police may view domestic violence as a civil dispute rather than a crime, or, in Durkheimian terms, an issue for restitutive not repressive law. In California, four women filed a class action suit in 1976 with the aim of obtaining effective police protection for battered women by reversing the police department's arrest-avoidance policy which they argued was discriminatory on the basis of sex, breached police officers' statutory arrest duty, and denied women equal legal protection. They also sought to educate the criminal justice system and the public about the problem of domestic violence.[1] The court decision prohibits 'arrest avoidance' policies and provides that domestic violence be treated like any other criminal behaviour and requires the city to obtain support services for battered victims (Gee 1983, pp. 554–62).

Police reticence to intervene is often criticised as indicating reluctance to 'intrude' in the private lives of individuals or implicit affirmation of a husband's right to physically sanction family members. Even though the message underlying these criticisms is that police are not doing their job, it is unclear what should be the role of the police: should it be to deal with the matter as if the parties were strangers? Policing domestic violence highlights the dilemmas of police work discussed in chapter 5. From the police point of view, ambiguities arise from balancing their law enforcement and welfare roles, from providing immediate protection for victims while respecting citizens' rights and civil liberties, and from responding to a situation where the victim wants something done, not necessarily an apprehension, to stop the violence.

Even where the official policy is to take formal action, police make few arrests in assaults involving intimate partners (Ferraro 1989, p. 61). In New South Wales, the Crimes (Domestic Violence) Act defines a range of existing offences from common assault to homicide, as domestic violence where they occur between currently or previously married or de facto couples. Victims, or police on behalf of a victim, can obtain an apprehended domestic violence order which may restrict the perpetrator's behaviour for up to six months. Breaching an order constitutes a criminal offence with a penalty of six months imprisonment and/or a fine not exceeding $2000. Despite these reforms police remain reluctant to intervene in domestic violence matters and to seek orders on behalf of victims, and lack of action on breached orders is widespread (Stubbs & Wallace 1988, p. 75). However, the swift imposition of a sanction of temporary incarceration seems to deter male offenders in domestic assault cases. Alternatively, the apparent recidivism might result from the victims' failure to report after an arrest because of the negative financial consequences of incarceration for the family, or offenders previously arrested might be less likely to remain on the scene after a new assault (Sherman & Berk 1984, pp. 268–70). Analyses of police contacts for domestic violence offences in Milwaukee and Dade County (Florida) reveal that arrest has no overall crime reduction effect but increases the rate of recidivism among those with a low stake in conformity, namely unmarried and unemployed men. Indeed, arrest is no more effective than other police interventions in reducing further violence. These findings support the labelling perspective and counter suppositions that legal sanctions have a deterrent effect on subsequent criminal activity (Berk et al. 1992, p. 698; Pate & Hamilton 1992, p. 695; Sherman et al. 1992, pp. 686–8).

Another reform aimed at curbing domestic violence and the harassment, intimidation and even murder of women by their former partners is 'anti-stalking' legislation, first passed in California in 1990 and introduced in South Australia (McMahon & Davids 1993, pp. 4–5). The laws criminalise such wilful and malicious conduct as harassment or pursuit intended to cause a person to fear for their safety or to harm them physically or psychologically.

Homicide and the battered woman syndrome

Recent attention addresses the situation in which a victim of domestic violence retaliates and murders the perpetrator. Of especial interest is the law's response and the applicability of available legal defences. A case study of the thirty-six women convicted of homicide in New South Wales between July 1979 and March 1980 finds that sixteen had killed their male partner, fourteen of whom had been assaulted physically, typically repeated and severe violence, by the man she killed. At least nine of these women had experienced non-physical oppression (Bacon & Lansdowne 1982, pp. 68–78). Most of the women indicated that they were motivated to kill their partners by a need for protection against serious physical harm from him. However, little detail of the extent or degree of the violence and the nature of the relationship was put to the court. This hiatus stemmed from poor communication between the woman and her lawyers, especially if the woman was not on bail, limitations on admissible evidence, the woman's reluctance to put herself on the stand and the narrow focus of the trial on the 'relevant' legal issues (Bacon & Lansdowne 1982, pp. 82–8).

Commentators demonstrate that the traditional defences to murder—self-defence and provocation—do not 'fit' circumstances where a woman kills her batterer (Greene 1989, pp. 152–6; O'Donovan 1991, pp. 221–8; Sheehy, Stubbs & Tolmie 1992, pp. 370–80). Successfully raising self-defence results in an acquittal but the defendant must show that the amount of force used was proportionate to the imminent danger. This is a problem for many women who are generally of smaller size and strength than men. As one writer suggests: 'the law of self-defence is stated as a one-time barroom brawl between two men of equal size and strength' (O'Donovan 1993, p. 429). Demonstrating provocation reduces murder to manslaughter and requires the defendant to show that the victim's actions caused her/him to lose self-control and act in the heat of passion; the killing cannot be pre-meditated or carried out in 'cold blood'. Judges may or may not consider cumulative violence over many years to constitute provocation (*R v. R* (1981) 28 SASR 321).

Evidence of the battered woman syndrome has been accepted in North American and Australian courts as remedying the limitations of conventional defences. Lenore Walker (1979; 1984), a clinical psychologist, pioneered the conceptualisation of the battered woman syndrome and provides expert evidence herself. She argues that women who suffer repeated violence become immobilised, unable to act or to escape from the situation, thus resulting in 'learned helplessness', a psychological condition. The image presented is of the woman so paralysed by fear that the only way to change the situation is to kill the batterer. She is the real victim. In the first

Australian case to admit evidence of the battered woman syndrome, one judge observes that:

> The primary thrust of the evidence is to establish a pattern of responses commonly exhibited by battered women ... It is designed to assist the court in assessing whether women of reasonable firmness would succumb to the pressure to participate in the offences. It also serves to explain why even a woman of reasonable firmness would not escape the situation rather than participate in criminal activity (*Runjanjic and Kontinnen v. R* (1991) 53 A Crim R 362 at 368).

On one level, courts' acceptance of the battered woman syndrome advances the position of women defendants, however, it places the interpretation of their deviance within a psychological or medical paradigm; psychological disturbance, not criminal intent or rational action, precipitated the killing. Indeed, the claim that women who experience 'learned helplessness' are capable of homicide seems illogical. The battered woman syndrome has been criticised as lacking scientific validity and specific links between the condition and an actual offence are tenuous (Freckelton 1994, p. 42). At any rate, introduction of this type of evidence reinforces the notion that women's evidence needs to be legitimated or corroborated by expert witnesses to enhance its credibility.

Sexual harassment

As violence in the home is becoming defined as deviant, so is harassment in the workplace coming under public scrutiny. Again, feminists have been central in promoting the awareness that sexual harassment is a serious social problem and in lobbying for legal change. In the quest to redefine the problem as a public issue they advance the classic social problems claims, namely, the incidence of the problem is widespread, victims suffer genuine harm, and social factors cause sexual harassment thus requiring institutional solutions, such as law reform (Gillespie & Leffler 1987, p. 492). Even though sexual harassment is a gender-neutral offence it is mostly a problem women face. A survey of federal employees in the USA showed that 42 per cent of women and 15 per cent of men had experienced some form of harassment (Collins & Blodgett 1981, p. 79). A study of workplace sexual assaults finds that 17 per cent of the total sample of 372 female employees reported at least one completed or attempted assault by an acquaintance—usually a co-worker or supervisor—from work. Most of the assaults involved the threat or actual use of physical force and emotional appeals, for example pleas for sympathy, while economic promises or threats were less often employed. Four-fifths of the women who experienced a workplace assault remained at their jobs, only one in five complained to the employing organisation and one in five quit (Schneider 1991, pp. 538–43).

In many jobs women are subject to unwanted or uninvited sexual advances or innuendos. Women may be hired (or rejected) because of such criteria as sexual attractiveness when appearance has nothing to do with the requirements of the job. Schur (1984, p. 143) calls this the 'display job' phenomenon where women's 'looks' continue to be treated as a relevant employment criterion. Moreover, where women are hired, male managers, co-workers or clients might consider sexual advances or comments acceptable simply because the employee is a woman. Until the mid-1970s such unwanted behaviour was not defined as sexual harassment and the recipient could do little about it, especially where the harassment came from an employer or supervisor. MacKinnon observes: 'Until 1976, lacking a term to express it [sexual harassment] was literally unspeakable, which made a generalised, shared, and social definition of it inaccessible' (1979, p. 27). The popular media, court cases and the activities of interest groups, especially the women's movement concerned with issues of equal opportunity, were instrumental in the emergence of sexual harassment as a public issue and an identifiable social problem. Court cases in the USA legitimised sexual harassment as a serious matter and as a legal problem with employers realising the financial risks of being sued (Weeks et al. 1986, p. 449).

The term 'sexual harassment' includes a broad range of activities, usually considered to constitute sex discrimination (MacKinnon 1979, p. 4). However, little consensus exists on the types of behaviour that should be assigned the label sexual harassment (Gillespie & Leffler 1987, p. 496). In Australia, the Commonwealth and some state governments, outlaw sexual harassment in employment and educational settings. The Commonwealth Sex Discrimination Act (1984) defines sexual harassment as 'an unwelcome sexual advance, or an unwelcome request for sexual favours, or ... other unwelcome conduct of a sexual nature' where the harassed person reasonably believes that rejecting the advance would or does disadvant-age the person's employment or work, including possible employment (ss 28(3)(a&b)). The Act also prohibits oral or written statements of a sexual nature about a person (s 28(4)). The Human Rights and Equal Opportunity Commission, which adjudicates sexual harassment cases, aims to resolve complaints by conciliation and seeks to 'enable the parties to negotiate with a view to settlement of the complaint by amicable arrangements' (Sex Discrimination Act 1984, s 73). The Commission is not a judicial forum and the proceedings are not adversarial as sexual harassment complaints are dealt with under administrative and tort, not criminal, law. The emphasis is on informal proceedings and alternative dispute resolution, nonetheless the Commission has considerable power. It can dismiss complaints, declare that the respondent has engaged in unlawful behaviour, order him or her to pursue a course of conduct, for example an apology, or pay damages as compensation for any loss or harm to the complainant, including injury to feelings, mental or physical health problems and loss of wages, or initiate proceedings in the Federal Court. The payment of damages is a civil or restitutive not a criminal sanction; its purpose is to restore the status quo rather constitute a punishment.

In line with the legal definition, sexual harassment includes leering, patting, pinching, touching, verbal abuse including repeated sexual innuendo, displays of offensive pictures, reference to the employee's body parts, as well as attempts at rape or sexual assault (Collins & Blodgett 1981, p. 79; Fain & Anderton 1987, p. 297; The Flinders University of South Australia n.d.; Schur 1984, p. 136). Sexual harassment can be distinguished from flirting, mutual attraction between people or workplace romances in that harassment is unwanted and potentially coercive or disruptive (Benson & Thomson 1982, p. 237). Reports of sexual harassment are increasing: from 1979–80 five complaints of sexual harassment were made to the South Australian Commissioner of Equal Opportunity, by 1987–88 the number increased to ninety which constitutes 15 per cent of all complaints (Equal Opportunity Commission 1979/80, p. 14; 1987/88, p. 19). In 1991–92, 46 per cent of the complaints lodged under the Commonwealth Sex Discrimination Act involved sexual harassment in employment (Australian Law Reform Commission 1993, p. 115).

MacKinnon (1979, p. 208) makes a useful distinction between specific incidents of sexual harassment that are prerequisites to hiring or promotional decisions and sexual harassment which is part of the general work environment. The United States Equal Employment Opportunity Commission's guidelines prohibiting sexual harassment reflect this distinction. They prohibit unwelcome sexual advances, requests for sexual favours and other physical or verbal conduct of a sexual nature when submission becomes a term of employment, or when it interferes with an individual's work performance or creates an intimidating, hostile, or offensive work environment (Schur 1988, pp. 159–60).

Little agreement exists on the kinds of jobs or employment settings in which sexual harassment is most likely to occur. Some argue that women in such male-dominated occupations as mining and blue-collar jobs, who are highly visible and already defined as deviating from gender norms are most likely to be harassed sexually. A survey of workers in a heavy manufacturing firm, a non-manufacturing firm and a public agency finds that women working in 'male' jobs or challenging male authority in other ways are most likely to experience discrimination and sexual harassment, and thus be aware of the sexualisation of the work environment, in other words, 'sex becomes the medium through which power games are exercised in the workplace' (Di Tomaso 1989, pp. 88–9). Others claim that it is women in traditionally female jobs, for example nurses and secretaries, who suffer the most because harassment is an institutionalised part of their occupation (Coles 1986, p. 87; Fain & Anderton 1987, p. 292; Gutek & Cohen 1987, pp. 100–1; Hemming 1985, p. 67; Schur 1984, pp. 135–45). This is especially true of jobs which involve emotional labour, for example flight attendants and nurses, where passengers or patients may interpret a nurturing and caring attitude as sexual availability or particular interest (Hochschild 1983 p. 171). Research on the work experiences of a sample (N=220) of women lawyers in a medium-sized city in the USA indicates that one in four reported being sexually harassed, that is, receiving unwanted sexual advances in a professional setting. The primary perpetrators were other lawyers, followed by clients, then judges and other legal personnel. Women under thirty-five years of age reported being harassed most frequently and respondents identified harassment as occurring far more often in private firms than in government agencies. Harassment was also accompanied by discrimination and disparagement entailing comments that focus attention to women's gender and tend to demean or reduce their status, for example the use of infantalising terms of address (Rosenberg, Perlstadt & Phillips 1993, pp. 423, 426).

Many studies point to differential power relations to explain sexual harassment at work and on university campuses, which in turn maintain the authority hierarchy. Even though women are entering the professions, most women work in the secondary labour market characterised by job instability, few promotional opportunities, little autonomy and predominantly male management and supervisors. Women's vulnerable position makes them candidates for sexual harassment, as they are powerless to do anything about it for fear of losing their jobs or being passed over in promotion decisions (Fain & Anderton 1987, p. 301; MacKinnon 1979, p. 4). A study of undergraduate women at a large university in the USA found a high degree of consensus that sexual harassment initiated by male lecturers is neither isolated nor rare (Benson & Thomson 1982, p. 241). The types of unwanted sexual attention ranged from verbal and physical advances to sexual bribery. Given their lack of power and vulnerability, the students adopted a range of management techniques such as suppressing their true responses, ignoring the advances, and avoiding contact with the lecturer. One student points to the difficulties of the situation: 'I tried to let him know I wasn't interested in a personal relationship with him. I couldn't be as rude as I would have liked to have been. At the time I felt I had to put up with it because I was trying to get into the honors program' (Benson & Thomson 1982, p. 243). Management techniques like avoidance or changing jobs can disadvantage a student's or employee's career prospects by placing the harassed person outside mentor relationships and decreasing self-confidence.

While consensus exists that the more serious forms of sexual harassment are deviant, disagreement surrounds what are seen as the more ambiguous incidents. It is sometimes said that women should be flattered by male attention, or at least they should tolerate 'normal' sexual attractions in the workplace. These views are exemplified by one controversial sexual harassment case where the former President of the Human Rights and Equal Opportunity Commission, Justice Einfeld said:

> isolated occasions when an employer simply places a hand on an employee or around a chair on which the employee is sitting, though not at all according with the employee's dignity or entitlement, are not sexual harassment within the meaning of the Act ... Light incidental touching and other minor physical contact, actual or

attempted casting of eyes or glances and the occasional use of words or suggestion or invitation, fall short of unlawful sexual harassment under this Act (*Hall & Ors v. Sheiban & Anor* (1988) EOC ¶92–227 at 146–7).

Justice Einfeld dismissed as trivial and insignificant the medical doctor's 'sporadic, assertive if unwanted attempts at closer physical or facial contact' directed toward the three receptionists. This is a good example of a situation where the legislation is clear on what constitutes sexual harassment but the courts, or enforcement agents, do not agree that the kinds of behaviour described constitute deviance. To the extent that incidents of sexual harassment differ from the 'classic rape' situation, they are less likely to be defined as deviant, and more likely to be considered as acceptable, trivial, or should be tolerable as part of normal everyday social interaction. A year later, the Federal Court reversed this decision and in a subsequent case, Justice Einfeld changed his position (probably due to the public outcry following the *Sheiban* case) and agreed that a single act or statement might constitute unwelcome conduct and 'all employees have a right to employment without sexuality or attempts at the introduction of sexuality, either direct or indirect' (*Bennett & Anor v. Everitt & Anor* (1988) EOC ¶92–244 at 280). Moreover, the amount of harm and damage done is determined in terms of what the complainant personally and genuinely suffered from the unlawful conduct.

Women and property crime

The discussion of women as victims of practices defined as deviant is only part of the story. Women are both victims and perpetrators of various crimes. As chapter 2 indicates, much debate centres on the extent of women's and girls' involvement in crime and the types of crimes they commit. Some authors argue that there are no gender differences in the kinds of crimes males and females commit; the differences reflected by crime statistics result from the differential processing of men and women by the police and the courts. Others maintain that for a variety of reasons women do commit different kinds of crime than do men.

Since the articulation of the Women's liberation thesis several Australian and overseas studies empirically document and offer alternative explanations for women's and girl's participation in criminal deviance. They question whether the criminal activities of women are becoming like those of men in kind and degree, particularly whether women are committing more 'masculine', violent and serious crimes. These investigations show that most relative gains by women are minimal; women still constitute a small proportion of all offenders, and the only significant increases in female offending occur in the area of minor property offending (Box & Hale 1983, p. 46; Challinger 1982, p. 123; Mukerjee & Fitzgerald 1981, pp. 161–2; Steffensmeier 1980b, pp. 1095–7; Steffensmeier & Cobb 1981, p. 45). Most of the research documenting female rates of offending analyses data for this century, usually since the 1960s, in part to test the effect of the women's liberation movement on crime. Feeley and Little suggest that by incorporating a wider time frame 'one of the central puzzles for students of gender and crime should be the vanishing female participation in the criminal process' (1991, p. 720). Their examination of criminal cases in the Old Bailey in London for 1687 until 1912 indicates that for much of the eighteenth century women constituted a significant proportion (almost half in some years) of all those indicted for felony offences, ranging from larceny to murder, compared with contemporary levels of 15 per cent. Women's involvement was greatest in larceny, burglary, theft, receiving stolen goods and uttering counterfeit coins. This finding concurs with research on women convicts transported to Australia who were largely convicted of property offences, contrary to contemporary and historical writings suggesting their major offence was prostitution (Oxley 1991, pp. 91–5). The decline in the proportion of women in the criminal courts from the early nineteenth century, Feeley and Little suggest, resulted from the changing role of women, the increased separation of the public and private spheres and women's greater subjection to private, informal social control (1991, pp. 741–7).

The most sophisticated in-depth longitudinal analysis of male and female involvement in criminal deviance over the course of the present century has been undertaken in the USA. Using national arrest data, the researchers found that women made the most significant gains in the petty property crimes of larceny, fraud, and forgery and in crimes of vagrancy and disorderly conduct. Increased opportunities for shoplifting (and getting caught) account for adolescent and adult female gains in arrests for larceny. While shoplifting is a relatively non-serious offence (Rossi et al. 1974, p. 229) retail stores consider it a substantial financial cost (Office of Crime Statistics 1982, p. 1). Most female arrests for fraud involve forging cheques and credit cards, falsifying identification, and welfare fraud. Women made few gains in traditionally male property offences such as robbery, burglary, motor vehicle theft, arson, vandalism or stolen property (Steffensmeier 1978, p. 578; Steffensmeier & Cobb 1981, pp. 42–5). The minimal increases in most offence categories cannot be attributed to changes in women's status, indeed their gains in larceny offences reflect extensions of traditional female role activities, specifically being consumers and doing the shopping, rather than new role patterns. This is not to assert that women are biologically or psychologically pre-disposed toward petty pilfering (Cameron 1964, pp. 159–66).

Central to the debate about women's involvement in criminal activity are questions about the interpretation of arrest data. As Kitsuse and Cicourel (1963, p. 135) point out, crime statistics are highly problematic and tell us more about the practices of organisations within the criminal justice system than the actual incidence of criminal deviance. Taking into account some of the problems with officially collected statistics, a number of explanations for the changes in women's involvement can be offered:

1 attitudes toward women and female offenders have become less sympathetic and chivalrous and more punitive. Citizens are more likely to report, police are more likely to arrest, and courts are more likely to convict female offenders rather than ignore or excuse them;

2 as a result of the increased pressure for the equal application of the law, police may be more attuned to charges of discrimination and unequal treatment of alleged male and female offenders, and therefore apply the same criteria.

3 the increasing professionalisation and bureaucratisation of police work suggests greater application of universalistic standards in decision-making and lack of concern for ascribed statuses, like sex. Additionally, improvements in data recording make police statistics more accurate and detailed;

4 the social control system has changed in relation to specific criminal acts which women are more likely than men to commit. Most retail stores have increased their surveillance mechanisms by installing video cameras, employing security personnel, and adopting policies of prosecuting shoplifters. Government departments, for example the Department of Social Security, set up elaborate surveillance procedures in order to stem welfare fraud. As most welfare recipients are women, such procedures increase the visibility of any offending.

Changes in law enforcement and reporting practices explain part of the change in arrest patterns, however, other factors, particularly the opportunity structure, also affect the increases in women's involvement in property crime. The greater reliance on self-service marketing and the purchasing of credit mean that women, being the primary consumers, are faced with growing opportunities for shoplifting and writing bad cheques (Steffensmeier 1980b, p. 1099; Steffensmeier & Cobb 1981, p. 47). Expanded opportunities for law-breaking have been accompanied by the economic marginalisation of women, the 'feminisation' of poverty, and increasing female unemployment which contribute to involvement in petty property offences and welfare fraud (Box & Hale 1983, p. 36). Even so, there is no clear cut extent to which women's unemployment is related to increases in property offending. Women who experience unemployment may seek other than criminal solutions to economic marginality, such as opting for early domesticity or single motherhood. Interviews with fifty unemployed young women in Melbourne suggest that, apart from marijuana use, most do not engage in criminal behaviour, with the exception of minor shoplifting (Alder 1986, p. 222). South Australian data show that female unemployment has exceeded male unemployment from 1966 to 1986 but women still offend less than men. The levels of female involvement in the crime of breaking and entering—a crime related to unemployment—remained low for the whole period (Naffine & Gale 1989, pp. 151–3). United States data on white-collar defendants shows that women constituted 45 per cent of convicted bank embezzlers, 18 per cent of postal fraud convictions, and for both credit fraud and false claims and statements women made up 15 per cent of those convicted. The numbers of women convicted of anti-trust violations, bribery and securities fraud were negligible (Daly 1989a, p. 775). Men's white-collar crimes were both petty and major while women's tended to be petty. Around half of the employed men were in managerial or professional positions whereas most of the employed women were clerical workers. Daly concludes that women's economic marginality, not mobility, best describes female fraud. She predicts that if female arrests for white-collar crimes increase then they will result from increasing numbers of women in highly monitored, clerical, sales or services jobs involving the handling of money and increasing numbers of poor and unemployed women attempting to defraud government agencies and financial institutions (Daly 1989a, pp. 789–90).

In sum, female involvement in criminal deviance has not changed markedly in recent history; women and girls still predominantly commit non-violent petty property offences. This, then, raises the question of why their involvement in crime differs from that of men's. Relying on some of the theories discussed in chapter 2, several factors are important:

1 *socialisation*: arguably, sex-role socialisation is linked to criminality in such a way that it accounts for the much lower rate of female, as compared to male, crime. Specifically, boys learn to be aggressive, adventurous and innovative while girls learn to be passive, unadventurous, and dependent (Naffine 1987, pp. 26–42; Smart 1976, pp. 66–70). However, there is little support for the thesis that female offenders conform less to traditional sex roles than do non-offenders (Box 1983, p. 175). Moreover, it is tautological to assume that law-abiding women conform to gender norms and female offenders do not.

2 *social control*: women and girls are subject to more informal social control within the family while men and boys are more subject to the formal social control of the criminal justice system. As a consequence of female family roles and responsibilities women and girls have fewer opportunities and less time to engage in criminal activities. In addition, female friendships seem to be more home- than street-centred and female peer groups reinforce compliance and passivity unlike male peer groups (Hagan, Simpson & Gillis 1979, pp. 34–5).

3 *opportunity structure*: just as sex segregation exists in the legitimate occupational structure so it exists in the illegitimate opportunity structure. Women are either excluded or allocated to less valued, secondary roles as accomplices or decoys reflecting assumptions that women do not possess the skills for crime commission or that they are untrustworthy (Steffensmeier 1983, pp. 1010–13).

4 *societal reaction*: as women are less likely to be imprisoned or stigmatised for illegal behaviour the chances of secondary deviance are reduced. Contact with the police seems to deter girls from subsequent deviance

but tends to amplify male delinquency (Keane et al. 1989, p. 348). Millman (1975, p. 253) observes that women's deviance is usually understood as deriving from gender norms such as falling in love with a deviant man (women's recent involvement in terrorism has often been explained by their particular relationship to a man), being impulsive and emotional (an assumed explanation for shoplifting), using their sexuality exploitatively (as in prostitution), but not very differently than other women. The suggestion is that members of the public and the criminal justice system do not really consider women deviant, just misguided, and are therefore less responsible for illegal behaviour but nevertheless requiring help and protection. This supports the earlier suggestion that women's deviance is more likely to be defined as illness, especially mental illness, rather than crime. It also appears that female prisoners become less criminalised than their male counterparts partly because the female prisoner population has relatively fewer 'hardened' career criminals, hence fewer criminal role models to emulate (Dobash, Dobash & Gutteridge 1986, pp. 90–7). Women offenders' integration into the community may be facilitated, as they are perceived as less dangerous and less aggressive than men. However, when women alone actually or allegedly commit offences which are seen as 'male' crimes, for example homicide or armed robbery, they become doubly deviant; deviant from the gender norms as well as from the criminal law, often resulting in harsher penalties. The media portrayal of Lindy Chamberlain during her trial for the murder of her baby exemplifies such double deviance (Chesney-Lind 1978, p. 218; Hiller 1982, pp. 73–5; Edwards 1986, p. 80).

Women and the criminal justice system

Another dominant theme in the discussion of women and crime is their treatment by the criminal justice system, not just as victims but as perpetrators. One pervasive argument is that women are treated leniently thus reflecting paternalism or chivalry on the part of male police and magistrates (Anderson 1976, pp. 350–1). Preferential treatment results from police and judges treating females in a fatherly, protective manner, or perceiving women as less capable than men of committing serious crimes (Parisi 1982, p. 207; Steffensmeier 1980a, p. 350). Pollak (1979, p. 39), for example, states: 'Men hate to accuse women and thus indirectly to send them to their punishment, police officers dislike to arrest them, district attorneys to prosecute them, judges and juries to find them guilty, and so on'.

Such a view has been questioned by research which demonstrates the conditions under which women, and which particular, women will be treated leniently. Moreover, it must be remembered that not all men are treated by the criminal justice system in the same fair and just way (see chapter 5). It has become clear that chivalry is not synonymous with lenient treatment. There is some evidence that women (for major non-sex-related offences) have benefited from police and judicial leniency when compared with men, as have girls on criminal charges; but where females (particularly under-age) transgress sexual and moral standards they received more severe treatment than many males would receive, suggesting a dual standard of morality still operates in legal and judicial processes (Chesney-Lind 1973, p. 58; 1978, pp. 211–17; Smart 1976, pp. 132–40).

An investigation of police reports and juvenile court records in Victoria finds girls more likely than boys to be presented to court on protection applications for juvenile 'status' offences, like running away from home, truancy, sexual delinquency, and ungovernability. Such behaviour, if committed by an adult, would not be illegal. A legalistic model operates for juvenile offenders against criminal laws and since females are typically infrequent and less serious law-breakers, girls on such charges can expect more lenient treatment from police and courts (Hancock & Chesney-Lind 1982, p. 109). However, where girls offend moral standards they are treated more harshly than males. The justification that girls need extra protection results in harsher treatment and greater infringement of rights than does a more legalistic approach. Comparable behaviour for boys rarely results in an application for protection let alone commitment to an institution (Hancock 1980, pp. 7–10). Carrington (1990a) questions this 'sexualisation thesis', that is the argument that the juvenile justice system operates on a double standard of morality punishing sexually active girls but not boys via welfare or status complaints. First, by privileging and isolating gender, the thesis omits race thereby failing to examine the specific experiences of Aboriginal women and the massive criminalisation rates of Aboriginal youth in general (Carrington 1993, p. 124). Second, New South Wales data indicate that courts deal more harshly with both girls and boys appearing on welfare matters as compared with criminal matters. Carrington suggests that this outcome relates to the influence of social work practices and recommendations within the court. She points out that: 'it has been too confidently assumed in essentialist readings of female delinquency that the vehicle of sexualisation is some patriarchal family or some male magistrate, father or police officer, rather than some female social worker, district officer, school counsellor or departmental psychologist' (Carrington 1990a, p. 25).

Paternalism, then, does not mean greater leniency and a distinction needs to be made between judicial concern for protecting women and a concern for protecting children and families (Daly 1989b, pp. 10–11). As women are typically responsible for their children, judges confront the practical problems of jailing women with children, which would result in family disruption and place considerable financial burden on the rest of society (Steffensmeier 1980a, p. 349). Carlen (1983, p. 63) argues that courts resolve a sentencing dilemma in a case where the offender is female on the basis of their assessment of the woman as mother. However, it seems that the critical issue is not gender but care of children. A study of sentencing in the USA suggests that, depending on the nature of the offence and the defendant's prior record, judges rationalise family-based sentencing disparities for both men and women as necessary for keeping families together (Daly 1989b, pp. 27–8). Judges also perceive that family men and women are better probation risks than the non-family men and women because their lives are more tightly bound by familial interdependencies, thus, subscribing to a control theory of deviance (see chapter 2).

Summary

This chapter demonstrates that the topic of women and deviance, in particular crime, currently receives more theoretical and empirical attention than previously. Such offences as rape, domestic violence and sexual harassment have been defined and re-defined as social problems, largely due to the actions of social movements. A wider range of behaviour has become 'deviant', indicating increasing formal social control and the extension of the law—but not necessarily the criminal law—into family and employment relations. The laws, in a sense, create more crime and deviance, but they also indicate formal recognition of practices which may have been considered unacceptable or harmful where victims had little scope or authority to do anything about them; they were viewed as private not public matters. New social polices and legal changes regarding rape, domestic violence and sexual harassment generally focus on the situation after the event, for example by expanding police powers, providing refuges and counselling, and making court procedures more accessible for the victims. Much of the discussion centres on the victim, thus reinforcing an individualistic approach to a social problem. Increasing medicalisation of these examples of deviance, through the development and application of concepts like 'rape trauma syndrome' and 'battered woman syndrome', reinforce the individual as the level of analysis and treatment.This emphasis diverts attention from the political and social contexts in which rape and violence occur. The emergence of these types of deviance as social problems provides sites of contestation between agents of the criminal justice system and other professional workers, such as medical personnel, psychologists and social workers.

The issues of women's participation in criminal deviance, as compared with men's participation, continue to be a major focus of research and discussion but remain relatively under-theorised. Certainly, women's and girls' deviance has been perceived as stemming from sexuality which criminal justice and social welfare agencies seek to control. Recent research examines female crime and deviance, including previously defined gender-specific crimes like prostitution and infanticide, in terms of women's location in the occupational structure and their economic situation. One reason why so few women are involved in white-collar crime is that most lack access to the high status occupations where those illegitimate opportunities exist.

Note

1 A class action suit involves obtaining a judicial decision that will benefit the members of a class of people—such as a group of employees, the users of particular product (for example the Dalkon Shield Inter-Uterine Device), or the members of a state, city or union—rather than an individual complainant. The purpose of class action suits is to change public policy. As a form of law reform, class action suits are not generally available in Australia.

Key terms

Rape
Victim-precipitation
Sex discrimination
Battered woman syndrome
Domestic violence
Self-defence
Women's movement
Chivalry
Judicial paternalism

'Classic rape'
Sexual harassment
Domestic violence
Wife battering
Family violence
Provocation
Feminism
Women's liberation thesis

Main points

1 Recently, a number of activities, including rape, sexual harassment and domestic violence, victims of which are mostly women, have been criminalised or deviantised. They have become public issues and the subject of legislative change.
2 Changes in the definitions of these activities largely resulted from the activities of the women's movement. Problems of enforcement remain. For example, police reticence to make an arrest in a situation of domestic violence is related to ambiguities surrounding the role of police and their perception that a prosecution would not eventuate.
3 Even though the legal and everyday definitions of rape have been widened, most incidents of rape are measured against the so-called 'classic rape' involving a sudden, brutal and armed attack by a stranger in a deserted place. While most rapes do not conform to this description, this is not the impression conveyed by the mass media, which sensationalise particularly heinous rapes. Crime statistics based on police data can be misleading as only around one quarter of sexual assault victims report the incident.
4 Unwanted sexual advances, requests or comments in the workplace have been defined as sexual harassment and prohibited under Commonwealth and state legislation. Administrative and tort rather than criminal laws prohibit sexual harassment. The primary resolution of complaints occurs through informal tribunal hearings not the adversarial court process. The aim of damages payments is to restore the status quo and compensate the victim for any harm to her or his emotions, mental or physical health or income.

5 Over the past twenty years, women's involvement in property crime has been increasing. However, these increases are relatively small with most being in the areas of minor property offending, especially fraud.

6 Considerable evidence documents the differential treatment of men and women by the criminal justice system. Many critics argue that women are treated more leniently because of police and judge's paternal orientation and view of women as incapable of intentionally committing serious offences. However, judicial paternalism can translate into more severe penalties if the offender is a young female and accused of a 'status' offence, such as 'ungovernability'.

Further reading

Brownmiller, Susan 1975, *Against Our Will: Men, Women and Rape*, Simon & Schuster, New York.

Carrington, Kerry 1993, *Offending Girls*, Allen & Unwin, Sydney.

MacKinnon, Catharine 1979, *Sexual Harassment of Working Women: A Case of Sex Discrimination*, Yale University Press, New Haven.

Morris, Allison 1987, *Women, Crime and Criminal Justice*, Basil Blackwell, Oxford.

National Committee on Violence 1990, *Violence: Directions for Australia*, Australian Institute of Criminology, Canberra.

Price, Barbara Raffel & Natalie J. Sokoloff eds 1995, *The Criminal Justice System and Women: Offenders, Victims and Workers*, 2nd edn, McGraw-Hill, New York.

Rafter, Nicole Hahn & Elizabeth A. Stanko eds 1982, *Judge, Lawyer, Victim, Thief: Women, Gender Roles and Criminal Justice*, Northeastern University Press, Boston.

Corporate crime

Crime statistics and news reports suggest that the volume of crime in society mainly consists of property and public order offences, offences against the person such as murder and assault and drug-related offences. Such crimes are committed disproportionately by young men with little education and few occupational skills. These are the crimes with which police departments and the criminal courts routinely deal. Thus, government ministers and policy makers often argue that the reduction of crime requires more police and more efficient courts. Similarly, many of the sociological theories discussed in chapter 2 focus on the lack of legitimate opportunities, poverty, social disorganisation and powerlessness to explain why some individuals are motivated to break the criminal law or are subject to deviant labels.

This account excludes a large range of illegal and deviant practices carried out by powerful individual and corporate members of society: business elites, professional people, public and private corporations and other organisations. Such concepts as white-collar crime, corporate crime, organisational crime, occupational crime and elite deviance attempt to distinguish this type of deviance from everyday or conventional crime and highlight the status of the perpetrator as a powerful individual or corporate actor. Traditional sociological theories of crime emphasising deprivation, economic inequality and poverty cannot explain illegal activities undertaken by the rich and powerful. Gottfredson and Hirschi's conclusion that most criminal acts are impulsive, unplanned and requiring little foresight or skill also inadequately describes corporate crime entailing co-ordination and planning between various actors with specific skills and knowledge. Some of the illegal activities referred to in discussions of corporate crime, for example the violation of taxation, discrimination or securities laws, are regulated by civil or administrative law. Technically, then, these are not crimes. Others, including insider trading, fraud and embezzlement are prohibited by criminal law. It is important not to conflate corporate crime with illegal corporate behaviour or offences against corporations laws (Baucus & Dworkin 1991, p. 231).

Since the late 1980s much greater attention has been given to publicising and prosecuting the alleged illegal activities of corporate actors. Several major corporate collapses, including the Qintex group of companies, Spedley Securities, Rothwells merchant bank, the Pyramid Building Society and the State Bank of South Australia, have led to government inquiries and attempts to prosecute in both civil and criminal courts such (formerly) high-profile entrepreneurs as Alan Bond, Christopher Skase and John Elliott . While it is no longer valid to conclude that the most economically significant deviance is the least publicised, investigated or punished, it is doubtful that there will be many successful prosecutions due to the resources available to corporate offenders, the complexity of the trials in which most of the evidence is documentary, and the difficulties for the prosecution in proving 'beyond reasonable doubt' cases of corporate crime.

The sociologist most closely associated with analysing crime and deviance among the powerful is Edwin H. Sutherland who proposed the concept of 'white-collar crime'. This has become a commonly understood term with direct translations into *crime en col blanc* (French), *criminalita in colletti bianchi* (Italian), *weisse-kragen-kriminalitat* (German), and *el delito de cuello blanco* (Spanish) (Geis & Meier 1977, p. 26; Geis & Goff, 1983, pp. xi–xii). Sutherland wrote prolifically on white-collar crime in the 1940s and in the wake of his work several other studies followed. An example is Cressey's *Other People's Money* which examines embezzlement. However, from the 1950s until recently, sociological research into white-collar crime was minimal. Stanton Wheeler claims, in his presidential address to the Society for the Study of Social Problems, that: 'In one particular area of criminality, we have been almost totally negligent. I refer to the patterns of illegal activity that lie at the core of large-scale corporate, industrial society' (Wheeler 1976, p. 525). Renewed interest in the concept of white-collar crime and sociological research on the incidence and control of corporate and professional illegality emerged in the 1970s and flourishes in the 1980s, particularly in Australia.

This chapter first addresses Sutherland's work and examines some of the definitional problems with his broad conception of white-collar crime. It suggests that occupational and corporate crimes need to be distinguished. The discussion also examines the concept of organised crime which is related to corporate crime: both concepts suggest co-ordination and co-operation in the pursuit of illegal activities and legitimate financial institutions may be used to launder income gained illegally. The chapter outlines recent research on illegal or harmful activities performed by high status individuals and corporations and focuses on the problems of studying and regulating such activities.

Sutherland on white-collar crime

In his 1939 Presidential Address to the American Sociological Association, Sutherland rejected theories of crime which blame poverty, broken homes and psychological pathology for illegal behaviour by observing that such factors cannot explain widespread law-breaking activity among persons in positions of power, especially corporate executives. Previous socio-logical theories had relied on official data, especially police and court records which Sutherland criticises as a biased sample of all criminal acts. A theory of crime must be able to explain the illegal activities of high-status individuals in the course of their occupations, or white-collar crime, as well as crime among the working class (Sutherland 1940, p. 2; 1945, p. 136). Sutherland's concept of white-collar crime is ambiguous; sometimes he emphasises the status of the offender, other times he focuses on the nature of the act. He defines white-collar crime as 'a crime committed by a person of *respectability and high social status* in the course of his [sic] occupation' (1983, p. 7, emphasis added), but indicates that: 'these varied types of white-collar crimes in business and the professions consist principally of *violation of delegated or implied trust*, and many of them can be reduced to two categories: misrepresentation of asset values and duplicity in the manipulation of power' (1940, p. 3, emphasis added).

Sutherland published *White Collar Crime* (1949), which documents the crimes perpetrated by the seventy largest private companies and fifteen public utility corporations in the USA. Dryden, the publishing company, demanded that the names of the companies be eliminated for fear of liability for damages because the book called certain corporations 'criminal' even though they had not been prosecuted under criminal statutes. However, as Cressey observes: 'Had the original manuscript been published, and had a libel suit been initiated, then Sutherland's contention that the listed offences are in fact crimes might have been tested in a court of law—a corporation might have argued that the statement is libellous because its behaviour is not a crime, with Sutherland giving the arguments presented in his book [*White Collar Crime*]' (Cressey 1961, p. vii). In 1983 an uncut version identifying the corporations was published.

Sutherland identifies the most frequent forms of white-collar criminality as misrepresentation in corporations' financial statements, manipulation in the stock exchange, commercial bribery, bribery of public officials in order to secure favourable contracts and legislation, misrepresentation in advertising and sales, embezzlement and misapplication of funds and tax fraud (Sutherland 1940, pp. 2–3). These varied types of white-collar crime all violate trust and make victims of consumers, competitors, stockholders and other investors, inventors and employees, as well as the state in the form of tax frauds and bribery of public employees. These crimes are not dis-crete and inadvertent violations of technical regulations, but are deliberate and pervasive.

Sutherland's central thesis is that the principal difference in the crimes of the upper and lower classes is the administrative procedures used in dealing with the offenders, but variations in administrative procedures are not significant in explaining crime causation (Sutherland 1983, p. 7). Police officers handle the crimes of the lower class and judges order penal sanctions in the form of fines, community work orders, imprisonment, and, in some places, death. Upper-class illegality results either in no official action or in suits for damages in civil courts, or is handled by inspectors, administrative boards or commissions whose sanctions range from warnings, orders to cease and desist, occasionally the loss of a license and only in extreme cases fines or prison sentences (Sutherland 1940, pp. 7–8).

For Sutherland, crime is the real and the actual (not the reported or prosecuted) incidence of criminal and regulatory offences. He hypothesises that white-collar criminality, like any other systematic criminality is learned in association with those who already practise the behaviour. Those who learn this criminal behaviour are segregated from frequent and intimate contacts with law abiding behaviour. Whether a person becomes a criminal or not is determined largely by the comparative frequency and intimacy of contacts with the two types of behaviour. In other words, the theory of differential association (see chapter 2) is a general theory applicable to crime across all social classes.

The broadness of Sutherland's conception of white-collar crime evokes criticism. Braithwaite, for example, says that it is 'an impotent construct for theory building in sociology' (1985, p. 3). Instead of guiding a coherent body of theory and research the term has generated often futile terminological disputes and stimulated the development of more specific terms, including 'elite deviance', 'corporate crime', 'organisational crime' and 'occupational deviance' (Aubert 1952, p. 264). The following section details some of the difficulties in Sutherland's notion of white-collar crime:

1 even though Sutherland seeks to develop a unitary theory of crime he separates crimes in terms of the social status of the perpetrator. He conflates characteristics of the perpetrator with the crime; whether crime is white-collar depends on the attributes of the actor. While proposing the theory of *differential association*, Sutherland distinguishes white-collar from ordinary crimes, thus conflating definition with explanation;

2 from his definition, it is impossible to separate crimes committed by management against the corporation, for example embezzlement and insider trading, and those crimes management commit to benefit the corporation, such as marketing unsafe products, misrepresentations to shareholders, pollution or tax avoidance. Moreover, Sutherland's concept of corporation becomes reified as he assumes that business organisations act as a coherent and singular entity. Instead, different parts of an organisation often come under different statutes and administrative regulations and each might be violating different laws simultaneously;

3 Sutherland's use of the term 'crime' is ambiguous. On one hand, he accepts legal definitions and states 'the essential characteristic of crime is that it is behaviour which is prohibited by the State as an injury to the State and against which the state may react, at least as a last resort, by punishment' (1983, p. 46). On the other, he goes beyond this by arguing that even though laws may not exist certain behaviour may be criminal because it is (morally) wrong or causes harm. Sutherland often cites actions that are not violations of law (or at least were not at the time he was writing) but which are socially injurious, including recalls of hazardous consumer products, or contract breaches which are civil matters only, as instances of white-collar crime, yet he is clear that white-collar crime is real crime in that it violates the criminal law (Braithwaite 1985, p. 4). As one contemporary, somewhat polemical, critic of Sutherland's writes: 'One seeks in vain for criteria to determine this white collar criminality. It is the conduct of one who wears a white collar and indulges in occupational behavior to which some particular criminologist takes exception' (Tappan 1947, p. 99).

At its most general, white-collar crime seems to mean abuse of power or violation of trust which encompasses a wide variety of deviant, illegal and criminal behaviour. In developing the concept of white-collar crime as an abuse of trust, Shapiro (1990) focuses on the role of fiduciary relationships in which a principal delegates power, property, responsibility and discretion to agents who have custody and control over these resources. Fiduciary relationships underpin the operation of most business enterprises, partnerships and professional/client relationships. While the owners of a public corporation are the shareholders they entrust its management to boards of directors who are the agents of the former (Redmond 1992, pp. 347–52). However, the scale of corporations and the often large number of shareholders raises problems of surveillance, control and accountability, especially as fiduciary relationships tend to be ill-defined, amorphous and lack specific guidance regarding the exercise of multiple agency roles. This opens up enormous opportunities for lying, stealing, misappropriation and self-dealing. Shapiro proposes that: 'The violation and manipulation of the norms of trust—of disclosure, disinterestedness, and role competence—represent the modus operandi of white-collar crime' (1990, p. 350). Problems of the social control of white-collar crime do not derive solely from the social status of the offenders but from the social organisation of trust. Specifically, 'abuses of trust are hard to detect, offending is collective, victimization subtle, offenses ongoing, culpability difficult to assign, conclusive evidence hard to amass, harsh penalties spill over to innocent parties, and so on' (Shapiro 1990, p. 358).

An investigation of the financial scandals and collapses in the United States savings and loan and insurance industries identifies their role as trustees of other people's money within a deregulated economy where profits are made from high-risk speculative investment as creating opportunities for collective embezzlement, defined as 'the siphoning off of company funds for personal use by top management' (Calavita & Pontell 1991, p. 94). These embezzlers participate in networks of co-conspirators both within and without the institution and are not lone lower-level employees. Ironically, the organisation is the vehicle for perpetrating crime against itself; it provides the structural opportunities for collective fraud and illegality which result in its own demise. 'The organization, in other words, is both weapon *and* victim' (Calavita & Pontell 1991, p. 103, emphasis in original). Even so, disagreement exists over the extent to which the crisis in this segment of finance capitalism is attributable to criminal conduct (Zimring & Hawkins 1993, pp. 262–73).

Some writers distinguish between *corporate* and *occupational* crime. They conceptualise corporate crime as the offences corporate officials commit to further the legitimate purpose of the corporation, and include bribery, corrupt practices, violations of companies and securities law, breaches of laws and regulations relating to taxation, environmental protection, occupational health and safety, consumer protection and discrimination. More generally, Schrager and Short define *organisational* crime as 'illegal acts of omission or commission of an individual or group of individuals in a legitimate formal organization in accordance with the operative goals of the organization, which have a serious physical or economic impact on employees, consumers or the general public' (1978, pp. 411–12). While corporate or organisational crime might benefit individual directors or managers, the illegal acts are not committed exclusively for personal gain (Clinard & Yeager 1980, p. 19; Grabosky 1984, p. 95). Occupational crime, in contrast, is committed by individuals or small groups of individuals in the course of their occupations for personal gain (Clinard & Quinney 1973, p. 188). It includes violations of law by business people, politicians, trade union members, lawyers, doctors, and employees who embezzle money, steal tools or equipment. Even though corporate and ocupational crime entail trust violations and it is often impossible to determine who is the ultimate beneficiary of the illegality, to facilitate clarity they are discussed separately.

Corporate Crime

Corporate crime is any act, punishable by the state, committed by corporations or, more accurately, by individuals within corporations, to achieve corporate goals. The illegal activity can be prohibited under administrative, civil or criminal law (Clinard & Yeager 1980, p. 16). Even so, divisions between the various types of law are somewhat arbitrary and they may not make much difference to the consequences of the illegal behaviour or to the victims. The nature of corporate bodies raises special problems for criminal law: they are legal fictions distinct from their members or founders and courts are reticent to 'pierce the corporate veil' and equate the activities of the corporation with those of managers, directors or shareholders; corporations can be created or wound up with relative ease—an ephemeral quality that human actors lack; assigning responsibility is difficult as evidence—in the form of documents, minutes of meetings, memoranda, invoices, contracts, cheques, ledgers, bank statements and computer data bases—is easily manipulated, circumvented or destroyed (Shapiro 1990, p. 354); and such criminal penalties as imprisonment are not available where a corporation is found criminally liable and fines often lack any deterrent or punitive value as their effects are passed on to consumers, employees or shareholders.

Tomasic (1994, pp. 255, 265–7) makes a useful distinction between a breach of the corporate criminal law by a corporation or its agents; and a breach of corporate criminal law involving manipulation of the corporate form itself, which might entail misuse of audited accounts, negligence or favourable bias on the part of supposedly independent company auditors, fabricating transactions to enable directors to receive fees and commissions, and directors moving their activities from one company to another after each is wrecked financially. A recent example involved the movement of money within the Qintex group of companies, the complexity of which made it difficult to identify any illegality. Schroders, a merchant bank, sold a large sum of yen to Qintex Television Ltd (QTL) which was used to service the debts of Qintex Australia Finance (QAF). Schroders took legal action to force QAF to repay the debt. The court had difficulty determining which company took out the loan, as the judge observes: 'where money is shuffled round the members of a groups of companies to those in most immediate need, it is an exercise in fiction to pinpoint ... the intention of the parties to the money movements as to the identity of the contracting parties (*Qintex Australia Finance Ltd v. Schroders Australia Ltd* (1991) 9 ACLC 109 at 113). However, it reaffirmed the separate corporate personalities of each of the subsidiary companies and held that the contract was between QTL, not QAF, and Schroders, thus the bank's attempt to obtain repayment from QAF, which actually used the money, failed. The judge expresses frustration that the rigid separation of corporate personalities does not reflect commercial reality and serves to obscure business practices which should be illegitimate.

The pressure for profit has been identified as 'the single most compelling factor behind deviance by industry, whether it be price fixing, the destruction of competition, or the misrepresentation of a product' (McCaghy 1976, p. 218). However, the literature documents criminality on such a scale among public organisations that the profit motive must be questioned as the most significant cause of corporate crime or illegality. Examples range from corruption in police departments, to the British and Australian armies' intentional exposure of soldiers to fall-out from nuclear explosions resulting in cancer and early deaths. All organisations experience pressure to resort to illegitimate means of goal attainment when legitimate ones are blocked, especially when they operate within a culture of competition, a central component of the culture of contemporary industrial capitalism (Coleman 1987, p. 420). Schrager and Short (1978, p. 413) criticise the overemphasis on economic gain as the impetus for organisational crime. They suggest a new conception comprising not only of illegal acts but including any act with a serious physical or economic impact on employees, consumers or the general public. An analysis of three well-known price fixing conspiracies in the heavy electrical equipment industry which took place in the USA in the 1950s demonstrates that secrecy was a paramount consideration and that the illegal networks involved high risks, major corporations, government buyers and the careers and reputations of eminent business people (Baker & Faulkner 1993, p. 844). Whereas efficiency motivates legal networks, secrecy motivates illegal organisation. The researchers identify a fundamental problem for illegal networks involving companies and their agents (employees): the dilemma of concealment versus co-ordination. On the one hand, the conspiracy can be maintained only through secrecy and concealment, yet, on the other, the scale of the conspiracy necessitates co-ordination which requires information management. Where illegal networks have low information-processing needs, secrecy results in decentralised structures which protect corporate executives from legal liability. Centralised structures, albeit more task-efficient, increase top management's vulnerability (Baker & Faulkner 1993, pp. 853–6).

Since Sutherland's statement that the only significant difference between white-collar and so-called ordinary crimes is their regulation, authors have struggled to accommodate other differences, including issues of intent and liability. A central element of most ordinary crimes is *mens rea* or a guilty mind. Even though a corporation is a legal person, that is, separate and distinct from its managers and directors, questions arise as to whether it has a mind that can form the necessary criminal intent (*Harvard Law Review* 1979, p. 1241). A corporation's policies may reflect illegal or deviant intentions, recklessness or negligence which are irreducible to the intentions of directors, officers or employees. Moreover, if violations result from standard operating procedures, it is difficult to hold particular individuals responsible as the responsibility is diffused among numerous employees (French 1979, pp. 212–13; Hopkins 1978, p. 227). Even though the corporation exists beyond its officers, it cannot be punished in the same way since it cannot be jailed. Sanctions usually take the form of a fine or the revocation of a licence, ultimately to be passed onto the consumer or customer. In Australia, a corporation will be liable for the criminal acts of its officers or employees done in the scope of their authority if it can be shown that those acts were, in fact, acts of the corporation, that is, that the person responsible was sufficiently senior in the company's management for his or her conduct to be able to be viewed as that of the company (Latimer 1988, p. 92).

Recent examples of corporate crimes or illegality include the sale of Thalidomide, the Dalkon Shield contraceptive and other pharmaceutical goods marketed without adequate testing or without heed of contrary results; the marketing or dumping of dangerous drugs in the developing world; such industrial accidents as the Union Carbide disaster at Bhopal in 1984 which killed more than 3000 people; nuclear explosions, for example Chernobyl and Three Mile Island; and the exposure of workers to toxic environments resulting in cancer, asbestosis, and other terminal illnesses. Braithwaite (1984, pp. 5–6) argues that among multinational corporations the pharmaceutical industry has the worst record of international bribery and corruption, a history of fraud in the safety-testing of drugs, and a disturbing record of criminal negligence in the unsafe manufacture of drugs.

Many of the injuries corporate persons cause, like asbestosis and silicosis, are 'insidious', as the links between their causes and manifest symptoms are often obscure, particularly when symptoms are of a general disease rather than a specific trauma (Calhoun & Hiller 1988, p. 162; McCulloch, Jock 1986). Establishing that asbestosis or cancer results from exposure to asbestos fibre becomes more difficult the weaker a person's relationship to an asbestos mine. For example, women who washed the overalls of miners have been exposed to asbestos dust, but seeking compensation from the mining corporations is very difficult. These factors increase the difficulties in assigning responsibility to corporate actors.

The emergence of corporate crime

Two factors are important in understanding the emergence of corporate crime. First, organisational scale and complexity diffuse responsibility and second, problems of detection and evidence make prosecutions and convictions rare. The absence of identifiable victims or the distance between the corporate decision-maker and the victim reduces the probability of complaints and prosecution. As Braithwaite comments: 'When a New York board meeting decides to continue marketing a dangerous drug in a Third World country, the victims could hardly be more remote from the killers' (1984, p. 4). This suggests a control theory of deviance; the lack of social control leaves deviant activities unchecked (see chapter 2).

Organisational culture often legitimates illegal activities by, among other things, providing employees with verbalisations which cloud the differences between business and crime. This echoes Sutherland's conception of differential association and focuses on the learning process and definition of the situation, not on the 'badness' of individual actors. Often heinous corporate crimes are perpetrated by very nice people (Braithwaite 1984, pp. 1–11). In fact, while business people violate laws and other societal norms, they are often conforming to organisational expectations. Each of these distinctive aspects of corporate crime will now be discussed.

Organisations face numerous uncertainties in their environments, including the rapid growth of science and technology, mergers and takeovers, the increasing role of government in all spheres of life, rapidly changing and unpredictable market conditions, and increasing interdependence, all of which may increase pressures to break the law to achieve organisational goals. Industries where several large firms compete, for example, might engage in illegal mergers, joint ventures and interlocking directorships in order to reduce competitive uncertainty. The opportunities to engage in anti-trust violations would be less attractive in industries where many firms operate, because such a conspiracy would require so many participants, thus jeopardising concealment (Coleman 1987, p. 428). Business enterprises may also feel compelled to engage in false advertising and bribery to sell their products. Firms in the recording industry, for example, often pay disc jockeys and radio station executives to play their records (Conklin 1977, pp. 34–5). Following Merton's conception of anomie it seems that where achievement of goals through such legitimate means as profit or expanded market share, is blocked then illegitimate means of goal attainment, namely crime, may be sought.

Unlike individuals, corporations can and do structure their affairs so that all of the pressures to break the law surface at a lower level of their own organisation or in another organisation to which it sub-contracts various tasks. Alternatively, many lower-level organisational actors perform their responsibilities with integrity and honesty, only to have their work used for dishonest purposes by people more senior in the organisation who might ignore or distort their advice. Some 'respectable' corporations engage contractors to do illegal dirty work, like disposing toxic and radioactive wastes or producing fraudulent scientific data about a product's safety. Such corporations also hire illegal immigrants enabling them to ignore occupational health and safety regulations with the knowledge that the workers cannot become 'whistle-blowers' without making their illegal status known. Finally, corporations frequently move offshore to countries like Malaysia, the Philippines and the Dominican Republic where laws regulating pay, working conditions and scientific testing are far less stringent than in developed countries.

On the one hand, it would seem that large corporations with access to good legal counsel and resources to pay any damages would be most likely to break the law. This was the case with the infamous Ford Pinto car in the USA, where the company knew of the fuel tank's combustibility in rear-end collisions but decided, on cost-benefit terms, that payment of any damages or compensation for death was more efficient than recall of the cars (Dowie 1977, p. 21; Simon & Eitzen 1986, pp. 98–9). Despite the fatal injuries caused and the callous nature of this management decision, Ford technically did not break the criminal law. Australian data on actions for breaches of environmental, consumer, taxation and companies legislation show that small and medium-sized firms are more frequent violators. Because of concern over image and public relations, large firms are less likely to violate the law if they can find a way to circumvent it. Case studies show the many ways, for example by retaining specialist and expensive lawyers or moving offshore, large firms can ensure that their activities, however anti-social or harmful, do not become labelled as criminal, or remain technically within the law (Sutton & Wild 1978, pp. 189–95; 1985, p. 249).

Invariably, small business white-collar offenders have been portrayed simplistically, especially in such consumer advocacy television programs as 'The Investigators', as small-scale confidence tricksters oper-ating individually, or as victims of circumstance. Leonard and Weber (1970, pp. 420–2) maintain that cheating by motor vehicle dealers in the USA is related directly to the control of the automotive industry by a few large firms which determine prices and marketing strategies. Dealers have to make the repair side of business as profitable as possible by cheating customers. These unethical practices, Leonard and Weber conclude, are coerced occupational crimes stemming from a market structure where the auto manufacturer has criminogenic power resulting from oligopolistic control of the market (1970, p. 416). Denzin (1977, pp. 913–17) finds similar conditions in the liquor industry, where distillers impose strict sales quotas on their distributors that force them to give retailers untaxed, under-the-table incentives in order to keep up their sales. Australian data suggest that used-car fraud, specifically turning back mileage readings, reflects highly competitive market conditions which encourage 'cutting corners' and obtaining an edge on competitors by engaging in criminal fraud (Braithwaite 1978, p. 118). These case studies suggest that small businesses are victims merely responding to their market situation and not actively seeking to violate the law.

By contrast, Sutton and Wild (1985, pp. 255–7) argue that even though large national and multinational corporations restrict small business people's life chances, their commitment to a particular lifestyle gives them immense tenacity to survive. They describe the example of Australian Factors Limited (AFL), a finance company set up in 1960 to lend money to small entrepreneurs, and suggest that because of its poor management and failure to check customers' credit-worthiness it had virtually become a 'Father Christmas' to struggling owners of small businesses. Many firms would not hesitate to present forged invoices to the AFL to obtain large funds in order to maintain their own operation and the associated status symbols. Small business crimes arise from the fact that large enterprises, as well as government fiscal policy, restrict the opportunities of the small business people.

Despite the opportunities, not all corporate actors break business laws. In addition to a corporation's location in the market or ability to achieve organisational goals, the cultural norms operating within a given corporation or even an industry may not be conducive to law violation. Stone (1975, p. 236) describes the culture of the corporation as a whole range of underlying institutional attitudes and forces, including a desire for profits, expansion, power; a desire for security; a fear of failure; feelings of omniscience; and corporate ethnocentrism.

Law-breaking can become a normative pattern within a corporation accompanied by rationalisations. Cressey suggests that management fraud committed on behalf of a company is like embezzlement from a company, as it is determined by neutralising ideologies which make it somehow 'all right' to violate the law. Business executives seeking to increase their corporation's profits through illegal or unethical means often transform a number of ideologies into neutralising verbalisations (Cressey 1986, p. 201). Examples of rationalisations include:

1 *honesty is the best policy, but business is business.* Bribery, kickbacks and payoffs often become part of the political and business culture. A manager in the Mexican subsidiary of a United States pharmaceutical company whom Braithwaite interviewed, comments: 'Our company policy is not to pay bribes. But sometimes if you want a price increase it is necessary. Some of them [local officials] they do ask for extra money. This is an unofficial position, but the pharmaceutical industry has to pay bribes like everyone else' (1984, p. 42);

2 *illegal transactions are necessary for survival.* Many business people hold the view that committing crime or behaving unethically is all right if doing so is a 'necessity'. Reduced profits, failures to increase profits according to stipulated goals, and declines in market share all get defined as tight spots. This definition stimulates the use of such verbalisations as: 'It is all right to cut corners'; 'It's worth the risk'; 'I've got to be practical'; 'Everybody does it'. One of the defendants in a price-fixing trial articulated this justification when asked whether he thought his behaviour was illegal, by responding: 'Illegal? Yes, but not criminal ... I thought that we were more or less working on a survival basis in order to try to make enough to keep our plant and our employees' (Geis 1977, p. 122);

3 *government regulation of business is socialistic and counterproductive.* This rationalises ignoring business regulations by arguing that they are contrary to business and not in the best interests of free trade and the market economy. Ironically, such business regulations as anti-trust laws which prohibit monopolies, price-fixing and cartels aim to protect free trade. Corporations often view the law not in terms of prohibitions or deterrents but as an aspect of the environment requiring management and avoidance. Many large corporations hire in-house counsel to provide them with continuous legal advice on how they can achieve their business goals (Spangler 1986, pp. 70–106).

Occupational Crime

Insider trading was the most sensational occupational crime of the 1980s. It involves obtaining and exchanging price-sensitive information about the stock market and proposed mergers before it becomes public. The Australian Stock Exchange identifies the following types of insider trading:

1 *classic insider trading*: when a company director or employee buys or sells shares before the release of a price-sensitive announcement, for example a merger, takeover or proposed liquidation;

2 *front-running*: when a broker, knowing that a client has a large or price-sensitive order, initiates an advantageous transaction on the broker's or another client's behalf;

3 *scalping*: trading prior to the release of a research report;

4 *piggy backing*: a broker who observes a client's successful investments, initiates similar transactions for other clients or for him or herself;

5 *inside market information*: when a broker disseminates information that certain transactions will occur which will affect share prices (Redmond 1992, p. 924).

This information enables traders to make investments which they know will result in large profits. Newspaper headlines like 'Insider Trading Blitz Rocks Finance World', 'Corporate Stars Trapped in a Web of Greed and Sleaze', 'Is your Closest Colleague a Supergrass?', '$100m Insider Trading Charges "Tip of Iceberg"' point to a convergence of business and crime. Indeed, the question emerges whether the practices are crime or just part of normal everyday business transactions. Reports present insider trading as a crime requiring urgent attention and immediate control. One national newspaper cover story, for example, announces: 'Australian corporate circles were rocked yesterday by allegations of a massive web of insider trading involving at least 50 people, 100 companies and share market transactions worth $100 million' (Gluyas 1989, p. 1). However, insider trading is not new. The 1974 Report of the Senate Select Committee on Securities and Exchange documents the widespread incidence of insider trading, manipulation and other abuses of the stockmarkets in Australia (Australia 1974, chapter 15). Insider trading is analogous to embezzlement, as the perpetrators are in positions of trust receiving privileged information which they are able to exploit for their own benefit.

In the 1950s, Cressey developed a theory of embezzlement to explain the psychological processes whereby an individual comes to violate a position of trust. To be included within Cressey's conception of embezzlement a person must have accepted a position of trust in good faith, that is, did not take up a job with the intention of embezzling money, and the person must have violated that trust by committing a crime (1953, p. 20). After interviews with prisoners convicted of embezzlement, forgery, fraud, confidence games, uttering fictitious cheques and larceny by bailee, Cressey hypothesises that the violation of trust depends on three essential conditions:

1 The feeling that a personal financial problem is not shareable. All the situations producing such problems involved attaining or maintaining status which had been threatened by other deviance like gambling, overconfidence, attempting to present a certain image, or blackmail. As one of Cressey's interviewees reflects: 'The more I think about it the more I'm inclined to think that before a person does a thing like that [embezzle money] he must have done something previously that the community wouldn't approve of. If he's in an environment and isn't leading a double life and doesn't have anything to hide, I can't conceive of him

starting with an embezzlement. He has to do something previously' (Cressey 1953, p. 40);

2 the awareness that this problem can be secretly resolved by violation of the position of financial trust. The potential embezzler must recognise the opportunities which the job provides to solve the problems. Recognition is neither self-evident nor automatic;

3 language enables the embezzler to re-define the trust violation as non-criminal, as justified, or as a part of a general irresponsibility for which the individual is not completely accountable. Applying verbalisations to illegal conduct enables the perpetrators to accommodate their self-conceptions as trusted persons with the act of embezzling (1953, p. 30). Another interviewee comments: 'In the real estate business you have to paint a pretty picture in order to sell the property. We did a little juggling and moving around, but everyone in the real estate business has to do that. We didn't do anything that they all don't do' (1953, pp. 104–5).

One of the former partners of the failed Australian merchant bank—Ward Knight and Dunn Ltd set up in 1978 to offer, among other things, tax evasion schemes—reflects this view when commenting on the two other partners arrested for fraud: 'I think they really got a hard deal. Back then everyone was playing the game. It was considered almost like sport between the government and business. Their main crime was, perhaps, to have been caught' (Shand 1989, p. 8). Trust violators who take funds over a period of time by rationalising that they are borrowing the money or that it is normal business practice, become criminals without intending to do so. An implication of this 'everybody does it' rationalisation is that it is unfair to condemn one violator while others get away with fraud and embezzlement (Coleman 1987, p. 413).

Tomasic and Pentony's (1988, 1989a, 1989b, 1989c) interviews with a wide range of market place participants in Australia, including lawyers and stock brokers, find similar verbalisations rendering insider trading acceptable. The verbalisations all suggest a laissez-faire view of the market which tolerates illegal activities if they provide competitive advantage. One broker describes the market as being 'like the racetrack. Everyone tries to get a piece of the action'. A lawyer comments: 'people will have a flutter. Insider trading is almost accepted as one of the risks of trading' (1989a, p. 4). Another broker sums up the prevailing view of insider trading by remarking that 'within the industry we are laid back about insider trading' (1988, p. 8). This research suggests that insider trading is widespread and 'normal' business practice, especially in relation to the shares of speculative, volatile, mining high-technology companies or in those owned by a small number of shareholders (1989c, p. 188). The Australian Corporations Law (1992) prohibits insider trading and provides both criminal and civil sanctions, however there have been few successful prosecutions.

The pervasiveness of insider trading and the view that it is a normal part of doing business ('everyone does it') suggest that the law is out of step with commercial reality but is maintained for ideological reasons reaffirming the values of free competition in the face of large corporate conglomerates. This is often the case with company laws, as commercial developments precede legal regulation; laws are often revised only when a spate of frauds demonstrates their inadequacies (Sutton & Wild 1979, p. 216). Difficulties in measuring and detecting insider trading, the lack of a vocal victim, its tolerance and encouragement within the securities industry, legal complexity including problems of proof, and the impersonal nature of the transaction impede prosecutions. Because the formal legal system does not reach very far into the regulation of the securities industry, insider trading is either left unregulated at all or dealt with by informal and private means. Indeed, participants' explanations for their actions may not be verbalisations if they do not perceive their activities as deviant and the law does not prohibit them. The existence of the regulatory agencies provides a degree of symbolic reassurance to the general public, whilst practitioners in the securities industry know they have little to fear from the regulators provided that they are not too blatant in their practices. The existence of criminal sanctions and regulatory structures which theoretically deal with insider trading has led many to see insider trading as a matter for the agencies and not for the industry itself (Tomasic & Pentony 1988). Unlike Sutherland, this is not to argue that the central difference between white-collar and ordinary crimes is administrative but that the issue is that many corporate crimes, such as tax evasion, fraud and insider trading are complex and embedded in the system making them difficult to prosecute. Regulatory agencies prefer civil remedies rather than criminal penalties in part because the standard of proof is lower (on the balance of probabilities not beyond a reasonable doubt) and they often can get higher fines in the civil courts.

One of the most highly publicised examples of tax evasion in Australia is the so-called 'bottom of the harbour' scheme which sparked a Royal (Costigan) Commission, reporting in 1982 and 1984, and an inquiry by the Victorian Corporate Affairs Office into the activities of the Federated Ship Painters and Dockers Union. The scheme involved union officials acting as 'bogus' or 'straw' company directors involved in tax evasion, drug importation and trafficking, Starting Price (SP) bookmaking, money laundering and social security fraud. Various court decisions in the 1970s limiting the Tax Commissioner's role created a legal environment conducive to tax avoidance on the part of professionals and small and medium-sized business sectors. The Commonwealth Tax Office could not make substantive judgements regarding whether an individual or company engaged in tax avoidance; it could only check whether they adhered to the letter of the law. Various tax offices also apparently declined to initiate or rigorously pursue prosecutions for tax evasion (Sutton 1989, pp. 3–6). The 'bottom of the harbour' scheme is an example of how laws create opportunities for deviant behaviour rather than deterring or punishing it. The emergence of such a scheme required three central conditions: low perceived risks of detection and prosecution; the opportunity to make vast amounts of money; and a number of people willing to act as directors in false companies without asking too many questions. As one participant comments: 'I don't ask questions. I never have. I find that being a painter and docker it was always the healthiest way, so I never ask questions' (Sutton 1989, p. 9).

Other prominent occupational crimes include medical fraud, the fudging of research data and misappropriation of clients' funds. Following newspaper accounts in 1981, the growing suspicion of widespread medical benefits fraud was confirmed early in 1982 when even the Australian Medical Association estimated that over 800 of its members were engaged in gross abuse of the medical benefits program (Grabosky & Braithwaite 1986, p. 154). The estimated costs of medical fraud and overservicing range from $130 to $200 million per annum which outweighs the national cost of burglary, estimated to be $73 million in 1979, and nears the total property loss from all conventional crime, estimated at $200 million per year (Cashman 1982a, p. 60; Wilson & Gorring 1985, p. 175). Fraud is the making of false or misleading statements on documents used to obtain medical benefits. Overservicing is more complex, and refers to services not reasonably required for a patient's adequate medical care. Overservicing can include unnecessary surgery performed only because a government or private insurance program will cover the cost, ordering superfluous laboratory tests, and encouraging unnecessary office visits or hospitalisation (Grabosky & Braithwaite 1986, p. 155; Opit 1983, pp. 240–1). The threat of malpractice litigation may be the cause of increased overservicing. The Commonwealth Department of Health estimates that between 900 and 2500 doctors are defrauding Medibank, the national health scheme (Wilson 1989, p. 78). Most fraud and overservicing would occur among private individual practitioners because of the low visibility of the actions and minimal chance of detection. The fee-for-service structure of medical practice creates opportunities for at least six principle forms of medical fraud (Pontell, Jesilow & Geis 1982, p. 118; Wilson 1989, pp. 80–1):

1 *time shuffling*: where doctors deliberately treat patients after hours and thus charge higher rates;
2 *upgrading*: charging for more services than were actually performed;
3 *injury enlargement*: exaggerating the nature and severity of the injury treated;
4 *ping-ponging*: making unnecessary referrals to other physicians or specialists. This might also involve fee-splitting, that is collusion between doctors whereby they agree to split the fees for a series of referrals;
5 *phantom treatment*: billing for services and operations never performed;
6 *assembly-line production*: seeing many patients for a small period of time yet charging the normal rate.

The impetus for professional deviance relates to occupational socialisation and the unique position members of the professions have regarding access to illegitimate opportunity structures combined with competition for patients or clients. Studies of medical and law students indicate that their professional education shifts their orientation from patient or client needs to remuneration, professional autonomy and the economics of the profession which strengthen their expectations about affluent lifestyles (Becker et al. 1961, chapter 1; Granfield & Koenig 1992; Wilson & Gorring 1985 p. 179). Additionally, solo practitioners often find the running of a small business difficult and their lack of training in financial management creates pressures for deviance. Not only do members of a profession working on a fee-for-service basis have greater access to legitimate opportunities, they also have more access to illegitimate activities with a low probability of detection and prosecution than the perpetrators of such conventional crimes as robbery and property theft. Even if fraud is suspected, difficulties relate to ascertaining and identifying the offences, the total money involved and obtaining evidence, especially as clients and patients are reticent to act as witnesses (Cashman 1982b, p. 118).

Moreover, because the professions generally are self-regulated, complaints against practitioners are initially handled within the profession by law societies and bar associations and criminal prosecutions are rare. Carlin's important investigation of the legal profession estimates that only 2 per cent of lawyers who violate professional norms are processed and less than 1 per cent are sanctioned officially (1966, p. 150–62). Arnold and Hagan (1992) identify three central factors influencing misconduct among lawyers: inexperience or lack of time in practice, a consequence of which is fewer clients and less income; stratification within the profession which places solo practitioners at the bottom of the hierarchy (Heinz & Laumann 1982); and economic recession which increases competition for a declining amount of legal work. Their research on lawyers against whom complaints were lodged with a Canadian provincial law society indicates that the cumulative effects of inexperience, solo practice and economic recession increase the probability of prosecution and that inexperienced solo practitioners are prosecuted for professional misconduct at a higher rate during a recession because they experience a heightened risk of surveillance. These findings support a labelling model of deviant careers whereby social control, rather than having a deterrent effect, increases the likelihood of subsequent prosecution independent of the distribution of the deviant behaviour (Arnold & Hagan 1992, pp. 778–9).

Another type of professional deviance is negligence, in particular medical negligence, which receives considerable public attention. Again, such cases are rarely prosecuted, in part because patients lack the expertise to evaluate medical services and the courts adopt a very narrow view of negligence when assessing professional personnel. Usually, the courts maintain that the medical action must be far beyond the boundaries of normal medical practice to constitute negligence. In a situation where a wife poisoned her husband with arsenic but the doctors diagnosed his condition as alcoholism and treated him accordingly, the court did not agree that the medical personnel contributed to the man's death (*R v. Bristow* (1960) SASR 210 at 217). In 1987, in South Australia, an anaesthetist was tried for the manslaughter of a woman by incorrectly inserting the oxygen tube into her oesophagus rather than the trachea during an operation resulting in oxygen deprivation. The prosecution argued that he had consumed a quantity of alcohol before the operation therefore impairing his judgement. The trial judge did not accept this allegation and acquitted the doctor finding no evidence of criminal negligence while agreeing that the misplaced tube ultimately led to death. The judge ordered that the anaesthetist's name be suppressed resulting in considerable controversy about freedom of speech and the court's protection of a high status individual. The Crown was successful in having the suppression order lifted (*R v. F* (1987) unreported, SA Supreme Court). This case demonstrates the near impossibility of prosecuting a doctor for criminal negligence. Research in the USA suggests that drug-addiction, alcoholism and psychiatric disorders among doctors which affect professional performance are more likely to be defined as medical issues for the profession to resolve rather than as legal or criminal problems (Morrow 1982, pp. 102–5). Nevertheless, civil actions for negligence may be more successful as Australian courts are being more specific and interventionist regarding the nature of a doctor's duty to the patient, the obligation to warn her or him of any risk inherent in a proposed treatment and the status of informed consent (*Rogers v. Whitaker* (1992) Australian Torts Rep, 81–189 at 673). A possible unintended consequence of increasing or clarifying medical practitioners' legal liability, is an increase in litigation, large court-ordered payments to complainants and problems in obtaining insurance. Medical malpractice crises emerged in the USA in the 1970s and 1980s and physicians responded by successfully lobbying for tort law reform (Hay 1992, p. 655).

Deviance in science resembles professional deviance: the effects are often harmful, problems exist in evaluating its prevalence, and rates of detection and punishment are low. The main difference is that scientists are oriented to professional kudos, not just financial success. A recent, much-publicised example of the fraudulent reporting of scientific experiments is Dr William McBride, a Sydney obstetrician, who falsified the results of a 1980 experiment on rabbits to support his case that the drug, Debendox, causes birth deformity. A special inquiry set up by Foundation 41, McBride's research institute (which had no legal powers, was not a trial, could not administer oaths or cross-examine witnesses), headed by a Former Chief Justice of the High Court, Sir Harry Gibbs, finds that deliberate falsification had occurred in a scientific paper. It concludes that McBride deviated from scientific method in conducting and reporting an experiment indicating dishonesty and an absence of scientific integrity (Nicol 1989, pp. 160–2). Ironically, McBride was one of the first medical researchers to suspect the connection between Thalidomide and deformed births, in 1961.

Like any other fraud, scientific falsification needs to be explained in terms of the political economy of scientific work which determines available opportunities as well as scientists' verbalisations which neutralise their deviant behaviour. Declining opportunities in science and the steep competition for jobs and for grant money in the second half of the 1970s contribute to the 'publish or perish' syndrome which places heavy pressure on young scientists (including social scientists). This pressure results in plagiarism, fudging, fraud, forgery and widespread destruction of laboratory data. Ben-Yehuda (1986) argues that because replication is not a major activity in science the probability of fraud detection is very low. Punishment for deviant scientists often does not become a matter of public knowledge because of concerns about the prestige and reputations of the research institute or the university and of other scientists. If the case is not blatant fraud and fabrication on a mass scale, the worst punishment is the deviant scientist loses his or her job. While this in itself is serious, it hardly compares with the punishments to which other convicted offenders are subjected (Ben-Yehuda 1986, p. 8).

The combination of a low probability of detection and non-harsh punishments provides a fertile context for deviance, including both occupational and corporate crimes.

Organised crime

The concept of organised crime suggests a co-ordinated structure or network of participants intentionally established or at least maintained to engage in illegal activities. Organised crime can be subject to the same kinds of sociological examination as any other kind of organisation including analyses of the degree of formalisation, the division of labour, the hierarchy of authority, the type, number and variety of participants and the complexity of tasks and transactions involved in everyday activities. While business corporations are not set up with the explicit goal of breaking the law, many of the illegal activities corporations and organised crime syndicates commit are similar, for example tax evasion and fraud. Moreover, criminal organisations are not engaged solely in criminal activity and may participate in legitimate business activities. Symbiotic relationships, perhaps entailing bribery and corruption, often exist between crime syndicates and such legitimate organisations as banks, the stock exchange, trade unions, business corporations, police forces and governments. Organised crime is linked also to occupational crime. Lawyers, accountants and financial advisers, knowingly or unknowingly, may provide information and advice to participants in criminal associations thereby facilitating the commission of crime and potentially rendering them an accessory to the illegality.

Organised crime encompasses a variety of offences but is perceived usually as comprising activities in illegal markets, for example drug trafficking, smuggling, prostitution and illegal gambling. The National Crime Authority (NCA) Act 1984 provides a comprehensive view of organised crime by defining 'relevant offence' as one:

(a) that involves 2 or more offenders and substantial planning and organization; (b) that involves, or is of a kind that ordinarily involves, the use of sophisticated methods and techniques; (c) that is committed, or is of a kind that is ordinarily committed, in conjunction with other offences of a like kind; and (d) that involves theft, fraud, tax evasion, currency violations, illegal drug dealings, illegal gambling, obtaining financial benefit by vice engaged in by others, extortion, violence, bribery or corruption of, or by, an officer of the Commonwealth, an officer of a State or an officer of a Territory, bankruptcy and company violations, harbouring of criminals, forging of passports, armaments dealings or illegal importation or exportation of fauna into or out of Australia, or that involves matters of the same general nature as one or more of the foregoing, or that is of any prescribed kind (NCA Act 1984 s. 4).

This definition is very broad and amorphous; it emphasises planning and organisation but these attributes are present in many criminal activities involving more than one person, and the list of crimes might involve a variety of actors, not just participants in a criminal organisation. Dickie suggests shifting attention from attempting to identify and control organised crime as a distinct but nebulous entity to addressing how crime is organised by examining the pattern of criminal organisation, the degree of influence over market or effective regulation and the significance of the illegal market or industry and relationship to the legal economy (1994, pp. 107–12). Illegal and legal markets are not mutually exclusive and separate; illegal economic activity can be viewed as part of the overall economic activity.

Discussions of organised crime often stress the ethnicity of the participants. Research indicates that Italian organised crime groups control the majority of cannabis production and distribution in Australia whereas ethnic Chinese groups—specifically the Triad societies, not all of which are engaged in criminal activity—dominate world heroin markets. Italian crime groups, for example the Mafia and the Italian–American La Cosa Nostra crime families, and criminally oriented Triads have similarities: both engage in extortion, protection rackets in certain industries, gambling and drug trafficking. The Mafia is structured around families and patron/client relationships whereas Triads consist of initiated members located within a hierarchy of power, authority and obedience (Kelly, Chin & Fagan 1993, p. 255). A study of Chinese organised crime in New York City suggests links between the expanding youth gangs and Chinese organised crime outside the USA. The gangs engage in four types of victimisation:

1 *protection* entailing a demand for money from the owner of a business to ensure that it will not be disturbed by that gang or by any other;
2 *extortion* or the periodic demand for money where the perpetrators do not promise any service in return. Extortion is one of the most prevalent crimes in the Chinese communities and when retail business owners refuse to pay, gang members vandalise, burglarise, burn or close the businesses down;
3 *forced sales* where gang members force business owners to buy goods with highly inflated prices from them;

4 *free goods and services* from the business for gang members.

The interviews with over 600 Chinese business owners in the New York metropolitian area reveal that most of the victims were other Chinese people, an estimated three-quarters of the restaurants compared with one in ten of the professional offices were victimised and the business owners offer little resistance. Except for paying protection money weekly or monthly, most victims are not exploited more than three times a year and gang activities did not seriously, financially disadvantage most businesses (Kelly, Chin & Fagan 1993, p. 259). Little overall financial cost and fear of recrimination by the gangs militate against invoking law enforcement or criminal sanctions.

Social control of corporate and organised crime

The financial cost of white-collar crime is probably several times as great as that of all the crimes customarily regarded as the 'crime problem', and the evidence suggests that corporate offenders persistently violate civil and criminal laws. Treasury's 1985 Draft White paper estimates revenue losses of $3 billion per year arising from tax fraud; a meat substitution scandal in 1981 threatened an export market worth $1 billion per year; hundreds of deaths and tens of thousands of serious injuries occur in Australian workplaces each year, often arising from occupational health and safety law violations; and illegal price fixing arrangements in the building industry in one capital city helped add an estimated $30 million in construction costs during the late 1970s (Grabosky & Braithwaite 1987, p. 1). In the USA, street crime costs around $4 billion which is less than 5 per cent of the average take from corporate crime. The savings and loan debacle in which over 300 companies have defaulted represents an astronomic cost to the governments underwriting them (Snider 1991, pp. 209–10; Zimring & Hawkins 1993, pp. 249–58). Nearly all of the seventy largest United States industrial and commercial corporations Sutherland investigated were recidivist in the sense of having two or more adverse court decisions against them.

It seems that none of the official procedures used on business people for law violation has been very effective in rehabilitating them or in deterring other businesses from similar behaviour. The illegal behaviour is much more extensive than the prosecutions and complaints indicate. Business people, or such other organisations as the government and the military, who violate laws designed to regulate their activities do not usually lose status. Business people customarily feel and express contempt for law, for government and for governmental personnel, as they are perceived as impeding business behaviour. For example, John Elliott, a former chief executive of Elders IXL (one of Australia's top companies) countered the Taxation Commissioner's aims to eliminate tax avoidance by claiming that the Australian Taxation Office (ATO) has 'been engaged in a trial by press release, accusing companies and individuals of tax avoidance who have in fact been acting in accordance with the law', and in usurping the policy-making role of the legislature (Tingle 1988, p. 1). The Australian Chamber of Commerce argues that Australia's systems of business regulation are a barrier to developing international competitiveness, difficult to understand, unnecessarily broad, increase costs for business investors, create uncertainty and inhibit risk-taking and enterprise (Chong 1994, p. 33).

Prospects for controlling corporate law violations appear negligible because of the problems of detection, the economic and political power of corporate organisations, the role of regulatory agencies, and difficulties in separating unacceptable from normal business activities. The likelihood of detection is low when corporate activity crosses several national boundaries, which allows international law evasion strategies that utilise Swiss banks, tax havens, for example the Marshall Islands in the South Pacific, pollution havens and international dumping of banned products and hazardous wastes in developing countries. Few individual law-breakers have such opportunities to cover their tracks. Moreover, in the aftermath of a corporate scandal, the corporation often has ample resources to initiate a large scale publicity campaign. The United States investment bank Drexel Burnham Lambert, involved in insider trading, for example, spent over $US140 million on its 'damage control' campaign including television commercials emphasising family values and patriotism (Perrett 1988, p. 15). Nevertheless, the court subsequently ordered Drexel to pay $650 million in fines and its former head, Michael Milken, was criminally indicted on 98 racketeering and securities fraud charges and sentenced to a ten-year prison term.

As Sutherland first pointed out, social control of ordinary crimes is radically different from that of white-collar offenders. To deal with the complexity of corporate illegality and organised crime, governments have established specialised regulatory and enforcement agencies. The Commonwealth government legislatively created the Australian Securities Commission (ASC), the National Crime Authority (NCA), the Trade Practices Commission (TPC), the Australian Federal Police (AFP) and Australian Taxation Office (ATO); the New South Wales parliament created the Independent Commission Against Corruption (ICAC) and Queensland established the Criminal Justice Commission (CJC) to counter organised crime. The Commonwealth government also enacted the Cash Transaction Reports Act 1988 as a way of reducing opportunities for money laundering and to sever links between legitimate and illegitimate business organisations. The legislation requires financial institutions to inform the ATO when $10 000 or more is deposited or transferred offshore. Additionally, criminal confiscation legislation provides for the tracing, freezing and confiscation of money or property derived from crime, especially significant in major crimes involving large profits and complex monetary transactions.

The specialised investigatory agencies have wide powers to search premises, seize documents and to interview witnesses and suspects. For example, the ASC, which replaces the National Companies and Securities Commission (NCSC) and began operations on 1 January 1991, can undertake an investigation if it suspects corporate illegality which might involve fraud or dishonesty, it can require persons to be examined and questioned on oath and hold hearings, can demand the production or seizure of company books and is not obliged to provide reasons for the investigation to the affected persons. The search and seizure powers of the Australian Taxation Office (ATO) were dramatically highlighted when thirty-seven of its officers entered and searched the premises of Citibank in the hope of locating clients' documents that would reveal a tax avoidance scheme, the estimated value of which was $100 million (*Commissioner of Taxation v. Citibank* (1989) 20 FCR 403 at 409). Newspaper reports and critics suggested that this 'raid' amounted to a fishing expedition, was an example of 'blowing up the door before knowing', and exemplified the magnitude of state incursion into individual privacy and personal liberty (Dirkis 1989, p. 63).

Legal commentators point to the tension between government concern to stem corporate crime and citizens' rights of privacy and protections against self-incrimination. They are also concerned about the role of lawyers and the fate of legal professional privilege (Boniface 1992, pp. 327–8, 332–7; Kluver 1992, pp. 31–2). In contrast to conventional crime, evidence of corporate crime typically is contained in written material frequently produced in the context of the professional–client relationship. According to one member of the AFP: 'The most sought after commodity during major fraud investigations is documentation ... [and in the vast majority of cases] the most lucrative source of these documents is professional offices such as legal and accounting firms' (Sing 1986, p. 33). Even though these communications and documents are protected by confidentiality, some of the special agencies have the power to obtain them. Lawyers feel that this undermines their professional integrity and will constrain them in advising clients, especially where they are obliged to report knowledge of a client's fraud or other illegality to a third party (Partlett & Szweda 1991, pp. 25–31).

After advising a corporation or association involved in criminal activity, a lawyer or accountant also might be prosecuted for corporate illegality as an accessory, accomplice or co-conspirator (Grabosky 1990, p. 74). In the USA, the Racketeering Influenced and Corrupt Organisations (RICO) Act enables victims of organised crime to sue the perpetrators and, if successful, they receive treble damages and legal fees. RICO's primary purpose is to reduce the infiltration of organised crime and racketeering into legitimate organisations. The legislation is broad, causing concern among professional advisers who potentially come within its parameters if 'they participate in the operation or management of the enterprise itself' (*California Lawyer* 1993, p. 3; *Reves v. Ernst & Young* 113 S Ct 1163 at 1173). In Australia, the complexity and uncertainty of taxation laws, the fear of penalties and a change in the attitude from tax avoidance to tax minimisation have transformed professional tax advisers' primary role as providing advice to clients to one where they attempt to ensure their clients' compliance to the regulations (Tomasic & Pentony 1991, p. 250). Legislative requirements and obligations to the ATO constrain the professional–client relationship; the tax adviser has become more concerned with enforcement and social control than previously.

Despite their wide powers and the penalties available, regulatory agencies usually view their primary objective as achieving substantive regulatory goals and rarely think of themselves as part of the criminal justice system. Their predominant strategy is 'compliance' through persuasion or other forms of inducement rather than prosecution and deterrence law enforcement. The ASC, for example, states that its:

> surveillance programs promote efficient and properly informed markets by concentrating on areas of perceived greatest risk [for example the activities of securities and investment advisers and of trustees and managers of collective investment schemes]. The programs aim to establish a climate of compliance, ethics and responsibility through education, monitoring of market activity and enforcement of the Law. Staff examined current policy issues, visited companies and talked to their directors and officers to resolve problems, and took enforcement action where individuals or firms did not comply adequately with the Law (Australian Securities Commission 1993, p. 15).

This surveillance program contrasts sharply with that of the Department of Social Security, for example (see chapter 9). Corporate owners or managers found violating regulatory laws rarely are prosecuted nor are their firms fined large amounts and 'made' to comply. For example, in 1988–89, Australian states and territories reported less than 100 prosecutions each under the companies law (Tomasic 1990, p. 371). However, it seems that the ASC's law enforcement role has increased in the wake of numerous corporate collapses and the excesses of the 1980s. It launched civil and criminal actions against the Bond Group, Rothwells Ltd and Spedley Securities and laid criminal charges against Christopher Skase relating to the alleged improper use of his position as an officer of a finance company. In 1992–93, of the 1038 criminal prosecutions initiated by the ASC, 64 per cent resulted in convictions, 0.6 per cent in acquittals and the remainder were discontinued. Of the 720 civil actions commenced, 80 per cent were decided in the ASC's favour (Australian Securities Commission 1993, pp. 24–5).

Carson (1970, p. 393) observes that substantial violations of the nineteenth-century British Factory Acts which specified minimum safety, health and welfare standards were countered almost exclusively by the use of such formal administrative procedures as regular inspections, repeated check visits, notification of matters requiring attention, and occasional threats. The inspectors felt that such strategies were most appropriate for achieving the legislation's purpose, namely compliance. A former chief New South Wales mining inspector's comments about the working conditions at an asbestos mine at Baryulgil also reflect this view: 'We wanted the plant to comply, yes ... Not to enforce. The danger I see with enforcement ... is that if you start prosecuting people for breaches of the Act your sources of information dry up. People will not talk to you' (Gunningham 1989, p. 225).

Regulatory agencies' reticence to prosecute is not due to insufficient evidence of crime or lack of statutory power to intervene and control corporate deviance. A number of factors make the relationship between the corporate offender and regulatory agency different from that of the individual offender and the police. Firstly, unlike most police work, enforcement agencies are proactive and often a complainant or an identifiable victim does not come forward. Victims may not be aware of the source of their complaint, indeed it is difficult to identify specific causes, and they may feel powerless in the face of large corporations and perceive litigation as useless. This is especially true in Australia where class action suits generally are not available. In the USA, class actions permit victims of a particular loss or injury to jointly sue the defendant. Usually, one member of the class notifies the others and sues on their behalf. Class action suits are available when the class is so large that union of all members is impractical, the questions of law and claims are common to the class and that the representative parties will equitably and adequately protect the interests of the class (Nelthorpe 1988, p. 28). This was the case with the A.H. Robbins litigation where 200 000 women throughout the world, who had used the Dalkon Shield contraceptive, were eligible for court-ordered damages payments (Breslin 1989, p. 46). Such actions overcome the reluctance of individual consumers to sue powerful corporations, but they can be very time-consuming and unwieldy processes and the resulting damages paid to individuals in a large class are often miniscule.

Secondly, the number of corporate offences detected and prosecuted is a function of the resources available to enforcement agencies. A major complaint of regulatory agencies is lack of funds, for example the Trade Practices Tribunal indicates that it is unable to afford the best legal counsel to handle big corporate takeovers and mergers. Henry Bosch, a former chair of the NCSC (the precursor of the ASC), admitted that between 1987 and 1990 only 10 per cent of the matters referred to the commission were investigated (Taylor 1988, p. 12; Tomasic 1990, p. 370). Due to the complexity and length of trials involving many corporations law violations, questions emerge regarding the appropriateness of spending sometimes millions of dollars on a single case, especially if it involves criminal allegations. This is because criminal prosecution requires higher standards of proof and criminal charges and convictions are more prone to contestation and appeal than are civil or administrative charges, thus representing greater cost and likelihood of failure to the prosecuting agency (Shapiro 1990, p. 359, fn 10). The trials of Sir Andrew Grimwade, involving fraud charges in relation to investments in the failed aviation company JetCorp, which lasted for more than seven years, are estimated to have cost between $15 and $20 million, an amount equivalent to the whole of the 1993 operating budget of the Victorian Director of Public Prosecutions (DPP). The trial court convicted Grimwade and his co-accused and ordered suspended prison sentences, but on appeal they were acquitted (Gluyas 1994, p. 23; Gunn 1994, p. 1). The DPP indicates that about half of its annual budget for outside counsel has been spent on two or three large, complex cases; most people accused of ordinary crimes plead guilty. Thirdly, as discussed above, members of regulatory agencies do not define themselves as police with the duties of arrest and prosecution but as educators obtaining compliance through information and persuasion.

Much research focuses on the enforcement practices of agencies—state consumer affairs departments, the trade practices commission and equal opportunity boards—which are responsible for obtaining industries' compliance with laws and regulations. This literature suggests that the regulation of corporate misconduct in Australia (as elsewhere) is largely symbolic. Grabosky and Braithwaite's (1986) study of ninety-six major federal, state and local government agencies involved in business regulation find them to be 'of manners gentle'. They initiate litigation or any adversarial encounter with industry only as a last resort. Most of the agencies possess statutory powers of entry, search, seizure and investigation which are often wider than those of the police. Fifty-one have specific power to order production to cease in a workplace, to order that a machine no longer be used, or to close down the workplace. One-third have the power to force people to answer questions even if their answers would be incriminating, and, unlike the police, most (77 per cent) can inspect private premises without a warrant. Of the agencies, 60 per cent work with principal statutes which define offences as strict liability, thus obviating the need to prove intent in order to secure a conviction (1986, p. 201).

Agencies' major strategies include appeals to industry to act responsibly, token enforcement, keeping the lid on problems which could blow up into scandals, and passing the buck to another agency when a scandal emerges. One-third of the agencies had not launched a prosecution in the most recent three years for which data were available. The prosecutions were overwhelmingly directed at companies rather than at individuals who acted on behalf of the company, but for more than half the agencies which do prosecute the average fine is under $200. The agencies view the use of enforcement and threats of enforcement primarily as a background which gives them authority and as bargaining chips in negotiation for compliance when faced with resistance. Over time, regulators become more concerned to serve the interests of the industry with which they are in regular contact, than the more remote and abstract public interest. The tendency for regulators, for example mine inspectors, to be recruited from the regulated industry also minimises their social control functions. Regulatory agencies' low record of prosecutions is not simply a result of their lack of motivation. It arises from difficulties in identifying corporate wrongdoing because it is often closely associated with legitimate business practices and the legal and practical difficulties in initiating legal action.

This situation is not distinctively Australian. Shapiro's (1984, 1985) investigation of the United States Securities Exchange Commission (SEC), the major protector of capital markets with responsibility for the regulation of publicly owned corporations, the securities markets and professionals who service them, indicates that while criminal dispositions are often appropriate they are rarely pursued to the sentencing stage. Out of every 100 suspects the SEC investigates, ninety-three have committed securities violations that carry criminal penalties. Legal action is taken against forty-six of them, but only eleven receive criminal sanctions. Six of these are indicted, five are convicted and three sentenced to prison (1985, p. 182). Moreover, regardless of the seriousness of the offence, the existence of civil or administrative sanctions increases the likelihood of legal action and reduces the risk of criminal prosecution (Shapiro 1990, p. 360).

The wide powers of investigatory agencies are used infrequently in part as a result of the fragmentation of Australian business regulation across overlapping and often unco-ordinated federal, state and local government entities. This is especially true in the area of organised crime where a number of inquiries suggest that the interrelationships between law enforcement bodies are characterised by lack of co-operation and jealousies (Corns 1992a, p. 170). The NCA's capacity to identify multiple and complex transactions depends on access to the information that customs, social security, taxation and state police departments collect. However, tension between the NCA and other agencies has emerged. Members of the Australian Federal Police view the NCA as impinging on their traditional police territory and argue that conventional police forces could achieve the same successes if they had received the funds supporting the NCA. Other agencies distrust the NCA because of a widespread perception that it is overly secretive and does not share information (Corns 1992a, pp. 179–81; Whittaker 1993, pp. 56, 59). The NCA's multi-disciplinary team approach also has led to conflict between police and lawyers; police criticise their exclusion from key policy decisions and administration and argue that lawyers do not understand the practical dimensions of criminal investigation (Corns 1992b, p. 247). These tensions thwart the effective operation of specialised regulatory and enforcement agencies.

Enforcement problems not only result from agencies' inaction, but are often built into the legislation. The Trade Practices Act 1974 (Commonwealth), which prohibited anti-competitive business practices and those which mislead or deceive consumers, overcame the problem of imputing intent to corporations by imposing strict liability on corporations for their behaviour. However, if the defendant company could show that it had made serious efforts to avoid contravening the Act it would not be held responsible for the violation (Hopkins 1980, pp. 202–3). In another example, Hopkins and Parnell (1984, pp. 181–5) show that despite the progressive expansion and updating of the safety regulations contained within the Mines Regulation Act (New South Wales), amendments making it easier for violators to escape prosecution undermine the possibility of enforcement. The principal provision weakens the regulations by specifying their application only if it is 'reasonably practicable' for management to comply. The Act makes the owner, agent and manager liable for violations occurring down the line, but the fact that a manager need only show that an order had been issued to employees to observe the regulations and had taken 'all reasonable means' to avoid liability dilutes the legal prohibitions. The Act also specifies that prosecutions under the vicarious liability provision cannot be brought by anyone other than an inspector except with the written consent of the Minister, effectively making it impossible for employees to prosecute owners or management.

The courts' and regulatory agencies' treatment of strict liability offences might also impede enforcement of business regulations. Some judges have held that strict liability offences can only be quasi-criminal because the central element of all real crime is mens rea (Sweet v. Parsley (1970) AC 132). Carson (1980, p. 163) demonstrates that the enforcement of the British Factory legislation, which created strict liability offences, foundered because inspectors insisted they would initiate criminal proceedings only when the offence stemmed from some concrete element of intention.

It is often argued that corporate crime is allowed to flourish because the community tolerates it and defines such deviance as necessary for business enterprise. This was one of Sutherland's main contentions. However, a national survey of attitudes toward white-collar crime shows that Australians perceive many forms of white-collar crime as more serious and deserving of more severe punishment than most forms of common crime (Grabosky, Braithwaite & Wilson 1987). The public perceives most types of individual homicide as more serious than all types of white-collar crime, but white-collar crimes which cause severe harm to persons are generally rated as more serious than all other types of crime. Respondents regarded the fatal incidence of industrial pollution and employer negligence resulting in the loss of a worker's leg as more serious than armed robbery and only less serious than fatal stabbing and heroin trafficking. Even so, the severity of penalties the public prescribes is inconsistent with the perceived seriousness of offences reported. The preferred penalty for corporate offending was a monetary fine, whereas respondents felt imprisonment to be appropriate for such conventional crimes as homicide, armed robbery, and break and enter. A further problem with this survey is that it presents white-collar crime as clear cut, identifiable and easy to prove, but rarely would a regulatory agency be confronted with evidence of gross negligence or the deliberate malpractices the survey uses as examples.

It appears that legal control of corporate crime is all but impossible. Snider suggests that this stems from the constant vigilance needed to secure even minimal enforcement of laws against corporate crime and the state's reticence to penalise corporations because of their role in amassing capital which affects gross domestic products, employment and inflation, that is, central components of government policy in late twentieth-century capitalism (1991, pp. 211, 214–15). In contrast to the traditional law enforcement approach emphasising punishment and deterrence, much corporate deviance might be controlled more effectively through informal social control by subjecting offending corporations to negative publicity, stigma and shaming (Braithwaite & Fisse 1983, p. 67). This is based on the premise that corporations value their prestige and reputation highly, as is indicated by their often elaborate advertising campaigns. Informal publicity successfully influenced and modified the marketing and selling of infant formula by the Nestlé company in developing countries (Gerber & Short 1986, pp. 210–12). In response to the company's promotional tactics relating to the preparation, storage and administration of the formula, ten nations, the World Health Organization (WHO) and the United Nations International Children's Emergency Fund (UNICEF) boycotted Nestlé products. The company subsequently altered its policies demonstrating the success of the campaign, at least in the short-term, and the power of social movements and of adverse publicity even against large multinational corporations. Unlike individuals, corporations will not respond to labelling by developing a deviant self-identity but attempt to project a positive image to displace negative labels.

Summary

The concept of white-collar (corporate and occupational) crime raises central issues for theories of deviance. Sometimes the activities of corporations and members of the professions are deemed criminal even if they do not technically violate any law. Business and professional people have access to a range of tax minimisation schemes due to loopholes in legislation and judicial interpretation of statutes. However, to most people, the differences between tax minimisation and evasion appear non-existent. This again reinforces the point that behaviour is not inherently deviant, but is rendered so by application of norms. Corporate organisations are regulated more by civil and administrative law than by the criminal law, whereas the opposite is true for individuals, thus the illegalities of the former are less likely to be labelled as crime. Following the reasoning of the labelling perspective, few corporations are deviant because few are identified and labelled publicly as law-breakers. If laws prohibit only some corporate activities and are enforced only rarely, and the behaviour is pervasive among business people who consider it a rational response to the market situation and their profit-maximising goals, then the question of whether it is deviant arises.

The following chapter examines the opposite situation of powerless individuals who are highly likely to be identified as violating the law, receive negative labels and be subject to surveillance and social control by government departments.

Key terms

White-collar crime
Occupational crime
Organised crime
Differential association
Embezzlement
Conspiracy
Medical negligence
Organisational culture
Compliance

Corporate crime
Organisational crime
Civil action
Insider trading
Fraud
Trust
Scientific fraud
Regulatory agency

Main points

1 Sutherland, the first sociologist to develop a theory of white-collar crime, defined it as the illegal activities of high-status individuals undertaken in the course of their occupations. He maintains that white-collar crime, like any other type of criminal deviance, is learned through social interaction.

2 It is useful to distinguish between occupational and corporate crime. Occupational crime is committed by individuals in the course of their jobs, principally for personal gain. Corporate crime involves criminal or harmful activities which benefit corporate goals of profit or efficiency maximisation.

3 Corporate and occupational crimes are rarely dealt with by the criminal courts. Regulatory agencies attempt to obtain conformity to the relevant legislation through persuasion, education and warnings rather than a punitive approach.

4 Scientific and medical fraud are examples of occupational deviance which needs to be explained in terms of opportunity structures and the absence of social control.

5 Recently, a large amount of research has been conducted in Australia regarding the deviant or harmful activities of corporations, including occupational safety issues, tax evasion and the marketing of unsafe products. Special problems arise regarding the culpability and intentions of corporate entities.

6 The concept of organised crime suggests a co-ordinated structure or network of participants whose primary rationale is illegal activity, including drug trafficking, extortion, illegal importation and exportation, prostitution and illegal gambling.

Further reading

Braithwaite, John 1985, 'White Collar Crime', *Annual Review of Sociology*, vol. 11, pp. 1–25.
Grabosky, Peter & John Braithwaite 1986, *Of Manners Gentle: Enforcement Strategies of Australian Business Regulatory Agencies*, Oxford University Press, Melbourne.

Grabosky, Peter & Adam Sutton eds 1989, *Stains on a White Collar: Fourteen Studies in Corporate Crime or Corporate Harm*, Hutchinson, Sydney.

Shapiro, Susan 1984, *Wayward Capitalists: Targets of the Securities and Exchange Commission*, Yale University Press, New Haven.

Shapiro, Susan 1990, 'Collaring the Crime Not the Criminal: Reconsidering the Concept of White-Collar Crime', *American Sociological Review*, vol. 55, pp. 346–65.

Sutherland, Edwin H. 1983, *White Collar Crime: The Uncut Version*, Yale University Press, New Haven.

CHAPTER

9

Poverty and social disadvantage

A range of activities and characteristics not usually defined as crime or illness nevertheless get labelled deviance, at least by some segments of society. Examples include unemployment, homelessness, begging, being disabled, single-parenting and poverty generally. Individuals within these categories may or may not receive government welfare benefits, but are typically subject to negative labelling or stigmatisation. Such terms as 'dole-bludger', 'welfare mother', 'problem' or 'dysfunctional family' connote deviance. As with all stigma they act like magnets and attract other deviant labels. It is often assumed that unemployed people are more likely to consume illicit drugs and engage in acquisitive crimes; that homeless people are more likely to be mentally ill than are other segments of the community. The social control of these deviant practices or individuals is the so-called welfare-state, which is less clearly a form of social control than the criminal justice system or the medical profession but which has strong links with both those systems.

The major elements of social welfare are health, education and training, housing, social security, income maintenance, legal aid and such personal social services as mental health programs or physical rehabilitation programs. Social policy refers to the application of the values and principles of the welfare state through government decisions (Graycar & Jamrozik 1993, p. 8). In defining welfare, emphasis is generally placed on assistance to disadvantaged groups, satisfaction of needs, enhancement of living conditions, and the provision of opportunities for equal participation in social life, especially in the labour market (Titmuss 1968, p. 74; Wilensky & Lebeaux 1965, p. 139). Welfare can be provided by families, the market, government agencies like the Department of Social Security, and such voluntary or charitable organisations as the Brotherhood of St Laurence or the Red Cross. Until recently, the trend has been for welfare responsibility and expenditure to shift from families and voluntary charities toward the central government. The organisation of welfare dispensed by governments is bureaucratic; departments formally apply universal criteria, not moral discretion, to determine the amount of payment or services available to eligible claimants who have a right to benefits by virtue of their citizenship.

The welfare state

The taken for granted everyday conception of the welfare system is its orientation to helping people, the alleviation of so-called social problems and the maintenance of living standards. The broad aims of social policy are the elimination of poverty, the maximisation of health and welfare, and the pursuit of equality (Briggs 1961, p. 229; Marshall 1970, pp. 11–12). This involves a range of activities and programs including material and financial assistance, counselling and guidance services. Generally, the welfare state is considered an appropriate and humane response to minimise the negative consequences of laissez-faire capitalism, industrialisation and urbanisation which generate unemployment, poverty, low housing standards at the same time as disrupting extended family networks (Quadagno 1987, pp. 110–13; Titmuss 1968, pp. 124–36; Wilensky & Lebeaux 1965, pp. 67–89; Zaretsky 1982, pp. 196–207; 1986, pp. 85–90). The perception of various commodities and services as essential for achieving basic living standards for the whole community justifies government intervention when there is no guarantee of their equitable and consistent provision by either the market or the family. According to Wilensky (1965, p. xii), the essence of the welfare state is 'government-protected minimum standards of income, nutrition, health, housing, and education for every citizen, assured to him [sic] as a political right, not as charity'. Graycar and Jamrozik suggest that the functions of the welfare state are twofold: the facilitating function enables the market to function and enables people to participate in the system by developing their capacities for production and consumption; and the maintenance function provides the means for physical survival for those individuals and groups who do not have access to these means through the market (1993, p. 9).

State provision of social welfare can be universal in scope, such as schooling and health services, or selective and focus on specific groups of people, for example unemployed or Aboriginal people. Welfare can take the form of cash transfers, for example pensions or benefits, or the provision of such services as health, education and training schemes. Two dominant conceptions of welfare prevail: residual and institutional (Wilensky & Lebeaux 1965, pp. 138–40):

1 *residual*: social welfare institutions offer assistance only when it is neither available nor accessible from the family or the market. The welfare system provides a safety net for the most extreme cases of disadvantage and deprivation;
2 *institutional*: social welfare services become accepted as a proper, legitimate function of industrial society to achieve social justice and help individual self-fulfilment. Government expenditure on housing, income maintenance, health and education aims to prevent or minimise poverty, homelessness, crime and delinquency by reducing social inequalities. The actual nature and scope of government welfare provision reflects a compromise between the values of economic individualism and free enterprise on one hand and security, equality and humanitarianism on the other.

The so-called 'welfare state' emerged after the Second World War with a principal goal of full employment, and commitment to Keynesian economics, asserting the centrality of government expenditure in alleviating poverty and stimulating economic growth. However, the beginnings of the welfare state in England are evident in the Elizabethan Poor Laws of 1597 and 1601. A pervasive theme running through the history of welfare provision distinguishes the able-bodied poor, who are able to work, from the physically and mentally ill, the old, abandoned or neglected children, and one-parent families, generally headed by women—unmarried women, widowed or deserted wives (Kumar 1984, p. 189). This latter category comprised the traditional 'deserving poor', who received private philanthropic and charitable gifts and endowments, usually administered by the church. The impetus for alms-giving was not alleviating the condition of the poor in this world, but improving the givers' chances for salvation in the next (Coser 1965, p. 141).

After the Reformation and the dissolution of the monasteries, the state partly took over this function through Poor Law institutions. Despite the establishment of workhouses, the able-bodied unemployed and those with insufficient wages were treated largely through a system of outdoor relief, as it was cheaper to make cash payments than to accommodate them. In Britain, only paupers too young, too old or too sick to care for themselves and with no one to look after them were relieved in workhouses (Kumar 1984, pp. 192–3). An 1834 law abolished the outdoor relief and effectively forced all the able-bodied poor into the workhouse. In the 1880s, unemployment as a concept was first recognised and in most industrialised societies 'full employment' became a policy goal from the 1890s to the 1940s, thus attesting to the deviant status of unemployment.

In Australia, as with all Western industrialised societies, welfare services are linked inextricably to governmental structures and bureaucratic administration. Details of welfare programs reflect the federal system which divides powers and responsibilities among Commonwealth, state and local governments. Moreover, welfare provision is tied up with political fortunes, as levels of expenditure and types of programs are always contested issues, especially during elections.

The history of welfare in Australia has seen a shift from voluntary charitable organisations to state (or colonial) governments, and especially since the Second World War to the Commonwealth, which has become the main dispenser of all social security measures (Kewley 1980, pp. 3–12). During the nineteenth century, voluntary agencies catered to the welfare needs of the sick, neglected children, the poor, including old people who were destitute, and 'fallen', pregnant and deserted women. Except for South Australia, no equivalent of the English poor law existed. Only the governments of Tasmania and South Australia played a central role in providing charitable relief, while in the eastern states the churches and such organisations as the Benevolent Society of New South Wales founded in 1813, were the main instrumentalities for aiding the destitute. These bodies offered both indoor and outdoor relief (Kewley 1980, p. 4). Various institutions, for example the Sydney Benevolent Asylum for 'friendless and fallen women', infants, inebriates and the aged and infirm, provided indoor relief, while outdoor relief included the supply of food, clothing and work tools. This form of charity conformed with the nineteenth-century opinion that full government responsibility undermined individual initiative. Relief to the able-bodied unemployed constituted no part of the charitable relief system; they received wages or goods in return for work, mostly on public projects (Gollan 1974, p. 178). Granting or withholding assistance was entirely discretionary, often depending on the whim of an official or volunteer who made judgements about individual moral worth, rather than a notion of welfare rights (Dickey 1980, p. 71)

Following the 1890s depression, the inadequacy of existing provisions became clear and the first major change to charitable relief was the implementation of old-age pensions. This signified a move away from the institutional method of care toward a conception of pensions as a right to be provided collectively through government redistribution of taxes. Between 1900 and 1908 three states passed Old Age Pension Acts and the Commonwealth government began to pay all old-age pensions in 1909. The scheme was non-contributory, and pensions were payable to people who could satisfy specified requirements regarding age, residence, character and means. Except for the scheme of maternity allowances in 1912, the federal government introduced no further social security measures until the Second World War.

In 1942 the Commonwealth government assumed overall responsibility for income tax collection. With this increase in financial power it began to enact social welfare legislation to constitute a national welfare scheme with provision for child endowment, widows' pensions, unemployment and sick benefits and expanded old-age and invalid pensions. A successful referendum in 1946 gave the Commonwealth the constitutional power to pass the Social Services Consolidation Act 1947, enabling it to implement the social welfare measures enacted during the war (Social Welfare Commission 1975, p. 20). This Act was repealed and replaced with the Social Security Act 1991.

Income maintenance payment is the primary component of government outlay on social security and welfare in Australia. The major payments cover the aged, people with disabilities and the sick, widows, sole parents and the unemployed. Other services like rent assistance, family payment, free pharmaceutical and telephone rental for certain groups, the Jobs Education and Training (JET) scheme for sole parent pensioners, the short-term Job Search Allowance (JSA) and a Newstart Allowance (NSA) for those unemployed for more than twelve months, and the Youth Social Justice Strategy which addresses the needs of disadvantaged young people also are provided. These latter schemes represent a change in social policy orientation from primarily providing income support to an emphasis on education, training and skills acquisition (Department of Social Security 1993, p. 42).

Over one-fifth of the adult population depends on government programs for their income, and 2 443 023 people received social security payments in 1992–93 (Department of Social Security 1993, p. 287, table 98; Graycar & Jamrozik 1989, p. 7). Table 9.1 presents the number and types of benefit and pension recipients for selected years from 1973 to 1993. Men are more likely to be recipients of invalid/disability, sickness and unemployment benefits than are women who are more likely to receive either the age or the sole parent pension. While the number of women and men receiving unemployment payments increased by a factor of twenty-three during the two decades, the proportions of women and men receiving the benefit remained relatively stable. However, there is evidence that women's rate of unemployment is higher than men's which is not reflected in figures on recipients of unemployment benefits (Cass 1988b, p. 52). On the other side, some evidence suggests that women are doing better than men because they are obtaining full- and part-time employment in the service industries, which is one of the few expanding sectors of the economy.

Australia relies more on general income tax to finance the welfare system than do most other countries (Jones 1980, p. 120). It also differs by financing the major income maintenance benefits through general tax revenues rather than adopting contributory requirements (Kewley 1980, p. 219). Due to its control of fiscal policy, the federal government is the single most important provider of welfare. Public expenditure on education, health, welfare and social security expanded in the decade 1968–69 to 1978–79. Despite these increases, the welfare component of Gross Domestic Product is low compared with other OECD (Organisation for Economic Cooperation and Development) countries (Graycar & Jamrozik 1993, p. 7). The Commonwealth government provides mostly income support, whereas the states administer a range of personal services and programs, such as community

Table 9.1 Number and type of pension recipients¹, Australia, 1973–93

Year ended 30 June	Age		Invalid/Disability		Sickness		Unemployment		Sole Parent²	
	N	Proportion Female	N	Proportion Female	N	Proportion Female	N	Proportion Female	N	Proportion Female
1973	931 812	.69	149 609	.43	18 744	.22	37 945	.36	—	—
1978	1 264 778	.69	204 944	.33	29 950	.2	268 480	.3	57 433	.96
1983	1 390 838	.67	220 289	.29	65 065	.23	626 825	.24	140 228	.94
1988	1 328 814	.69	296 913	.26	74 936	.27	470 845	.27	182 007	.94
1993	1 515 682	.68	406 572	.28	45 226	.32	889 566	.27	298 444	.97

TYPE OF PENSION RECIPIENTS

1 The table includes the major types of pensions/benefits, those not presented include recipients of rehabilitation allowance, mobility allowance, child disability allowance, widowed person allowance, additional family payment, double orphan pension and special benefits.

2 Supporting mothers' benefit began in 1973 and was renamed supporting parent's benefit and extended to supporting fathers in 1977. From 1989 the sole parent pension replaced the supporting parent's pension and also covered a widow with a qualifying dependent child in her care.

Source: Department of Social Security 1989, *Annual Report 1988–89*, table 18, p. 167, DSS, Canberra; 1993, *Annual Report 1992–93*, table 58, p. 251; table 62, p. 255; table 71, p. 263; table 81, p. 271; table 95, p. 285, DSS, Canberra; Australian Bureau of Statistics 1975, *Year Book of Australia 1974*, ABS, Canberra, p. 426.

(formerly child) welfare departments, mental health services, and education, and in some cases, emergency financial relief.

After two decades of unprecedented expansion the growth of government expenditures on welfare ceased in most industrialised societies from the mid 1970s. Many critics link large government expenditures with some aspect of the recession of the late 1970s and early 1980s. Currently, social policies aim to restructure welfare provision by reducing government expenditure and achieving privatisation, that is the transfer of welfare responsibilities from the state to voluntary or community agencies, private providers or contractors, the family and individuals (Johnson 1989, p. 17; Kosonen 1987, p. 282; Robinson 1986, p. 1). There is greater emphasis on allocating scarce resources and efficiency. For example, in 1985, the Commonwealth government and state governments established the Home and Community Care (HACC) Program to fund organisations and groups which provide home and community support services namely, transport, nursing care and food services for the frail elderly and people with disabilities to enable them to remain living at home. The government sees this program as a cost-effective alternative to long-term residential accommodation. A second example involves the tightening eligibility criteria for various payments, for example unemployment benefits, thereby encouraging people to rely on other sources of assistance. Increasingly, the family is being sought out as a private care agent for its dependent family members. This policy assumes that family members exist who are willing and able to provide additional support. The rising numbers of homeless people and the increase in begging, combined with the fact that most people receiving benefits come from relatively poor families, suggest that such an assumption is erroneous. Greater reliance on families for welfare provision has implications for women's status and participation in the labour force because women as wives, mothers, daughters or volunteers typically provide care and welfare to family members (McIntosh 1984, pp. 232–4). Finch and Groves propose that insufficiently funded community care programs result in a 'double equation', as 'in practice community care equals care by the family, and in practice care by the family equals care by women' (1980, p. 494).

Poverty

In Western cultures, which place considerable value on wealth and monetary success, consumption, individual achievement and worth, poverty is deviant, often attributed to such individual deficiencies as lack of education or intelligence, skills, responsibility, motivation or morality. Ryan (1971, pp. 10–15) describes this definitional process as 'blaming the victim', a process in which 'victim blamers' identify the ill, jobless, and slum tenants as strange or different. Social problems are explained in terms of individual deviance rather than social structural factors, especially income inequality, unequal access to education, or discrimination. Even so, poverty itself may not be deemed reprehensible; religious personnel who reject material wealth are defined as virtuous. There are, however, recent examples of religious leaders who profited from their 'calling' and pursued extravagant lifestyles and who have been publicly humiliated, even imprisoned. It seems that acceptance of certain forms of assistance indicates deviance, not poverty itself. Coser (1965, p. 142) maintains that as long as people continue to be defined primarily in terms of their occupational status they will not be stigmatised as poor. Nonetheless, if welfare provision is defined as government assistance, then people on low incomes are not the only beneficiaries. Three sorts of parallel and overlapping welfare states are discernible:

1 *the visible welfare state* which delivers minimal resources in the form of income security payments to people who exist below or near the poverty line. Only the beneficiaries of this assistance are viewed as the welfare poor;
2 *the less visible welfare state* grants access to quality education, health care and fairly high grade community resources from which middle-class people largely benefit;
3 *the hidden welfare state*, or occupational welfare, provides for expensive transfers, including superannuation concessions, tax rebates for work-related expenses and condones tax minimisation, which benefit the affluent segments of the community (Graycar & Jamrozik 1993, pp. 75–80).

Measuring poverty

How to define and measure poverty is a constant question in the welfare literature. The central issue is determining the point of reference. For example, if we compare income, housing and living standards (however measured) between Australia and a developing country like India, we would conclude that there is no or little poverty in Australia, but if we compare the current situation with that of the period of economic expansion and high employment in the 1950s and 1960s the conclusion would be that poverty exists. What is sociologically relevant is that poverty is a socially recognised condition: a social status (Coser 1965, p. 141). Like all forms of deviance, the boundaries of poverty and the number and types of people considered poor depend on a process of definition and the application of varying norms.

Poverty lines provide a device for determining the proportion of the population in poverty. They generate considerable controversy and inevitably reflect values about what constitutes poverty or an adequate standard of living as well as political rivalry (Beeghley 1984, p. 322; Saunders 1980, p. 388). Obviously, raising or lowering the poverty line will determine the number of people in poverty, thus affecting social policy and government expenditure on welfare programs.

Poverty emerged as an important social issue in the 1970s with the findings of the Commission of Inquiry into Poverty (known as the Henderson Report), published in 1975. The Commission undertook two national surveys on income and families receiving social security benefits, and organised specific research reports on migrants, Aborigines, families, housing, the aged and juveniles. Based on this research, the Report defines 'primary poverty' as inadequate income, which for a two-parent family with two dependent children was equivalent to the then basic wage plus child endowment (now family allowance). The Report maintains that as the poverty line is so low those below it are indisputably 'very poor' (Commission of Inquiry into Poverty 1975, p. 13). The investigations show that over 10 per cent of income units were below the poverty line, and nearly 75 per cent of them were not in the labour force. Aboriginal people, migrants from non-English speaking backgrounds and fatherless families experienced the greatest poverty (1975, pp. 27–8). An analysis of 1986 census data provides the first estimates of the proportion of Aboriginal families with children below the Henderson poverty line. The results show that poverty rates are much higher among Aboriginal families, 40 per cent of which live on or below the poverty line, than among their non-Aboriginal counterparts. While the Aboriginal children accounted for 2.7 per cent of all children in 1986, they accounted for 7.1 per cent of children in poverty; nearly half of all Aboriginal children live in families with below poverty-line incomes. The primary contributing factor is the very high rates of unemployment among the adult Aboriginal population (Ross & Whiteford 1992, pp. 107–10).

The Henderson poverty line (which is updated twice a year) measures minimum physical survival not minimal social functioning, which centres welfare debates on income maintenance rather than on other aspects of welfare such as engaging in useful and productive work, personal autonomy and economic independence (Graycar & Jamrozik 1993, pp. 30–6). Perhaps the most sophisticated measure of poverty is Townsend's (1979, pp. 1173–6; 1987, pp. 136–7) notion of multiple deprivation which includes such indicators of *material deprivation* as lack of clothing, physical and mental health, housing, household facilities or favourable working conditions, and such *social deprivation* factors as lack of access to employment, education, social support or recreation. Finally, the anti-poverty Family Care Program initiated by the Brotherhood of St Laurence in Melbourne characterises poverty as rooted in the institutional structure of society not in the personal defects of individuals, and seeks to alleviate poverty by facilitating the target groups' access to power over resources, relationships, information and decision-making (Benn 1981, p. 92).

Families and poverty

Recent discussions of poverty centre on the situation of children, and a related phenomenon, the 'feminisation' of poverty. Since 1980, the proportion of children in poverty has increased from 8 to 19 per cent. Children comprised one-third of poor people in the 1970s; a decade later they constituted 44 per cent. By 1985–86 over 800 000 children lived in families in poverty compared with 233 000 in 1966 (Graycar & Jamrozik 1993, p. 36; Saunders & Whiteford 1987, p. 4). This increase results from the greater economic vulnerability of families with dependent children, subjected to long-term unemployment and other barriers to labour force participation, including sole parenthood. The Commission of Inquiry into Poverty found that female-headed households were the largest proportion of very poor people; 37.5 per cent of fatherless families compared with 15.9 per cent of all motherless families were below the poverty line (1975, p. 199). Research in the USA suggests that growing up in a female-headed family increases the risks of poverty by lowering chances of educational attainment, but rejects the notion that the long-term absence of a male role model is the explanation (McLanahan 1985, p. 898).

In 1973, the Commonwealth government introduced the supporting mothers' benefit, which in 1977 was renamed the supporting parent's benefit and thus extended to supporting fathers. In 1989, the sole parent pension covered widows with one or more qualifying children and supporting parents. Despite the extension of these benefits to men most—in 1992–93, 94 per cent or 280 915—sole parent pensioners are women (Department of Social Security 1993, p. 285, table 95). Moreover, the number of children in sole pensioner families more than doubled between 1974 and 1986 (Saunders & Whiteford 1987, p. 5). In 1987, child poverty became a high-profile political issue with the Hawke Labor government pledging during the election campaign that by 1990 no child will live in poverty.

The 'feminisation of poverty' is a term coined to refer to the increasing proportion of the poor who are female or who live in female-headed households (Pearce 1978, pp. 28–36). The most frequently mentioned cause is the change in family structure and household composition, including the increase in marital disruption and non-marital births leading to single motherhood. Data for Australia and the USA show that the proportion of women in poverty has increased relative to men since the 1950s. The sex differences in poverty rates are related to increases of single parenthood for women and the high cost of child care facilities combined with women's lower earning capacity deriving in part from the fact that in a segmented occupational structure women's work pays less than men's (Cass 1988a, p. 123; McLanahan, Sorensen & Watson 1989, pp. 119–22). One-parent families in Australia usually result from divorce or separation of partners. The number of sole parent beneficiaries reflects this pattern. Most sole parent pensioners (72.5 per cent of women and 83.5 per cent of men) are divorced or separated from partners. Unmarried mothers constitute 19.1 per cent of all female sole parent pensioners compared with 4.6 per cent of male sole parent pensioners who are unmarried fathers (Department of Social Security 1993, p. 286, table 97). These trends indicate that women are more likely to rely on government income transfers by virtue of their status as mothers, whereas men are more likely to receive benefits as a result of their labour market position. This represents a major change in policy orientation for welfare states which traditionally have focused primarily on the needs of the male worker and his dependants via the concept of the family wage and unemployment benefits (Papadakis 1993, p. 349).

Unemployment

The status of unemployment as deviant and associated with other forms of deviance has a long history and was reflected in the passage of the first vagrancy law in England in 1349. The statute made it a crime to give alms to anybody who was unemployed while being of sound mind and body. An impetus for this legislation was drastic shortages in the supply of adequate cheap labour, in part a result of the Black Death. Beggars and vagabonds were not subject to social control within the family and thereby were perceived as disruptive to social order, the maintenance of which was deemed essential for safe transportation throughout the countryside with the coming of mercantilism. During the following century the penalties for vagrancy increased in severity to periods of imprisonment, and ultimately it became a felony punishable by death. By 1571 a new statute provided:

> All rogues, vagabonds, and sturdy beggars shall ... be committed to the common gaol ... he [sic] shall be grievously whipped and burnt thro' the gristle of the right ear with a hot iron of the compass of an inch ... And for the second offence, he [sic] shall be adjudged a felon, unless some person will take him [sic] for two years in to his [sic] service. And for the third offence, he [sic] shall be adjudged guilty of felony without benefit of clergy (quoted in Chambliss 1964, p. 73).

It covered idle persons, confidence tricksters and frauds, including minstrels and travelling actors, pedlars, jugglers and counterfeiters. The vagrancy laws had little to do with the subject of poor relief. They were directed to the prevention of crime, the preservation of good order and the maintenance of available labour supplies.

Similarly, in Australia, during periods of labour shortages in the nineteenth century, laws were enacted to penalise absence from work or apparent unproductivity indicated by loitering, drunkenness, gambling, and even lodging or wandering in company with Aborigines (Grabosky 1977, pp. 62–3). Where not repealed, contemporary vagrancy laws are infamous for providing the police with a general law to sanction a range of activities from begging, loitering, being in public places to prostitution and congregating in groups.

At the present time, unemployment is probably one of the most serious social issues in industrialised capitalist societies. While unemployment is a deviant status, some unemployed people are projected as more deviant than others. This is translated into a perception that lowering unemployment among certain groups, notably married men with dependent children, should be a priority. As the legitimacy of women's employment is not complete, they often experience negligible support from partners and families when they become involuntarily unemployed (Ratcliff & Bogdan 1988, p. 61). Indeed, unemployment among certain groups, specifically Aboriginal people and older workers may become normalised or at least expected.

Since the late 1970s, unemployment has been increasing rapidly in Australia, particularly among young people.[1] During 1983, unemployment rates peaked at almost 10 per cent for men and women, and since 1985 the unemployment rates of women in the labour force have been higher than for men. In 1987, young people (fifteen to nineteen years) comprised 24 per cent of all the unemployed, and those between twenty and twenty-four constituted a further 21 per cent. Aboriginal people are also highly vulnerable to unemployment, due to compounded disadvantages including lack of access to education and training, rural location and labour market discrimination. Estimated rates of unemployment for Aboriginal people are almost five times those of non-Aboriginal people (Cass 1988b, pp. 24, 52).

Structural changes in the economy, notably in the manufacturing sector, the increasing use of technology, the growing number of jobs which are insecure, low paying, lacking career structure all increase employees' vulnerability and contribute to unemployment. People in these jobs are most likely to be the youngest or oldest in the labour force, women, people from ethnic or racial minorities, and those with few educational qualifications or skills (Sinfield 1981, p. 18; Windschuttle 1979, pp. 11–15). Changes in the occupational structure also mean a changing opportunity structure regarding access to material resources, including the rates of pay, relative security of tenure and the quality of work, which favours persons with professional middle-class occupations (Graycar & Jamrozik 1993, p. 193).

As well as numerical growth the duration of unemployment has increased. Little agreement exists on the definition of long-term unemployment. The Poverty Inquiry took six weeks as its working definition but applying this benchmark would now mean that most unemployment benefit recipients would fall within the category of long-term unemployed. In May 1993 the median duration a beneficiary received the Job Search and Newstart allowances (which replaced the unemployment benefit in 1988 and 1991 respectively) was thirty-five weeks (a decrease of two weeks from the previous year) and the mean duration was sixty-six weeks, compared with fifty weeks in May 1992 (Department of Social Security 1993, p. 272, table 82). The Social Security Review in 1987–88 defines long-term unemployment as being without employment for at least six months (Cass 1988b, p. 179). The category has been further expanded as the Department of Social Security's special programs for long-term unemployed people are available only to those in receipt of unemployment benefits for one year or more. The Newstart Allowance is paid to men aged eighteen to sixty-four and to women aged between eighteen and fifty-nine who have been registered with the Commonwealth Employment Service for more than twelve months. This 'stretching' of the short-term category indicates the normalisation of longer periods of unemployment.

Distinguishing long-term from short-term unemployment is useful as recipients in the two categories are likely to differ, especially in terms of their relationship to the formal job market. As the length of unemployment increases, the likelihood of returning to work declines. Only around 30 per cent of people on unemployment benefits for one year or more will probably return to work, and 50 per cent will remain on benefit (Cass 1988b, p. 181). The most likely groups to be unemployed for a long period are older men, Aboriginal people, and those with relatively low levels of educational attainment or employed in declining industries with non-transferable skills. Numerous studies of the psychological impact of long-term unemployment point to the loss of self-confidence, self-esteem, erosion of skills and an overall discouragement in relation to the labour market.

Another consequence, albeit unintended, of distinguishing between short- and long-term unemployment is the creation of a new category of deviance and source of discrimination. Employers tend to perceive long periods of unemployment as indicating unemployability or a bad recruitment risk, further marginalising long-term unemployed persons (Cass 1988b, p. 185; Sinfield 1981, p. 96).

A pervasive view is that unemployed people should place a high priority on finding a job; that any kind of work, including voluntary services, is preferable to being unemployed. For example, eligibility for the Job Search Allowance requires that a person be actively seeking and willing to undertake suitable (however defined) paid work, to participate in a course that will assist in seeking work and not be unemployed as a result of industrial action, applicable only while the industrial action is in force (Department of Social Security 1993, p. 115). Bill Wyman, one of the former Rolling Stones, encapsulates an everyday interpretation of unemployment (held by employed or wealthy people) when he asserts: 'If I was out of work I'd take any job. I would sweep the road, I would do anything if I didn't have any money. They [unemployed people] just look up there [boards displaying job vacancies] and they go, no, and they go home and collect their £70 or £80 a week' (Trinca 1994, p. 11). The Calvinist underpinnings of our culture are evident in assumptions about unemployed people as being lazy, unproductive, free riders, indolent and lethargic. These views are juxtaposed by the tolerance and even positive acclaim of people who evade their taxes or receive such other government assistance as employment benefits which people receive by participation in the workforce as employees, for example paid public holidays, annual recreation leave and tax deductions for work-related expenses. Typically, these benefits and payments are not viewed as social welfare services but as part of the conditions or fringe benefits of employment (Bright 1978, p. 161; Graycar & Jamrozik 1993, pp. 197–207).

The notion of the dole-bludger is one aspect of the process of 'blaming the victim' which holds individuals responsible for their unemployment because of a failure to learn appropriate skills and values within the education system or from an unwillingness to move geographically in search of work. This view treats unemployed people as lacking moral fibre, tenacity or capacity for hard work. The media fuel and reinforce this image with periodic headlines proclaiming the luxurious lifestyle of the presumed large numbers of people cheating the welfare system (Windschuttle 1979, pp. 155–79). The increasing entry of women into the labour force is also viewed as contributing to rises in unemployment. Both young people and married women have been scapegoats for unemployment; the former because of a perception that they are unwilling to work, and the latter because they are viewed as not needing to work in paid labour (Power 1980, p. 42).

There is evidence that such individualistic sentiments are declining. Economic and work-related measures emphasising the need to preserve and create jobs rather than to simply change the outlook and attributes of unemployed people are now generally recognised as the most important means for alleviating unemployment. Nevertheless, individualistic explanations remain, among clerical and manual workers as well as business leaders and managers (Graetz 1987, pp. 328–9). A study of clients' compliance with the Department of Social Security's rules indicates that many recipients sought to distinguish themselves from those whom they perceived as 'bludgers' who were 'abusing the system'. Interviewees commented that they accepted the departmental requirements because: 'it's the only way they have to check on dole bludgers'; 'it's a good way to keep tabs on us, we've got to keep trying'; and 'it encourages you to go for a job' (Weatherley 1993, p. 30). Some suggested that meeting the requirements enabled them to assuage their feelings of shame about being unemployed, requiring help and being 'on the dole'; in their own eyes their deviance is reduced by conforming to the bureaucratic procedures. The widespread negative public opinion regarding the character of welfare recipients, doubts about their honesty and desire to seek employment, plus the stability of individualistic explanations of poverty facilitate the success of welfare cutbacks (Kluegel 1987, pp. 96–7).

In contrast to the 'blaming the victim' approach, negative orientation toward employment among unemployed people is a component of the development of a deviant self-identity, rather than deriving from the nature of people who become unemployed. Prolonged unemployment reduces self-confidence, and unemployed people often withdraw from social relationships and participation. Unemployed people experience a number of stages:

1 *shock and disbelief* about the loss of employment;
2 *optimism* about finding a job soon;
3 *pessimism* marked by eroding self-confidence and concern about ability to find work;
4 *fatalism* involving a redefinition of self-identity and a withdrawal from labour market participation (Cass 1988b, p. 132).

The long-term unemployed convince themselves that they are worthless or that their unemployment results from choice (Windschuttle 1979, pp. 58–60). Young people (fifteen to twenty-four years) unemployed for at least five months are more likely to exhibit physical inactivity, decreased contact with friends, disorganisation of sleeping and eating patterns, and to use alcohol, tobacco and medical services more than their age peers unemployed for less than five months (Turtle & Ridley 1984, pp. 35–6). These findings suggest that the experience of long-term unemployment results in anti-work attitudes, rather than vice versa. The longer a person is unemployed the more likely it is that she or he will conform to the dole-bludger stereotype. This denotes a self-fulfilling prophecy (Merton 1968, p. 477) or secondary deviation (Lemert 1951, pp. 75–6), whereby an individual conforms to an originally false conception and thereby verifies it.

A second specious element of the dole-bludger theme is the assumption that being unemployed equates with not working. At least some unemployed people do participate in an informal, local economy where the mode of exchange is not necessarily monetary (Bansemer 1987, p. 68; Henry 1982, p. 460; Sommerlad & Altman 1986, p. 8). Studies of voluntarily unemployed people in rural areas show that they often engage in a wide range of jobs such as painting, child-minding, repair work, producing items for sale, growing and selling agricultural products. This refutes the notion that unemployed people do not want to work, are not innovative, and are lazy, unproductive members of the community. Of course, not all unemployed people will have access to such informal opportunities and their orientation to the formal economy will reflect their location in it, their skills, and the available job opportunities.

In a participant observation study of long-term unemployed Afro-American men, Liebow finds that obtaining, retaining and performing well at a job are clearly low priorities (1967, p. 34). He argues that this is not due to the men's laziness, but that as they lacked skills the jobs they obtained tended to be low-paid service work, or construction work which was better paid but seasonal and irregular (1967, p. 58). Low-paying jobs do not offer prestige, respect, interesting work, opportunity for learning and advancement or any other compensation. Additionally, a study of long-term unemployed in rural South Australia suggests that many voluntarily unemployed people consciously choose to opt out of the labour market for lifestyle reasons. Being unemployed while working in an informal economy enhances autonomy, and reduces routinisation and pressures to increase production and productivity (Bansemer 1987, p. 52).

Unemployment and crime

It is frequently asserted, both in the daily press and in academic writing, that unemployment is an important cause of crime. A popular variant of the argument is that unemployed people have plenty of time to engage in criminal activity—the notion that 'the devil makes work for idle hands'. Many of the early sociological studies of delinquency focused on unemployment and restricted job opportunities to explain criminal deviance, particularly property crime. The traditional explanation is that unemployment is an indicator of economic need, which some may satisfy by resorting to property crime. However, as chapter 8 demonstrates, employees in high-status and high-paying jobs are not immune from crime commission, only to detection. Others stress a break down in ties to conventional society leading to a perception among the 'new marginal youth' that education will provide few opportunities, thus resulting in a gradual drift toward troublesome peers and ultimately crime (Polk 1984, pp. 471–2)

The relationship between crime and unemployment remains ambiguous and underresearched. In a thorough review of the findings of sixty-three studies that examine the unemployment–crime relationship, Chiricos argues that the consensus of doubt is premature, concluding instead that most cross-sectional and time-series studies support the existence of a positive, frequently significant relationship (1987, p. 203). The most consistent finding is that unemployment is related to property crimes, particularly burglary and larceny, rather than crimes involving personal violence (Cantor & Land 1985, p. 317).

Several problems arise regarding the measurement of crime and unemployment, and the interpretation of any relationship:

1 the official measure of unemployment taps job-seeking not joblessness, and the former may reflect commitment to employment rather than to illegitimate activities. It also assumes that unemployed people are not working, have access to illegitimate opportunities, and are motivated to break criminal laws. Much sociological theory and research, including anomie and differential association theories, dispute such simplistic assumptions;

2 the problem of the ecological fallacy. Aggregate data for cities or states showing a relationship between crime and unemployment rates do not demonstrate that it is unemployed people who are engaged in criminal offending;

3 crime and unemployment rates are highest for young people, which might mean that age is the important determinant of an observed unemployment–crime relationship. It is therefore important to investigate the manner in which the unemployment–crime relationship may differ among age groups and for different offences.

4 increases in crime may not be due to unemployment, but to underemployment or economic marginality signified by low wages, few hours and discouraged workers who have given up looking for work, and who do not appear in unemployment statistics.

Allan and Steffensmeier (1989, pp. 118–19) find that for juveniles, the availability of work reduces the attractiveness of delinquent activities, while for young adults the quality of employment is more important. Low-wage and/or part-time employment that may seem acceptable or even status-enhancing to juvenile first-job holders still living at home appears constraining and unsatisfactory to young adults seeking greater independence. They suggest that when marginal sorts of employment dominate labour market opportunities, young adults may find incentives to progress further into a lifestyle that deviates increasingly from the mainstream.

Welfare: assistance or social control?

As well as providing resources and real benefits for individuals and groups of people, state intervention and welfare provision constitute a form of social control. The welfare state has contradictory effects: it enhances social welfare by buffering the effects of the market and concurrently regulates individuals' activities and autonomy (Galper 1975, p. 46; Gough 1979, pp. 11–12). Rather than redistributing wealth and reducing inequalities, welfare provision reinforces commitment to the social structure, specifically the labour market, which actually generates the inequities (Galper 1975, p. 47). Government welfare policies and practices regulate the labour market by varying unemployment benefits, thus encouraging people to enter or withdraw from employment, and regulate families by intervening to establish particular family patterns.

Regulating the labour market

Piven and Cloward (1971, 1982) offer the most explicit statement on the role of welfare payments in regulating the demand and supply of labour. They identify two functions of welfare expenditure. Firstly, during periods of mass unemployment resulting in mass protest, unemployment relief expands in order to moderate political disorder. They maintain that the expansion of relief programs in the USA during the 1960s was a response to disorder relating to civil rights for blacks rather than a greater concern for social welfare or response to need. Welfare expenditures were greatest in northern cities which had received an influx of blacks migrating from the south, where there was massive unemployment resulting from modernisation of agriculture and job discrimination. The anti-poverty programs effectively absorbed many of the agitational elements in the black population, thereby quelling unrest (1971, pp. 189–99). More generally, welfare payments can be interpreted as a policy to calm any kind of disorder or protest by various groups. In contrast, in Australia during the depression of the late 1920s and early 1930s, large-scale unemployment resulted in mass protests in the streets but the Commonwealth government did not introduce unemployment benefits until 1945. Much of the unrest was controlled by criminal sanctions (Grabosky 1977, p. 121).

Secondly, when unemployment levels are low people receiving welfare payments are degraded and humiliated, thereby reasserting individualistic theories of social problems and reinforcing work norms. This reflects the notion of 'blaming the victim' and echoes Marx's description of a 'reserve army' of unemployed people who effectively deter employed workers from industrial action for fear of losing their jobs. It would seem that welfare payments are adopted as a form of social control when unemployment is viewed as resulting from structural changes in the economy, whereas criminal penalties prevail when individualistic explanations predominate.

Social services exert social control by requiring clients to conform to organisational regulations and offering incentives to people to behave in certain ways. Indeed, the very granting of relief and assignment of a person to the category of welfare recipient involves degradation thereby facilitating compliance (Coser 1965, p. 144). Payments can be suspended or terminated for failure to conform to welfare agencies' regulations and complicated eligibility criteria. Individuals must continuously demonstrate their eligibility by furnishing personal and ordinarily private information. Additional surveillance techniques include extensive interviewing and unannounced home visits to check the veracity of the information welfare recipients provide. In this respect, social welfare workers act as judges assessing the moral character of people applying for welfare benefits, and separating the 'deserving' from the 'non-deserving' poor (Matza 1971, pp. 642–3).

The social control activities of the Department of Social Security (DSS) is a good example of its role in regulating the labour force. The Department states explicitly that the major objective of its unemployment program is to promote job seeking (Cass 1988b, p. 141). Eligibility criteria include being unemployed for the period covered by the benefit, for men being between sixteen and sixty-four years of age and for women being between sixteen and fifty-nine years old, actively seeking work and registration with the Commonwealth Employment Service (which also provides the DSS with information about claimants). Recipients must report fortnightly in person to a Social Security office providing details of their efforts to find work and cohabitation status. Social Security and Employment Service staff have advisory and supervisory responsibilities: they are expected to assist unemployed people in looking for suitable employment or training, at the same time as ensuring they are genuinely available for and seeking work (Wikeley 1989, p. 297).

Following the large increases in unemployment, the DSS instigated a system of mobile review teams initially to verify the efforts of unemployment beneficiaries to find work. Since 1986, the number and types of teams have been increased to review a range of payments and circumstances; in 1988–89 these teams conducted over 84 000 reviews, by 1992–93 they undertook almost 200 000 reviews. The Department also implemented a data-matching program in 1990 which enables the verification of identification and income information that clients provide by using tax file numbers. The DSS identifies three central objectives in its accountability strategy: to identify possible overpayments promptly; to implement recovery action; and to identify cases where offences have been committed and to refer them to the Director of Public Prosecutions. This strategy aims to deter clients from defrauding the government.

The reviews involve targeting the groups and individuals that a team considers to be high risks for fraud and overpayment, notably unemployment benefit recipients between eighteen and twenty, long-term unemployed, invalid pensioners, and sole parents. In 1992–93, of the 134 314 recipients of the Job Search and Newstart Allowance reviewed, 13 per cent had their payments varied downward (reduced or cancelled) and 1.6 per cent had them varied upward. Of the 51 238 sole parent pensioners reviewed, 10 per cent had their benefits reduced, while 1 per cent had them increased. During 1992–93, 75.6 per cent of prosecutions under the Social Security Act 1991 were for breaches of unemployment benefits and 15.3 per cent of prosecutions related to sole parent pensioners. Moreover, nearly all the prosecutions result in convictions: 99 per cent of those prosecuted for social security fraud were convicted in 1992–93, with custodial penalties being imposed on 11 per cent of the men and 7 per cent of the women convicted (Department of Social Security 1993, pp. 88–7, table 13). Prosecution is facilitated by the fact that the Department of Social Security maintains comprehensive files on all of its recipients. Such measures, also adopted in Britain, exploit a popular mythology of benefit fraud and abuse and maintain the traditional distinction between the 'deserving' and the 'undeserving' poor (Wikeley 1989, p. 304). Nevertheless, a study of compliance with social security rules and procedures found little basis for the belief that fraud is rampant; only 5 per cent of the clients interviewed declared that they would not report income. Three-quarters of the interviewees indicated that they would report additional sources of income for reasons of honesty, fairness to others or fear of detection. For 20 per cent, the reporting of extra income depends on how much it is and the extent of their debts, thus the ethic of doing the right thing is subordinate to the capacity to make ends meet (Weatherley 1993, pp. 31–6).

Regulating the labour market also involves providing incentives to certain groups to withdraw from the formal economy, thereby reducing the competition for jobs in a period of high unemployment. For example, women are not eligible for the Job Search or the Newstart Allowance beyond the age of fifty-nine, whereas the cut-off age for men is sixty-four. Additionally, in 1988, unemployment benefits for sixteen- to seventeen-year-olds were replaced by a job search allowance ($53.55 per week in 1989) explicitly aimed at encouraging young unemployed people to take up training and employment opportunities rather than become dependent on unemployment benefits long-term. It also removed any financial incentives to leave school early. The allowance was subject to a parental income test, increasing the young person's dependence on parents, and providing the Department with information not only about the claimant but about his or her family. This scheme can be seen as an attempt to increase individuals' bonds to other sites of social control, namely the family or the school, and decreases the autonomy which a monetary payment would enhance. The

Job Search Allowance now replaces the unemployment benefit for all those people aged sixteen and above who have been unemployed for less than twelve months.

Regulating families

Another dimension of social control involves the ways various social policies serve to reinforce a family form or household structure based on a division of labour between a male 'breadwinner' and female domesticity, the latter economically dependent on the former (Gordon 1988, pp. 628–9 ; McIntosh 1978, p. 255; Zaretsky 1982, p. 195). Bryson (1983, p. 131) suggests that the welfare system reinforces the patriarchal family system and thus helps maintain women's subordination and dependency. In some respects, payments have increased women's autonomy by enabling a degree of economic independence from male partners but the means test restricts women's capacity to obtain paid employment. Coupled with the lack of affordable child care, this reinforces women's domestic roles, increases their dependency and subjects them to surveillance by government departments. Rather than increasing independence in an absolute sense, women's dependence on male partners is diverted to the state. Even though the sole parent benefit is available to men and women, 93 per cent of the recipients were female in 1993. In effect, such a benefit may reinforce patriarchal or viriarchal (rule by adult males) social relations by limiting mothers' participation in the paid labour force and reaffirming their parenting roles (Waters 1989b, p. 203). Nonetheless, in 1988–89 the federal government implemented the Jobs, Education and Training (JET) program which specifically provides to sole parent pensioners vocational advice and job search assistance, in order to facilitate their entry or re-entry into employment. Family policies often indicate most clearly the contradictory nature of welfare, with many benefits providing real gains which conservative critics maintain destroy the 'family' but whose operation often shores up traditional relationships.

The first example of the way public policy supports a particular family structure is the Harvester judgment in 1907, which established the 'family' or 'living' wage, measured in terms of the rights of adult male workers to a basic minimum wage enabling them to provide their wives and dependent children with a decent living standard. When it came to fixing the living wage for women, the arbitration court applied different principles and assigned separate and lower minimum rates for jobs normally held by women, reasoning that women were not usually legally responsible for the maintenance of a family (Cass 1983, p. 61). Even so, historical research demonstrates that it was not exceptional for women, especially those from the working class, to support their families. The implementation of a child endowment scheme in 1941 aimed to provide mothers and children with an income which was not means tested. While such payments did increase women's economic independence they were an adjunct to wage restraint and acted as an incentive, especially in the 1950s, to keep women out of the labour force by reaffirming their role as mothers.

Formal social policy provisions are presently more universal in their application, however, in effect, they can result in different outcomes for male and female beneficiaries. For example, taxation rebates for dependent spouses, while gender-neutral, are more likely to benefit men, as they are more likely to have dependent spouses than are women (Bryson 1983, p. 132). The 'cohabitation rule'—where benefits are terminated or reduced when a beneficiary cohabits—is more likely to disadvantage women, because they constitute the vast majority of recipients, and it assumes that they are economically dependent on their male partners. The Department of Social Security (1993, pp. 140–1) indicates that the most frequent reason for cancelling sole parent pensions is that the recipient is in a marriage-like relationship with their former or another partner, and it is the recipient who must prove that there is no marriage-like relationship. Cohabitation is not the major reason for terminating unemployment or other benefits. The existence of a marriage-like relationship, rather than evidence that the man is financially supporting the women, appears to be the significant factor in the denial or termination of the sole parent pension (Neave 1992, p. 795). In 1989, the criteria for determining whether such a relationship exists were formalised in legislation. The Department considers any financial arrangements and the nature of the relationship, including living arrangements and the distribution of household tasks; it can presume that men and women who live together pool their income. A possible rationale for this policy is that men should not benefit from the payments or that people living together should not be advantaged over a married couple in similar financial circumstances. Another plausible explanation might be that women should not receive income from the state and a male partner simultaneously, perhaps because it smacks of adultery, prostitution, or immorality. It is always assumed that cohabitation involves economic exchange. In effect, the rule means that a woman must be dependent on the man with whom she cohabits thereby regulating both men and women's behaviour (Bryson 1983, p. 141; Gordon 1988, p. 617). However, the Australian Law Reform Commission points out that 'a woman presumed to be in a marriage-like relationship may be ineligible for a benefit but have no legal means to oblige her partner to support her and their children' (Australian Law Reform Commission 1993, p. 129). In most Australian states de facto wives have no legally enforceable right to maintenance (Neave 1992, p. 794).

A focus on children further illustrates the regulatory aspects of welfare whereby certain families are 'policed' and specific family forms encouraged. In the middle of the eighteenth century an abundant literature began to flourish on the theme of the preservation of children, accompanied by increasing surveillance of family life (Donzelot 1979, p. 9). Together with widespread humanitarianism and concern for penal reform, the theme of the preservation of children is linked to two social phenomena: the child-saving movement, and the emergence of social work as an occupation.

In the late nineteenth century, in the USA, the child-savers were mostly politically conservative, 'native' born, protestant, middle-class women whose major achievement was the recognition of juvenile delinquency (the labelling of youthful deviance) and the development of the juvenile justice system, consisting of special judicial and correctional institutions (see chapter 4; Platt 1969, p. 3). Their concern with child welfare became the rationale for reforms in education, health, labour and the environment and dominated the Progressive Era (approximately between 1890 and the 1920s). The child-savers viewed themselves as humanitarian and altruistically dedicated to rescuing those less fortunately placed in the social order. Despite the wide acceptance of biological theories of deviance, they stressed the value of redemption and prevention through early identification and intervention in the form of education and training. Their quest to prevent juvenile delinquency involved concentrating on children in urban slums, which were thought to be the source of family breakdown and moral degeneration characterised by illegitimacy, abandonment of children, drinking, gambling, violence, bad habits, idleness and disease. In other words, they viewed the city slums as lacking social control and their residents in need of social reform. (Sutton 1990, p. 1368)

Like many sociologists of the time, the child-savers sought to reaffirm parental authority, home education, rural life, and integrity of the family apparently threatened by urbanism, industrialism and cultural diversity. Despite defending the family, they advocated the removal of children from homes which failed, in their estimation, to conform to the image of the ideal family girded by parental discipline (Platt 1969, p. 98). Child-savers' efforts were concentrated on the impoverished working classes whose children they regarded as innocent victims of incompetent, irresponsible and almost inhuman adults. These moral entrepreneurs focused specifically on the largely Catholic immigrant culture and viewed immigrant children most in need of supervision and socialisation. The New York Association for the Improvement of the Condition of the Poor stated that: 'To keep such families together either by occasional relief or employment, is to encourage their depravity ... These nurseries of indolence, debauchery, and intemperance, are moral pests of society and should be broken up' (quoted in Piven & Cloward 1988, p. 637).

While espousing disinterested humanitarian values, the child-saving movement was not simply a benevolent project to reform the lower classes. One of the effects (perhaps intended) of child labour legislation, removing children from their homes, and compulsory education was to render children unavailable for employment. This benefited the large industrialists by squeezing out of the market the small manufacturers who relied on cheap child labour (Platt 1974, p. 369). Numerous private, benevolent organisations emerged, for example the New York Children's Aid Society which established industrial schools and placed children in healthy, rural family homes (Block & Hale 1991, p. 229).

The child-savers aims were twofold: they sought to replace the practice of voluntary charity with a system of child welfare organised and funded by central governments; and they sought to change the punitive responses to delinquency and crime among young people via reforms emphasising preventative techniques, including family casework and foster care, designed to preserve the family and facilitate rehabilitation and socialisation. The result was a fusion of the distinction between delinquent and dependent children. Nominally, the distinction remained but delinquency was seen as evidence of problematic family life which in turn was seen as a potential environment for delinquency to occur; accordingly, a child deemed dependent or delinquent might receive the same treatment. The reforms had unanticipated consequences, in particular an expansion in the number of children held in public and private reformatories and benevolent institutions. Private institutions, unlike their public counterparts, were classified as benevolent in purpose and claimed to be less coercive and more therapeutic; they tended to house the dependent, neglected and 'wayward' children, who previously were beyond the reach of institutions. Growth of public institutions was not as dramatic as they had primary responsibility for juvenile delinquents. Ironically, the private sector expanded by detaining the types of children the child-savers were most concerned should avoid coercion and punishment (Block & Hale 1991, pp. 228–31; Sutton 1990, pp. 1368–71).

The moral depravity of the poor also became a concern in Sydney toward the end of the nineteenth century, with a particular focus on 'larrikins', loosely referring to young men from the working classes who exhibited assumed delinquent tendencies. Supposedly, the dominant causes of 'larrikinism' were large families, parental neglect and the disproportionate number of public houses, dancing halls and gaming establishments (Grabosky 1977, pp. 84–95). Similar views underlay child welfare and adoption laws which justified the removal of Aboriginal children from their families and placement with European parents (Chisholm 1985, pp. 72, 104).

The child-savers' emphasis on children's dependency and malleability became institutionalised in the juvenile justice system which brought within the ambit of governmental control a set of youthful activities that previously had been ignored or handled informally (Platt 1969, p. 139). The official rationale behind establishing special courts is to divert young people from the stigma and punitiveness of the criminal courts. Juvenile or children's courts are characterised by a special judge, confidential records and informal sessions not open to public viewing. Moreover, according to the welfare or treatment orientation the appropriate status of young people is dependency and therefore they cannot be responsible for their actions; their delinquency is attributed to conditions of their family life. Accordingly, punishment for a crime is replaced by treatment or re-education of a child (see chapter 5 for recent changes in the orientation to juvenile justice).

Social workers

In the development of the juvenile justice system, social workers assumed a key role as 'experts' in assessing the needs of children and ensuring child welfare. In determining the conditions where delinquency or neglect might occur, social welfare workers (who may or may not possess formal social work qualifications) place families under scrutiny, particularly poorer or working-class families living in public housing or otherwise not conforming to the nuclear family ideal type. Social workers, especially those employed by community welfare departments, focus on two dimensions of child welfare:

1 *those whose upbringing and education are deemed inadequate.* Here the role of the social worker is to provide in-depth information and assessment of family life, arrangements, resources and discipline. In response, the social worker might offer short-term counselling, advice on parenting skills or family discipline and make suggestions about other welfare services available in the community. Alternatively, an application might be made to the court claiming that a child is 'in need of care' or 'at risk' because of neglect, abuse (physical, sexual or emotional), abandonment or orphaning by parents or guardians. Essentially, on the advice and recommendations of community welfare workers, the court judges a child's family life in order to determine whether he or she should be placed in the custody or guardianship of the minister for community welfare. Guardianship is not the same as state wardship and custody agreements between the minister and the guardians of a child may be 'voluntary'. The general trend within child welfare is to reduce the number of children under residential care, to reduce the size of these facilities and to have more care provided by non-government agencies. Foster care is the most prevalent type of placement of children under guardianship (Graycar & Jamrozik 1993, p. 228);
2 *children charged with criminal or status offences,* including drinking, truancy, running away or uncontrollability. Again, the family context is viewed as causing the deviant behaviour and social workers provide social background reports to the court. As the aim of the court order is rehabilitation, social welfare departments usually administer it by providing counselling, guidance and supervision of children and their parents.

The social control of families is complex and diffuse. It operates under the guise of the welfare of children, or to use current terminology 'the best interests of the child' and aims to prevent delinquency and child abuse. Orientation to the family is ambivalent; intervention occurs when social workers judge that family relationships deviate or are likely to deviant from the 'normal' form. A child is defined as 'at risk' if she or he is being abused or neglected or if the guardians of the child are unable or unwilling either to maintain the child or to exercise 'adequate supervision and control over the child' or if the child 'has been persistently absent from school without satisfactory explanation of the absence' (Child Protection Act 1993, SA, s. 6 (2)). Like the child-savers, welfare departments regard parents as having the primary responsibility for child care but where this duty is not performed adequately, it has the responsibility to advocate, and if necessary intervene on behalf of the child and inquire into the nature of family relationships and type of supervision. The South Australian Department for Family and Community Services (FACS) states that:

> It is the business of the Department to focus attention on strengthening families in the community to cope with the demands of life and at the same time ensure that the interests of children are protected ... Despite the best efforts of early intervention and family preservation, for some children for whom safety and care cannot be guaranteed, there is a need for permanent alternative family care to be provided (Department for Family and Community Services 1993, p. 1).

Legislation provides that FACS always exercise its powers in the best interests of the child, simultaneously giving serious consideration to the desirability of keeping the child with his or her family, preserving and strengthening family relationships, not withdrawing the child from their familiar environment and preserving the child's sense of racial, ethnic, religious or cultural identity (Children's Protection Act 1993, SA, s. 4 (1 & 2)). Nevertheless, welfare departments adopt deficit discourses and evaluate families in terms of deviation from social and familial norms which can result in welfare intervention and surveillance. It is the welfare department which determines whether families are performing adequately. Carrington demonstrates how deficit discourses connect truancy with family malfunction and result in 'failing children' from working-class families being subject to legal and welfare discipline which aims to 'normalise' the child and the family (1990b, pp. 264–7).

The child-saving orientation is currently manifest in discussion and policies regarding child protection. The conservative, socially prominent middle-class child-savers have been replaced by social workers, physicians and child psychologists. The notion of child protection conveys a concern to protect children from parents who do, or are likely to, abuse their children. Broad definitions of child abuse or neglect include sexual abuse, physical or emotional abuse or neglect to the extent that 'the child has suffered, or is likely to suffer, physical or psychological injury detrimental to the child's wellbeing; or the child's physical or psychological development is in jeopardy' (Children's Protection Act 1993, SA, s. 6 (1) (a & b)). This definition provides wide scope for social workers and psychologists to make assessments regarding whether a child's development is 'normal', and if not whether deviant parental practices are the cause. The 'discovery' of child abuse provides welfare departments with investigative, surveillance and policing roles. Indeed, a medical practitioner, nurse, psychologist, social worker, teacher, police officer or other specified employee who fails to report any suspicion that a child is being abused or neglected could be fined. Ultimately, welfare departments can apply for a court order to have a child taken out of the family situation for a period of time and placed under the guardianship of the minister or director general of the community welfare department.

Welfare workers perceive their preventative role as offering a range of voluntary services and programs oriented to influencing parents and children before abuse occurs. However, such programs also alert the welfare department to locations where abuse is most likely to occur, as that will be defined in terms of those participating in the voluntary programs. The preventative dimension of social work may involve targeting groups perceived to be vulnerable, for example teenage parents, families with members who have disabilities, families of non-English speaking background and those experiencing multiple disadvantage, including those in rural or remote areas.

While welfare workers stress the paramountcy of the interests of the child, those interests are not natural but are defined by social policies. Given the view of children as dependent, innocent and not responsible for their situation—at least so long as they have not committed a violent or serious crime—they are deemed incapable of specifying their own interests. Courts, for example, are ambivalent about accepting a child's testimony in abuse cases often viewing children as incapable of deciphering the truth either because of an inherent mendacity or through fear of their parents or the judge. Consequently, the state, specifically social workers, becomes the representative, indeed the determinant of the child's interests (McIntosh 1984, p. 228).

In sum, community welfare departments intervene in the lives of certain families and children, only some of whom have actually deviated from the law. Even though they seek to distance themselves from the formal system of social control, child welfare cannot be considered different and alternative to the criminal justice system as strong links exist between the two systems. Welfare workers often view juvenile delinquency or youth crime as stemming directly from abuse or neglect within their family. Second, being placed in the care or under the supervision of a department of community welfare can be a court order, therefore a punishment. The emergence of child welfare and juvenile justice represents a fragmentation of the power to punish and a blurring of the distinction between assistance and punishment. Certain families are subject to more discipline, surveillance and intervention in the name of child protection and prevention of delinquency. Donzelot suggests that social workers' 'sphere of intervention ... follows the contours of the "less-favored" classes. Within these social strata, they focus on a privileged target, the pathology of children in its dual form: children in danger—those whose upbringing and education leaves something to be desired, and dangerous children, or delinquent minors' (1979, p. 96).

Summary

The foregoing discussion demonstrates the ambiguous location of social welfare in the constellation of social control. The ideology of government-funded welfare programs and services is to assist disadvantaged individuals, but their provision involves surveillance, supervision and stigmatisation. Although theorists of social welfare concentrate on the structural causes of 'need'—lack of employment opportunities, the capitalist market, discrimination—most welfare programs are oriented to helping individuals thereby reinforcing an individualistic focus and the labelling of individuals.

Note

1 The Australian Bureau of Statistics defines people as unemployed if they are without a job (from which they obtain pay, profit, commission or payment in kind) but are available and actively seeking full- or part-time employment (Cass 1988b, pp. 1–2). Officially, then, the unemployment benefit introduced in 1945 provides for the income support needs of unemployed people who are *actively* seeking work. This definition excludes persons without a job who state that they do want to work and are available to start but who have given up actively looking for work because of discouragement about their job prospects. People on other benefits, such as sole parents, who are actively seeking work, or others like unemployed married women not eligible because their husband's income is means tested or, if he is unemployed, he receives benefit at the married rate and therefore his partner receives the income indirectly, are also excluded from this definition of unemployment. Consequently, unemployment statistics are likely to under-estimate the extent of unemployment.

Key Terms

Welfare	Welfare state
Income maintenance	Poverty
Feminisation of poverty	Poverty line
Unemployment	Social security
Long-term unemployment	Social control
Child-savers	Social work
Child protection	

Main points

1 The broad purposes of the welfare state are the elimination of poverty, the maximisation of health and welfare, and the enhancement of living conditions. In Australia, as in all Western industrialised societies, welfare provision is linked inextricably to governmental structures and bureaucratic administration. The Commonwealth government is especially central in Australia because it collects income tax, the major source of revenue.

2 Since the English Poor Laws of the seventeenth century, governments have made a distinction between the undeserving and the deserving poor. The Department of Social Security's rules of eligibility for unemployment benefits reflect this distinction.

3 As success and achievement usually are held to reflect individuals' efforts, so are poverty and unemployment which are deemed deviant and undesirable. Often, financially disadvantaged and unemployed people are blamed for their situation, which is attributed to a lack of skills, education, motivation or morality. This is a central component of child-saving ideology which views children as innocent victims of bad parents and who therefore should be removed, or at least not dealt with in a punitive way, if they have been apprehended for violating the law.

4 As with poverty, numerous myths surround unemployment. Many people assume that unemployed people do not want to work, are lazy, 'dole-bludging' freeloaders, especially if they are young. In contrast, research indicates that unemployment is not synonymous with not working and that unemployed people participate in informal economies. Structural changes in the economy, especially in manufacturing with the introduction of new technology and the reduction of tariffs, are essential for understanding the recent increases in unemployment rates.

5 While welfare benefits provide people with some assistance, they also constitute a form of social control and surveillance. Recipients of government benefits must meet eligibility criteria, conform to rules and regulations, and be subject to check-ups and reviews in order to verify information given. Payments are suspended or terminated if violations occur.

6 Rather than altering social inequalities, welfare provision often reinforces existing social arrangements. For example, payments to families, while formally universal and gender-neutral, effectively reinforce a traditional division of labour. Over 90 per cent of the recipients of this benefit are women, and its receipt requires non-participation in the paid labour force, thereby affirming women's domestic and parenting roles and their dependency.

Further reading

Cass, Bettina 1988, 'Income Support for the Unemployed in Australia: Towards a More Active System', *Social Security Review*, Issues Paper no. 4, AGPS, Canberra.

Donzelot, Jacques 1979, *The Policing of Families*, Hutchinson, London.

Graycar, Adam & Adam Jamrozik 1993, *How Australians Live: Social Policy in Theory and Practice*, 2nd edn, Macmillan, Melbourne.

Piven, Frances Fox & Richard Cloward 1971, *Regulating the Poor: The Functions of Public Welfare*, Pantheon Books, New York.

Platt, Anthony 1969, *The Child Savers: The Invention of Delinquency*, University of Chicago Press, Chicago.

Quadagno, Jill 1987, 'Theories of the Welfare State', *Annual Review of Sociology*, vol. 13, pp. 109–28.

Conclusion

The central argument in this book is that deviance forms an integral part of social life. It is not something outside or peripheral to it. Indeed, notions of conformity, following rules or 'doing the right thing', make sense only because notions of deviance exist. The aim of this concluding chapter is to pull together the arguments and ideas presented in the preceding chapters.

The most frequent definition of deviance is behaviour which violates social norms. Such a conception implies a simplicity which is not reflected in the complexity of social life. Deviance can be seen as comprising two central elements: the norm-breaking process and the definitional or labelling process. Norms are not static phenomena, nor are they completely fluid and *ad hoc*. They are shaped by social contexts, situations and societies. As conceptions of deviance are socially constructed, no behaviour is inherently deviant; it depends on social definitions and the application of norms. Often conceptions of deviance are not a product of a general agreement among members of a particular community, but result from the activities of specific groups which attempt to have their conceptions of right and wrong, of appropriate and inappropriate behaviour, translated into law and enforced. Examples covered in this book include abortion, pornography, prostitution and the use of illegal drugs.

Frequently, deviance and deviants are viewed as synonymous but for the sociologist there is a considerable difference. While everybody breaks social norms probably at least once a day their deviance is usually rationalised, ignored or not visible to actors motivated to do something about it. The purpose of an explanation for doing something which appears to others to violate their expectations is to rationalise away the deviance. A simple question, such as 'where have you been?' or 'why did you do that?' indicates that the questioner perceives the person to have broken a social norm and is offering an opportunity for the apparent offender to normalise the social relations. In fact, these questions are forms of informal social control as they usually produce some embarrassment or discomfort, which subsequently may deter other people from violating those same social rules. Most norm-breaking in everyday life is explained away so the apparent deviance disappears; it was not really breaking rules, it was an accident, or unforeseen circumstances prevented conformity. Thus, techniques of rationalisation neutralise any deviant intention on the part of the actor (Sykes & Matza 1957). In everyday life as well as in criminal law, norm-breaking activities without the requisite intention do not constitute deviance. However, there are limits on the types and frequency of excuses or accounts that can be used to deny that deviance occurred.

The transition from deviance to deviant is a complicated process involving identification, sanctions and public labelling, all of which are contingent on who identifies the alleged deviance and whether they are motivated and have the power or authority to respond and apply sanctions. For example, while considerable law-breaking occurs, the police come into contact only with a small, certainly not random proportion, of illegal behaviour. This means that certain kinds of people are more likely to be apprehended, arrested, charged, prosecuted, convicted and sentenced, not necessarily because they break more laws than do other people. The situation of Aboriginal people and their overrepresentation in the criminal justice system is the prime example in Australian society. While there is evidence of racial discrimination by the police, this is only part of the story. As Aboriginal people are more likely to use public places for their leisure, they are more visible to the police, and police intervention can escalate deviance rather than control it.

It is ironic that such an economically deprived and powerless group in our society should be subject to high levels of police surveillance. However, it is the lack of power which makes the application of deviant labels so effective. Stereotypes of the typical 'Aboriginal offender', include assumptions about alcohol consumption, drunkenness, public disturbance and violence. In contrast, social control agents tend to perceive the typical corporate offender as a businessperson oriented to profit and rational action. It is not difficult to understand that corporate offenders are rarely seen as truly deviant. They will also have access to legal counsel and advertising campaigns to launder any stains on their white collars.

Therefore, no discussion of deviance can ignore issues of social inequality. Lack of power, resources and opportunities might be factors in motivating individuals to violate social norms, but their presence might also stimulate deviant behaviour. People in powerful positions, including scientists, politicians, business people, legal and medical practitioners, are confronted with many opportunities to defraud members of the public. Moreover, their rationalisations are more likely to be believed by regulatory agencies and the courts because of their high social status. 'Elite' deviants are much more likely to avoid detection and are more likely to be informally reprimanded by their peers, in the form of professional associations, than be prosecuted in the criminal justice system. When elite deviants are prosecuted the general public is more likely to perceive them as the 'bad apples', while their professional colleagues remain unblemished. On the other hand, the public perception of Aboriginal people, youths, unemployed people and welfare recipients who come into contact with the criminal justice system is more likely to be along the lines of 'what can you expect anyway, they are all like that'.

The criminal justice system is only one site of deviance designation and social control. The medical and welfare systems also provide 'deviant roles' and involve surveillance techniques. Both medical and welfare personnel map out areas of behaviour they deem to be inappropriate, and which therefore require their intervention. However, patient and welfare recipient statuses are not available to everyone. Women, for example, are more likely to seek medical assistance than men, and their 'conditions' are more likely to be defined by the medical profession as illness, especially mental illness, whereas men's deviance is more likely to be given a criminal designation. Generally, welfare payments are available only to people on low or no income. While such people may not previously have violated any laws, the welfare system provides new opportunities for fraud. Despite an ideology of care and assistance welfare departments' scrutiny and surveillance of beneficiaries underscores their policing functions.

Another central theme in this book regards the changing conceptions of deviance, some of which are reflected in legislation. A glance through the daily newspapers suggests that the major kinds of deviance requiring social control at the moment are drug trafficking, youth offending, homelessness, domestic violence, environmental pollution and tobacco consumption. While these activities have always existed they have not always been considered deviant. Moral entrepreneurs and social movements often play a central role in changing definitions of deviance.

Deviance definitions can be altered in a number of ways. In recent years there have been attempts to decriminalise certain activities and remove the stigma of the deviant labels. Examples include prostitution, abortion, homosexuality, personal marijuana use and drug and alcohol consumption. Decriminalisation does not necessarily mean a reduction in social control, but often indicates its displacement from the criminal justice system to the medical or welfare systems. In many instances, they create deviance rather than controlling it. For example, welfare workers use categories like 'problem family' or 'at-risk person', indicating a deviance designation and implying that the welfare agency will 'keep an eye' on them thereby increasing surveillance.

While proponents of decriminalisation seek to remove deviant labels from certain activities, there is a reverse trend oriented to applying deviant and criminal definitions to certain practices. For example, the feminist movement seeks to widen legal definitions of rape, apply assault laws to domestic violence, identify and prohibit sexual harassment and outlaw pornography, thereby criminalising a greater variety of activities. The feminist movement is a good example of a group oriented to both criminalising and decriminalising certain behaviour.

Given the heterogeneity of social groups and the unequal distribution of power in Australian society, it is not surprising that conceptions of deviance and conformity remain in continual flux, demonstrating the 'elasticity of evil'. As group and individual identity rests on defining certain activities and behaviour as unacceptable, immoral or harmful, then deviance prevails.

While its existence, even its inevitability, is indisputable, theoretical development and research findings have not provided consistent explanations of deviance. In a 1990 book review, Erich Goode laments that: 'Two qualities characterise contemporary deviance theory: fragmentation and stagnation ... we have no real community of discourse' (p. 5). Of all the subfields of sociology, it seems that the investigation of deviance suffers most from theories which are often non-complementary and research which is frequently atheoretical, because of an uncritical reliance on officially collected data or on small-scale studies adopting inductive methodologies. Moreover, many theorists of deviance (as well as of other subdisciplines) devote most of their energy to criticising or 'deconstructing' theories and constructing their own. While criticism and debate are at the core of theoretical analyses, the future development of the sociology of deviance requires empirical investigations which take into account the multidimensionality of deviance. Such a direction is essential for the development of complementary theoretical perspectives each contributing to an understanding and explanation of the definition, emergence, continuation or disappearance of deviance.

Sample questions for essays and examinations

1 Choose an example of deviant behaviour and assume that you have been called before a Royal Commission that wants to know if there is any established knowledge that can help it formulate policy recommendations about the behaviour in question. What do you advise the Commission? Specify the alternative value premises that underlie the different policy implications of your 'knowledge'. State explicitly the theoretical, substantive, and value assumptions that underlie the policy you favour. Back up your theoretical and substantive arguments with evidence and support the value assumptions in a reflective way.

2 Critically analyse Durkheim's notion that even in a 'society of saints' crime will be found.

3 Everyone has ideas about what constitutes norm-breaking and illegal behaviour, and views about how to control or eradicate deviance. However, in many situations rule infraction, whether it be violation of an informal norm or violation of the law, is ignored or tolerated. Explain this discrepancy, giving examples. In other words, under what conditions are rules and laws enforced?

4 Review and evaluate the criticisms of official crime statistics as measures of 'criminal activity'. Note that this can be done on methodological and theoretical levels.

5 How does the labelling perspective aid an explanation of the status of women as deviant? Do you think this approach is useful? Explain.

6 Different legal sanctions are based on different conceptions of the causes of crime, and how to control or prevent crime. Describe and analyse the assumptions and rationale upon which the rehabilitative ideal, deterrence and justice models of corrections are based.

7 Critically examine the proposition that certain kinds of deviance are more amenable to medicalisation than others.

8 In terms of financial, social and economic costs the illegal or deviant activities of corporate entities far exceed those stemming from the commission of 'common crimes'. Discuss the kinds of deviant activities corporate and professional actors commit and explain why they frequently remain undetected. Why is corporate and professional deviance so difficult to police and sanction despite the often detrimental consequences for employees, consumers and the general public?

9 A prevailing view is that deviance is behaviour that violates rules. If we know what somebody has done and we know the rules, we know whether a deviant activity has occurred. Another view is that it is impossible to construct a theory of deviance on the basis of such notions. Rules are resources that are invoked in the course of social interaction and are manipulated by the parties concerned to provide accounts for their actions, to justify labelling, or to avoid being labelled. Rules, then, cannot provide an objective criterion for distinguishing deviant and non-deviant behaviour. Examine the concerns of deviance theory in the light of each of these two perspectives. Discuss the logic, merits, and problems of each. Is either perspective more defensible than the other, or is an alternative formulation of deviance more appropriate?

10 Assess the merits of Cohen's 'subcultural theory' for an understanding of deviance. In what ways, if any, would it need to be modified in order to discuss delinquent girls?

11 Definitions of deviance change. Giving examples, critically analyse the processes of criminalisation and decriminalisation within the criminal justice system in contemporary Australian society.

12 Select two or three types of deviance from the following list:
   a homosexuality
   b drug use
   c rape
   d environmental pollution
   e insider trading
   f juvenile delinquency
   g mental illness
   h prostitution
   I traffic violations
   j obesity
   k corporate crime
   l vandalism
   m pornography

n   abortion
o   theft
p   unemployment
q   domestic violence
r   cigarette smoking

Discuss the concept of deviance with reference to the examples you select. First define deviance, then explain why, how, and by whom the examples are defined as deviant. What kinds of social control attaches to the examples of deviance? Discuss the factors affecting the effectiveness or otherwise of the sanctions applied.

13 Discuss three types of deviant behaviour from two different theoretical perspectives. Assess the strengths and weaknesses of the theories in explaining the incidence of deviance in society.

14 Discuss the prison as a sentencing option and type of punishment within our criminal justice system. Explain whether the goals of imprisonment are achievable and reflect on why crime persists despite this formal sanction.

15 Compare and contrast the law, medicine and social welfare as forms of social control.

16 It is often stated that women are less likely to be involved in criminal activities than are men. Alternatively, it is claimed that women are more likely to be labelled sick thereby avoiding criminal labels. Are these viewpoints incompatible? Explain.

17 Compare and contrast the arguments and strategies of social movements that seek to decriminalise or criminalise (or at least legally prohibit) such behaviour and activities as abortion, pornography, homosexuality, tobacco consumption and marijuana use.

18 To what extent are conventional theories of deviance capable of explaining women's involvement in criminal activities? What scope exists for a distinct feminist criminology?

19 Critically examine recent changes in the operation and focus of juvenile justice systems from both a sociological and public policy perspective.

20 Critically evaluate Braithwaite's concept of 'reintegrative shaming'. What kinds of assumptions are made by this theory? In your view, does it represent a synthesis of previous theories or a new general theory of crime?

21 Assess Sutherland's contribution to the analysis of corporate crime. How relevant is his conception of white-collar crime to a discussion of corporate deviance? Do we need separate theories to explain corporate crime or can a general theory of deviance explain both corporate and individual crime?

22 Explain Sellin's observation that: 'The value of a crime rate for index purposes decreases as the distance from the crime itself in terms of procedure increases. In other words, police statistics, particularly those of "crimes known to the police", are most likely to furnish a good basis

for a crime index' (1931, p. 346, emphasis omitted). Identify the strengths and limitations of the different sources of crime data.

23 In what ways does greater attention to the rights of victims change the nature of our criminal justice system?

24 Research suggests that certain segments of society are less at risk of victimisation than are others, yet some of these segments express the greatest fear of crime. Explain this apparent paradox.

25 What implications do 'deinstitutionalisation', 'decarceration' and 'privatisation' have for the scope and nature of formal and informal social control?

Bibliography

Abbott, Andrew 1988, *The System of Professions: An Essay on the Division of Expert Labor*, University of Chicago Press, Chicago.

Abrahamson, Mark 1978, *Functionalism*, Prentice Hall, Englewood Cliffs, New Jersey.

Adams, Phillip 1994, 'Criminal Behaviour Down South', *The Weekend Australian Review*, May 7–8, p. 2.

Adler, Freda 1975, *Sisters in Crime: The Rise of the New Female Criminal*, McGraw-Hill, London.

Adler, Freda & Simon, Rita eds 1979, *The Criminology of Deviant Women*, Houghton Mifflin, Boston.

Alder, Christine 1984, 'Gender Bias in Diversion', *Crime and Delinquency*, vol. 30, pp. 400–14.

Alder, Christine 1986, 'Unemployed Women Have Got it Heaps Worse', *Australian & New Zealand Journal of Criminology*, vol. 19, pp. 210–24.

Alder, Christine 1992, 'The Young People', in *Perceptions of the Treatment of Juveniles in the Legal System: Report to the National Youth Affairs Research Scheme*, eds C. Alder, I. O'Connor, K. Warner & R. White, National Clearing House for Youth Studies, Hobart.

The Advertiser 1988, 'Recording Shows Herbert "lied" About Drugs Network', 30 September, p. 4.

Allan, Emilie Andersen & Steffensmeier, Darrell J. 1989, 'Youth, Underemployment, and Property Crime: Differential Effects of Job Availability and Job Quality on Juvenile and Young Adults' Arrest Rates', *American Sociological Review*, vol. 54, pp. 107–23.

Allen, Francis A. 1972, 'Raffaele Garofalo', in *Pioneers in Criminology*, 2nd edn, ed. Hermann Mannheim, Patterson Smith, Montclair, New Jersey.

Allen, Hilary 1984, 'At the Mercy of Her Hormones: Premenstrual Tension and the Law', *M/F*, vol. 9, pp. 19–44.

Allen, Judith 1986, 'Desperately Seeking Solutions: Changing Battered Women's Options Since 1880', *National Conference on Domestic Violence*, vol. 1, ed. Suzanne E. Hatty, Australian Institute of Criminology, Canberra.

Allen, Judith 1988, 'The "Masculinity" of Criminality and Criminology: Interrogating Some Impasses', in *Understanding Crime and Criminal Justice*, eds Mark Findlay & Russell Hogg, The Law Book Company, Sydney.

Allen, Judith 1989, 'Men, Crime and Criminology: Recasting the Questions', *International Journal of the Sociology of Law*, vol. 17, pp. 19–39.

Amir, Menachim 1967, 'Victim Precipitated Forcible Rape', *Journal of Criminal Law, Criminology and Police Science*, vol. 58, pp. 493–502.

Amir, Menachim 1971, *Patterns in Forcible Rape*, University of Chicago Press, Chicago.

Anderson, Etta A. 1976, 'The "Chivalrous" Treatment of the Female Offender in the Arms of the Criminal Justice System: A Review of the Literature', *Social Problems*, vol. 23, pp. 350–7.

Aneshensel, Carol S., Rutter, Carolyn, & Lachenbruch, Peter A. 1991, 'Social Structure, Stress, and Mental Health: Competing Conceptual and Analytic Models', *American Sociological Review*, vol. 56, pp. 166–78.

Arnold, Bruce, & Hagan, John 1992, 'Careers of Misconduct: The Structure of Prosecuted Professional Deviance Among Lawyers', *American Sociological Review*, vol. 57, pp. 771–80.

Ashworth, Andrew J. 1992, 'Sentencing Reform Structures', *Crime & Justice: An Annual Review of Research*, vol. 16, pp. 181–241.

Aubert, Vilhelm 1952, 'White-Collar Crime and Social Structure', *American Journal of Sociology*, vol. 58, pp. 263–71.

Aubert, Vilhelm & Messinger, Sheldon L. 1958, 'The Criminal and The Sick', *Inquiry*, vol. 1, pp. 137–60.

Australia 1974, *Australian Securities Markets and Their Regulation*, vol. 1, Report from the Senate Select Committee on Securities and Exchange, AGPS, Canberra.

Australia 1988, *Report of the Joint Select Committee on Video Material*, vol. 1, AGPS, Canberra.

Australia 1989, *Drugs, Crime and Society*, Report by the Parliamentary Joint Committee on the National Crime Authority, AGPS, Canberra.

Australian Bureau of Statistics 1975, *Year Book of Australia 1974*, ABS, Canberra.

Australian Bureau of Statistics 1986, *Victims of Crime Australia 1983*, Cat. no. 4506.0, ABS, Canberra.

Australian Bureau of Statistics 1989, *Census of Population and Housing 30 June 1986, Characteristics of In-Patients of Health Institutions, Australia*, Cat. no. 4347.0, ABS, Canberra.

Australian Bureau of Statistics 1991a, *1989–90 National Health Survey: Users' Guide, Australia*, Cat. no. 4363.0, ABS, Canberra.

Australian Bureau of Statistics 1991b, *1989–90 National Health Survey: Summary of Results, Australia*, Cat. no. 4364.0, ABS, Canberra.

Australian Bureau of Statistics 1991c, *1989–90 National Health Survey: Cardiovascular and Related Conditions, Australia*, Cat. no. 4372.0, ABS, Canberra.

Australian Bureau of Statistics 1992a, *1989–90 National Health Survey: Health Status Indicators, Australia*, Cat no. 4370.0, ABS, Canberra.

Australian Bureau of Statistics 1992b, *1989–90 National Health Survey: Health Related Actions, Australia*, Cat. no. 43750, ABS, Canberra.

Australian Bureau of Statistics 1993a, *Deaths, Australia 1992*, Cat. no. 3302.0, ABS, Canberra.

Australian Bureau of Statistics 1993b, *Year Book Australia, 1994*, ABS, Canberra, Cat. no. 1301.0.

Australian Bureau of Statistics 1994a, *Crime and Safety Australia 1993*, Cat. no. 4509.0, ABS, Canberra.

Australian Bureau of Statistics 1994b, *Information Paper: National Crime Statistics*, Cat. no. 4511.0, ABS, Canberra.

Australian Bureau of Statistics 1994c, *National Crime Statistics: January–December 1993*, Cat. no. 4510.0, ABS, Canberra.

Australian Law Reform Commission 1980, *Sentencing Federal Offenders*, AGPS, Canberra.

Australian Law Reform Commission 1993, *Equality Before the Law*, Discussion Paper 54, ALRC, Sydney.

Australian Securities Commission 1993, *Annual Report 1992/93*, ASC, Sydney.

Bacon, Wendy & Lansdowne, Robyn 1982, 'Women Who Kill Husbands: The Battered Wife on Trial', in *Family Violence in Australia*, eds Carol O'Donnell & Jan Craney, Longman Cheshire, Melbourne.

Baker, Wayne E. & Faulkner, Robert R. 1993, 'The Social Organization of Conspiracy: Illegal Networks in the Heavy Electrical Equipment Industry', *American Sociological Review*, vol. 58, pp. 837–60.

Bansemer, Oliver 1987, Work and the Welfare State: The Dolesville Case, Honours thesis, The Flinders University of South Australia.

Barker-Benfield, Ben 1975, 'Sexual Surgery in Late Nineteenth-Century America', *International Journal of Health Services*, vol. 5, pp. 279–98.

Barnard, Marina A. 1993, 'Violence and Vulnerability: Conditions of Work for Street-Working Prostitutes', *Sociology of Health & Illness*, vol. 15, pp. 683–705.

Baron, Larry 1987, 'Immoral, Inviolate or Inconclusive?', *Society*, vol. 24, pp. 6–12.

Bassuk, Ellen L. 1984, 'The Homelessness Problem', *Scientific American*, vol. 251, pp. 28–33.

Bassuk, Ellen L. & Gerson, Samuel 1978, 'Deinstitutionalization and Mental Health Services', *Scientific American*, vol. 238, pp. 46–53.

Bates, Erica & Linder-Pelz, Susie 1990, *Health Care Issues*, 2nd edn, Allen & Unwin, Sydney.

Baucas, Melissa A. & Dworkin, Terry Morehead 1991, 'What is Corporate Crime? It is Not Illegal Corporate Behaviour', *Law & Policy*, vol. 13, pp. 231–44.

Bayley, David H. 1989, 'Community Policing in Australia: An Appraisal', in *Australian Policing: Contemporary Issues*, eds Duncan Chappell & Paul Wilson, Butterworths, Sydney.

Becker, Gay & Nachtigall, Robert D. 1992, 'Eager for Medicalisation: The Social Production of Infertility as a Disease', *Sociology of Health & Illness*, vol. 14, pp. 456–71.

Becker, Howard S. 1953, 'Becoming a Marijuana User', *American Journal of Sociology*, vol. 59, pp. 235–42.

Becker, Howard S. 1963, *Outsiders: Studies in the Sociology of Deviance*, The Free Press, New York.

Becker, Howard S. 1973, 'Labelling Theory Reconsidered', in *Outsiders: Studies in the Sociology of Deviance*, Howard S. Becker, The Free Press, New York.

Becker, Howard S., Geer, Blanche, Hughes, Everett C. & Strauss, Anselm 1961, *Boys in White: Student Culture in Medical School*, University of Chicago Press, Chicago.

Beeghley, Leonard 1984, 'Illusion and Reality in the Measurement of Poverty', *Social Problems*, vol. 31, pp. 322–33.

Beirne, Piers 1979, 'Empiricism and the Critique of Marxism on Law and Crime', *Social Problems*, vol. 26, pp. 373–85.

Beirne, Piers 1988, 'Heredity Versus Environment: A Reconsideration of Charles Goring's *The English Convict* (1913)', *The British Journal of Criminology*, vol. 28, pp. 315–39.

Beisel, Nicola 1990, 'Class, Culture and Campaigns Against Vice in Three American Cities, 1872–1892', *American Sociological Review*, vol. 55, pp. 44–62.

Beisel, Nicola 1993, 'Censorship, the Politics of Interpretation, and the Victorian Nude', *American Sociological Review*, vol. 58, pp. 145–62.

Bell, Susan E. 1987, 'Changing Ideas: The Medicalization of Menopause', *Social Science and Medicine*, vol. 6, pp. 535–42.

Benn, Concetta 1981, 'Innovation in Welfare', in *The Welfare States: Strategies for Australian Social Policy*, ed. Ronald F. Henderson, Institute of Applied Economic and Social Research, Melbourne.

Benson, Donna J. & Thomson, Gregg E. 1982, 'Sexual Harassment on a University Campus: The Confluence of Authority Relations, Sexual Interest and Gender Stratification', *Social Problems*, vol. 29, pp. 236–51.

Ben-Yehuda, Nachman 1980, 'The European Witch Craze of the 14th to 17th Centuries: A Sociologist's Perspective', *American Journal of Sociology*, vol. 86, pp. 1–31.

Ben-Yehuda, Nachman 1986, 'Deviance in Science', *British Journal of Criminology*, vol. 26, pp. 1–27.

Ben-Yehuda, Nachman 1992, 'Criminalization and Decriminalization as Properties of the Social Order', *Sociological Review*, vol. 40, pp. 73–108.

Berk, Richard A., Campbell, Alec, Klap, Ruth & Western, Bruce 1992, 'The Deterrent Effect of Arrest in Incidents of Domestic Violence: A Bayesian Analysis of Four Field Experiments', *American Sociological Review*, vol. 57, pp. 698–708.

Berk, Sarah Fenstermaker & Loseke, Donileen R. 1981, 'Handling Family Violence: Situational Determinants of Police Arrest in Domestic Disturbances', *Law & Society Review*, vol. 15, pp. 315–46.

Best, Joel ed. 1989, *Images of Issues: Typifying Contemporary Social Problems*, Aldine de Gruyter, New York.

Biles, David 1986, 'Prisons and Their Problems', in *The Australian Criminal Justice System: The Mid 1980s*, eds Duncan Chappell & Paul Wilson, Butterworths, Sydney.

Biles, David, McDonald, David & Fleming, Jillian 1989a, 'Australian Deaths in Police Custody 1980–1988: An Analysis of Aboriginal and Non-Aboriginal Deaths', Research Paper no. 10, Royal Commission into Aboriginal Deaths in Custody, Canberra.

Biles, David, McDonald, David & Fleming, Jillian 1989b, 'Australian Deaths in Prisons 1980–1988: An Analysis of Aboriginal and Non-Aboriginal Deaths', Research Paper no. 11, Royal Commission into Aboriginal Deaths in Custody, Canberra.

Bittner, Egon 1967, 'Police on Skid Row', *American Sociological Review*, vol. 32, pp. 699–715.

Bittner, Egon 1968, 'The Structure of Psychiatric Influence', *Mental Hygiene*, vol. 52, pp. 423–30.

Black, Donald 1970, 'Production of Crime Rates', *American Sociological Review*, vol. 35, pp. 733–48.

Black, Donald 1971, 'Social Organization of Arrest', *Stanford Law Review*, vol. 23, pp. 1087–111.

Black, Donald 1976, *The Behavior of Law*, Academic Press, New York.

Black, Donald & Reiss, Albert 1970, 'Police Control of Juveniles', *American Sociological Review*, vol. 35, pp. 63–77.

Blank, Robert H. 1990, *Regulating Reproduction*, Columbia University Press, New York.

Blau, Peter M. & Scott, W. Richard 1962, *Formal Organizations: A Comparative Approach*, Chandler Publishing Company, San Francisco.

Block, Kathleen J & Hale, Donna C. 1991, 'Turf Wars in Progressive Era Juvenile Justice: The Relationship of Private and Public Child Care Agencies', *Crime & Delinquency*, vol. 37, pp. 225–41.

Blumberg, Abraham S. 1985, 'The Police and the Social System: Reflections and Prospects', in *The Ambivalent Force: Perspectives on the Police*, 3rd edn, eds Abraham S. Blumberg & Elaine Niederhoffer, Holt, Rinehart & Winston, New York.

Blumer, Herbert 1971, 'Social Problems as Collective Behaviour', *Social Problems*, vol. 18, pp. 298–306.

Boniface, Dorne J. 1992, 'Legal Professional Privilege and Disclosure Powers of Investigative Agencies: Some Interesting and Troubling Issues Regarding Competing Public Policies', *Criminal Law Journal*, vol. 16, pp. 320–49.

Boswell, Bryan 1989, 'Panama Diehards Battle US Troops', *The Weekend Australian*, 23–24 December, pp. 1, 7.

Box, Steven 1983, *Power, Crime and Mystification*, Tavistock, London.

Box, Steven & Hale, Chris 1983, 'Liberation and Female Criminality in England and Wales', *British Journal of Criminology*, vol. 23, pp. 35–49.

Box, Steven, Hale, Chris & Andrews, Glen 1988, 'Explaining Fear of Crime', *British Journal of Criminology*, vol. 28, pp. 340–56.

Braithwaite, John 1978, 'An Exploratory Study of Used Car Fraud', in *Two Faces of Deviance: Crimes of the Powerless and the Powerful*, eds Paul R. Wilson & John Braithwaite, University of Queensland Press, St. Lucia.

Braithwaite, John 1982, 'Challenging Just Deserts: Punishing White Collar Criminals', *The Journal of Criminal Law & Criminology*, vol. 73, pp. 723–63.

Braithwaite, John 1984, *Corporate Crime in the Pharmaceutical Industry*, Routledge & Kegan Paul, London.

Braithwaite, John 1985, 'White Collar Crime', *Annual Review of Sociology*, vol. 11, pp. 1–25.

Braithwaite, John 1989, *Crime, Shame and Reintegration*, Cambridge University Press, Cambridge.

Braithwaite, John & Fisse, Brent 1983, 'Asbestos and Health: A Case of Informal Social Control', *Australian & New Zealand Journal of Criminology*, vol. 16, pp. 67–80.

Breines, Wini & Gordon, Linda 1983, 'The New Scholarship on Family Violence', *Signs: Journal of Women in Culture and Society*, vol. 8, pp. 490–531.

Breslin, Catharine 1989, 'Day of Reckoning', *MS*, June, pp. 46–52.

Brice, Chris 1988, 'How Life Ticks by for Geoff and His Electronic Jailer', *The Advertiser*, 16 December, p. 4.

Bright, Robin Anne 1978, 'Dole Bludgers or Tax Dodgers: Who is the Deviant', in *Two Faces of Deviance: Crimes of the Powerless and the Powerful*, eds Paul Wilson & John Braithwaite, University of Queensland Press, St. Lucia.

Briggs, Asa 1961, 'The Welfare State in Historical Perspective', *European Journal of Sociology*, vol. 2, pp. 221–58.

Brody, S.R. 1976, *The Effectiveness of Sentencing—A Review of the Literature*, Her Majesty's Stationery Office, London.

Brown, Beverly 1986, 'Women and Crime: The Dark Figures of Criminology', *Economy and Society*, vol. 15, pp. 355–402.

Brown, Beverley 1990, 'Reassessing the Critique of Biologism', in *Feminist Perspectives in Criminology*, eds Loraine Gelsthorpe & Allison Morris, Open University Press, Milton Keynes.

Brown, David & Hogg, Russell 1992, 'Essentialism, Radical Criminology and Left Realism', *Australian & New Zealand Journal of Criminology*, vol. 25, pp. 195–230.

Browne, Angela & Williams, Kirk R. 1993, 'Gender, Intimacy, and Sexual Violence: Trends from 1976 Through 1987', *Gender & Society*, vol. 7, pp. 78–98.

Brownmiller, Susan 1975, *Against Our Will: Men, Women and Rape*, Simon & Schuster, New York.

Bryan, James H. 1965, 'Apprenticeships in Prostitution', *Social Problems*, vol. 12, pp. 287–97.

Bryson, Lois 1983, 'Women as Welfare Recipients: Women, Poverty and the State', in *Women, Social Welfare and the State in Australia*, eds Cora V. Baldock & Bettina Cass, George Allen & Unwin, Sydney.

Bucher, Rue 1962, 'Pathology: A Study of Social Movements Within a Profession', *Social Problems*, vol. 9, pp. 40–51.

Bucher, Rue & Stelling, Joan 1969, 'Characteristics of Professional Organizations', *Journal of Health and Social Behavior*, vol. 10, pp. 3–15.

Bucher, Rue & Strauss, Anselm 1961, 'Professions in Process', *American Journal of Sociology*, vol. 66, pp. 325–34.

Bullington, Bruce, Sprowls, James, Katkin, Daniel & Phillips, Mark 1978, 'A Critique of Diversionary Juvenile Justice', *Crime & Delinquency*, vol. 24, pp. 59–71.

Bullough, Vern & Bullough, Bonnie 1987, *Women and Prostitution: A Social History*, Prometheus Books, Buffalo, New York.

Burr, Angela 1987, 'Chasing the Dragon: Heroin Misuse, Delinquency and Crime in the Context of South London Culture', *British Journal of Criminology*, vol. 27, pp. 333–57.

Bury, M.R. 1986, 'Social Constructionism and the Development of Medical Sociology', *Sociology of Health and Illness*, vol. 8, pp. 137–69.

Busfield, Joan 1988, 'Mental Illness as Social Product or Social Construct: A Contradiction in Feminists' Arguments?', *Sociology of Health & Illness*, vol. 10, pp. 521–42.

Busfield, Joan 1989, 'Sexism and Psychiatry', *Sociology*, vol. 23, pp. 343–64.

Cain, Maureen 1990, 'Towards Transgression: New Directions in Feminist Criminology', *International Journal of the Sociology of Law*, vol. 18, pp. 1–18.

Cain, Maureen & Hunt, Alan 1979, *Marx and Engels on Law*, Academic Press, New York.

Cain, Maureen & Sadigh, Susan 1982, 'Racism, The Police and Community Policing: A Comment on the Scarman Report', *Journal of Law & Society*, vol. 9, pp. 87–102.

Calavita, Kitty & Pontell, Henry N. 1991, '"Other People's Money" Revisited: Collective Embezzlement in the Savings and Loan and Insurance Industries', *Social Problems*, vol. 38, pp. 94–112.

Calhoun, Craig & Hiller, Henryk 1988, 'Coping with Insidious Injuries: The Case of Johns-Manville Corporation and Asbestos Exposure', *Social Problems*, vol. 35, pp. 162–81.

California Lawyer 1993, 'Counsel or Conspirator? The Supreme Court Leaves the Door Open for Professional Liability under RICO', June, pp. 33–4, 36.

Cameron, Mary Owen 1964, *The Booster and the Snitch*, The Free Press, Glencoe.

Campbell, Donald T. & Ross, H. Laurence 1968, 'The Connecticut Crackdown on Speeding: Time–Series Data in Quasi-Experimental Analysis', *Law & Society Review*, vol. 3, pp. 33–54.

Cantor, David & Land, Kenneth C. 1985, 'Unemployment and Crime Rates in the Post-World War II United States: A Theoretical and Empirical Analysis', *American Sociological Review*, vol. 50, pp. 317–32.

Carlen, Pat 1983, *Women's Imprisonment: A Study in Social Control*, Routledge & Kegan Paul, London.

Carlin, Jerome E. 1966, *Lawyers' Ethics: A Survey of the New York City Bar*, Russell Sage, New York.

Carrington, Kerry 1990a, 'Feminist Readings of Female Delinquency', *Law in Context*, vol. 8, pp. 5–31.

Carrington, Kerry 1990b, 'Truancy, Schooling and Juvenile Justice: "She Says She Hates School"', *Australian & New Zealand Journal of Criminology*, vol. 23, pp. 259–68.

Carrington, Kerry 1993, *Offending Girls*, Allen & Unwin, Sydney.

Carson, W.G. 1970, 'White-Collar Crime and the Enforcement of Factory Legislation', *British Journal of Criminology*, vol. 10, pp. 383–98.

Carson, W.G. 1980, 'The Institutionalization of Ambiguity: Early British Factory Acts', in *White Collar Crime: Theory and Research*, eds Gilbert Geis & E. Stotland, Sage, Beverly Hills.

Cashman, Peter 1982a, 'Medical Benefit Fraud: Prosecution and Sentencing of Doctors Part 1', *Legal Service Bulletin*, vol. 7, pp. 58–61.

Cashman, Peter 1982b, 'Medical Benefit Fraud: Prosecution and Sentencing of Doctors Part 2', *Legal Service Bulletin*, vol. 7, pp. 116–21.

Cass, Bettina 1983, 'Redistribution to Children and to Mothers: A History of Child Endowment and Family Allowances', in *Women, Social Welfare and the State in Australia*, eds Cora V. Baldock & Bettina Cass, George Allen & Unwin, Sydney.

Cass, Bettina 1988a, 'The Feminisation of Poverty', in *Crossing Boundaries: Feminism and the Critique of Knowledge*, eds Barbara Caine, E.A. Grosz & Marie de Lepervanche, Allen & Unwin, Sydney.

Cass, Bettina 1988b, 'Income Support for the Unemployed: Towards a More Active System', *Social Security Review*, Issues Paper no. 4, AGPS, Canberra.

Cass, Deborah Z. 1992, 'Casenote: Hakopian', *Criminal Law Journal* 16, pp. 200–4.

Chait, Linda R. 1986, 'Pre-Menstrual Syndrome and Our Sisters in Crime: A Feminist Dilemma', *Women's Rights Law Reporter*, vol. 9, pp. 267–93.

Challinger, Dennis 1982, 'Crime, Females and Statistics', *Australian & New Zealand Journal of Criminology*, vol. 15, pp. 123–8.

Chambliss, William 1964, 'A Sociological Analysis of Vagrancy', *Social Problems*, vol. 12, pp. 67–77.

Chambliss, William J. 1967, 'Types of Deviance and The Effectiveness of Legal Sanctions', *Wisconsin Law Review*, Summer, pp. 703–19.

Chambliss, William J. ed. 1969, *Crime and the Legal Process*, McGraw-Hill, New York.

Chambliss, William 1974, 'The State, The Law, and the Definition of Behaviour as Criminal or Delinquent', in *Handbook of Criminology*, ed. Daniel Glaser, Rand McNally, Chicago.

Chambliss, William J. 1978, 'The Political Economy of Smack: Opiates, Capitalism and Law', in *Research in Law and Sociology*, ed. Rita Simon, JAI Press, Greenwich, CT.

Chambliss, William J. 1979, 'On Law-Making', *British Journal of Law & Society*, vol. 6, pp. 149–71.

Chambliss, William & Seidman, Robert 1982, *Law, Order, and Power*, 2nd edn, Addison-Wesley Publishing Company, Reading, Mass.

Chan, Janet B.L. 1992, 'The Privatisation of Punishment: A Review of Key Issues', *Australian Journal of Social Issues*, vol. 27, pp. 223–47.

Chan, Janet & Zdenkowski, George 1986a, 'Just Alternatives—Part I: Trends and Issues in the Deinstitutionalization of Punishment', *Australian & New Zealand Journal of Criminology*, vol. 19, pp. 67–90.

Chan, Janet & Zdenkowksi, George 1986b, 'Just Alternatives—Part II', *Australian & New Zealand Journal of Criminology*, vol. 19, pp. 131–54.

Chappell, Duncan & Wilson, Paul eds 1994, *The Australian Criminal Justice System: The Mid 1990s*, Butterworths, Sydney.

Chesler, Phyllis 1971, 'Women as Psychiatric and Psychotherapeutic Patients', *Journal of Marriage and The Family*, vol. 33, pp. 746–59.

Chesler, Phyllis 1972, *Women and Madness*, Doubleday, Garden City.

Chesney-Lind, Meda 1973, 'Judicial Enforcement of the Female Sex Role: The Family Court and the Female Delinquent', *Issues in Criminology*, vol. 8, pp. 51–69.

Chesney-Lind, Meda 1978, 'Chivalry Re-examined: Women and the Criminal Justice System', in *Women, Crime and the Criminal Justice System*, ed. Lee H. Bowker, Lexington Books, Lexington, Mass.

Chesney-Lind, Meda 1986, 'Women and Crime: The Female Offender', *Signs: Journal of Women in Culture and Society*, vol. 12, pp. 78–96.

Chibnall, Steve 1975, 'The Crime Reporter: A Study in the Production of Commercial Knowledge', *Sociology*, vol. 9, pp. 49–66.

Chibnall, Steve 1977, *Law-And-Order News: An Analysis of Crime Reporting in the British Press*, Tavistock, London.

Chiricos, Theodore G. 1987, 'Rates of Crime and Unemployment: An Analysis of Aggregate Research Evidence', *Social Problems*, vol. 34, pp. 187–212.

Chisholm, Richard 1985, *Black Children, White Welfare? Aboriginal Child Welfare Law and Policy in New South Wales*, Social Welfare Research Centre, University of New South Wales.

Chong, Florence 1994, 'The Ties that Bind', *The Australian*, 20 April, p. 33.

Cicourel, Aaron V. 1968, *The Social Organization of Juvenile Justice*, John Wiley & Sons, New York.

Clark, Lorenne & Lewis, Debra 1977, *Rape: The Price of Coercive Sexuality*, Women's Press, Toronto.

Clarke, Alan 1987a, 'Moral Reform and the Anti-Abortion Movement', *Sociological Review*, vol. 35, pp. 123–49.

Clarke, Alan 1987b, 'Moral Protest, Status Defence and the Anti-Abortion Campaign', *The British Journal of Sociology*, vol. 38, pp. 235–55.

Clinard, Marshall B. & Quinney, Richard 1973, *Criminal Behaviour Systems: A Typology*, 2nd edn, Holt, Rinehart & Winston, New York.

Clinard, Marshall B. & Yeager, Peter C. 1980, *Corporate Crime*, The Free Press, New York.

Cloward, Richard A. & Ohlin, Lloyd E. 1960, *Delinquency and Opportunity: A Theory of Delinquent Gangs*, The Free Press, New York.

Cocozza, Joseph J. & Steadman, Henry J. 1978, 'Prediction in Psychiatry: An Example of Misplaced Confidence in Experts', *Social Problems*, vol. 25, pp. 265–76.

Coe, Rodney M. 1978, *Sociology of Medicine*, 2nd edn, McGraw-Hill, New York.

Cohen, Albert K. 1955, *Delinquent Boys: The Culture of the Gang*, The Free Press, New York.

Cohen, Albert K. 1965, 'The Sociology of the Deviant Act: Anomie Theory and Beyond', *American Sociological Review*, vol. 30, pp. 5–15.

Cohen, Albert K. 1966, *Deviance and Control*, Prentice Hall, Englewood Cliffs, New Jersey.

Cohen, Albert K. 1968, 'Deviant Behaviour', in *International Encyclopedia of the Social Sciences*, ed. David Sills, Macmillan, New York.

Cohen, Albert K. 1974, *The Elasticity of Evil: Changes in the Social Definition of Deviance*, Basil Blackwell, Oxford.

Cohen, Albert K. 1983, 'Crime Causation: Sociological Theories', *Encyclopedia of Crime and Justice*, vol. 1, ed. Sanford Kadish, The Free Press, New York.

Cohen, Albert K. & Short, James F. Jr. 1958, 'Research in Delinquent Subcultures', *Journal of Social Issues*, vol. 14, pp. 20–37.

Cohen, Lawrence E. & Felson, Marcus 1979, 'Social Change and Crime Rate Trends: A Routine Activity Approach', *American Sociological Review*, vol. 44, pp. 588–608.

Cohen, Stanley 1979, 'The Punitive City: Notes on the Dispersal of Social Control', *Contemporary Crises*, vol. 3, pp. 339–63.

Cohen, Stanley 1980, *Folk Devils and Moral Panics: The Creation of the Mods and Rockers*, Basil Blackwell, Oxford.

Cohen, Stanley 1985, *Visions of Social Control: Crime, Punishment and Classification*, Polity Press, Cambridge.

Coleman, James William 1987, 'Toward an Integrated Theory of White-Collar Crime', *American Journal of Sociology*, vol. 93, pp. 406–39.

Coleman, Karen 1988, 'The Politics of Abortion in Australia: Freedom, Church & State', *Feminist Review*, vol. 29, pp. 75–97.

Coles, Frances S. 1986, 'Forced to Quit: Sexual Harassment Complaints and Agency Response', *Sex Roles*, vol. 14, pp. 81–95.

Collins, Eliza G.C. & Blodgett, Timothy B. 1981, 'Sexual Harassment ... Some See It ... Some Won't', *Harvard Business Review*, vol. 59, March/April, pp. 76–95.

Commission of Inquiry into Poverty 1975, *Poverty in Australia, First Main Report*, (Prof. R.F. Henderson, Chair) AGPS, Canberra.

Conklin, John E. 1977, *Illegal But Not Criminal: Business Crime in America*, Prentice Hall, Englewood Cliffs, New Jersey.

Connell, R.W. 1992, 'A Very Straight Gay: Masculinity, Homosexual Experience, and the Dynamics of Gender', *American Sociological Review*, vol. 57, pp. 735–51.

Connell, R.W., Davis, M.D. & Dowsett, G.W. 1993, 'A Bastard of a Life: Homosexual Desire and Practice Among Men in Working-Class Milieux', *The Australian & New Zealand Journal of Sociology*, vol. 29, pp. 112–35.

Conrad, Peter & Schneider, Peter 1980, *Deviance and Medicalization: From Badness to Sickness*, The C.V. Mosby Company, St. Louis.

Corns, Christopher 1988, 'Policing and Social Change', *Australian & New Zealand Journal of Sociology*, vol. 24, pp. 32–46.

Corns, Christopher 1992a, 'Inter-agency Relations: Some Hidden Obstacles to Combatting Organised Crime?', *Australian & New Zealand Journal of Criminology*, vol. 25, pp. 169–85.

Corns, Christopher 1992b, 'Lawyers and Police: An Uneasy Marriage in the National Crime Authority's Fight Against Organised Crime', *Australian & New Zealand Journal of Criminology*, vol. 25, pp. 231–54.

Coser, Lewis A. 1965, 'The Sociology of Poverty', *Social Problems*, vol. 13, pp. 140–8.

Costigan, Frank 1984, *Royal Commission on the Activities of the Federated Ship Painters and Dockers Union*, vols 1–4, AGPS, Canberra.

Couch, Murray 1988, Workers' Health and Safety in the Broken Hill Mining Industry, Honours thesis, The Flinders University of South Australia.

Cousens, Penelope & Crawford, June 1988, 'Moving the Mentally Ill into the Community: The Problem of Acceptance and the Effect of Contact', *Australian Journal of Social Issues*, vol. 28, pp. 196–207.

Cressey, Donald R. 1953, *Other People's Money: The Social Psychology of Embezzlement*, The Free Press, New York.

Cressey, Donald R. 1958, 'Achievement of an Unstated Organizational Goal: An Observation on Prisons', *The Pacific Sociological Review*, vol. 1, pp. 43–9.

Cressey, Donald R. 1961, 'Foreword', in *White Collar Crime*, Edwin H. Sutherland, Holt, Rinehart and Winston, New York.

Cressey, Donald 1986, 'Why Managers Commit Fraud', *Australian & New Zealand Journal of Criminology*, vol. 19, pp. 195–209.

Cunneen, Chris 1988, 'The Policing of Public Order: Some Thoughts on Culture, Space and Political Economy', in *Understanding Crime and Criminal Justice*, eds Mark Findlay & Russell Hogg, The Law Book Company, Sydney.

Currie, Elliot P. 1968, 'Crimes Without Criminals: Witchcraft and Its Control in Renaissance Europe', *Law & Society Review*, vol. 3, pp. 7–32.

Daly, Kathleen 1988, 'The Social Control of Sexuality: A Case Study of the Criminalization of Prostitution in the Progressive Era', *Research in Law, Deviance and Social Control*, vol. 9, pp. 171–206.

Daly, Kathleen 1989a, 'Gender and Varieties of White-Collar Crime', *Criminology*, vol. 27, pp. 769–93.

Daly, Kathleen 1989b, 'Rethinking Judicial Paternalism: Gender, Work–Family Relations and Sentencing', *Gender & Society*, vol. 3, pp. 9–36.

Daly, Kathleen & Chesney-Lind, Meda 1988, 'Feminism and Criminology', *Justice Quarterly*, vol. 5, pp. 497–537.

Davis, Kingsley 1937, 'The Sociology of Prostitution', *American Sociological Review*, vol. 2, pp. 745–55.

Davis, Nanette J. 1978, 'Prostitution: Identity, Career and Legal Economic Enterprise', in *The Sociology of Sex*, eds James M. Henslin & Edward Sagarin, Schocken Books, New York.

Davis, Nanette J. 1986, 'Abortion and Legal Policy', *Contemporary Crises*, vol. 10, pp. 373–97.

Davis, Nanette J. 1993, 'Systematic Gender Control and Victimisation Among Homeless Female Youth', *Socio-Legal Bulletin*, no. 8, Summer.

Denzin, Norman 1977, 'Notes on the Criminogenic Hypotheses: A Case Study of the American Liquor Industry', *American Sociological Review*, vol. 42, pp. 905–20.

Denzin, Norman 1984, 'Toward a Phenomenology of Domestic Family Violence', *American Journal of Sociology*, vol. 90, pp. 483–513.

Department of Community Services and Health 1988a, *AIDS: A Time To Care, A Time To Act: Towards a Strategy for Australians*, A Policy Discussion Paper, AGPS, Canberra.

Department of Community Services and Health 1988b, *Health for All Australians: Report to the Australian Health Ministers' Advisory Council and the Australian Health Ministers' Conference*, AGPS, Canberra.

Department of Correctional Services & The Office of Crime Statistics 1989, *The Impact of Parole Legislation Changes in South Australia*, Government Printer, Adelaide.

Department for Family and Community Services 1993, *Strategies: Program 4, Families and Children at Risk*, FACS, Adelaide, SA.

Department of Health, Housing and Community Services 1992, *Statistics on Drug Abuse in Australia 1992*, AGPS, Canberra.

Department of Social Security 1989, *Annual Report 1988–89*, AGPS, Canberra.

Department of Social Security 1993, *Annual Report 1992–93*, AGPS, Canberra.

Diamond, Irene 1980, 'Pornography and Repression: A Reconsideration', *Signs: Journal of Women in Culture and Society*, vol. 5, pp. 686–701.

Diamond, Stanley 1971, 'The Rule of Law Versus the Order of Custom', *Social Research*, vol. 38, pp. 42–72.

Di Chiara, Albert & Galliher, John F. 1994, 'Dissonance and Contradictions in the Origins of Marihuana Decriminalization', *Law & Society Review*, vol. 28, pp. 41–77.

Dickey, Brian 1980, *No Charity There: A Short History of Social Welfare in Australia*, Allen & Unwin, Sydney.

Dickie, Phil 1994, 'Organising Crime: Towards a Research–Regulatory Approach to Organised Crime', in *The Australian Criminal Justice System: The Mid 1990s*, eds Duncan Chappell & Paul Wilson, Butterworths, Sydney.

Dirkis, M. J. 1989, 'An Orwellian Spectre: A Review of the Commissioner of Taxation's Powers to Seek Information and Evidence under Section 264 of the Income Tax Assessment Act 1936 and Under Section 10 of the Crimes Act 1914 (Cth)', *Adelaide Law Review*, vol. 12, pp. 63–81.

Di Tomaso, Nancy 1989, 'Sexuality in the Workplace: Discrimination and Harassment', in *The Sexuality of Organization*, eds Jeff Hearn, Deborah L. Sheppard & Peta Tancred-Sheriff, Sage, London.

Dixon, David, Coleman, Clive & Bottomley, Keith 1990, 'Consent and the Legal Regulation of Policing', *Journal of Law and Society*, vol. 17, pp. 345–62.

Dobash, R. Emerson & Dobash, Russell 1979, *Violence Against Wives: A Case Against the Patriarchy*, The Free Press, New York.

Dobash, Russell P. & Dobash, R. Emerson 1981, 'Community Response to Violence Against Wives: Charivari, Abstract Justice and Patriarchy', *Social Problems*, vol. 28, pp. 563–81.

Dobash, Russell P., Dobash, R. Emerson & Gutteridge, Sue 1986, *The Imprisonment of Women*, Oxford, Basil Blackwell.

Dobinson, Ian 1993, 'Pinning a Tail on the Dragon: The Chinese and the International Heroin Trade', *Crime & Delinquency*, vol. 39, pp. 373–84.

Dobson, A.T., Gibberd, R.W., Leeder, S.R. & O'Connell, D.L. 1985, 'Occupational Differences in Ischemic Heart Disease Mortality and Risk Factors in Australia', *American Journal of Epidemiology*, vol. 122, pp. 283–90.

Dohrenwend, Bruce P. 1966, 'Social Status and Psychological Disorder: An Issue of Substance and an Issue of Method', *American Sociological Review*, vol. 31, pp. 14–34.

Dohrenwend, Bruce P. & Dohrenwend, Barbara Snell 1976, 'Sex Differences and Psychiatric Disorders', *American Journal of Sociology*, vol. 81, pp. 1447–54.

Donnerstein, Edward 1984, 'Pornography: Its Effect on Violence Against Women', in *Pornography and Sexual Aggression*, eds Neil Malamuth & Edward Donnerstein, Academic Press, Orlando.

Donzelot, Jacques 1979, *The Policing of Families*, Hutchinson, London.

Dowie, Mark 1977, 'Pinto Madness', *Mother Jones*, September/October, pp. 18–24, 28–32.

Driver, Edwin D. 1972, 'Charles Buckman Goring', in *Pioneers in Criminology*, 2nd edn, ed. Hermann Mannheim, Patterson Smith, Montclair, New Jersey.

Duggan, Lisa, Hunter, Nan & Vance, Carole S. 1984, 'False Promises: Feminist Antipornography in the US', in *Women Against Censorship*, ed. Varda Burstyn, Douglas & McIntyre, Vancouver.

Duke, Marshall P. & Nowicki, Stephen Jr 1986, *Abnormal Psychology: A New Look*, Holt, Rinehart & Winston, New York.

Dunt, David R. 1982, 'Recent Mortality Trends in the Adult Australian Population and its Principal Ethnic Groupings', *Community Health Studies*, vol. 6, pp. 217–22.

Durkheim, Emile 1933, *The Division of Labour in Society*, trans. George Simpson, The Free Press, New York.

Durkheim, Emile 1938, *The Rules of Sociological Method*, trans Sarah A. Solovay & John H. Mueller, ed. George E.G. Catlin, The Free Press, New York.

Durkheim, Emile 1970, *Suicide: A Study in Sociology*, trans John A. Spaulding & George Simpson, Routledge & Kegan Paul, London.

Durkheim, Emile 1973, 'Two Laws of Penal Evolution', trans T. Anthony Jones & Andrew T. Scull, *Economy and Society*, vol. 2, pp. 285–308.

Durkheim, Emile 1986, 'The Positive Science of Morality in Germany', trans. Frank Pearce, *Economy and Society*, vol. 15, pp. 346–54.

Dusevic, Tom & Carruthers, Rona 1994, 'City of Churches: Our Crime Capital', *The Australian*, 1 June, p. 3.

Duster, Troy 1970, *The Legislation of Morality: Law, Drugs, and Moral Judgement*, The Free Press, New York.

Dworkin, Andrea 1983, *Ring-Wing Women*, Perigree Books, New York.

Easthope, Gary 1993, 'The Response of Orthodox Medicine to the Challenge of Alternative Medicine in Australia', *The Australian & New Zealand Journal of Sociology*, vol. 29, pp. 289–301.

Eck, John E. & Spelman, William 1987, 'Who Ya Gonna Call? The Police as Problem Busters', *Crime & Delinquency*, vol. 33, pp. 31–52.

Eckersley, Robyn 1987, 'Whither the Feminist Campaign? An Evaluation of Feminist Critiques of Pornography', *International Journal of the Sociology of Law*, vol. 15, pp. 149–78.

Edwards, Susan 1986, 'Neither Bad Nor Mad: The Female Violent Offender Reassessed', *Women's Studies International Forum*, vol. 9, pp. 79–87.

Edwards, Anne R. 1989, 'Sex/Gender, Sexism and Criminal Justice', *International Journal of the Sociology of Law*, vol. 17, pp. 165–84.

Egger, Sandra & Findlay, Mark 1988, 'The Politics of Police Discretion', in *Understanding Crime and Criminal Justice*, eds Mark Findlay & Russell Hogg, Law Book Company, Sydney.

Egger, Sandra & Harcourt, Christine 1993, 'Prostitution in NSW: The Impact of Deregulation', in *Women and the Law*, eds Patricia Weiser Easteal & Sandra McKillop, Australian Institute of Criminology, Canberra.

Ehrenreich, Barbara 1974, 'Gender and Objectivity in Medicine', *International Journal of Health Services*, vol. 4, pp. 617–23.

Ehrenreich, Barbara & English, Deirdre 1978, *For Her Own Good: 150 Years of the Experts' Advice to Women*, Pluto Press, London.

Eisenstein, Hester 1984, *Contemporary Feminist Thought*, Unwin, Sydney.

Eisenstein, Zillah 1991, 'Privatizing the State: Reproductive Rights, Affirmative Action, and the Problem of Democracy', *Frontiers*, vol. 12, pp. 98–125.

Elling, Ray H. 1981, 'The Capitalist World-System and International Health', *International Journal of Health Services*, vol. 11, pp. 21–51.

Engels, Frederick 1972, *The Origin of the Family, Private Property and the State*, International Publishers, New York.

Equal Opportunity Commission 1979/80–1987/88, *Annual Report*, Government Printer, Adelaide.

Ericson, Richard V. 1991, 'Mass Media, Crime, Law, and Justice', *British Journal of Criminology*, vol. 31, pp. 219–49.

Ericson, Richard V., Baranek, Patricia M. & Chan, Janet B.L. 1989, *Negotiating Control: A Study of News Sources*, University of Toronto Press, Toronto.

Erikson, Kai T. 1962, 'Notes on the Sociology of Deviance', *Social Problems*, vol. 9, pp. 307–14.

Erikson, Kai 1966, *Wayward Puritans: A Study in the Sociology of Deviance*, John Wiley & Sons, New York.

Fagan, Jeffrey & Deschenes, Elizabeth Piper 1990, 'Determinants of Judicial Waiver Decisions for Violent Juvenile Offenders', *Journal of Criminal Law & Criminology*, vol. 81, pp. 314–47.

Fain, T. & Anderton, D. 1987, 'Sexual Harassment: Organizational Context and Diffuse States', *Sex Roles*, vol. 15, pp. 291–311.

Faris, Robert E.L. & Dunham, H. Warren 1939, *Mental Disorders in Urban Areas*, Hafner Publishing, New York.

Faupel, Charles E. & Klockars, Carl B. 1987, 'Drug-Crime Connections: Elaborations from the Life Histories of Hard Core Heroin Addicts', *Social Problems*, vol. 34, pp. 54–68.

Feeley, Malcolm M. & Little, Deborah L. 1991, 'The Vanishing Female: The Decline of Women in the Criminal Process, 1687–1912', *Law & Society Review*, vol. 25, pp. 719–57.

Feld, Barry C. 1993, 'Criminalizing the American Juvenile Court', *Crime & Justice: An Annual Review of Research*, vol. 17, pp. 197–280.

Ferguson, David 1984, 'The "New" Industrial Epidemic', *Medical Journal of Australia*, vol. 17, March, pp. 318–19.

Ferraro, Kathleen J. 1989, 'Policing Woman Battering', *Social Problems*, vol. 36, pp. 61–74.

Ferraro, Kathleen J. & Johnson, John M. 1983, 'How Women Experience Battering: The Process of Victimization', *Social Problems*, vol. 30, pp. 325–39.

Figlio, Karl 1978, 'Chlorosis and Chronic Disease in 19th Century Britain: The Social Constitution of Somatic Illness in a Capitalist Society', *International Journal of Health Services*, vol. 8, pp. 589–617.

Figlio, Karl M. 1982, 'How Does Illness Mediate Social Relations? Workmen's Compensation and Medico-Legal Practices, 1890–1940', in *The Problem of Medical Knowledge*, eds Peter Wright & Andrew Treacher, Edinburgh University Press, Edinburgh.

Finch, Janet & Groves, Dulcie 1980, 'Community Care and the Family: A Case for Equal Opportunities', *Journal of Social Policy*, vol. 9, pp. 487–511.

Finch, Lyn & Stratton, Jon 1988, 'The Australian Working Class and the Practice of Abortion 1880–1939', *Journal of Australian Studies*, vol. 23, pp. 45–64.

Findlay, Mark & Hogg, Russell eds 1988, *Understanding Crime and Criminal Justice*, Law Book Company, Sydney.

Fishman, Mark 1978, 'Crime Waves as Ideology', *Social Problems*, vol. 25, pp. 531–43.

Fitzgerald, G.E. 1989, *Commission of Inquiry into Possible Illegal Activities and Associated Police Misconduct*, Report of a Commission of Inquiry Pursuant to Orders in Council, Queensland Government Printer, Brisbane.

Flinders University of South Australia n.d., *Sexual Harassment is Unacceptable Behaviour.*

Foley, Matthew 1984, 'Aborigines and the Police', in *Aborigines and the Law*, eds Peter Hanks & Bryan Keon-Cohen, George Allen & Unwin, Sydney.

Foucault, Michel 1975, *The Birth of the Clinic: An Archaeology of Medical Perception*, trans. A.M. Sheridan Smith, Vintage Books, New York.

Foucault, Michel 1978, 'About the Concept of the "Dangerous Individual" in 19th-Century Legal Psychiatry', trans Alain Baudot & Jane Couchman, *International Journal of Law and Psychiatry*, vol. 1, pp. 1–18.

Foucault, Michel 1979, *Discipline and Punish: The Birth of the Prison*, trans. Alan Sheridan, Vintage Books, New York.

Foucault, Michel 1981, *The History of Sexuality: An Introduction*, trans. Robert Hurley, Penguin, Harmondsworth.

Foucault, Michel 1988, *Madness and Civilization: A History of Insanity in the Age of Reason*, trans. Richard Howard, Vintage Books, New York.

Fox, Richard G. 1971, 'The XYY Offender: A Modern Myth?', *Journal of Criminal Law, Criminology & Police Science*, vol. 62, pp. 59–73.

Freckelton, Ian 1994, 'Contemporary Comment: When Plight Makes Right—The Forensic Abuse Syndrome', *Criminal Law Journal*, vol. 18, pp. 29–49.

Freckelton, Ian & Selby, Hugh 1988, 'The Politics of Police Discretion', in *Understanding Crime and Criminal Justice*, eds Mark Findlay & Russell Hogg, Law Book Company, Sydney.

Freeman, Jody 1993, 'The Disciplinary Function of Rape's Representation: Lessons from the Kennedy Smith and Tyson Trials', *Law and Social Inquiry*, vol. 18, pp. 517–46.

Freeman, Richard B. 1983, 'Crime and Unemployment', in *Crime and Public Policy*, ed. James Q. Wilson, ICS Press, San Francisco, California.

Freiberg, Arie 1993, 'Abolish Children's Courts? Juveniles, Justice and Sentencing', *Current Issues in Criminal Justice*, vol. 4, pp. 240–62.

Freidson, Eliot 1986, *Professional Powers: A Study of the Institutionalization of Formal Knowledge*, University of Chicago Press, Chicago.

Freidson, Eliot 1988, *Profession of Medicine: A Study of the Sociology of Applied Knowledge*, University of Chicago Press, Chicago.

French, Peter A. 1979, 'The Corporation as a Moral Person', *American Philosophical Quarterly*, vol. 16, pp. 207–15.

Frieze, Irene Hanson 1983, 'Investigating the Causes and Consequences of Marital Rape', *Signs: Journal of Women in Culture and Society*, vol. 8, pp. 532–53.

Fuszara, Matgorzata 1991, 'Legal Regulation of Abortion in Poland', *Signs: Journal of Women in Culture and Society*, vol. 17, pp. 117–28.

Gagnon, John H. 1974, 'Sexual Conduct and Crime', in *Handbook of Criminology*, ed. Daniel Glaser, Rand McNally, Chicago.

Gallagher, Eugene B. 1976, 'Lines of Reconstruction and Extension in the Parsonian Sociology of Illness', *Social Science and Medicine*, vol. 10, pp. 207–18.

Gallagher, Janet 1987, 'Prenatal Invasions and Interventions: What's Wrong with Fetal Rights', *Harvard Women's Law Journal*, vol. 19, pp. 9–58.

Gale, Fay & Wundersitz, Joy 1987, 'Police and Black Minorities: The Case of Aboriginal Youth in South Australia', *Australian & New Zealand Journal of Criminology*, vol. 20, pp. 78–94.

Galper, Jeffrey H. 1975, *The Politics of Social Services*, Prentice Hall, Englewood Cliffs, New Jersey.

Gardner, Carol Brooks 1990, 'Safe Conduct: Women, Crime, and Self in Public Places', *Social Problems*, vol. 37, pp. 311–28.

Gardner, Julie 1990, *Victims and Criminal Justice*, Office of Crime Statistics, Adelaide.

Gardner, Julie 1994, 'Violence Against Women', *JUSTATS: An Occasional Bulletin on Criminal Justice*, Attorney-General's Department, Adelaide.

Garfinkel, Harold 1956, 'Conditions of Successful Degradation Ceremonies', *American Journal of Sociology*, vol. 61, pp. 420–4.

Gawenda, Michael 1988, 'Law and Disorder', *Time Magazine*, 3 October, pp. 12–27.

Gee, Pauline 1983, 'Ensuring Police Protection for Battered Women: The *Scott* v. *Hart* Suit', *Signs: Journal of Women in Culture and Society*, vol. 8, pp. 554–67.

Gearty, Conor 1992, 'The Politics of Abortion', *Journal of Law and Society*, vol. 19, pp. 441–53.

Geis, Gilbert 1977, 'The Heavy Electrical Equipment and Anti-trust of 1961', in *White-Collar Crime: Offenses in Business, Politics and the Professions*, eds Gilbert Geis & Robert F. Meier, The Free Press, New York.

Geis, Gilbert & Goff, Colin 1983, 'Introduction', in *White Collar Crime: The Uncut Version*, Edwin H. Sutherland, Yale University Press, New Haven.

Geis, Gilbert & Meier, Robert F. eds 1977, *White-Collar Crime: Offenses in Business, Politics and the Professions*, The Free Press, New York.

Gelles, Richard J. 1976, 'Abused Wives: Why Do They Stay?', *Journal of Marriage and the Family*, vol. 38, pp. 659–68.

Gelsthorpe, Loraine & Morris, Allison eds 1990, *Feminist Perspectives in Criminology*, Open University Press, Milton Keynes.

George, Amanda 1988, 'Home Detention: The Privatization of Corrections', *The Legal Service Bulletin*, vol. 13, pp. 211–13.

Gerber, Jurg & Short, James F. Jr 1986, 'Publicity and the Control of Corporate Behaviour: The Case of Infant Formula', *Deviant Behaviour*, vol. 7, pp. 195–216.

Gerhardt, Uta 1979, 'The Parsonian Paradigm and the Identity of Medical Sociology', *The Sociological Review*, vol. 27, 229–51.

Giallombardo, Rose 1966, *Society of Women: A Study of a Women's Prison*, John Wiley & Sons, New York.

Gibbs, Jack P. 1966, 'Conceptions of Deviant Behaviour: The Old and the New', *Pacific Sociological Review*, vol. 9, pp. 9–14.

Gibbs, Jack P. 1982, 'The Notion of Social Control', in *Social Control: Views from the Social Sciences*, ed. Jack P. Gibbs, Sage Publications, Beverly Hills.

Gibson, Suzanne 1990, 'Continental Drift: The Question of Context in Feminist Jurisprudence', *Law and Critique*, vol. 1, pp. 173–200.

Gillespie, Dair L. & Leffler, Ann 1987, 'The Politics of Research Methodology in Claims-Making Activities: Social Science and Sexual Harassment', *Social Problems*, vol. 34, pp. 490–501.

Ginsburg, Faye D. 1989, *Contested Lives: The Abortion Debate in an American Community*, University of California Press, Berkeley.

Glassner, Barry 1989, 'Fitness and the Postmodern Self', *Journal of Health and Social Behaviour*, vol. 30, pp. 180–91.

Glueck, Sheldon 1925, *Mental Disorders and The Criminal Law*, Little, Brown, New York.

Glueck, Sheldon & Glueck, Eleanor 1956, *Physique and Delinquency*, Harper, New York.

Glueck, Sheldon & Glueck, Eleanor 1974, *Of Delinquency and Crime: A Panorama of Years of Search and Research*, Charles C. Thomas, Springfield, Illinois.

Gluyas, Richard 1989, '$100m Insider Trading Charges "Tip of Iceberg"', *The Weekend Australian*, 4–5 March, pp. 1, 34.

Gluyas, Richard 1994, 'He Fought the Law …', *The Weekend Australian*, April 30–May 1, p. 23.

Goffman, Erving 1961, *Asylums: Essays on the Social Situation of Mental Patients and Other Inmates*, Penguin, Harmondsworth.

Goffman, Erving 1963, *Stigma: Notes on the Management of Spoiled Identity*, Penguin, Harmondsworth.

Goldstein, Herman 1987, 'Toward Community-Oriented Policing: Potential, Basic Requirements, and Threshold Questions', *Crime & Delinquency*, vol. 33, pp. 6–30.

Goldstein, Michael S. 1984, 'Creating and Controlling a Medical Market: Abortion in Los Angeles after Liberalization', *Social Problems*, vol. 31, pp. 514–29.

Gollan, R.A. 1974, 'Nationalism, the Labour Movement and the Commonwealth', in *Australia: A Social and Political History*, ed. Gordon Greenwood, Angus & Robertson, Sydney.

Goode, Erich 1990, 'Review of *Seductions of Crime: Moral and Sensual Attractions of Doing Evil*, Jack Katz', *Contemporary Sociology*, vol. 19, pp. 5–12.

Gordon, Linda 1988, 'What Does Welfare Regulate?', *Social Research*, vol. 55, pp. 609–30.

Gottfredson, Michael R. 1986, 'Substantive Contributions of Victimization Surveys', in *Crime and Justice: An Annual Review of Research*, eds Michael Tonry & Norval Morris, University of Chicago Press, Chicago.

Gottfredson, Michael R. & Hirschi, Travis 1990, *A General Theory of Crime*, Stanford University Press, Stanford, CA.

Gough, Ian 1979, *The Political Economy of the Welfare State*, Macmillan, London.

Gouldner, Alvin W. 1968, 'The Sociologist as Partisan: Sociology and the Welfare State', *American Sociologist*, vol. 3, pp. 103–16.

Gove, Walter R. 1972, 'The Relationship Between Sex Roles, Marital Status, and Mental Illness', *Social Forces*, vol. 51, pp. 34–44.

Gove, Walter R. 1975, 'Labelling and Mental Illness: A Critique', in *The Labelling of Deviance: Evaluating a Perspective*, ed. Walter R. Gove, John Wiley & Sons, New York.

Gove, Walter R. 1978, 'Sex Differences in Mental Illness Among Adult Men and Women: An Evaluation of Four Questions Raised Regarding the Evidence on the Higher Rates of Women', *Social Science and Medicine*, vol. 12B, pp. 187–98.

Gove, Walter R. & Tudor, Jeanette F. 1972, 'Adult Sex Roles and Mental Illness', *American Journal of Sociology*, vol. 78, pp. 812–35.

Grabosky, Peter N. 1977, *Sydney in Ferment: Crime, Dissent and Official Reaction 1788–1973*, Australian National University Press, Canberra.

Grabosky, Peter 1984, 'Corporate Crime in Australia: An Agenda for Research', *Australian & New Zealand Journal of Criminology*, vol. 17, pp. 95–107.

Grabosky, Peter 1989, *Wayward Governance: Illegality and Its Control in the Public Sector*, Australian Institute of Criminology, Canberra.

Grabosky, Peter & Braithwaite, John 1986, *Of Manners Gentle: Enforcement Strategies of Australian Business Regulatory Agencies*, Oxford University Press, Melbourne.

Grabosky, Peter & Braithwaite, John 1987, *Corporate Crime in Australia*, Australian Institute of Criminology, Canberra.

Grabosky, Peter, Braithwaite, John & Wilson, Paul 1987, 'The Myth of Community Tolerance Toward White-Collar Crime', *Australian & New Zealand Journal of Criminology*, vol. 20, pp. 33–44.

Grabosky, Peter & Sutton, Adam eds 1989, *Stains on a White Collar: Fourteen Studies in Corporate Crime or Corporate Harm*, Hutchinson, Sydney.

Grabosky, Peter & Wilson, Paul 1989, *Journalism and Justice: How Crime is Reported*, Pluto Press, Sydney.

Grabosky, Peter 1990, 'Professional Advisers and White Collar Criminality: Towards Explaining and Excusing Professional Failure', *University of New South Wales Law Review*, vol. 13, pp. 73–96.

Graetz, Brian 1987, 'Unemployment, Social Policy and Public Opinion', *Australian Journal of Social Issues*, vol. 22, pp. 321–31.

Graham, Saxon & Reeder, Leo G. 1979. 'Social Epidemiology of Chronic Diseases', in *Handbook of Medical Sociology*, ed. Howard E. Freeman, Englewood Cliffs, New Jersey.

Granfield, Robert & Koenig, T. 1992, 'The Fate of Elite Idealism: Accommodation and Ideological Work at Harvard Law School', *Social Problems*, vol. 39, pp. 315–31.

Gray, Susan 1982, 'Exposure to Pornography and Aggression Toward Women: The Case of the Angry Male', *Social Problems*, vol. 29, pp. 387–98.

Graycar, Adam & Jamrozik, Adam 1993, *How Australians Live: Social Policy in Theory and Practice*, 2nd edn, Macmillan, Melbourne.

Greenberg, David F. 1975, 'Problems in Community Corrections', *Issues in Criminology*, vol. 10, pp. 1–33.

Greenberg, David 1988, *The Construction of Homosexuality*, Chicago, University of Chicago Press.

Greenberg, David F. & Bystryn, Marcia H. 1982, 'Christian Intolerance of Homosexuality', *American Journal of Sociology*, vol. 88, pp. 515–48.

Greene, J. 1989, 'A Provocation Defence for Battered Women Who Kill', *Adelaide Law Review*, vol. 12, pp. 145–63.

Greil, Arthur L. 1991, 'A Secret Stigma: The Analogy Between Infertility and Chronic Illness and Disability', *Advances in Medical Sociology*, vol. 2, pp. 17–38.

Greil, Arthur L., Leitko, Thomas A. & Porter, Karen L. 1988, 'Infertility: His and Hers', *Gender & Society*, vol. 2, pp. 172–99.

Griffin, Susan 1981, *Pornography and Science: Culture's Revenge Against Nature*, Harper & Row, New York.

Gunn, Michelle 1994, 'Aquittal Ends Grimwade Saga', *The Weekend Australian*, April 23–24, pp. 1, 4.

Gunningham, Neil 1989, 'Asbestos Mining at Baryulgil: A Case of Corporate Neglect', in *Stains on a White Collar: Fourteen Studies in Corporate Crime or Corporate Harm*, eds Peter Grabosky & Adam Sutton, Hutchinson, Sydney.

Gurr, Ted Robert 1976, *Rogues, Rebels and Reformers: A Political History of Urban Crime and Conflict*, Sage Publications, Beverly Hills.

Gusfield, J. 1963, *Symbolic Crusade: Status Politics and the American Temperance Movement*, University of Illinois Press, Urbana, Illinois.

Gusfield, J. 1967, 'Moral Passage: The Symbolic Process in Public Designations of Deviance', *Social Problems*, vol. 15, pp. 175–88.

Gutek, Barbara A. & Cohen, Aaron Groff 1987, 'Sex Ratios, Sex Role Spillover and Sex at Work: A Comparison of Men's and Women's Experiences', *Human Relations*, vol. 40, pp. 97–115.

Haber, Lawrence D. & Smith, Richard, T. 1971, 'Disability and Deviance: Normative Adaptations in Role Behaviour', *American Sociological Review*, vol. 36, pp. 87–97.

Hagan, John 1980, 'The Legislation of Crime and Delinquency: A Review of Theory, Method and Research', *Law & Society Review*, vol. 14, pp. 603–28.

Hagan, John & Leon, Jeffrey 1977, 'Rediscovering Delinquency: Social History, Political Ideology and the Sociology of Law', *American Sociological Review*, vol. 42, pp. 587–98.

Hagan, John, Simpson, John H. & Gillis A.R. 1979, 'The Sexual Stratification of Social Control: A Gender Based Perspective on Crime and Delinquency', *British Journal of Sociology*, vol. 30, pp. 25–38.

Hakeem, Michael 1958, 'A Critique of the Psychiatric Approach to Crime and Correction', *Law and Contemporary Problems*, vol. 23, pp. 650–82.

Hale, Sir Matthew 1971, *Historia Placitorum Coronae*, vol. 1, Professional Books Limited, London.

Hall, Stuart, Critcher, Chas, Jefferson, Tony, Clark, John & Roberts, Brian 1978, *Policing the Crisis: Mugging, The State and Law and Order*, Macmillan, London.

Halpern, Sydney A. 1992, 'Dynamics of Professional Control: Internal Coalitions and Cross Professional Boundaries', *American Journal of Sociology*, vol. 97, pp. 994–1021.

Hancock, Linda 1980, 'The Myth that Females are Treated More Leniently than Males in the Juvenile Justice System', *Australian & New Zealand Journal of Sociology*, vol. 16, pp. 4–14.

Hancock, Linda & Chesney-Lind, Meda 1982, 'Female Status Offenders and Justice Reforms: An International Perspective', *Australian & New Zealand Journal of Criminology*, vol. 15, pp. 109–22.

Harbutt, Karen & Hogarth, Murray, 1988, '12,000 Pages On, It's Time for the Results', *The Weekend Australian* 16–17 July, pp. 6–7. ·

Harding, Geoffrey 1986, 'Constructing Addiction as a Moral Failing', *Sociology of Health & Illness*, vol. 8, pp. 75–85.

Harding, Richard 1987, 'Prison Overcrowding: Correctional Policies and Political Constraints', *Australian & New Zealand Journal of Criminology*, vol. 20, pp. 16–32.

Harris, Anthony R. 1977, 'Sex and Theories of Deviance: Toward a Functional Theory of Deviant Type-Scripts', *American Sociological Review*, vol. 42, pp. 3–16.

Harvard Law Review 1979, 'Developments in the Law—Corporate Crime: Regulating Corporate Behaviour Through Criminal Sanctions', vol. 92, pp. 1227–375.

Haug, Marie 1973, 'Deprofessionalization: An Alternative Hypothesis for the Future', *Sociological Review Monograph*, vol. 20, pp. 195–211.

Haug, Marie 1975, 'The Deprofessionalization of Everyone?', *Sociological Focus*, vol. 8, pp. 197–213.

Hay, Iain 1992, 'Place, Power, and Medical Liability Insurance in the United States', *Environment and Planning*, vol. 24, pp. 645–61.

Heidensohn, Frances 1968, 'The Deviance of Women: A Critique and an Enquiry', *British Journal of Sociology*, vol. 19, pp. 160–75.

Heidensohn, Frances 1985, *Women and Crime*, Macmillan, London.

Heinz, John & Laumann, Edward O. 1982, *Chicago Lawyers: The Social Structure of the Bar*, Russell Sage Foundation and American Bar Foundation, New York,.

Hemming, Heather 1985, 'Women in a Man's World: Sexual Harassment', *Human Relations*, vol. 38, pp. 67–79.

Henry, Stuart 1982, 'The Working Unemployed: Perspectives on the Informal Economy and Unemployment', *Sociological Review*, vol. 30, pp. 460–77.

Hepworth, Mike & Turner, Bryan S. 1982, *Confession: Studies in Deviance and Religion*, Routledge & Kegan Paul, London.

Herman, Dianne 1979, 'The Rape Culture', in *Women: A Feminist Perspective*, 2nd edn, ed. Jo Freeman, Mayfield Publishing, Palo Alto, California.

Heyl, Barbara Sherman 1977, 'The Madam as Teacher: The Training of House Prostitutes', *Social Problems*, vol. 24, pp. 545–55.

Hicks, Ron 1989, 'The Troubles of Sharleen', *The Australian Magazine*, 25–26 November, pp. 71–4.

Hiller, Anne Edwards 1982, 'Women, Crime and Criminal Justice: The State of Current Theory and Research in Australia and New Zealand', *Australian & New Zealand Journal of Criminology*, vol. 15, pp. 69–89.

Hirschi, Travis 1969, *Causes of Delinquency*, University of California Press, Berkeley, California.

Hirst, Paul Q. 1972, 'Marx and Engels on Law, Crime and Morality', *Economy & Society*, vol. 1, pp. 28–56.

Hochschild, Arlie Russell 1983, *The Managed Heart: Commercialization of Human Feeling*, University of California Press, Berkeley.

Hogg, Russell 1988, 'Taking Crime Seriously: Left Realism and Australian Criminology', in *Understanding Crime and Criminal Justice*, eds Mark Findlay & Russell Hogg, Law Book Company, Sydney.

Hollingshead, August B. & Redlich, Frederick C. 1958, *Social Class and Mental Illness: A Community Study*, John Wiley & Sons, New York.

Hopkins, Andrew 1978, 'The Anatomy of Corporate Crime', in *Two Faces of Deviance: Crimes of the Powerless and the Powerful*, eds Paul R. Wilson & John Braithwaite, University of Queensland Press, St. Lucia.

Hopkins, Andrew 1980, 'Controlling Corporate Deviance', *Criminology*, vol. 18, pp. 198–214.

Hopkins, Andrew 1983, 'Marxist Theory and Australian Monopoly Law', in *Essays in the Political Economy of Australian Capitalism*, eds E.L. Wheelwright & Ken Buckley, Australia & New Zealand Book Company, Sydney.

Hopkins, Andrew & Parnell, Nina 1984, 'Why Coal Mine Safety Regulations in Australia are not Enforced', *International Journal of the Sociology of Law*, vol. 12, pp. 179–94.

Horney, Julie 1978, 'Menstrual Cycles and Criminal Responsibility', *Law and Human Behaviour*, vol. 2, pp. 25–36.

Hughes, Everett C. 1945, 'Dilemmas and Contradictions of Status', *American Journal of Sociology*, pp. 353–59.

Humphries, Drew 1981, 'Serious Crime, News Coverage, and Ideology', *Crime & Delinquency*, vol. 27, pp. 191–205.

Hunter, Nan D. & Law, Sylvia 1987–88, 'Brief *Amici Curiae* of Feminist Anti-censorship Taskforce et al.', in *American Booksellers Association v. Hudnut, Journal of Law Reform*, vol. 21, pp. 69–136.

Inciardi, James A. ed. 1980, *Radical Criminology: The Coming Crisis*, Sage Publications, Beverly Hills.

Jacobs, Patricia A., Brunton, Muriel & Melville, Marie M. 1965, 'Aggressive Behaviour, Menial Subnormality & the XYY Male', *Nature*, vol. 208, pp. 1351–52.

Johnson, Norman 1989, 'The Privatization of Welfare', *Social Policy and Administration*, vol. 23, pp. 17–30.

Jones, Michael Anthony 1980, *The Australian Welfare State*, George Allen & Unwin, Sydney.

Kallen, Horace M. 1963, 'Morals', in *Encyclopeadia of the Social Sciences*, ed. Edwin R.A. Seligman, Macmillan, New York.

Kantor, Glenda Kaufman & Straus, Murray A. 1987, 'The "Drunken Bum" Theory of Wife Beating', *Social Problems*, vol. 34, pp. 213–30.

Kaplan, Howard B., Johnson, Robert J., Bailey, Carol A. & Simon, William 1987, 'The Sociological Study of AIDS: A Critical Review of the Literature and Suggested Research Agenda', *Journal of Health and Social Behavior*, vol. 28, pp. 140–57.

Karlen, Arno 1978, 'Homosexuality: the Scene and its Students', in *The Sociology of Sex: An Introductory Reader*, eds James M. Henslin & Edward Sagarin, Schocken Books, New York.

Kawashima, Takeyoshe 1982, 'Dispute Settlement in Japan', in *The Social Organization of Law*, eds Donald Black & Maureen Mileski, Seminar Press, New York.

Keane, Carl, Gillis, A.R. & Hagan, John 1989, 'Deterrence and Amplification of Juvenile Delinquency by Police Contact', *British Journal of Criminology*, vol. 29, pp. 336–52.

Kelly, Robert J., Chin, Ko–Lin & Fagan, Jeffrey A. 1993, 'The Dragon Breathes Fire: Chinese Organized Crime in New York City', *Crime, Law and Social Change*, vol. 19, pp. 245–69.

Kersten, Joachim 1993, '"Street Youths", *Bosozoku* and *Yakuza*: Subculture Formation and Societal Reactions in Japan', *Crime & Delinquency*, vol. 39, pp. 277–95.

Kewley, Thomas Henry 1980, *Australian Social Security Today: Major Developments from 1900 to 1978*, Sydney University Press, Sydney.

Kinsey, Alfred C., Pomeroy, Wardell B. & Martin, Clyde E. 1948, *Sexual Behavior in the Human Male*, W.B. Saunders Company, Philadelphia.

Kinsey, Alfred C., Pomeroy, Wardell B., Martin, Clyde E. & Gebhard, Paul H. 1953, *Sexual Behavior in the Human Female*, W.B. Saunders Company, Philadelphia.

Kinsey, Richard, Lea, John & Young, Jock 1986, *Losing the Fight Against Crime*, Basil Blackwell, Oxford.

Kitsuse, John 1962, 'Societal Reaction to Deviant Behaviour', *Social Problems*, vol. 9, pp. 247–56.

Kitsuse, John I. & Cicourel, Aaron V. 1963, 'A Note on the Use of Official Statistics', *Social Problems* vol. 11, pp. 131–9.

Kitsuse John I. & Spector, Malcolm 1973, 'Toward a Sociology of Social Problems: Social Conditions, Value-Judgements, and Social Problems', *Social Problems*, vol. 20, pp. 407–19.

Klein, Dorie 1973, 'The Etiology of Female Crime: A Review of the Literature', *Issues in Criminology*, vol. 8, pp. 3–30.

Klein, Malcolm W. 1979, 'Deinstitutionalisation and Diversion of Young Offenders', *Crime & Justice: An Annual Review of Research*, vol. 1, pp. 145–201.

Kluegel, James R. 1987, 'Macro-economic Problems, Beliefs About the Poor and Attitudes Toward Welfare Spending', *Social Problems*, vol. 34, pp. 82–99.

Kluver, John 1992, 'ASC Investigations and Enforcement: Issues and Initiatives', *University of New South Wales Law Journal, vol.* 15, pp. 31–60.

Knapp Commission 1984, 'Police Corruption in New York City', in *Deviant Behavior: A Text–Reader in the Sociology of Deviance*, 2nd edn, ed. Delos H. Kelly, St. Martin's Press, New York.

Kosonen, Pekka 1987, 'From Collectivity to Individualism in the Welfare State', *Acta Sociologica*, vol. 30, pp. 281–93.

Kumar, Krishan 1984, 'Unemployment as a Problem in the Development of Industrial Societies: The English Experience', *Sociological Review*, vol. 32, pp. 185–233.

Kurz, Demie 1989, 'Social Science Perspectives on Wife Abuse: Current Debates and Future Directions', *Gender & Society*, vol. 3, pp. 489–505.

La Free, Gary D. 1981, 'Official Reactions to Social Problems: Police Decisions in Sexual Assault Cases', *Social Problems*, vol. 28, pp. 582–94.

Larson, Magali Sarfatti 1977, *The Rise of Professionalism: A Sociological Analysis*, University of California Press, Berkeley, California.

Lasch, Christopher 1977, *Haven in a Heartless World: The Family Besieged*, Basic Books, New York.

Latimer, Paul 1988, *Australian Business Law*, CCH Australia Ltd, Sydney.

Laub, John H. & Sampson, Robert J. 1991, 'The Sutherland–Glueck Debate: On the Sociology of Criminological Knowledge', *American Journal of Sociology*, vol. 96, pp. 1402–40.

Law Reform Commission of Victoria 1986, *Rape and Allied Offences: Substantive Aspects*, Discussion Paper No. 2, Government Printer, Melbourne.

Law Reform Commission of Victoria 1988, *Rape and Allied Offences: Procedure and Evidence*, Discussion Paper No. 13, Government Printer, Melbourne.

Le Grand, Camille, E. 1973, 'Rape and Rape Laws: Sexism in Society and Law', *California Law Review*, vol. 61, pp. 919–41.

Lemert, Edwin M. 1951, *Social Pathology*, McGraw-Hill, New York.

Lemert, Edwin M. 1967, *Human Deviance, Social Problems, and Social Control*, Prentice Hall, Englewood Cliffs, New Jersey.

Leonard, William N. & Weber, Marvin Glenn 1970, 'Automakers and Dealers: A Study of Criminogenic Market Forces', *Law & Society Review*, vol. 4, pp. 407–24.

Lerman, Paul 1980, 'Trends and Issues in the Deinstitutionalisation of Youths in Trouble', *Crime & Delinquency*, vol. 26, pp. 281–98.

Levine, Sol & Kozloff, Martin 1978, 'The Sick Role: Assessment and Overview', *Annual Review of Sociology*, vol. 4, pp. 317–43.

Liazos, Alexander 1972, 'The Poverty of the Sociology of Deviance: Nuts, Sluts and Preverts', *Social Problems*, vol. 20, pp. 103–20.

Liebow, Elliot 1967, *Tally's Corner: A Study of Negro Streetcorner Men*, Little, Brown & Co., Boston.

Liem, Ramsay & Liem, Joan 1978, 'Social Class and Mental Illness Reconsidered: The Role of Economic Stress and Social Support', *Journal of Health and Social Behavior*, vol. 19, pp. 139–56.

Ligertwood, Andrew 1993, *Australian Evidence*, 2nd edn., Butterworths, Sydney.

Lindesmith, Alfred R. 1938, 'A Sociological Theory of Drug Addiction', *American Journal of Sociology*, vol. 43, pp. 593–613.

Lindesmith, Alfred R. 1940, 'The Drug Addict as Psychopath', *American Sociological Review*, vol. 5, pp. 914–20.

Lindesmith, Alfred & Levin, Yale 1937, 'The Lombrosian Myth in Criminology', *American Journal of Sociology*, vol. 42, pp. 653–71.

Liska, Allen E. & Baccaglini, William 1990, 'Feeling Safe by Comparison: Crime in the Newspapers', *Social Problems*, vol. 37, pp. 360–74.

Liska, Allen E. & Warner, Barbara 1991, 'Functions of Crime: A Paradoxical Process', *American Journal of Sociology*, vol. 96, pp. 1441–63.

Lizotte, Alan J. 1978, 'Extra-Legal Factors in Chicago's Criminal Courts: Testing the Conflict Model of Criminal Justice', *Social Problems*, vol. 25, pp. 564–80.

Lombroso, Cesare 1968, *Crime: Its Causes and Remedies*, trans. Henry P. Horton, Patterson Smith, Montclair, New Jersey.

Lombroso, Cesare & Ferrero, William 1895, *The Female Offender*, T. Fisher Unwin, London.

Lombroso, Cesare & Ferrero, William 1979, 'Criminals and Prostitutes', in *The Criminology of Deviant Women*, eds Freda Adler & Rita James Simon, Houghton Mifflin, Boston.

Lorber, Judith 1975, 'Good Patients and Problem Patients: Conformity and Deviance in a General Hospital', *Journal of Health and Social Behavior*, vol. 16, pp. 213–25.

Lorber, Judith 1988, '*In Vitro* Fertilization and Gender Politics', *Women & Health*, vol. 13, pp. 117–33.

Loseke, Donileen & Cahill, Spencer E. 1984, 'The Social Construction of Deviance: Experts on Battered Women', *Social Problems*, vol. 31, pp. 296–310.

Luker, Kristin 1984, *Abortion and the Politics of Motherhood*, University of California Press, Berkeley.

Lukes, Steven & Scull, Andrew 1983, *Durkheim and the Law*, Basil Blackwell, Oxford.

Lyons, John 1994, 'Showtime for Justice', *The Australian Magazine*, 21–22 May, pp. 12–15, 17–18.

Mack, Julian W. 1909, 'The Juvenile Court', *Harvard Law Review*, vol. 23, pp. 104–22.

Mack, Kathy 1993, 'Continuing Barriers to Women's Credibility: A Feminist Perspective on the Proof Process', *Criminal Law Forum*, vol. 4, pp. 327–53.

MacKinnon, Catharine 1979, *Sexual Harassment of Working Women: A Case of Sex Discrimination*, Yale University Press, New Haven, Connecticut.

MacKinnon, Catharine 1983, 'Feminism, Marxism, Method, and the State: Toward Feminist Jurisprudence', *Signs: Journal of Women in Culture and Society*, vol. 8, pp. 635–58.

MacKinnon, Catharine 1986, 'Pornography: Not a Moral Issue', *Women's Studies International Forum*, vol. 9, pp. 63–78.

MacKinnon, Catharine 1987, *Feminism Unmodified: Discourses on Life and Law*, Harvard University Press, Cambridge, Massachusetts.

Macquarie Dictionary 1987, 2nd rev. edn, Macquarie University, Sydney.

Maher, L. & Curtis, R. 1992, 'Women on the Edge of Crime: Crack, Cocaine and the Changing Contexts of Street-Level Sex Work in New York City', *Crime, Law and Social Change*, vol. 18, pp. 221–58.

Makkai, Toni & McAllister, Ian 1993, *Trends in Drug Use in Australia, 1985–91*, AGPS, Canberra.

Makkai, Toni, McAllister, Ian & Moore, Rhonda 1994, 'Illicit Drug Use in Australia: Trends, Policies and Options', in *The Australian Criminal Justice System: The Mid 1990s*, eds Duncan Chappell & Paul Wilson, Butterworths, Sydney.

Malamuth, Neil M. 1984, 'Agression Against Women: Cultural and Individual Causes', in *Pornography and Sexual Aggression*, eds Neil Malamuth & Edward Donnerstein, Academic Press, Orlando.

Mannheim, Hermann ed. 1960, *Pioneers in Criminology*, Stevens & Sons, London, and 2nd edn 1972, Patterson Smith, Montclair, New Jersey.

Manning, Peter K. 1971, 'The Police: Mandate, Strategies and Appearances', in *Crime and Justice in American Society*, ed. Jack D. Douglas, Bobbs-Merrill, Indianapolis.

Markle, Gerald & Troyer, Ronald J. 1979, 'Smoke Gets in Your Eyes: Cigarette Smoking as Deviant Behaviour', *Social Problems*, vol. 26, pp. 611–25.

Marshall, T.H. 1970, *Social Policy*, Hutchinson University Library, London.

Martin, Karin A. 1993, 'Gender and Sexuality: Medical Opinion on Homosexuality, 1900–1950', *Gender & Society*, vol. 7, pp. 246–60.

Martinson, Robert, 1974, 'What Works—Questions and Answers About Prison Reform', *The Public Interest*, vol. 35, pp. 22–54.

Marx, Gary T. 1981, 'Ironies of Social Control: Authorities as Contributors to Deviance through Escalation, Nonenforcement and Covert Facilitation', *Social Problems*, vol. 28, pp. 221–46.

Marx, Karl & Engels, Friedrich 1964, *The Communist Manifesto*, Monthly Review Press, New York.

Marx, Karl & Engels, Friedrich 1975, *Collected Works*, vol. 1, International Publishers, New York.

Matthews, Eric 1988, 'AIDS and Sexual Morality', *Bioethics*, vol. 2, pp. 118–28.

Matthews, Roger & Young, Jock 1986, 'Editors' Introduction: Confronting Crime', in *Confronting Crime*, eds Roger Matthews & Jock Young, Sage, London.

Matza, David 1971, 'Poverty and Disrepute', in *Contemporary Social Problems*, 3rd edn, eds Robert K. Merton & Robert Nisbet, Harcourt Brace Jovanovich, New York.

McAllister, Ian & Makkai, Toni 1991, 'Patterns of Cocaine Use in Australia, 1985–88', *Australian Journal of Social Issues*, vol. 25, pp. 107–21.

McAllister, Ian, Moore, Rhonda & Makkai, Toni 1991, *Drugs in Australian Society: Patterns, Attitudes and Policy*, Melbourne, Longman Cheshire.

McAsey, Jennifer 1994, 'Pregnancy Test', *The Australian*, April 20, p. 9.

McCaghy, Charles H. 1976, *Deviant Behaviour: Crime, Conflict, and Interest Groups*, Macmillan, New York.

McCord, William 1983, 'Psychopathy', in *Encyclopedia of Crime and Justice*, vol. 4, ed. Sanford Kadish, The Free Press, New York.

McCulloch, Jock 1986, *Asbestos: Its Human Cost*, University of Queensland Press, St. Lucia.

McCulloch, Jude 1986, 'Police Response to Domestic Violence, Victoria', *National Conference on Domestic Violence* vol. 2, ed. Suzanne E. Hatty, Australian Institute of Criminology, Canberra.

McDonald, David & Biles, David 1991, 'Who Gets Locked Up? The Australian Police Custody Survey', *Australian & New Zealand Journal of Criminology*, vol. 24, pp. 190–203.

McIntosh, Mary 1968, 'The Homosexual Role', *Social Problems*, vol. 16, pp. 182–92.

McIntosh, Mary 1978, 'The State and the Oppression of Women', in *Feminism and Materialism*, eds A. Kuhn & A.M. Wolpe, Routledge & Kegan Paul, London.

McIntosh, Mary 1984, 'The Family, Regulations and the Public Sphere', in *Slave and Society in Contemporary Britain: A Critical Introduction*, eds Gregor McLennan, David Held & Stuart Hall, Polity Press, Cambridge.

McLanahan, Sara S. 1985, 'Family Structure and the Reproduction of Poverty', *American Journal of Sociology*, vol. 90, pp. 873–901.

McLanahan, Sara S., Sorensen, Annemetta, & Watson, Dorothy 1989, 'Sex Differences in Poverty, 1950–1980', *Signs: Journal of Women in Culture and Society*, vol. 15, pp. 102–22.

McLean, Athena 1990, 'Contradictions in the Social Production of Clinical Knowledge: The Case of Schizophrenia', *Social Science & Medicine*, vol. 30, pp. 969–85.

McMahon, Marilyn & Davids, Cindy 1993, 'Anti-Stalking Legislation: A New Strategy in the Fight Against Domestic Violence?', *Socio-Legal Bulletin* no. 10, pp. 4–7.

McMichael, A.J. 1985, 'Social Class (as estimated by occupational prestige) and Mortality in Australian Males in the 1970s', *Community Health Studies*, vol. 9, pp. 220–30.

McMichael, A.J. & Bonett, Anton 1981, 'Cancer Profiles of British and Southern-European Migrants', *Medical Journal of Australia*, 7 March, pp. 229–32.

Mechanic, David 1978, *Medical Sociology*, 3rd edn, The Free Press, New York.

Meier, Robert F. 1977, 'The New Criminology: Continuity in Criminological Theory', *Journal of Criminal Law and Criminology*, vol. 67, pp. 461–9.

Meier, Robert F. 1982, 'Perspectives on the Concept of Social Control', *Annual Review of Sociology*, vol. 8, pp. 35–55.

Meier, Robert F. & Miethe, Terance D. 1993, 'Understanding Theories of Criminal Victimization', *Crime and Justice: An Annual Review of Research*, vol. 17, pp. 459–99.

Meile, Richard L. & Whitt, Hugh P. 1981, 'Cultural Consensus and Definition of Mental Illness', *Social Science & Medicine*, vol. 15A, pp. 231–42.

Merton, Robert K. 1938, 'Social Structure and Anomie', *American Sociological Review*, vol. 3, pp. 672–83.

Merton, Robert K. 1968, *Social Theory and Social Structure*, The Free Press, New York.

Merton, Robert K. 1971, 'Social Problems and Sociological Theory', in *Contemporary Social Problems*, 3rd edn, eds Robert K. Merton & Robert Nisbet, Harcourt Brace Jovanovich, New York.

Miall, Charlene E. 1986, 'The Stigma of Involuntary Childlessness', *Social Problems*, vol. 33, pp. 268–82.

Miller, Walter B. 1958, 'Lower Class Culture as a Generating Milieu of Gang Delinquency, *The Journal of Social Issues*, vol. 14, pp. 5–19.

Millman, Marcia 1975, 'She Did It All For Love: A Feminist View of the Sociology of Deviance', in *Another Voice*, eds Marcia Millman & Rosabeth Moss Kanter, Anchor Books, New York.

Mills, C. Wright 1943, 'The Professional Ideology of Social Pathologists', *American Journal of Sociology*, vol. 49, pp. 165–80.

Mills, Elizabeth Ann 1982, 'One Hundred Years of Fear: Rape and the Medical Profession', in *Judge, Lawyer, Victim, Thief: Women, Gender Roles, and Criminal Justice*, eds Nicole Hahn Rafter & Elizabeth Anne Stanko, North Eastern University Press, Boston.

Mohr, James C. 1978, *Abortion in America: The Origins and Evolution of National Policy, 1800–1900*, Oxford University Press, New York.

Molotch, Harvey & Lester, Marilyn 1974, 'News as Purposive Behaviour: On The Strategic Use of Routine Events, Accidents and Scandals', *American Sociological Review*, vol. 39, pp. 101–12.

Monachesi, Elio 1960, 'Cesare Beccaria', in *Pioneers in Criminology*, ed. Hermann Mannheim, Stevens & Sons, London.

Montgomery, Bruce 1994, 'Lavarch Poised to Banish the Bedroom Police', *The Weekend Australian*, April 9–10, p. 11.

Moore, David 1992, 'Beyond the Bottle: Introducing Anthropological Debate to Research into Aboriginal Alcohol Use', *Australian Journal of Social Issues*, vol. 27, pp. 173–93.

Moore, Mark Harrison 1992, 'Problem-solving and Community Policing', *Crime and Justice: A Review of Research*, vol. 15, pp. 99–158.

Moran, Richard 1978, 'Biomedical Research and the Politics of Crime Control', *Contemporary Crises*, vol. 2, pp. 335–57.

Morris, Allison 1987, *Women, Crime and Criminal Justice*, Basil Blackwell, Oxford.

Morris, Norval 1974, 'The Future of Imprisonment: Toward a Punitive Philosophy', *Michigan Law Review*, vol. 72, pp. 1161–80.

Morris, Norval & Hawkins, Gordon 1970, *The Honest Politician's Guide to Crime Control*, University of Chicago Press, Chicago.

Morrow, Carol Klaperman 1982, 'Sick Doctors: The Social Construction of Professional Deviance', *Social Problems*, vol. 30, pp. 92–108.

Morrow, Ross 1994, 'The Sexological Construction of Sexual Dysfunction', *The Australian & New Zealand Journal of Sociology*, vol. 30, pp. 20–35.

Mukherjee, Satyanshu K. & Fitzgerald, R. William 1981, 'The Myth of Rising Female Crime', in *Women and Crime*, eds Satyanshu K. Mukherjee & Jocelynne A. Scutt, George Allen & Unwin, Sydney.

Mukherjee, Satyanshu K., Scandia, Anita, Dagger, Dianne & Matthews, Wendy 1989, *Sourcebook of Australian Criminal & Social Statistics 1804–1988*, Bicentennial Edition, Australian Institute of Criminology, Canberra.

Mukherjee, Satyanshu K. & Dagger, Dianne 1990, *The Size of the Crime Problem in Australia*, 2nd edn, Australian Institute of Criminology, Canberra.

Mukherjee, Satyanshu K. & Dagger, Dianne 1993, *Size of the Crime Problem in Australia: Updates*, Australian Institute of Criminology, Canberra.

Murphy, B. 1988, *Data Comparability and Problems with Selected Crime Statistics*, National Police Research Unit, Adelaide.

Nader, Laura & Metzger, Duane 1963, 'Conflict Resolution in Two Mexican Communities', *American Anthropologist*, vol. 65, pp. 584–92.

Naffine, Ngaire 1987, *Female Crime: The Construction of Women in Criminology*, Allen & Unwin, Sydney.

Naffine, Ngaire 1992, 'Windows on the Legal Mind: The Evocation of Rape in Legal Writings', *Melbourne University Law Review*, vol. 18, pp. 741–67.

Naffine, Ngaire & Gale, Fay 1989, 'Testing the Nexus: Crime, Gender and Unemployment', *British Journal of Criminology*, vol. 29, pp. 144–56.

Nathanson, Constance 1975, 'Illness and the Feminine Role: A Theoretical Review', *Social Science & Medicine*, vol. 9, pp. 57–62.

National Committee on Violence 1990, *Violence: Directions for Australia*, Australian Institute of Criminology, Canberra.

Navarro, Vicente 1980, 'Work Ideology and Science: The Case of Medicine', *International Journal of Health Services*, vol. 10, pp. 523–50.

Navarro, Vicente 1983, 'Radicalism, Marxism and Medicine', *International Journal of Health Services*, vol. 13, pp. 179–202.

Neave, Marcia 1985a, *Inquiry into Prostitution: Final Report*, vol. 1, Government Printer, Melbourne.

Neave, Marcia 1985b, *Inquiry into Prostitution: Final Report*, vol. 2, Government Printer, Melbourne.

Neave, Marcia 1988, 'The Failure of Prostitution Law Reform', *Australian & New Zealand Journal of Criminology*, vol. 21, pp. 202–13.

Neave, Marcia 1992, 'From Difference to Sameness—Law and Women's Work', *Melbourne University Law Review*, vol. 18, pp. 768–809.

Neff, James Alan, McFall, Stephenie L. & Cleaveland, Timothy D. 1987, 'Psychiatry and Medicine in the US: Interpreting Trends in Medical Specialty Choice', *Sociology of Health & Illness*, vol. 9, pp. 45–61.

Neill, Rosemary 1994a, 'A Woman's Right to a Life', *The Weekend Australian,* April 23–24, p. 23.

Neill, Rosemary 1994b, 'Our Shame: How Aboriginal Women and Children are Bashed in their Own Community—then Ignored', *The Weekend Australian Review* 18–19 June, pp. 1–2.

Nelson, Steve & Amir, Menachim 1975, 'The Hitch-Hiker Victim of Rape: A Research Report', in *Victimology*, eds Israel Drapkin & Emilio Viano, vol. v, Lexington Books, Lexington.

Nelthorpe, Denis 1988, 'Consumer Law: Class Actions—the Real Solution', *Legal Service Bulletin*, vol. 13, pp. 26–8.

Nicol, Bill 1989, *McBride: Behind the Myth*, Australian Broadcasting Corporation, Sydney.

Nisbet, Robert 1971, 'The Study of Social Problems', in *Contemporary Social Problems*, 3rd edn, eds Robert K. Merton & Robert Nisbet, Harcourt Brace Jovanovich, New York.

Nolan Sybil & Lynch, Paul 1988, 'Herbert Netted $1m from Corruption', *The Australian*, 13 September, pp. 1–2.

Note 1990, 'Rethinking (M)Otherhood: Feminist Theory and State Regulation of Pregnancy', *Harvard Law Review*, vol. 103, pp. 1325–43.

O'Connell, Terry & Moore, David 1992, ' Wagga Juvenile Cautioning Process: The General Applicability of Family Group Conferences for Juvenile Offenders and Their Victims', *Rural Society*, vol. 2, pp. 16–19.

O'Connor, Rory 1984, 'Alcohol and Contingent Drunkenness in Central Australia', *Australian Journal of Social Issues*, vol. 19, pp. 173–83.

O'Donnell, Carol & Saville, Heather 1982, 'Domestic Violence and Sex and Class Inequality', in *Family Violence in Australia*, eds Carol O'Donnell & Jan Craney, Longman Cheshire, Melbourne.

O'Donovan, Katherine 1991, 'Defences for Battered Women Who Kill', *Journal of Law and Society*, vol. 18, pp. 219–40.

O'Donovan, Katherine 1993, 'Law's Knowledge: The Judge, The Expert, the Battered Woman, and Her Syndrome', *Journal of Law and Society*, vol. 20, pp. 427–37.

Office of Crime Statistics 1982, *Shoplifting in South Australia*, Research Bulletin No. 1, Attorney-General's Department, Adelaide.

Office of Crime Statistics 1986a, *Decriminalising Drunkenness in South Australia*, Research Bulletin No. 4, Attorney-General's Department, Adelaide.

Office of Crime Statistics 1986b, *Law and Order in South Australia: An Introduction to Crime and Criminal Justice Policy*, 2nd edn, Attorney-General's Department, Adelaide.

Office of Crime Statistics 1992, *Crime and Justice in South Australia 1991*, Attorney-General's Department, Adelaide.

Office of Crime Statistics 1993, *Crime and Justice in South Australia 1992*, Attorney-General's Department, Adelaide.

Office of Multicultural Affairs 1989, *National Agenda for a Multi-cultural Australia … Sharing Our Future*, AGPS, Canberra.

Office of Technology Assessment 1988, *Infertility: Medical and Social Choices*, US Government Printing Office, Washington D.C.

O'Malley, Pat 1983, *Law, Capitalism and Democracy: A Sociology of Australian Legal Order*, Allen & Unwin, Sydney.

Opit, Louis J. 1983, 'Wheeling, Healing and Dealing: The Political Economy of Health Care in Australia', *Community Health Studies*, vol. 11, pp. 238–46.

Opit, Louis J., Oliver, R. Graeme & Salzberg, Michael 1984, 'Occupation and Blood Pressure', *The Medical Journal of Australia*, vol. 140, pp. 760–4.

Owen, D.R. 1972, 'The 47 XYY Male: A Review', *Psychological Bulletin*, vol. 78, pp. 209–33.

Oxley, Deborah 1991, 'Women Transported: Gendered Images and Realities', *Australian & New Zealand Journal of Criminology*, vol. 24, pp. 83–98.

Pagelow, Mildred Daley 1981, *Women-Battering: Victims and Their Experiences*, Sage, Beverly Hills.

Pakulski, Jan 1991, *Social Movements: The Politics of Moral Protest*, Longman Cheshire, Melbourne.

Papadakis, Elim 1993, 'Public Opinion, Sexual Difference and the Welfare State', *Australian & New Zealand Journal of Sociology*, vol. 29, pp. 343–66.

Parisi, Nicolette 1982, 'Are Females Treated Differently? A Review of the Theories and Evidence on Sentencing and Parole Decisions', in *Judge, Lawyer, Victim, Thief: Women, Gender Roles, and Criminal Justice*, eds Nicole Hahn Rafter & Elizabeth A. Stanko, Northeastern University Press, Boston.

Parks, Evelyn L. 1970, 'From Constabulary to Police Society', *Catalyst*, vol. 5, pp. 76–97.

Parsons, Talcott 1951a, 'Illness and the Role of the Physician: A Sociological Perspective', *American Journal of Orthopsychiatry*, vol. 21, pp. 452–66.

Parsons, Talcott 1951b, *The Social System*, The Free Press, New York.

Parsons, Talcott 1975, 'The Sick Role and the Role of the Physician Reconsidered', *The Milbank Memorial Fund Quarterly*, vol. 53, pp. 257–78.

Parsons, Talcott 1979, 'Definitions of Health and Illness in the Light of American Values and Social Structure', in *Patients, Physicians and Illness: A Source Book in Behavioural Science and Health*, 3rd edn, ed. E. Gartly Jaco, The Free Press, New York.

Partlett, David & Szweda, Eric A. 1991, 'An Embattled Profession: The Role of Lawyers in the Regulatory State', *University of New South Wales Law Journal*, vol. 14, pp. 8–45.

Pate, Antony M. & Hamilton, Edwin E. 1992, 'Formal and Informal Deterrents to Domestic Violence: The Dade County Spouse Assault Experiment', *American Sociological Review*, vol. 57, pp. 691–7.

Patton, Cindy 1988, 'AIDS: Lessons from the Gay Community', *Feminist Review*, vol. 30, pp. 105–11.

Pearce, Diana 1978, 'The Feminization of Poverty: Women, Work and Welfare', *Urban and Social Change Review*, vol. 11, pp. 28–36.

Perrett, Janine, 1988, 'Drexel Mounts Publicity War Against Charges', *The Australian*, 16 September, p. 15.

Perrucci, Robert & Targ, Dena B. 1982, *Mental Patients and Social Networks*, Auburn House Publishing Company, Boston.

Pescosolido, Bernice A. 1992, 'Beyond Rational Choice: The Social Dynamics of How People Seek Help', *American Journal of Sociology*, vol. 97, pp. 1096–1138.

Petchesky, Rosalind Pollack 1986, *Abortion and Woman's Choice: The State, Sexuality, and Reproductive Freedom*, Verso, London.

Petchesky, Rosalind Pollack 1987, 'Fetal Images: The Power of Visual Culture in the Politics of Reproduction', *Feminist Studies*, vol. 13, pp. 263–92.

Petersen, Kerry A. 1993, *Abortion Regimes*, Dartmouth Publishing, Aldershot.

Pfohl, Stephen J. 1977, 'The "Discovery" of Child Abuse', *Social Problems*, vol. 24, pp. 310–23.

Phillips, Derek L. & Segal, Bernard E. 1969, 'Sexual Status and Psychiatric Symptoms', *American Sociological Review*, vol. 34, pp. 58–72.

Piliavin, Irving & Briar, Scott 1964, 'Police Encounters with Juveniles', *American Journal of Sociology*, vol. 49, pp. 206–14.

Pitts, Jesse R. 1968, 'Social Control: The Concept', in *International Encyclopedia of the Social Sciences*, ed. David Sills, Macmillan, New York.

Piven, Frances Fox & Cloward, Richard A. 1971, *Regulating the Poor: The Functions of Public Welfare*, Pantheon Books, New York.

Piven, Frances Fox & Cloward, Richard A. 1982, *The New Class War*, Pantheon Books, New York.

Piven, Frances Fox & Cloward, Richard A. 1988, 'Welfare Dosen't Shore Up Traditional Family Roles: A Reply to Linda Gordon', *Social Research*, vol. 55, pp. 631–47.

Pixley, Jocelyn 1991, 'Wowser and Pro-Woman Politics: Temperance Against Australian Patriarchy', *Australian & New Zealand Journal of Sociology*, vol. 27, pp. 293–314.

Pizzey, Erin 1974, *Scream Quietly or the Neighbours Will Hear*, Penguin, Harmondsworth.

Platt, Anthony 1969, *The Child Savers: The Invention of Delinquency*, The University of Chicago Press, Chicago.

Platt, Anthony 1974, 'The Triumph of Benevolence: The Origin of the Juvenile Justice System in the United States', in *Criminal Justice in America,* ed. Richard Quinney, Little, Brown, Boston.

Polk, Ken 1984, 'The New Marginal Youth', *Crime & Delinquency*, vol. 30, pp. 462–80.

Pollak, Otto 1979, 'The Masked Character of Female Crime', in *The Criminology of Deviant Women,* eds Freda Adler & Rita James Simon, Houghton Mifflin, Boston.

Pontell, Henry N., Jesilow, Paul D. & Geis, Gilbert 1982, 'Policing Physicians: Practitioner Fraud and Abuse in a Government Medical Program', *Social Problems*, vol. 30, pp. 117–25.

Power, M. 1980, 'Unemployed Women: Scapegoats of the Recession, in *Australia and World Capitalism,* eds Greg Crough, E.L. Wheelwright & Ted Wiltshire, Penguin, Melbourne.

Price, Barbara Raffel & Natalie J. Sokoloff eds 1995, *The Criminal Justice System and Women: Offenders, Victims and Workers*, 2nd edn, McGraw-Hill, New York.

Punch, Maurice 1985, *Conduct Unbecoming: The Social Construction of Police Deviance and Control,* Tavistock, London.

Quadagno, Jill 1987, 'Theories of the Welfare State', *Annual Review of Sociology*, vol. 13, pp. 109–28.

Quinney, Richard 1970, *The Social Reality of Crime*, Little, Brown & Company, Boston.

Quinney, Richard 1974, *Critique of Legal Order: Crime Control in Capitalist Society*, Little, Brown & Company, Boston.

Quinney, Richard 1977, *Class, State and Crime: On the Theory and Practice of Criminal Justice*, Longman, New York.

Radcliffe-Browne, A.R. 1952, *Structure and Function in Primitive Society*, Cohen & West, London.

Ragg, Mark 1994, 'Sticking Point', *The Weekend Australian*, April 9–10, p. 20.

Ratcliff, Kathryn Strother & Bogdan, Janet 1988, 'Unemployed Women: When "Social Support" Is Not Supportive', *Social Problems*, vol. 35, pp. 54–63.

Rafter, Nicole Hahn & Stanko, Elizabeth A. eds 1982, *Judge, Lawyer, Victim, Thief: Women, Gender Roles, and Criminal Justice*, Northeastern University Press, Boston.

Redmond, Paul 1992, *Companies and Securities Law: Commentary and Materials*, 2nd edn, Law Book Company, Sydney.

Reinarman, Craig & Levine, Harry G. 1989, 'The Crack Attack: Politics and Media in America's Latest Drug Scare', in *Images of Issues: Typifying Contemporary Social Problems*, ed. Joel Best, Aldine de Gruyter, New York.

Reiner, R. 1985, *The Politics of the Police*, Wheatsheaf Books, London.

Reiner, Robert 1992, 'Police Research in the United Kingdom: A Critical Review', in *Crime and Justice: A Review of Research*, vol. 15, pp. 435–508.

Reiss, Albert 1960, 'Sex Offenses: The Marginal Status of the Adolescent', *Law and Contemporary Problems*, vol. 25, pp. 309–33.

Ricketson, Matthew 1988, 'Rambo Movie: A Blueprint for Queen Street Massacre', *The Australian*, 7 October, p. 6.

Rintoul, Stuart 1990, 'The Street that Whites Fear to Tread', *The Weekend Australian*, 17–18 February, pp. 4–5.

Risman, Barbara & Schwartz, Pepper 1988, 'Sociological Research on Male and Female Homosexuality', *Annual Review of Sociology*, vol. 14, pp. 125–47.

Rittenhouse, C. Amanda 1991, 'The Emergence of Premenstrual Syndrome as a Social Problem', *Social Problems*, vol. 38, pp. 412–25.

Roach Anleu, Sharyn L. 1992, 'Critiquing the Law: Themes and Dilemmas in Anglo-American Feminist Legal Theory', *Journal of Law and Society*, vol. 19, pp. 423–40.

Roach Anleu, Sharyn L. 1993, 'Reproductive Autonomy: Infertility, Deviance and Conceptive Technology', *Law in Context*, vol. 11, pp. 17–40.

Roach Anleu, Sharyn L. 1995, 'Lifting the Lid: Perspectives on Social Control, Youth Crime and Juvenile Justice', in *Ways of Resistance: Social Control and Young People in Australia*, eds Cheryl Simpson & Richard Hil, Hale & Iremonger, Sydney.

Robbins, Ira 1986, 'Privatization of Corrections: Defining the Issues', *Judicature*, vol. 69, pp. 324–31.

Robinson, Cyril & Scaglion, Richard 1987, 'The Origin and Evolution of the Police Function in Society: Notes Toward a Theory', *Law & Society Review*, vol. 21, pp. 108–53.

Robinson, Kay 1986, 'Restructuring the Welfare State: An Analysis of Public Expenditure 1979/80–1989/85', *Journal of Social Policy*, vol. 15, pp. 1–21.

Rodriguez, Noelie Maria 1988, 'Transcending Bureaucracy: Feminist Politics at a Shelter for Battered Women, *Gender & Society*, vol. 2, pp. 214–27.

Room, Robin 1976, 'Ambivalence as a Sociological Explanation: The Case of Cultural Explanations of Alcohol Problems', *American Sociological Review*, vol. 41, pp. 1047–65.

Rose, Vicki McNickle 1977, 'Rape as a Social Problem: A Byproduct of the Feminist Movement', *Social Problems*, vol. 25, pp. 75–89.

Rosenbaum, Dennis P. 1987, 'The Theory and Research Behind Neighborhood Watch: Is it a Sound Fear and Crime Reduction Strategy?', *Crime & Delinquency*, vol. 33, pp. 107–34.

Rosenberg, Dorothy J. 1991, 'Shock Therapy: GDR Women in Transition from a Socialist Welfare State to a Social Market Economy', *Signs: Journal of Women in Culture and Society*, vol. 17, pp. 129–51.

Rosenberg, Janet, Perlstadt, Harry & Phillips, William R. 1993, 'Now that We are Here: Discrimination, Disparagement, and Harassment at Work and the Experience of Women Lawyers', *Gender & Society*, vol. 7, pp. 415–33.

Rosenhan, D.L. 1973, 'On Being Sane in Insane Places', *Science*, vol. 179, pp. 250–8.

Ross, Edward Alsworth 1896, 'Social Control', *American Journal of Sociology*, vol. 1, pp. 513–35.

Ross, Russell & Whiteford, Peter 1992, 'Poverty in 1986: Aboriginal Families with Children', *Australian Journal of Social Issues*, vol. 27, pp. 92–111.

Rossi, Peter H., Waite, Emily, Bose, Christine E. & Berk, Richard E. 1974, 'The Seriousness of Crimes: Normative Structure and Individual Differences', *American Sociological Review*, vol. 39, pp. 224–37.

Rotenberg, Mordechai 1974, 'Self-labelling: A Missing Link in the Societal Reaction Theory of Deviance', *Sociological Review*, vol. 22, pp. 335–54.

Rothman, Barbara Katz 1983, 'Midwives in Transition: The Structure of a Clinical Revolution', *Social Problems*, vol. 30, pp. 262–71.

Rothman, Barbara Katz 1986, *The Tentative Pregnancy: Prenatal Diagnosis and the Future of Motherhood*, Viking, New York.

Rothman, David S. 1971, *The Discovery of the Asylum: Social Order and Disorder in the New Republic*, Little, Brown, Boston.

Rowe, David C. & Osgood, D. Wayne 1984, 'Heredity and Sociological Theories of Delinquency: A Reconsideration', *American Sociological Review*, vol. 49, pp. 526–40.

Rust, Paula C. 1993, '"Coming Out" in the Age of Social Constructionism: Sexual Identity Formation Among Lesbian and Bisexual Women', *Gender & Society*, vol. 7, pp. 50–77.

Ryan, William 1971, *Blaming The Victim*, Vintage Books, New York.

SA Attorney-General's Department n.d., *Information for Victims of Crime*, South Australia, Government Printer.

Sagarin, Edward 1985, 'Positive Deviance: An Oxymoron', *Deviant Behaviour*, vol. 6, pp. 169–81.

Sagarin, Edward & Kelly, Robert J. 1987, 'Deviance: A Polymorphous Concept', *Deviant Behaviour*, vol. 8, pp. 13–25.

Sallmann, Peter A. 1986, 'Perspectives on the Police and Criminal Justice Debate', in *The Australian Criminal Justice System: The Mid 1980s*, eds Duncan Chappell & Paul Wilson, Butterworths, Sydney.

Sampson, Robert J. & Laub, John H. 1990, 'Crime and Deviance over the Life Course: The Salience of Adult Social Bonds', *American Sociological Review*, vol. 55, pp. 609–27.

Sandelowski, Margarete J., Holditch-Davis, Diane & Harris, Betty G. 1990, 'Living the Life: Explanations of Infertility', *Sociology of Health & Illness*, vol. 12, pp. 195–215.

Sarre, Rick, Sutton, Adam & Pulsford, Tim 1989, *Cannabis: The Expiation Notice Approach*, Office of Crime Statistics, Attorney-General's Department, Adelaide.

Sarri, Rosemary C. 1986, 'Gender and Race Differences in Criminal Justice Processing', *Women's Studies International Forum*, vol. 9, pp. 89–99.

Saunders, Peter 1980, 'What's Wrong With The Poverty Line?', *The Australian Quarterly*, vol. 51, pp. 388–97.

Saunders, Peter & Whiteford, Peter 1987, *Ending Child Poverty: An Assessment of the Government's Family Package*, Social Welfare Research Centre, University of New South Wales.

Scheff, Thomas J. 1966, *Being Mentally Ill: A Sociological Theory*, Aldine, Chicago.

Schneider, Beth E. 1991, 'Put Up and Shut Up: Workplace Sexual Assaults', *Gender & Society*, vol. 5, pp. 533–48.

Schneider, Joseph W. 1978, 'Deviant Drinking as Disease: Alcoholism as a Social Accomplishment', *Social Problems*, vol. 25, pp. 361–72.

Schneider, Joseph W. 1985, 'Social Problems Theory: The Constructionist View', *Annual Review of Sociology*, vol. 11, pp. 209–29.

Schrager, Laura Shill & Short, James F. Jr 1978, 'Toward a Sociology of Organizational Crime', *Social Problems*, vol. 25, pp. 407–19.

Schuessler, Karl F. & Cressey, Donald R. 1950, 'Personality Characteristics of Criminals', *American Journal of Sociology*, vol. 55, pp. 476–84.

Schur, Edwin M. 1965, *Crimes Without Victims: Deviant Behaviour and Public Policy: Abortion, Homosexuality, Drug Addiction*, Prentice Hall, Englewood Cliffs, New Jersey.

Schur, Edwin M. 1971, *Labeling Deviant Behaviour: Its Sociological Implications*, Harper & Row, New York.

Schur, Edwin M. 1984, *Labeling Women Deviant: Gender, Stigma and Social Control*, Random House, New York.

Schur, Edwin M. 1988, *The Americanization of Sex*, Temple University Press, Philadelphia.

Schur, Edwin M. & Bedau, Hugo Adam 1974, *Victimless Crimes: Two Sides of a Controversy*, Prentice Hall, Englewood Cliffs, New Jersey.

Schwartz, Richard D. 1954, 'Social Factors in the Development of Legal Control: A Case Study of Two Israeli Settlements', *Yale Law Journal*, vol. 63, pp. 471–91.

Schwartz, Richard D. & Miller, James 1964, 'Legal Evolution and Societal Complexity', *American Journal of Sociology*, vol. 70, pp. 159–69.

Scott, Ellen Kaye 1993, 'How to Stop the Rapists? A Question of Strategy in Two Rape Crisis Centers', *Social Problems*, vol. 40, pp. 343–61.

Scott, Marvin B. & Lyman, Stanford M. 1968, 'Accounts', *American Sociological Review*, vol. 33, pp. 46–62.

Scritchfield, Shirley A. 1989, 'The Social Construction of Infertility: From Private Matter to Social Concern', in *Images of Issues: Typifying Contemporary Social Problems*, ed. Joel Best, Aldine de Gruyter, New York.

Scull, Andrew T. 1975, 'From Madness to Mental Illness: Medical Men as Moral Entrepreneurs', *Archives Europeènnes de Sociologie*, vol. 16, pp. 218–61.

Scull, Andrew T. 1977a, *Decarceration: Community Treatment and the Deviant: A Radical View*, Prentice Hall, Englewood Cliffs, New Jersey.

Scull, Andrew T. 1977b, 'Madness and Segregative Control: The Role of the Insane Asylum', *Social Problems*, vol. 24, pp. 337–51.

Scull, Andrew T. 1986, 'Mental Patients and the Community', *International Journal of Law and Society*, vol. 9, pp. 383–92.

Scully, Diana & Marolla, Joseph 1984, 'Convicted Rapists' Vocabulary of Motive: Excuses and Justifications', *Social Problems*, vol. 31, pp. 530–44.

Scully, Diana 1988, 'Convicted Rapists' Perceptions of Self and Victim: Role Taking and Emotions', *Gender & Society*, vol. 2, pp. 200–13.

Scutt, Jocelynne A. 1979, *Probation as an Option for Sentencing*, Research Paper No. 8, Australian Law Reform Commission, Sydney.

Scutt, Jocelynne A. 1986, 'Sexual Assault and the Australian Criminal Justice System', in *The Australian Criminal Justice System: The Mid 1980s*, eds Duncan Chappell & Paul Wilson, Butterworths, Sydney.

Sellin, Thorsten 1931, 'The Basis of a Crime Index', *Journal of Criminal Law and Criminology*, vol. 22, pp. 335–56.

Sellin, Thorsten 1972, 'Enrico Ferri', in *Pioneers in Criminology*, 2nd edn, ed. Hermann Mannheim, Patterson Smith, Montclair, New Jersey.

Senate Standing Committee on Legal and Constitutional Affairs 1994, *Gender Bias and the Judiciary*, Commonwealth of Australia, Canberra.

Seymour, John 1988, *Dealing with Young Offenders*, Law Book Company, Sydney.

Shand, Adam 1989, 'Bank's Scheme Evaded Tax, But Not the Law', *The Weekend Australian*, 6–7 May, p. 8.

Shapiro, Susan P. 1984, *Wayward Capitalists: Target of the Securities and Exchange Commission*, Yale University Press, New Haven.

Shapiro, Susan, P. 1985, 'The Road Not Taken: The Elusive Path to Criminal Prosectuion for White-Collar Offenders', *Law & Society Review*, vol. 19, pp. 179–217.

Shapiro, Susan P. 1990, 'Collaring the Crime, not the Criminal: Reconsidering the Concept of White-Collar Crime', *American Sociological Review*, vol. 55, pp. 346–65.

Sheehy, Elizabeth A., Stubbs, Julie & Tolmie, Julia 1992, 'Defending Battered Women on Trial: The Battered Woman Syndrome and its Limitations', *Criminal Law Journal*, vol. 16, pp. 369–94.

Sheldon, William 1949, *Varieties of Delinquent Youth*, Harper, New York.

Sheley, Joseph F. & Hanlon, John J. 1978, 'Unintended Effects of Police Decisions to Actively Enforce Laws: Implications for Analyses of Crime Trends', *Contemporary Crises*, vol. 2, pp. 265–75.

Sherman, Lawrence W. & Berk, Richard A. 1984, 'The Specific Deterrent Effects of Arrest for Domestic Assault', *American Sociological Review*, vol. 49, pp. 261–71.

Sherman, Lawrence W. & Smith, Douglas with Schmidt, Janell D. & Rogan, Dennis, P. 1992, 'Crime, Punishment, and Stake in Conformity: Legal and Informal Control of Domestic Violence', *American Sociological Review*, vol. 57, pp. 680–90.

Silver, Allan 1967, 'The Demand for Order in Civil Society: A Review of Some Themes in the History of Urban Crime, Police, and Riot', in *The Police: Six Sociological Essays*, ed. David Bordua, John Wiley, New York.

Simmel, Georg 1971, *On Individuality and Social Forms*, University of Chicago Press, Chicago.

Simon, David R. & Eitzen, D. Stanley 1986, *Elite Deviance*, 2nd edn, Allyn & Bacon, Boston.

Simon, William & Gagnon, John H. 1967, 'Homosexuality: The Formulation of a Sociological Perspective', *Journal of Health and Social Behavior*, vol. 8, pp. 177–85.

Simpson, Sally S. 1989, 'Feminist Theory, Crime, and Justice', *Criminology*, vol. 27, pp. 605–31.

Sinclair, Ken & Ross, Michael W. 1986, 'Consequences of Decriminalization of Homosexuality: A Study of Two Australian States', *Journal of Homosexuality*, vol. 12, pp. 119–27.

Sinfield, Adrian 1981, *What Unemployment Means*, Martin Robertson, Oxford.

Sing, A.J. 1986, 'Search Warrants and Legal Professional Privilege', *Criminal Law Journal*, vol. 10, pp. 32–48.

Siskind, V., Najman, J.M. & Copeman, R. 1987a, 'Socioeconomic Status and Mortality: A Brisbane Area Analysis', *Community Health Studies*, vol. 11, pp. 15–23.

Siskind, V., Najman, J.M. & Copeman, R. 1987b, 'Infant Mortality in Socioeconomically Advantaged and Disadvantaged Areas of Brisbane', *Community Health Studies*, vol. 11, pp. 24–30.

Skogan, Wesley 1987, 'The Impact of Victimization on Fear', *Crime & Delinquency*, vol. 33, pp. 135–54.

Smart, Carol 1976, *Women, Crime and Criminology: A Feminist Critique*, Routledge & Kegan Paul, London.

Smart, Carol 1979, 'The New Female Criminal: Reality or Myth?', *British Journal of Criminology*, vol. 19, pp. 50–9.

Smart, Carol 1989, *Feminism and the Power of Law*, Routledge, London.

Smith, Barbara Ellen 1981, 'Black Lung: The Social Production of Disease', *International Journal of Health Services*, vol. 11, pp. 343–59.

Smith, David James 1994, 'Little Devils', *The Weekend Australian Review*, 8–9 January, pp. 1, 4.

Snider, Laureen 1991, 'The Regulatory Dance: Understanding Reform Processes in Corporate Crime', *International Journal of the Sociology of Law*, vol. 19, pp. 209–86.

Snow, David A., Baker, Susan G., Anderson, Leon & Martin, Michael 1986, 'The Myth of Pervasive Mental Illness Among the Homeless', *Social Problems*, vol. 33, pp. 407–23.

Social Welfare Commission 1975, *Progress Report on Social Welfare Manpower*, Australian Government Social Welfare Commission, Canberra.

Sommerlad, Elizabeth A. & Altman, Jon C. 1986, 'Alternative Rural Communities: A Solution to Unemployment?', *Australian Journal of Social Issues*, vol. 21, pp. 3–15.

Sontag, Susan 1977, *Illness as Metaphor*, Farrar, Straus & Giroux, New York.

Sontag, Susan 1990, *AIDS and Its Metaphors*, Penguin, New York.

Soothill, Keith, Walby, Sylvia & Bagguley, Paul 1990, 'Judges, the Media, and Rape', *Journal of Law and Society*, vol. 17, pp. 211–33.

South Australia 1993, *Parliamentary Debates: House of Assembly*, 1 April, Government Printer, Adelaide.

South Australian Police Department 1989, unpublished data, Adelaide.

Spangler, Eve 1986, *Lawyers for Hire: Salaried Professionals at Work*, Yale University Press, New Haven.

Special Committee on Pornography and Prostitution (Canada) 1985, *Pornography and Prostitution in Canada*, vol. 1, Canadian Government Publishing Service, Ottawa, Ontario.

Spector, Malcolm 1977, 'Legitimizing Homosexuality', *Society*, vol. 14, pp. 52–6.

Spitzer, Steven & Scull, Andrew T. 1977, 'Privatization and Capitalist Development: The Case of the Private Police', *Social Problems*, vol. 25, pp. 18–29.

Stanton, Alfred H. & Schwartz, Morris 1954, *The Mental Hospital: A Study of Institutional Participation in Psychiatric Illness and Treatment*, Basic Books, New York.

Steffensmeier, Darrell J. 1978, 'Crime and the Contemporary Woman: An Analysis of Changing Levels of Female Property Crime, 1960–75', *Social Forces*, vol. 57, pp. 566–84.

Steffensmeier, Darrell J. 1980a, 'Assessing the Impact of the Women's Movement on Sex–Based Differences in the Handling of Adult Criminal Defendants', *Crime and Delinquency*, vol. 76, pp. 344–57.

Steffensmeier, Darrell J. 1980b, 'Sex Differences in Patterns of Adult Crime, 1965–77: A Review and Assessment', *Social Forces*, vol. 58, pp. 1080–1108.

Steffensmeier, Darrell J. 1983, 'Organization Properties and Sex-Segregation in the Underworld: Building a Sociological Theory of Sex Differences in Crime', *Social Forces*, vol. 61, pp. 1010–32.

Steffensmeier, Darrell J. & Cobb, Michael J. 1981, 'Sex Differences In Urban Arrest Patterns, 1934–79', *Social Problems*, vol. 29, pp. 37–50.

Stone, Christopher 1975, *Where the Law Ends: The Social Control of Corporate Behaviour*, Harper & Row, New York.

Stothard, Peter & Bone, James 1989, 'Nation Rallies Behind Bush's Hunt for the "Rat"', *The Weekend Australian*, 23–24 December, p. 7.

Strauss, Anselm, Schatzman, Leonard, Ehrlich, Danuta, Bucher, Rue & Sabshin, Melvin 1963, 'The Hospital and its Negotiated Order', in *The Hospital in Modern Society*, ed. Eliot Freidson, The Free Press, Glencoe.

Strickler, Jennifer 1992, 'The New Reproductive Technology: Problem or Solution?' *Sociology of Health & Illness*, vol. 14, pp. 111–32.

Stubbs, Julie & Wallace, Alison 1988, 'Protecting Victims of Domestic Violence?', in *Understanding Crime and Criminal Justice*, eds Mark Findlay & Russell Hogg, The Law Book Company, Sydney.

Sudnow, David 1965, 'Normal Crimes: Sociological Features of the Penal Code in a Public Defender's Office', *Social Problems*, vol. 12, pp. 255–76.

Sullivan, Barbara 1991, 'The Business of Sex: Australian Government and the Sex Industry', *Australian & New Zealand Journal of Sociology*, vol. 27, pp. 3–18.

Sullivan, Deborah & Weitz, Rose 1988, *Labor Pains: Modern Midwives and Home Birth*, Yale University Press, New Haven.

Sullivan, Rohan 1994, 'Wife Joins Storm over Sex Remarks', *The Australian*, January 13, pp. 1–2.

Sumner, The Hon. C.J. 1987, 'Victim Participation in the Criminal Justice System', *Australian & New Zealand Journal of Criminology*, vol. 20, pp. 195–217.

Sutherland, Edwin H. 1940, 'White-Collar Criminality', *American Sociological Review*, vol. 5, pp. 1–12.

Sutherland, Edwin H. 1945, 'Is "White Collar Crime" Crime?', *American Sociological Review*, vol. 10, pp. 132–39.

Sutherland, Edwin H. 1950, 'The Diffusion of Sexual Psychopath Laws', *American Journal of Sociology*, 1950, vol. 56, pp. 142–8.

Sutherland, Edwin H. 1983, *White Collar Crime: The Uncut Version*, Yale University Press, New Haven.

Sutherland, Edwin H. & Cressey, Donald R. 1978, *Criminology*, 10th edn, Lippincott, New York.

Sutton, Adam 1989, 'Bottom of the Harbour Tax Evasion Schemes', in *Stains on a White Collar: Fourteen Studies in Corporate Crime or Corporate Harm*, eds Peter Grabosky & Adam Sutton, Hutchinson, Sydney.

Sutton, Adam 1994, 'Community Crime Prevention: A National Perspective', in *The Australian Criminal Justice System: The Mid 1990s*, eds Duncan Chappell & Paul Wilson, Butterworths, Sydney,.

Sutton, Adam & Wild, Ronald 1978, 'Corporate Crime and Social Structure', in *Two Faces of Deviance: Crimes of the Powerless and the Powerful*, eds Paul R. Wilson & John Braithwaite, University of Queensland Press, St. Lucia.

Sutton, Adam & Wild, Ronald 1979, 'Companies, the Law and the Professions: A Sociological View of Australian Companies Legislation', in *Legislation and Society in Australia*, ed. Roman Tomasic, The Law Foundation of New South Wales and Allen & Unwin, Sydney.

Sutton, Adam & Wild, Ronald 1985, 'Small Business: White-Collar Villains or Victims', *International Journal of the Sociology of Law*, vol. 13, pp. 247–59.

Sutton, John 1990, 'Bureaucrats and Entrepreneurs: Institutional Responses to Deviant Children in the United States, 1890–1920s', *American Journal of Sociology*, vol. 95, pp. 1367–1400.

Sutton, John R. 1991, 'The Political Economy of Madness: The Expansion of the Asylum in Progressive America', *American Sociological Review*, vol. 56, pp. 665–78.

Sykes, Gresham M. 1956, 'The Corruption of Authority and Rehabilitation', *Social Forces*, vol. 34, pp. 257–63.

Sykes, Gresham M. 1958, *The Society of Captives: A Study of a Maximum Security Prison*, Princeton University Press, Princeton, New Jersey.

Sykes, Gresham M. & Matza, David 1957, 'Techniques of Neutralization: A Theory of Delinquency', *American Sociological Review*, vol. 22, pp. 664–70.

Sykes, Richard E., Fox, James C. & Clark, John P. 1985, 'A Socio-Legal Theory of Police Discretion', in *The Ambivalent Force: Perspectives on the Police*, 3rd edn, eds Abraham S. Blumberg & Elaine Niederhoffer, Holt, Rinehart & Winston, New York.

Szasz, Thomas S. 1960, 'The Myth of Mental Illness', *The American Psychologist*, vol. 15, pp. 113–18.

Szasz, Thomas S. 1961, *The Myth of Mental Illness*, Holber-Harper, New York.

Szasz, Thomas S. 1973, *Ideology and Insanity: Essays on the Psychiatric Dehumanization of Man*, Colder & Boyars, London.

Tannenbaum, Frank 1938, *Crime and the Community*, Columbia University Press, New York.

Tappan, Paul 1946, 'Treatment Without Trial', *Social Forces*, vol. 24, pp. 306–11.

Tappan, Paul W. 1947, 'Who is the Criminal?', *American Sociological Review*, vol. 12, pp. 96–102.

Taylor, Ian, Walton, Paul & Young, Jock 1973, *The New Criminology: For a Social Theory of Deviance*, Routledge & Kegan Paul, London.

Taylor, Mike 1988, 'Corporate Watchdogs Being Starved of Funds', *The Weekend Australian*, 22–23 October, p. 12.

Taylor, Ralph B. & Covington, Jeanette 1993, 'Community Structural Change and Fear of Crime', *Social Problems*, vol. 40, pp. 374–95.

Thomson, Neil & Smith, Leonard 1985, 'An Analysis of Aboriginal Mortality in NSW Country Regions, 1980–81', *The Medical Journal of Australia*, Special Supplement, vol. 143, pp. S49–S54.

Tierney, Kathleen 1982, 'The Battered Women Movement and the Creation of the Wife Beating Problem', *Social Problems*, vol. 29, pp. 207–20.

Tingle, Laura 1988, 'Boucher Comes Out Fighting on Avoidance', *The Weekend Australian*, 19–20 November, p. 1.

Titmuss, Richard M. 1968, *Commitment to Welfare*, George Allen & Unwin, London.

Tomasic, Roman 1990, 'Corporate Crime: Making the Law More Credible', *Company and Securities Law Journal*, December, pp. 369–80.

Tomasic, Roman 1994, 'Corporate Crime', in *The Australian Criminal Justice System: The Mid 1990s*, eds Duncan Chappell & Paul Wilson, Butterworths, Sydney.

Tomasic, Roman & Pentony, Brendan 1988, Insider Trading and Business Ethics in Australia, paper prepared for presentation at the 6th Australian Law and Society Conference, La Trobe University, 2–4 December.

Tomasic, Roman & Pentony, Brendan 1989a, 'Insider Trading', *Legal Service Bulletin*, vol. 14, pp. 3–5.

Tomasic, Roman & Pentony, Brendan 1989b, 'The Prosecution of Insider Trading: Obstacles to Enforcement', *Australian & New Zealand Journal of Criminology*, vol. 22, pp. 65–81.

Tomasic, Roman & Pentony, Brendan 1989c, 'Crime and Opportunity in the Securities Markets: The Case of Inside Trading in Australia', *Company and Securities Law Journal*, vol. 7, pp. 186–98.

Tomasic, Roman & Pentony, Brendan 1991, 'Taxation Law Compliance and the Role of Professional Tax Advisers', *Australian & New Zealand Journal of Criminology*, vol. 24, pp. 241–57.

Townsend, Peter 1979, *Poverty in the United Kingdom*, Allen Lane & Penguin Books, Harmondsworth.

Townsend, Peter 1987, 'Deprivation', *Journal of Social Policy*, vol. 16, pp. 125–46.

Townsend, Peter & Davidson, Nick eds 1982, *Inequalities in Health: The Black Report*, Penguin, Harmondsworth.

Trice, Harrison & Roman, Paul 1970, 'Delabeling, Relabeling and Alcoholics Anonymous', *Social Problems*, vol. 17, pp. 538–46.

Trinca, Helen 1994, 'Stone Turns Squarely to the Tories', *The Weekend Australian*, June 18–19, p. 11.

Tuchman, Gaye 1973, 'Making News by Doing Work: Routinizing the Unexpected', *American Journal of Sociology*, vol. 79, pp. 110–31.

Turk, Austin T. 1966, 'Conflict and Criminality', *American Sociological Review*, vol. 31, pp. 338–52.

Turk, Austin 1976a, 'Law as a Weapon in Social Conflict', *Social Problems*, vol. 23, pp. 276–91.

Turk, Austin T. 1976b, 'Law, Conflict and Order: from Theorizing Toward Theories', *The Canadian Review of Sociology and Anthropology*, vol. 13, pp. 282–94.

Turner, Bryan S. 1987, *Medical Power and Social Knowledge*, Sage, London.

Turtle, Alison M. & Ridley, Anne 1984, 'Is Unemployment a Health Hazard? Health Related Behaviours of a Sample of Unemployed Sydney Youth in 1980', *Australian Journal of Social Issues*, vol. 19, pp. 27–42.

Uggen, Christopher 1993, 'Reintegrating Braithwaite: Shame and Consensus in Criminological Theory, *Law & Social Inquiry*, vol. 18, pp. 481–99.

van der Poel, Sari 1992, 'Professional Male Prostitution: A Neglected Phenomenon', *Crime, Law and Social Change*, vol. 18, pp. 259–75.

van Maanen, John 1975, 'Police Socialization: A Longitudinal Examination of Job Attitudes in an Urban Police Department', *Administrative Science Quarterly*, vol. 20, pp. 207–28.

von Hirsch, Andrew 1976, *Doing Justice: The Choice of Punishment*, Hill and Wang, New York.

von Hirsch, Andrew 1982, 'Desert and White-Collar Criminality: A Response to Dr Braithwaite', *The Journal of Criminal Law and Criminality*, vol. 73, pp. 1164–75.

Walker, John 1994, 'Trends in Crime and Criminal Justice', in *The Australian Criminal Justice System: The Mid 1990s*, eds Duncan Chappell & Paul Wilson, Butterworths, Sydney.

Walker, John assisted by Dianne Dagger 1993, *Crime in Australia: As Measured by the Australian Component of the International Crime Victim Survey 1992*, Australian Institute of Criminology, Canberra.

Walker, John & Salloom, Sue 1993, *Australian Prisoners 1992: Results of the National Prison Census 30 June 1992*, Australian Institute of Criminology, Canberra.

Walker, Lenore E. 1979, *The Battered Woman*, New York, Harper & Row.

Walker, Lenore E. 1983, 'The Battered Woman Syndrome Study', in *The Dark Side of Families*, eds David Finkerhor, Richard J. Gelles, Gerald T. Hotaling & Murray A. Straus, Sage, Beverly Hills,.

Walker, Lenore E. 1984, *The Battered Woman Syndrome*, Springer, New York.

Waller, L. & Williams, C.R. 1993, *Criminal Law: Texts and Cases*, 7th edn, Sydney, Butterworths.

Warhurst, John & Merrill, Vance 1982, 'The Abortion Issue in Australia: Pressure Politics and Policy', *The Australian Quarterly*, Winter, pp. 119–35.

Ward, Patricia & Dobinson, Ian 1988, 'Heroin: A Considered Response?', in *Understanding Crime and Criminal Justice*, eds Mark Findlay & Russell Hogg, The Law Book Company, Sydney.

Warr, Mark 1984, 'Fear of Victimization: Why are Women and the Elderly More Afraid?', *Social Science Quarterly*, vol. 65, pp. 681–702.

Warr, Mark 1985, 'Fear of Rape among Urban Women, *Social Problems*, vol. 32, pp. 238–50.

Waters, Malcolm 1989a, 'Collegiality, Bureaucratization, and Professionalization: A Weberian Analysis', *American Journal of Sociology*, vol. 94, pp. 945–72.

Waters, Malcolm 1989b, 'Patriarchy and Viriarchy: An Exploration and Reconstruction of Concepts of Masculine Domination', *Sociology*, vol. 23, pp. 193–211.

Weatherburn, Don 1985, 'Appellate Review, Judicial Discretion, and the Determination of Minimum Periods', *Australian & New Zealand Journal of Criminology*, vol. 18, pp. 272–83.

Weatherburn, Don 1988, 'Note: Front-End Versus Rear-End Solutions to Prison Overcrowding: A Reply to Professor Harding', *Australian & New Zealand Journal of Criminology*, vol. 21, pp. 117–20.

Weatherley, Richard 1993, 'Doing the Right Thing: How Social Security Claimants View Compliance', *Australian New Zealand Journal of Sociology*, vol. 29, pp. 21–39.

Weber, Max 1954, *On Law in Economy and Society*, ed. Max Rheinstein, Harvard University Press, Cambridge.

The Weekend Australian 1989, 'Black Magic Dictator "Still in the Country"', 23–24 December, p. 7.

Weekley, Kelly J.C. 1986, *Rape: A Four Year Police Study of Victims*, South Australian Police Department, Adelaide.

Weeks, Elaine Lunsford, Boles, Jacqueline M., Garbin, Albeno P. & Blount, John 1986, 'The Transformation of Sexual Harassment from a Private Trouble into a Public Issue', *Sociological Inquiry*, vol. 56, pp. 432–55.

Weinburg, Martin S. & Williams, Colin J. 1974, *Male Homosexuals: Their Problems and Adaptations*, Oxford University Press, New York.

Weis, Kurt & Borges, Sandra S. 1973, 'Victimology and Rape: The Case of the Legitimate Victim', *Issues in Criminology*, vol. 8, pp. 71–115.

Wells, Celia 1985, 'Law Reform, Rape and Ideology', *Journal of Law and Society*, vol. 12, pp. 63–75.

West, Jennifer 1994, *Unley & Mitcham Home Protection Project: Victims' Survey, Consultant's Report*, SA Police, City of Mitcham and City of Unley, South Australia.

Wheeler, Stanton 1976, 'Trends and Problems in the Sociological Study of Crime', *Social Problems*, vol. 23, pp. 525–34.

White, Rob 1993, 'Young People and the Policing of Community Space', *Australian & New Zealand Journal of Criminology*, vol. 26, pp. 207–18.

Whitt, Hugh P. & Meile, Richard L. 1985, 'Alignment, Magnification,and Snowballing: Processes in the Definition of Symptoms of Mental Illness', *Social Forces*, vol. 63, pp. 682–97.

Whittaker, Mark 1993, 'Inside the NCA: Gang Busters Inc.', *The Australian Magazine* 12–13 June, pp. 54–9.

Wikeley, Nick 1989, 'Unemployment Benefit, The State, and The Labour Market', *Journal of Law & Society*, vol. 16, pp. 291–309.

Wilensky, Harold 1965, 'The Problems and Prospects of the Welfare State', 'Introduction' in *Industrial Society and Social Welfare*, Harold L. Wilensky & Charles N. Lebeaux, The Free Press, New York.

Wilensky, Harold L. & Lebeaux, Charles N. 1965, *Industrial Society and Social Welfare*, The Free Press, New York.

Wilkie, Meredith 1992, 'Crime (Serious and Repeat Offenders) Sentencing Act 1992: A Human Rights Perspective', *Western Australian Law Review*, vol. 22, pp. 187–96.

Williams, Joan 1991, 'Gender Wars: Selfless Women and the Republic of Choice', *New York University Law Review*, vol. 66, pp. 1559–1634.

Williams, Linda S. 1984, 'The Classic Rape: When Do Victims Report?', *Social Problems*, vol. 31, pp. 459–67.

Willis, Evan 1986, 'Commentary: RSI as Social Process', *Community Health Studies*, vol. 10, pp. 210–19.

Willis, Evan 1989, *Medical Dominance: Division of Labour in Australian Health Care*, Allen & Unwin, Sydney.

Wilson, James Q. 1975, *Thinking About Crime*, Basic Books, New York.

Wilson, Paul R. 1989, 'Medical Fraud and Abuse in Medical Benefit Programmes', in *Stains on a White Collar: Fourteen Studies in Corporate Crime or Corporate Harm*, eds Peter Grabosky & Adam Sutton, Hutchinson, Sydney.

Wilson, Paul R. & Gorring, Pam 1985, 'Social Antecedents of Medical Fraud and Overservicing: What Makes A Doctor Criminal?', *Australian Journal of Social Issues*, vol. 20, pp. 175–87.

Windschuttle, Keith 1979, *Unemployment: A Social and Political Analysis of the Economic Crisis in Australia*, Penguin, Melbourne.

Wolfenden, Sir John (Chair) 1957, *Report of the Committee on Homosexual Offences and Prostitution*, Her Majesty's Stationery Office, London.

Wolfgang, Marvin E. 1972, 'Cesare Lombroso', in *Pioneers in Criminology*, 2nd edn, ed. Hermann Mannheim, Patterson Smith, Montclair, New Jersey.

Wright, James D. 1988, 'The Mentally Ill Homeless: What is Myth and What is Fact', *Social Problems*, vol. 35, pp. 182–91.

Wright, Peter & Treacher, Andrew eds 1982, *The Problem of Medical Knowledge: Examining the Social Construction of Medicine*, Edinburgh University Press, Edinburgh.

Wundersitz, Joy 1992, 'The Net-Widening Effect of Aid Panels and Screening Panels in the South Australian Juvenile Justice System, *Australian & New Zealand Journal of Criminology*, vol. 25, pp. 115–34.

Wundersitz, Joy 1993, 'Some Statistics on Youth Offending: An Inter-Jurisdictional Comparison', in *Juvenile Justice: Debating the Issues*, eds Fay Gale, Ngaire Naffine & Joy Wundersitz, Allen & Unwin, Sydney.

Wundersitz, Joy & Gale, Fay 1988, 'Disadvantage and Discretion: The Results for Aboriginal Youth in Relation to the Adjournment Decision', *Adelaide Law Review*, vol. 11, pp. 248–58.

Yarrow, Marian Radke, Schwartz, Charlotte Green, Murphy, Harriet S. & Deasy, Leila Calhoun 1955, 'The Psychological Meaning of Mental Illness in the Family', *Journal of Social Issues*, vol. 11, pp. 12–24.

Yeo, S. 1987, 'Ethnicity and the Objective Test in Provocation', *Melbourne University Law Review*, vol. 16, pp. 67–82.

Yin, Peter 1980, 'Fear of Crime Among the Elderly: Some Issues and Suggestions', *Social Problems*, vol. 27, pp. 492–504.

Yin, Peter 1982, 'Fear of Crime as a Problem for the Elderly', *Social Problems*, vol. 30, pp. 240–45.

Young, Jock 1971, 'The Role of the Police as Amplifiers of Deviancy, Negotiators of Reality and Translators of Fantasy: Some Consequences of Our Present System of Drug Control as Seen in Notting Hill', in *Images of Deviance*, ed. Stanley Cohen, Penguin, Harmondsworth.

Young, Jock 1986, 'The Failure of Criminology: The Need for a Radical Realism', in *Confronting Crime*, eds Roger Matthews & Jock Young, Sage, London.

Zaretsky, Eli 1982, 'The Place of the Family in the Origins of the Welfare State', in *Rethinking the Family: Some Feminist Questions*, ed. Barrie Thorne with Marilyn Yalom, Longman, New York.

Zaretsky, Eli 1986, 'Rethinking the Welfare State: Dependence, Economic Individualism and Family', in *Family, Economy & State: The Social Reproduction Process Under Capitalism*, eds James Dickinson & Bob Russell, Croom Helm, London.

Zdenkowski, George 1994, 'Contemporary Sentencing Issues', in *The Australian Criminal Justice System: The Mid 1990s*, eds Duncan Chappell & Paul Wilson, Butterworths, Sydney.

Zdenkowski, George & Brown, David 1982, *The Prison Struggle: Changing Australia's Penal System*, Penguin, Ringwood.

Zielinska, Eleonora 1993, 'Recent Trends in Abortion Legislation in Eastern Europe, with Particular Reference to Poland', *Criminal Law Forum*, vol. 4, pp. 47–93.

Zimring, Franklin E. & Hawkins, Gordon 1993, 'Crime, Justice, and the Savings and Loan Crisis', *Crime and Justice: An Annual Review of Research*, vol. 18, pp. 247–92.

Zola, Irving Kenneth 1972, 'Medicine as an Institution of Social Control', *Sociological Review*, vol. 20, pp. 487–504.

Zola, Irving Kenneth 1977, 'Healthism and Disabling Medicalization', in *Disabling Professions*, eds Ivan Illich, Irving Kenneth Zola, John McKnight, Jonathan Caplan & Harley Shaiken, Marion Boyars, London.

Zurcher, L.A., Kirkpatrick, R.G., Cushing, R.G. & Bowman, C.K. 1971, 'The Anti-Pornography Campaign: A Symbolic Crusade', *Social Problems*, vol. 19, pp. 217–38.

Zussman, Robert 1993, 'Life in the Hospital: A Review', *The Milbank Quarterly*, vol. 71, pp. 167–85.

Index